Four Views on Free Will

Great Debates in Philosophy
Series Editor: Ernest Sosa

Dialogue has always been a powerful means of philosophical exploration and exposition. By presenting important current issues in philosophy in the form of a debate, this series attempts to capture the flavor of philosophical argument and to convey the excitement generated by the exchange of ideas. Each author contributes a major, original essay. When these essays have been completed, the authors are each given the opportunity to respond to the opposing view.

Four Views on Free Will

Second Edition

John Martin Fischer
University of California Riverside
Riverside, CA

Robert Kane
The University of Texas at Austin
Austin, TX

Derk Pereboom
Cornell University
Ithaca, NY

Manuel Vargas
University of California San Diego
La Jolla, CA

WILEY Blackwell

This edition first published 2024
© 2024 John Wiley & Sons Ltd

The right of John Martin Fischer, Robert Kane, Derk Pereboom, and Manuel Vargas to be identified as the authors of this work has been asserted in accordance with law.

Registered Offices
John Wiley & Sons, Inc., 111 River Street, Hoboken, NJ 07030, USA
John Wiley & Sons Ltd, The Atrium, Southern Gate, Chichester, West Sussex, PO19 8SQ, UK

For details of our global editorial offices, customer services, and more information about Wiley products visit us at www.wiley.com.

Wiley also publishes its books in a variety of electronic formats and by print-on-demand. Some content that appears in standard print versions of this book may not be available in other formats.

Library of Congress Cataloging-in-Publication Data applied for

Cover Design: Wiley
Cover Image: © Henry Moore Foundation: Standing Figures, 1950 by Henry Moore

Set in 10/12.5pt Adobe Caslon Pro by Straive, Pondicherry, India

Printed and bound by CPI Group (UK) Ltd, Croydon, CR0 4YY

C9781394161966_170124

Contents

Notes on Authors

John Martin Fischer is Distinguished Professor in the Department of Philosophy at the University of California, Riverside, where he has held a UC President's Chair. He is the author of *The Metaphysics of Free Will: An Essay on Control* (1994) and, with Mark Ravizza, S.J., *Responsibility and Control: A Theory of Moral Responsibility* (1998). He has published four collections of essays on the topics of this debate: *My Way: Essays on Moral Responsibility* (2006), *Our Stories: Essays on Life, Death, and Free Will* (2009), *Deep Control: Essays on Free Will and Value* (2012), and *Our Fate: Essays on God and Free Will* (2016). In 2017 he was appointed by the Board of Regents as the first and only philosopher to hold a University Professorship in the University of California.

Robert Kane is University Distinguished Professor of Philosophy and Law Emeritus at The University of Texas at Austin. He is the author of ten books and over eighty articles on the philosophy of mind and action, free will, moral and legal responsibility, ethics, and the theory of values, including *Free Will and Values* (1985), *Through the Moral Maze* (1993), *The Significance of Free Will* (1996), *A Contemporary Introduction to Free Will* (2005), *Ethics and the Quest for Wisdom* (2010), and, with Carolina Sartorio, *Do We Have Free Will? A Debate* (2022), and *The Complex Tapestry of Free Will: A Philosophical Odyssey* (accepted for publication). He is editor of two editions of *The Oxford Handbook of Free Will* (2002 and 2011) among other edited anthologies. The recipient of fifteen major teaching awards at the University of Texas, he was named an inaugural member of the Academy of Distinguished Teachers in 1995 and in 2017 was awarded the Albert Nelson Marquis Lifetime Achievement Award by Marquis Who's Who.

Derk Pereboom is the Susan Linn Sage Professor of Philosophy and Ethics in the Philosophy Department at Cornell University and Senior Associate Dean for Arts and Humanities in Cornell's College of Arts and Sciences. His areas of research include free will and moral responsibility, philosophy of mind, and early modern philosophy, especially Kant. He is the author of *Living Without Free Will* (2001), *Consciousness and the Prospects of Physicalism* (2011), *Free Will, Agency, and Meaning in Life* (2014), and *Wrongdoing and the Moral Emotions* (2021). He has published articles on free will and moral responsibility, consciousness and physicalism, nonreductive materialism, and Kant's metaphysics and epistemology.

Manuel Vargas is Professor of Philosophy at the University of California San Diego. He is the author of *Building Better Beings: A Theory of Moral Responsibility* (2013), which won the 2015 APA Book Prize. He is a coeditor of *Rational and Social Agency: The Philosophy of Michael Bratman* (2014) and the *Oxford Handbook of Moral Psychology* (2022). He also publishes on the history of Latin American philosophy and is the author of the forthcoming *Mexican Philosophy*.

Preface to the Second Edition

All the chapters of this second edition of *Four Views on Free Will* have been updated, and even entirely rewritten from the first edition.

Acknowledgments

We wish to thank the many teachers and readers of the first edition, especially those who shared with us their experiences using that edition. We hope this volume is even more useful to you.

JMF: Over the years I have had the benefit of comments and conversations with many colleagues and students, too numerous to mention, which have significantly shaped my contribution. Thank you so very much. I am also honored by the opportunity to write this book with such distinguished philosophers, from whom I have learned throughout my career, as well as here. I appreciate the ideas, inspiration, and gracious collaboration.

RK: Thanks to the other three authors for their cogent comments, and to Manuel for his diligent organizational efforts.

DP: Thanks from me to Manuel Vargas, Robert Kane, John Fischer, Seth Shabo, David Christensen, and Sarah Adler.

MV: I'd like to thank my coauthors for agreeing to do the first edition of this book with a very green philosopher all those years ago, and for being game to get the band back together again. The ideas presented in this edition of my chapters have benefitted from the feedback of many colleagues and students over the years. In this edition my chapters have especially benefitted from the feedback of Michael Bratman, Federico Burdman, Joseph Martinez, Dana Nelkin, Sam Ridge, Dan Speak, and Satya Vargas.

Some Terms and Concepts

Basic Terms: Free Will, Moral Responsibility, and Determinism

Perhaps the three most important concepts in philosophical work on free will are **free will**, **moral responsibility**, and **determinism**.

The notion of freedom at stake in philosophical discussions is usually distinguished from a variety of other freedom concepts, including things like religious and political freedom. Usually, **free will** is also treated as distinct from several other concepts associated with human agency, such as autonomy and authenticity. As we will see in the chapters that follow, there are many ways of thinking about the nature of free will, and there are serious disagreements about what would constitute an adequate theory of free will. Much of the tradition has taken free will to be a kind of power or ability to make decisions of the sort for which one can be morally responsible, but philosophers have also sometimes thought that free will might be required for a range of other things, including moral value, originality, and self-governance. Two other claims often made about free will are hotly disputed among philosophers. One is the claim that free will requires "alternative possibilities" or the power to do otherwise, and the other is the claim that free will requires that we are the "ultimate sources" of our free actions or the ultimate sources of our wills to perform free actions. The authors of this volume will take different sides on these claims.

Important to many discussions of free will is the idea of **moral responsibility**. In the context of discussions of free will, moral responsibility is often understood as a kind of status connected to judgments and/or practices of moral praise and blame. This meaning is distinct from another, perhaps more commonly used, sense of responsibility: responsibilities as obligations (e.g. when we talk about what responsibilities a parent has to a child). There are important connections between responsibility of the sort concerned with praise and blame and responsibility of the sort concerned with obligations. However, philosophers writing on free will and moral responsibility are typically concerned with the former and not the latter.

Determinism is a third concept that is often important for philosophical discussions of free will. For present purposes, we can treat determinism as the thesis that at any time (at least right up to the very end, if there is one) the universe has exactly one physically possible future. Something is deterministic if it has only one physically possible outcome.

It is important to bear in mind that a definition of determinism is just that – a characterization of what things would have to be like *if* things were deterministic. It does not follow that the universe is actually deterministic. Compare: "A creature is a gryphon if it has the hindquarters of a lion and the head and claws of an eagle." Nothing about the definition of "gryphon" shows that there are such creatures in our universe. It simply tells us something about what sorts of things would count as gryphons. Similarly, to offer a definition of determinism does not show that the universe is deterministic. It only defines a term, and we may find that the term never properly applies to the world we live in.

When discussing these issues, it is natural to wonder whether the world is deterministic. Most physicists and philosophers think that the answer is no, but the technical issues are extremely complex. Nevertheless, if we accept that the universe isn't deterministic, there are still good reasons to think about the compatibility of free will and determinism. First, it could turn out that future physicists conclude that the universe is deterministic, contrary to the contemporary consensus about at least quantum mechanics. It is notoriously difficult to predict how future science will turn out, and it might be useful to have an answer to the question in advance of the scientific issues getting sorted out. Second, even if the universe were not fully deterministic, determinism might hold locally (either as a matter of how local spacetime is constructed or as a matter of how the physics for nonquantum physical objects operates). Third, we could be interested in whether free will is compatible with a broadly scientific picture of the universe. Since some aspects of the universe seem deterministic and others do not, we might ask if free will is compatible with determinism as a first step to answering the more general question of whether free will is compatible with a broadly scientific picture of the universe.

Philosophical Options on the Free Will Problem

One particularly important issue for contemporary philosophers thinking about free will is whether we could have free will in a deterministic universe. Call this issue – whether free will could exist if the universe were deterministic – the **compatibility issue**. There is a long-standing tradition of dividing up the conceptual terrain in light of the main answers to the compatibility issue. Traditionally, **incompatibilists** are those who think that free will is incompatible with the world being deterministic. **Compatibilists**, conveniently enough, are those who hold that free will is compatible with the universe being deterministic.

It is important to recognize that the compatibility issue is distinct from the issue of whether we have free will. You could be an incompatibilist and maintain that we do have free will. Or you might be an incompatibilist and think that we lack free will. (You could even think that irrespective of how the compatibility issue is settled, there are threats to free will apart from determinism.)

In the philosophical literature, **libertarianism** is the view that we have free will and that free will is incompatible with determinism. In this volume, it is the view presented by Robert Kane. Libertarianism as it is used in the context of free will is distinct from libertarianism in political philosophy. (Indeed, "libertarianism" in the free will sense is the original meaning – it was only later appropriated as the label for a view in political philosophy.) One might be a libertarian in both political and free will senses, but you can be a libertarian about free will without being a libertarian in political philosophy. And, perhaps, you could also be a political libertarian without being a free will libertarian (although some political libertarians are also free will libertarians).

Following Derk Pereboom, we will label as **hard incompatibilism** any view that holds that (i) incompatibilism is true and (ii) we lack free will. Historically, most hard incompatibilists were what William James called **hard determinists**. (Indeed, Pereboom's coining of the term "hard incompatibilism" reflects James's older terminology.) Hard determinists think we lack free will *because the world is deterministic*. Contemporary hard determinists are few and far between. What is more common are views that hold that we have no free will irrespective of whether the world is deterministic, and views that hold that although freedom might not be conceptually incompatible with determinism (or indeterminism, for that matter), we nevertheless lack it. As with the other views, Pereboom's version of this view represents one among several ways one can be a hard incompatibilist.

To summarize then: a traditional way of dividing up the terrain concerns answers to the compatibility issue. The two main approaches are incompatibilism and compatibilism. We have been considering the incompatibilist fork, where the two main species of incompatibilism are libertarianism and hard incompatibilism. Both forms of incompatibilism have further species we have not discussed in this brief introduction.

The remaining fork of the compatibility debate is **compatibilism**. There are many varieties of compatibilism. Some compatibilists have emphasized a particular understanding of "can," others have emphasized a kind of identification with one's motives or values, and others emphasize the role of responsiveness to reasons. One influential variation, however, is the view that holds that responsibility is compatible with determinism, combined with agnosticism about whether free will, understood in one important way, is compatible with determinism. This view is **semicompatibilism**, and its most prominent defender is John Martin Fischer.

Lastly, there are views that resist some or other aspects of traditional formulations of positions or methods in debates about free will. **Revisionism** is one such view, and it is the view defended by Manuel Vargas. The core idea of revisionism is that the picture of free will and moral responsibility embedded in common sense needs revision, but not abandonment. That is, the revisionist holds that the correct account of free will and moral responsibility conflicts with common sense. As is the case with libertarianism, hard incompatibilism, and compatibilism, this view can take a variety of more specific forms. In this volume, the view recommends a compatibilist repair to our incompatibilist thinking, given a diverse set of theoretical, empirical, and moral considerations.

For a diagram and discussion of these and some other possible positions in philosophical debates about free will, see the appendix at the end of this volume.

1
Libertarianism

Robert Kane

There is a disputation that will continue till mankind is raised from the dead, between the necessitarians and the partisans of free will.
Jalalu'ddin Rumi, thirteenth-century Persian poet and mystic

1 Introduction: An Ancient Problem with Modern Significance

The problem of free will and necessity or determinism of which Jalalu'ddin Rumi spoke has arisen in history whenever humans have reached a higher stage of self-consciousness about how profoundly the world may influence their behavior in ways unknown to them and that they do not control. The rise of doctrines of determinism or necessity in the history of ideas is an indication that this higher stage of self-consciousness has been reached. People have wondered at various times whether their actions might be determined by Fate or by God, by the laws of physics or the laws of logic, by evolution, genes or environment, unconscious motives, upbringing, psychological or social conditioning, or, with the latest scientific threats from the neurosciences, by the activity of the neurons of their brains of which they are not conscious.

There is a core idea running through all these historical doctrines of determinism or necessity, whether they are religious, secular, or scientific,

Four Views on Free Will, Second Edition. John Martin Fischer, Robert Kane, Derk Pereboom, and Manuel Vargas.

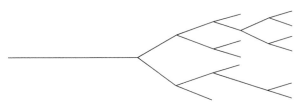

Figure 1.1 Garden of forking paths.

that shows why many people have felt they are a threat to free will. This core idea may be stated as follows:

> **Determinism**: given the past at any time and the laws governing the universe, there is only one possible future. Whatever happens is therefore inevitable; it cannot but occur, given the past and laws.

> **Free will**: by contrast, this implies (i) an open future, with multiple possible paths into the future and that (ii) it is sometimes "up to us" which of these possible paths we will take.

Such a picture of an open future that free will seems to require is often illustrated by an image made famous in a short story by the well-known South American writer Jorge Luis Borges. It is the image of a "garden of forking paths" illustrated in Figure 1.1. At each juncture there are forking paths into the future. If we believe our choices about which of these paths we will take at such times are *free* choices, we must believe both options are "open" to us while we are deliberating. We could choose different paths into the future at various points in our lives; and it would be "up to us" and no one and nothing else which of these paths will be taken.

I believe such a picture of different possible paths into the future, at least at some times in our lives, is essential to our understanding of free will. Such a picture is also important, we might even say, to what it means to be a person and to live a human life. Yet determinism, if true, would seem to threaten this picture. For it implies that there really is, at all times, only one possible path into the future, not many. We may *believe* there are multiple paths available to us. But in reality, if determinism is true, only one of them would be possible.

2   Modern Debates and Views

Like Rumi and many other thinkers of the past, I had always believed there was some kind of conflict lurking here that was very deep and could not be easily dismissed by facile arguments. Yet I was also aware that many philosophers and scientists, especially in the modern era, have argued that doctrines of determinism pose no real threat to free will, or at least to any free will "worth wanting." These thinkers are usually called "compatibilists":

> **Compatibilists**: believe that free will is compatible with determinism, so that we can have all the free will that is possible and worth wanting, even if determinism should be universally true.

Even in a determined world, these compatibilists argue, we would want to distinguish persons who are free from such things as physical restraint, addiction or neurosis, coercion, compulsion, covert control by others, or political oppression from persons who are not free from these things; and we could affirm that these freedoms could exist and would be preferable to their opposites *even in a determined world*. In addition, these modern compatibilists commonly argue that requiring that free actions must be *un*determined would not do anything to enhance our freedom, but would rather reduce our freedom to mere chance or luck or mystery.

In modern debates about free will, compatibilist views of these kinds are opposed by:

> **Incompatibilists**: those who deny that every kind of freedom "worth wanting" is compatible with determinism.

I will be defending such an incompatibilist view in this debate. While many kinds of freedom may be compatible with determinism, as the preceding paragraph suggests, I believe there is one important kind of freedom – traditionally called the "freedom of the will" – that is also worth wanting but that is not compatible with determinism.

Freedom of will of this incompatibilist kind satisfies the two conditions mentioned earlier that seem to be threatened by determinism, that is (i) at least at some points in our lives, we face a genuinely open future, with forking paths into that future, either of which we may choose, and (ii) at these crucial times, it is "up to us" and no one and nothing else, which of these possible paths into the future will be taken. We determine our future at such times and the kinds of persons we will become. Those who believe there is an important kind of freedom of will that we can possess satisfying these conditions which is not compatible with determinism are usually called "libertarians" about free will in contemporary debates (from the Latin *liber* meaning "free").[1]

> **Libertarians about free will** believe there is an important kind of freedom of will we can possess that is *incompatible* with determinism and satisfies the following conditions: (i) at some points in our lives, we face a genuinely open future, with forking paths into that future, either of which we may choose, and (ii) at these

crucial times, it is "up to us," and no one and nothing else, which of these possible paths into the future will be taken.

I will be defending such a libertarian and incompatibilist view of free will in this debate. Many thinkers believe that a free will of the kind libertarians defend – a free will that is not compatible with determinism – is not even possible or intelligible. It is not a kind of freedom, they argue, we *could* have. This worry has a long history and is related to an ancient dilemma: if free will is not compatible with determinism, it does not seem to be compatible with *indeterminism* either. Arguments have been made since the time of the ancient Stoics that *undetermined* events would occur spontaneously and hence could not be controlled by agents in the way that free and responsible actions would require.

If, for example, a choice occurred by virtue of some undetermined quantum events in one's brain, it would seem to be a fluke or accident rather than a responsible choice. Undetermined events occurring in brains or bodies, it is commonly argued, would not seem to enhance our freedom and control over, and hence responsibility for, actions, but rather to diminish freedom, control, and responsibility. Arguments such as these and many others have led to often-repeated charges throughout history that undetermined choices or actions such as a libertarian free will would require would be "arbitrary," "random," "irrational," "uncontrolled," "mere matters of luck," or "chance," and hence could not be free and responsible actions at all.

In response, libertarians about free will throughout history have often appealed to special and unusual forms of agency or causation to explain undetermined free actions, while their opponents have cried magic or mystery. Indeterminism might provide "causal gaps" in nature, libertarians frequently reasoned, but that was only a negative condition for free will. Some special form of agency or causation was needed that went beyond familiar modes of causation in the natural order to "fill" those causal gaps in nature left by indeterminism. And thus we had historical appeals to "extra factors," such as noumenal selves outside space and time (e.g. Immanuel Kant); immaterial minds (e.g. René Descartes); or uncaused causes, nonevent agent causes, or prime movers unmoved that might account for an otherwise undetermined free will.

A tempting way to think, to be sure. But such traditional ways of thinking have also prompted charges by compatibilists and free will skeptics and many other modern critics of libertarian free will. These critics argue that one cannot make sense of an undetermined free will without appealing to magical or mysterious forms of agency which have no place in the modern scientific picture of the world and of human beings.

Friedrich Nietzsche summed up this prevailing modern skepticism in his inimitable prose when he said that such a traditional notion of freedom of the will that would underwrite an ultimate responsibility (UR) for our actions and require that one somehow be an undetermined "cause of oneself" was "the best self-contradiction that has been conceived so far" by the human mind (1989: Section 17.8).

I agree that a traditional idea of free will that would require its being incompatible with determinism is likely to appear utterly mysterious and unintelligible in a modern context unless we learn to think about it in new ways, hence my long struggle in attempting to defend and make sense of such an idea of free will without reducing it to mere chance, on the one hand, *or* to mystery, on the other. Yet the struggle seemed worth the effort. For, like many another issue of modernity, the question is whether *something* of this traditional idea of free will in what Nietzsche called "the superlative metaphysical sense" can be retrieved from the dissolving acids of modern science and secular learning. Or would it become, along with other aspects of our self-image, yet another victim of the "disenchantments" of modernity?

Yet I came to realize that any retrieval of this idea of free will that would require its being incompatible with determinism would be no simple matter, if it were possible at all. Such a retrieval would require answering not one question but a whole host of questions. And it would require rethinking the relations of many different and related notions: agency, choice, mind, action, selfhood, will, control, responsibility, power, and many others.[2] I will be addressing many of these questions and topics here, beginning with the following central question in contemporary debates about free will.

3   The Compatibility Question, Alternative Possibilities, and Ultimate Responsibility

Why might one believe there is an important kind of free will worth wanting that is not compatible with determinism? The first step in answering this question is recognizing that – as this so-called Compatibility Question is usually formulated in many modern discussions of free will, "Is *freedom* compatible or incompatible with determinism?" – the question is too simple. For, as noted in Section 2, *there are many meanings of "freedom"* (as one would expect from such a much-disputed and debated term) and many of these meanings *are* compatible with determinism. Even in a determined world, as noted, we would want to distinguish persons who are *free* from such things as physical restraint, addiction, coercion, and political oppression from persons not free from these things. And we should acknowledge that these freedoms *are* significant ("worth wanting") – having them would be preferable to their opposites – even in a determined world.

Those of us who are libertarians about free will (who believe in a free will that is incompatible with determinism) should, I contend, concede this point to compatibilists: many freedoms worth wanting are compatible with determinism.

What **libertarians about free will** should insist upon is that *there is at least one kind of freedom that is also worth wanting and is not compatible with determinism.* This further freedom is **freedom** *of will*, which I define as: "**the power to be the ultimate source and sustainer to some degree of one's own ends or purposes.**"

To understand what this notion of free will amounts to, return to the two features mentioned in Section 2 that have historically led persons to believe that free will is threatened by determinism. We believe we have free will when we view ourselves as agents capable of influencing the world in various ways. Open alternatives seem to lie before us (a "garden of forking paths" in the earlier image). We reason and deliberate among them, and choose. We feel (i) it is "up to us" what we choose and how we act, and this means we "could have chosen or acted otherwise" or that we had "alternative possibilities." This "up-to-us-ness" also suggests that (ii) the ultimate sources of our actions lie to some degree in us and not entirely outside us in factors beyond our control.

Most modern debates about whether such a free will is or is not compatible with determinism have tended to focus on the first of these two requirements, which might be called the:

> **Condition of alternative possibilities (AP):** free agents must have "alternative possibilities" or "open alternatives" for choice or action, which implies that they "could have chosen or acted otherwise."

But arguments about whether or not this much-discussed condition of alternative possibilities (AP) is compatible with determinism have led to contentious debates in modern philosophy. These debates in turn have tended to stalemate over differing interpretations of what it means to say that agents have alternative possibilities, or that agents "could have done otherwise" than they actually did, or that they had the "power" or "ability" at a given time to act *or* to act otherwise.

I believe these contentious debates about the meaning of such expressions as "could have done otherwise" and the resulting stalemates about the role of this AP condition in modern debates about free will are symptoms of a deeper problem. The deeper problem is that focusing on alternative possibilities alone is too thin a basis on which to rest the case for the incompatibility of free will and determinism. It is not that alternative possibilities and the power to do otherwise are unimportant for free will. Far from it. They are very important and we will return shortly to consider why. It is rather that other considerations must also be brought into the picture in arguing for the incompatibility of free will and determinism if we are to fully understand historical and contemporary debates about free will. The Compatibility Question concerning free will and determinism cannot be resolved by focusing on alternative possibilities or the power to do otherwise alone.

Realizing this, I have argued that one must revisit the long history of debates about free will to see where else to look. When doing so, one finds there is another historical condition fueling incompatibilist intuitions that to my mind is even more important than the alternative possibilities condition. This other condition is related to the second of the two requirements for the "up-to-us-ness" of freedom of will mentioned, namely that "the ultimate sources of our actions must lie to some degree in us and not entirely outside us in factors beyond our control." I call this further condition:

> **The condition of ultimate responsibility (UR)**: the basic idea is that to be ulti-mately responsible for an action, an agent must be responsible to some degree for anything that is a sufficient reason (a sufficient condition, cause, or motive) for the action's occurring.

If, for example, a choice were to issue from, and can be sufficiently explained by, an agent's character and motives (together with background conditions) at the time, then to be ultimately responsible for the choice, the agent must be at least in part responsible by virtue of choices or actions voluntarily performed in the past for *having* the character and motives he or she now has. Compare Aristotle's claim that if a man is responsible for wicked acts that flow from his character, he must at some time in the past have been responsible for forming the wicked character from which these acts flow (Aristotle 1985: 67).

This condition of UR accounts for the *ultimate* in the original definition of free will given earlier: "the power of agents to be the ultimate sources and sus-tainers to some degree of their own ends or purposes."

4 Self-forming Actions

Importantly, such a condition of ultimate responsibility (UR) does not require that we could have done otherwise (AP) for *every* act done "of our own free wills." This UR condition thus partially vindicates compatibilists and others who insist that we can be held morally responsible for many acts even when we could not have done otherwise than perform them. But the vindication is only partial. For this UR con-dition *does* require that we could have done otherwise with respect to *some* acts in our life histories by which we *formed* or *shaped* our present characters, motives, and purposes (i.e. our wills). I call these character and will-forming actions:

> **Self-forming actions (SFAs)**: those acts by which we form and reform our wills (our characters, motives, and purposes) and for which we could have done otherwise, that must occur at some times in our lives, if we are to be ultimately responsible for having the wills we have and hence for being the kinds of persons we become.

To bring out the importance of these self-forming actions (SFAs), consider a familiar line of argument purporting to show that moral responsibility does not require alternative possibilities or the power to do otherwise *at all*, a line of argument illustrated by compatibilist Daniel Dennett's much-discussed example of Martin Luther (1984: 131–133). When finally breaking with the Church at Rome, Luther said, "Here I stand, I can do no other." Suppose, says Dennett, Luther was literally right about himself at that moment. Given his character and motives, he literally could not then have done otherwise. Does this mean he was not morally responsible? Not at all, Dennett says. In saying, "I can do no other," Luther was not disowning responsibility for his act, but taking full responsibility for it. Thus, compatibilist Dennett concludes, "could have done otherwise (AP) is *not* required for free will in a sense demanded by moral responsibility."

In response, I would argue that incompatibilists about free will may, and indeed should, grant that Luther could have been responsible for this act, *even ultimately responsible in the sense of UR*, though he could not have done otherwise then and there, even if his act were determined by his existing will at that moment. But this would be so, incompatibilists should argue, to the extent that Luther was responsible for his present *motives and character* (his will) by virtue of some earlier struggles and self-forming choices (SFAs) that *brought him to this point where he could do no other.*

> **Acting of "our *own* free will"**: often we act from a will already formed, but it is "our *own* free will" by virtue of the fact that we formed it by other choices or actions in the past (*self-forming choices or actions* or SFAs) for which we could have done otherwise. If this were not so, *there is nothing we could have ever done differently in our entire lifetimes to make ourselves different than we are* – a consequence, I believe, that is incompatible with our being (at least to some degree) ultimately responsible for being the way we are.

5   Freedom of Action and Freedom of Will: AP and UR

Focusing on this condition of ultimate responsibility (UR) tells us something else of importance about the traditional problem of free will. It tells us why it is a problem about the freedom *of the will* and not just about the freedom *of action* and why these freedoms must be distinguished if the Compatibility Question and other questions about free will are to be adequately addressed.

There has been a tendency in the modern era of philosophy, beginning with Thomas Hobbes and John Locke in the 17th century, and coming to fruition in the 20th century, to reduce the problem of free will to a problem of free action. I believe such a reduction oversimplifies the problem.

Free will is not just about free action, though it involves free action. *Free will is about self-formation*, about the *formation of our "wills"* or how we got to be the kinds of persons we are, with the characters, motives, and purposes we now have. Were we ultimately responsible to some degree for having the wills (characters, motives, and purposes) we do have, or can the sources of our wills be completely traced back to something over which we had no control, such as Fate or the decrees of God, heredity and environment, social conditioning, or hidden controllers, and so on? Therein, I believe, lies the core of the traditional problem of "free will."

John Locke (1690/1975, Book II, Chapter xxi: 134) famously said in the 17th century that the so-called problem of free will which had so exercised medieval and earlier philosophers was really a problem about *free agency*, or the freedom *of the agent*, and not about the freedom *of the will*. Like other thinkers of the modern era, Locke was skeptical of medieval references to the "will" in general which often made it out to be a mysterious inner homunculus or power capable of influencing actions and events in ways not countenanced, Locke believed, by the new emerging sciences of his day.

Many moderns down to the present time have followed Locke in this skepticism. They argue, as did Ludwig Wittgenstein (1953) and Gilbert Ryle (1949) in the mid-20th century, that references to the *will* and *acts of will* were outdated remnants of pre-modern modes of thought and should go the way of witches and phlogiston. Even some modern libertarians and incompatibilists about free will have joined compatibilists in arguing that the historical "problem of free will" is really about the freedom of agency and hence about the freedom of action and not about the freedom of the will.

I believe this is a mistake. It is *not* wrong, to be sure, to say as Locke does that the traditional problem of free will is really a problem about *free agency*. But it *is* wrong to say it is not therefore *also* about the freedom of the will. For, as described in these paragraphs, *freedom of will is an important aspect of free agency*; and moreover *free will is that particular aspect of free agency that has been the subject of historical debates about whether it is or is not compatible with determinism.*

For if the case for the incompatibility of free will and determinism cannot be made by appealing to the condition of alternative possibilities (AP) alone, the case can be made if UR is added. I have thus argued that UR should be moved to center stage in free will debates. To be ultimately responsible for an action in the sense required by UR, an agent must be responsible to some degree for anything that is a sufficient reason (cause or motive) for the action's occurring. And this implies, as noted, that if a choice or action can be sufficiently explained by an agent's present character, motives, and purposes, then to be ultimately responsible for the choice or action, the agent must be at least in part responsible by virtue of choices or actions voluntarily performed in the past for *having* the character, motives, and purposes he or she now has. But this being the case, an impossible infinite regress of past choices or actions would be required unless *some* choices or actions in the agent's life history (self-forming actions, or SFAs) did *not* have *sufficient* causes or motives (and hence were not determined).[3]

Yet if one could arrive at the incompatibility of free will and determinism from this condition of ultimate responsibility (UR) alone in this manner, one might wonder whether appeals to alternative possibilities (AP) are needed at all for free will. Some recent philosophers who are impressed by arguments of the above kind for incompatibilism (they are sometimes called "source incompatibilists") have suggested that appeals to alternative possibilities and the power to do otherwise are not needed at all for free will.

I believe this is also a mistake. *Both conditions – UR and AP – are needed for free will.* But the reasons why both conditions are needed are more subtle than is generally realized; and understanding them requires further steps in rethinking the Compatibility Question.

6   Plurality Conditions and Plural Voluntary Control

The first of these further steps concerns what I call "plurality conditions" for free will. When we wonder about whether the wills of agents are free, it is not merely whether they could have done otherwise that concerns us, *even if the doing otherwise is undetermined.* What interests us is whether agents could have done otherwise *voluntarily* (or *willingly*), *intentionally* and *rationally*. Or to put it more generally, we are interested in whether agents could have acted voluntarily, intentionally, and rationally *in more than one way*, rather than in only one way, and in other ways merely by accident or mistake, unintentionally, involuntarily, or irrationally. I call such conditions:

> **Plurality conditions for free will** (Kane 1996: 107–111): the power of agents to act voluntarily, intentionally, and rationally *in more than one way*, rather than in only one way, and in other ways merely by accident or mistake, unintentionally, involuntarily, inadvertently, or irrationally.

Such conditions seem to be deeply embedded in our intuitions about free choice and action. Most of us naturally assume that freedom and responsibility would be deficient if it were always the case that we could *only* do otherwise by *accident* or *mistake, unintentionally, involuntarily,* or *irrationally.*

To illustrate, imagine a world in which there is a considerable amount of genuine indeterminism or chance in human affairs as well as in nature. In this world, people set out to do things – kill prime ministers, press buttons on machines, punch computer keys, hit targets, etc. – usually succeeding, but sometimes failing by mistake or accident. Suppose an assassin, who usually hits his targets, is aiming to kill a prime minister from a distance with a high-powered rifle, when some undetermined events in his nervous system lead to a wavering of his arm and he misses his target. Or suppose I approach a coffee machine meaning to push the button for black coffee when, due to an undetermined brain cross, I accidentally press the button for coffee with cream.

Now imagine further that *all* actions in this world in the lifetimes of agents, whether the agents succeed in their purposes or not, are such that their reasons, motives, and purposes for wanting and trying to act as they do are always preset or settled by prior circumstances of heredity, environment, social conditioning, and other formative circumstances. Whether the assassin misses the prime minister or not, his *intention* to kill is already *settled* prior to his attempt, by his past formative circumstances. Whether I succeed in pressing the button for coffee without cream, my wanting to do so because of my dislike of cream is already *settled* by my formative circumstances. And so it is, we are to assume, for all persons and all their actions in this imagined world.

I would argue that persons in such a world lack free *will*, even though it may often be the case that they have (i) *alternative possibilities* and that their actions are (ii) *undetermined*. For they can sometimes do otherwise than they do in a manner that is undetermined, but only inadvertently or unintentionally, by mistake or accident, as in the case of the assassin or my pressing the wrong button on the coffee machine – and this is a limited kind of freedom at best. What they cannot do is *will* otherwise than they do. Their reasons, motives, and purposes have been already "set one way" before and when they act, so that if they act otherwise, it will *not* be "*in accordance with their wills*," but rather by chance or accident.

What this shows is that when we wonder about whether the *wills* of agents are free, it is not only whether they could have done otherwise that concerns us, even if their doing otherwise is undetermined. What interests us is whether they could have done otherwise *voluntarily* (in accordance with their wills), *intentionally* (knowingly rather than inadvertently and on purpose rather than accidentally), and *rationally* (having reasons for so acting and acting for those reasons). Or to put it more generally, we are interested in whether they could at some times have acted voluntarily, intentionally, and rationally *in more than one way*, rather than in only one way, and in other ways merely by accident or mistake, unintentionally, inadvertently, or irrationally.

We thus arrive at an answer to the question of why these "plurality conditions" are so deeply embedded in our intuitions about free choice and action. We naturally assume that freedom and responsibility would be deficient if it were always the case that we could *only* do otherwise by accident or mistake, unintentionally, involuntarily, or irrationally, in short, *unwillingly*. To have freedom of will, we must not only be able to do otherwise: we must be able to do otherwise *willingly* or *at will*. If free *will* involves more than alternative possibilities and indeterminism, these plurality conditions appear to be among the significant additional requirements.

Reflecting on these plurality conditions tells us something else of importance about free will. For, satisfying such plurality conditions implies that agents must be able to exercise a certain kind of control over some of their actions that I refer to as:

> **Plural voluntary control (PVC)**: agents have PVC over a set of options (e.g. choices or actions) when (i) they are able to bring about *either* of the options *voluntarily* (without being coerced or compelled or otherwise controlled by other agents or mechanisms), *intentionally* (knowingly and on purpose, rather than merely by accident or mistake) and *rationally* (for *reasons* that they then and there wish to act upon) and (ii) *whichever* option they do bring about by exercising such PVC will have been brought about by them voluntarily, intentionally, and rationally in these senses.

These conditions can be summed up by saying, as we sometimes do, that the agents can act or choose either way "at will" or, alternatively, that it is "up to them" which way they will choose or act when they choose or act.

7   Will-setting and Self-formation

Focusing in this way on plurality conditions and plural voluntary control (or PVC) also leads to a further important and often-neglected topic in free will debates that I call "will-setting" (Kane 1996: 113–115). In the imagined scenario in Section 6, all of the motives and purposes of agents in every situation are already "preset" or "set one way" before they act. The assassin's desires and purposes are set on killing the prime minister, not on missing or killing an aide. My desires and purposes are set on pressing the button for black coffee and not any other button. In such cases, where the motives and purposes of agents are already set one way before they act, we may say:

> Their actions are **will-settled**, meaning that the wills of agents, their motives and purposes, are already set one way on doing something *before* they act.

By contrast:

> Actions are **will-setting** when the wills of agents, their motives and purposes, are *not* already preset or set one way *before* they act. Rather the agents set their wills one way or another *in the performance of the actions themselves*.

Choices or decisions, which are self-forming actions (SFAs), in the sense defined here, are will-setting in this sense. The agents' wills are not already set one way before they choose, but they set their wills, one way or the other, voluntarily, intentionally, and rationally, *in the act of choosing itself.* Such self-forming actions would thus satisfy the plurality conditions.

The imagined world in which all the motives and purposes of agents are already set one way whenever they act thus provides a clue to the deep connection between will-setting, ultimate responsibility (UR), free will, and the plurality conditions. If we are to be to some degree ultimate determiners of our own wills, as UR requires, some actions in our lifetimes (self-forming actions, or SFAs) must be will-setting in the above sense and hence must satisfy the plurality conditions. But these self-forming actions will then satisfy the condition of alternative possibilities (AP) as well. For if one can do or do otherwise, voluntarily, intentionally, and rationally either way, it follows that one can do or do otherwise. One has alternative possibilities. AP would therefore be necessary for free will after all, *at least sometimes in our lives when we engage in self-formation.*

8 The Compatibility Question Revisited: Free Will and Moral Responsibility

Focusing on both ultimate responsibility (UR) and alternative possibilities (AP) when discussing the Compatibility Question, rather than merely on AP alone, has another significant consequence. It shows why issues about free will have been so deeply entangled throughout history with issues about *moral responsibility* for actions. This entanglement is no accident. It has to do with the very meaning of freedom *of will* (which involves both UR and AP). Reflecting on this entanglement of free will and moral responsibility leads to further arguments relating to whether freedom of will is or is not compatible with determinism – arguments having to do with our ordinary practices of holding persons responsible for their actions in everyday moral and legal contexts.

Many contemporary compatibilists and other philosophers have been influenced on these topics by a seminal 1962 article by British philosopher P.F. Strawson. In this influential article, entitled "Freedom and Resentment," Strawson focused on our ordinary practices of holding persons morally responsible and on what he called the:

> **Reactive attitudes:** attitudes toward persons usually associated with ordinary practices of holding persons morally responsible, including attitudes such as blame, resentment, indignation, guilt, moral approval, and moral praise.

Strawson argued that our ordinary practices of holding people responsible, including these reactive attitudes, were basic to our human form of life and could be wholly "insulated" from traditional abstract philosophical and scientific concerns about free will and determinism. To believe, he argued, that our ordinary practices of holding persons responsible in everyday life and the reactive attitudes related to them would have to be qualified in some ways – or even possibly abandoned – if we found that all their actions were determined by prior causes was to "overintellectualize" the issues.

This "insulation thesis" (as it has sometimes been called) is a controversial feature of Strawson's article, and it has had numerous proponents and critics. Interestingly, one of the most prominent of the critics was Strawson's son, Galen Strawson, who in his 1986 book *Freedom and Belief* took issue with his father's contention in "Freedom and Resentment" that ordinary practices of blaming and other reactive attitudes *could* be entirely "insulated" from metaphysical concerns about determinism. Against this contention, Galen Strawson argued that "the roots of the incompatibilist intuition" (that free will is incompatible with determinism) "lie deep" in our ordinary practices and in the reactive attitudes associated with those practices. These ordinary practices and the reactive attitudes associated with them, he argued, "enshrine the incompatibilist intuition," rather than being "insulated" from it (Strawson 1986: 89).

I agree with Galen Strawson on this issue, though my reasons are not all the same as his. Like him, I believe our ordinary practices of holding persons morally responsible and related questions about blameworthiness and the reactive attitudes cannot be *entirely* insulated from philosophical worries about free will and determinism that have engaged philosophers for centuries. This genie cannot be kept in the bottle, annoying as he may be. There are a number of ways to show this that I will explore in Section 9.

9   Fair Opportunity to Avoid Wrongdoing: Hart and Others

The first way focuses on ordinary practices of ascribing responsibility, culpability, and blame in courts of law and other legal contexts. A widely cited condition among legal theorists for such ascriptions was stated by the influential British legal theorist H.L.A. Hart (1968). It may be called:

> **The fair opportunity condition**: a necessary condition for ascribing responsibility and culpability to agents in legal contexts according to which the agents must have had a "fair opportunity to avoid wrongdoing," or more generally, a "fair opportunity to have done otherwise" than they have done.

In an important article, David Brink and Dana Nelkin (2013) argue persuasively that this "fair opportunity" criterion of Hart's is not only crucial for understanding legal and criminal responsibility but also crucial for understanding moral responsibility in general, in an accountability sense that would justify blame, sanction, and punishment. Hart's fair opportunity condition, they argue, is thus a crucial part of the "architecture" of ordinary practices of ascribing moral as well as legal responsibility (Brink and Nelkin 2013: 284).

If this is the case, as I believe it is, it has implications concerning whether our ordinary practices of ascribing responsibility can *be* insulated from traditional philosophical debates about free will and determinism. For, appeals to Hart's fair opportunity criterion for assigning responsibility in ordinary legal and moral practices lands one squarely in the center of traditional philosophical debates that have concerned incompatibilists about whether causal determinism rules out the freedom to do otherwise and whether and to what degree the freedom to do otherwise is required for moral responsibility.

To show this, it is instructive to consider the following: if causal determinism were true, anything you might have done differently in the course of your life to make yourself different than you are would have been *causally impossible* in the following sense:

> **Causal impossibility**: an event E's occurring at a time t is *causally impossible* just in case the following is true: "If the past prior to t is as it is in the actual world and the laws of nature are as they are in the actual world, then E cannot possibly occur at t."

If causal determinism was true, *anything you might have done differently in the course of your life* to make yourself different than you are at any time – your character, your motives, your dispositions, your intentions, the quality of your will – would have been causally impossible in this sense. For, as we have seen in Section 1, causal determinism implies that given the past and the laws governing the universe at any time, there is only one causally possible future. And if an agent's avoiding wrongdoing was causally impossible in this sense, it would certainly appear that the agent lacked a "fair opportunity" to avoid doing it.

An important qualification, however, must immediately be added here – a qualification that is crucial for understanding not only Hart's fair opportunity criterion but also ascriptions of responsibility in ordinary moral contexts generally. The qualification is that the causal impossibility of avoiding wrongdoing *in certain particular circumstances* will not always imply that agents are excused from moral responsibility *in those circumstances*. It implies this only in certain conditions.

For example, if it could be shown that it was causally impossible for a drunk driver to have avoided hitting a pedestrian on a dark and rainy night, given all the circumstances at the moment of the accident, that fact alone will not excuse the driver of responsibility. For one must also ask whether the driver was responsible by virtue of earlier actions or omissions for the existence of some of those crucial circumstances that made it now causally impossible for him to have avoided the accident, such as his prior decisions to drink and then drive. The causal impossibility of avoiding doing something *now* (e.g. avoiding the accident when it occurred) will not excuse an agent of responsibility, if some of the crucial circumstances that made it now causally impossible to avoid doing it were the results of actions or omissions by the agent in the past, *which the agent had a "fair opportunity to avoid" when they occurred.* And this last phrase is crucial. For the problem is that if determinism is true, there would be no actions or omissions in an agent's past that were not causally impossible for the agent to have avoided doing when *they* occurred.

10   Reactive Attitudes, Criminal Trials, and Transference of Responsibility

Another significant way of highlighting problems with the thesis that issues about responsibility and the reactive attitudes can be insulated from philosophical concerns about determinism is discussed by a number of other writers. It is discussed, for example, by Shaun Nichols in his book *Bound: Essays on Free Will and Responsibility* (2015). Nichols's book focuses on the implications of new research in empirical psychology and experimental philosophy for traditional philosophical debates about free will and moral responsibility. The passages of interest here in his book are where Nichols discusses Galen Strawson's claim, mentioned in Section 8, that our ordinary practices of holding responsible, and the reactive attitudes related to them, "enshrine" incompatibilist intuitions about freedom and responsibility rather than being entirely "insulated" from such intuitions.

In discussing what he takes to be important arguments supporting this claim of Galen Strawson's, Nichols introduces two examples that play a pivotal role in his discussion. One of these examples is from Gary Watson's (1987) well-known and much-discussed account of the ruthless murderer, Robert Harris, on death row in California for multiple murders. The other example Nichols (2015) considers in his book is taken from my own writing about the trial of a young man who assaulted and raped a teenage girl. The examples have similar import. But I will focus on my example because it brings out some key points that Watson does not emphasize. As Nichols points out, my example is roughly based on experience, triggered by the trial of the young man accused of the assault and rape.

My initial reactions attending the trial of this young man were filled with anger and resentment against him, since we knew the family of the teenage girl who was his victim and who lived in our neighborhood. But as I listened daily to the testimony of how the young man came to have the mean character and perverse motives he did have – a sordid story of parental rejection, sexual abuse, bad role models, and other such factors (not entirely unlike Watson's case of Robert Harris) – some of my resentment toward the young man decreased and was directed toward other persons who abused and influenced him. But – and here is a key point – I wasn't yet ready to shift all the blame away from the young man himself. I resisted this "transference of responsibility" entirely to others and wondered whether some residual responsibility and blame might not belong to the young man himself. My question became: Was his behavior *all* a matter of bad parenting, neglect, and abuse, and like factors, or did he have any crucial role to play in choosing it?

We know that parenting and society, genetic makeup, and upbringing have a profound influence on what we become and what we are. But were these influences entirely *determining*, or did they "leave anything over" for the young man to be responsible for? Note that:

> The question of whether the young man was merely a victim of bad circumstances or had some residual responsibility for being the way he is – the question, that is, of **whether he became the person he is to any degree *of his own free will* – seems to depend on whether these other factors were or were not *entirely* determining**. It seems to depend, in other words, on whether or not it was *ever causally possible for the young man to have resisted the influences of his genetics and upbringing* and to have acted differently at some points in his life to make himself different than he now is. And if determinism were true, acting differently than he actually did at *any* time in his lifetime would have been *causally impossible*.

One might argue here that my particular reactions at this trial to the young man, the fact that my reactive attitudes of resentment and blame toward him were mitigated to some degree and transferred to others when I learned about his sad history, were the reactions of a "philosopher" and not the reactions of ordinary folk. But this was far from being the case. My wife and I sat in this courtroom with friends and other neighbors of the young girl's family, none of whom were philosophers. They were firemen, businesswomen, store owners, high school football coaches, teachers, and many others; and all had similar reactions to ours. Keep in mind that, like us, they all resisted mightily transferring responsibility entirely away from the young man. But their reactive attitudes, including retributive ones, were nonetheless mitigated to some degree and influenced by hearing the sordid stories of his history.

Moreover, if there *were* any persons in that courtroom whose retributive attitudes were not in any way influenced by listening to the history of the young man (as I am sure there were), then I would not want to see those persons anywhere near a jury deciding the fate of persons I cared about, or any other persons whatever. For they would not be capable of responding in ways I believe would be *fair* to those they judge. They would not be capable of responding fairly, if they were not capable of appreciating that, to the extent that the young man's sad history made it *causally impossible* for him to have turned out differently, to that extent he would not have had a "fair opportunity to avoid wrongdoing."

11 Transference of Responsibility and Compatibility Questions

It is worth reflecting further on this interesting notion of "transference of responsibility." We are inclined to do this to some degree to other persons who may have influenced agents to be the way they are and act as they do, to the extent we believe that the influences of these others *were difficult for the agents to have resisted when they occurred.* In such cases, we are inclined to "transfer" at least some of the responsibility and blame to those others who so strongly influenced the agents (parents, caregivers, role models, abusers, and so on) and to mitigate the responsibility of the agents accordingly. In some extreme cases, such as Watson's Robert Harris or the young man of my example, we might possibly conclude that the influences were so strong that resisting them to any degree was not causally possible. We could be wrong about this. Such judgments are fallible and should be made with great caution. But the crucial point is that *such judgments are relevant to our ordinary practices of holding agents responsible and blameworthy*, including who should be held responsible and to what degree.

Moreover, as noted, such judgments seem to depend on whether or not it was ever causally possible for the agents to have resisted the influences of their environment and upbringing and to have acted differently at some points in their lives to make themselves different than they are. And if determinism were true, this would never have been causally possible.

There are further interesting and relevant implications of this notion of transference of responsibility for free will debates. Many compatibilists – Daniel Dennett (1984) being a prominent example – are willing to concede that this transference of responsibility and related reactive attitudes, such as blame and resentment, to other persons who may have abused or otherwise exerted powerful influences over agents is indeed a normal feature of our ordinary practices of holding persons responsible. But these compatibilists go on to argue, as does Dennett, that such transference is only reasonable if the responsibility, blame, resentment, etc., is transferred to some other *persons*. If the influences on the agent's behavior and quality of will are due to natural causes alone and no other persons can be implicated, these compatibilists say, then it is not reasonable to transfer responsibility and other reactive attitudes, such as blame and resentment, to nature. For, as Dennett succinctly puts it, "nature is not a person."

This is true enough so far as it goes and should be admitted by incompatibilists. It is an important fact about this transference phenomenon that transference of moral and legal responsibility must be to other *persons* and cannot be to natural causes alone. Indeed, this fact is related to something important about the reactive attitudes, such as resentment, indignation, and blame, in general, namely that they are appropriately directed only at beings who are themselves capable of *responsible agency*. But rather than providing a decisive argument for compatibilism, further reflection on this significant fact can take us in an opposing direction.

To see why, return for a moment to the young man on trial. Since he seems to have acted voluntarily and intentionally from a perverse and vicious will, our reactive attitudes of blame and resentment were initially focused entirely on him. But when we heard more about his past, we wondered whether some of the blame at least should be transferred to the sexually abusive father and others who may have enabled the father. But now suppose we learn that the abusive father was as he was because *he* was sexually abused by his father and so on back indefinitely. Perhaps it was all in some bad genes. Or suppose the young man's having the perverse will from which he acted was all a matter of determining genetic mutations in his fetal development for which we cannot blame the father *or* any other persons.

Suppose further that, as evidence unveiled in the courtroom made clear, the young man's acting from his perverse will in this incident satisfied familiar compatibilist conditions for free and responsible agency: he acted voluntarily, without being coerced or forced by others; he acted intentionally, knowing exactly what he was doing and doing it on purpose; he was reasons-responsive in the sense that he was calculating and would have altered his behavior appropriately, if his beliefs, desires, and circumstances had been different in various ways. Nor was he acting compulsively, as in Harry Frankfurt's (1971) description of the unwilling addict, who wanted to resist the desire to take a drug, but could not resist taking it anyway. On the contrary, this young man had, in Frankfurt's terms, "the will he wanted to have" and was "wholehearted" and not ambivalent in his commitment to act in accordance with the will he had, perverse though it might be.

It was indeed the evidence of all this, coming to light in the proceedings, that led most of those present in the courtroom to our initial attitudes of resentment and moral anger toward the young man. Most of us, to be sure, transferred these reactive attitudes to some degree to others when we learned more about the sordid details of his upbringing. But we are now imagining a different situation. We are now supposing that the young man's having the perverse will from which he acted was a matter of determining genetic mutations in his fetal development for which we cannot blame an abusive father or any other persons. So we cannot blame any other *persons* for the young man's having the perverse will he does have. Yet it seems we can't blame *nature* either, which is not a person. And this prompts the following reflections.

Imagine two young men, possessing exactly the same wills and motives as this young man, and satisfying all the same compatibilist criteria for responsibility (uncoerced, reasons-responsive, etc.). Yet one of these young men was determined to be so by the actions of other persons, like the abusive father; the other young man was determined to be so by natural, impersonal causes alone (such as mutations in his genetic development). The first young man is not fully responsible, we might say, to the degree that the actions of other persons made him this way. The responsibility transfers at least in part to those others. But then should we say the second young man *is* fully responsible because no other persons, but only natural causes, made him the way he is – in other words, because we cannot find anyone *else* to blame?

Such reasoning seems not only perverse but also completely unfair to the second young man. For the question that begs to be answered *in both cases* is whether it was ever *causally possible* for either young man to have resisted the circumstances that influenced him, and to have made himself different than he turned out to be, whether those influencing circumstances were the result of the actions of other agents or the results of natural causes alone. And if these circumstances were *determining* either way, it would not have been causally possible for either young man to resist them. Neither of the young men would have had a "fair opportunity" to have turned out otherwise.

12 Two Dimensions of Responsibility

Reflections such as these suggest that if full justice is to be done to our understanding of moral and legal responsibility and to our practices of holding persons responsible, two dimensions of responsibility must be distinguished. Both dimensions, I would argue, are necessary for a fully adequate account of these practices, and neither dimension alone is sufficient. The first dimension is responsibility for *expressing the will* (the character, motives, and purposes) *one has in action*, and doing so *voluntarily* and *intentionally*.

The second dimension of responsibility is another matter. It is not responsibility for expressing in action the true quality of will one has or the real self one is, but responsibility for *forming* and thus *having* the quality of will one *expresses* and thus *being* the kind of self one *is*. The distinction put succinctly is between:

> **First dimension of responsibility**: responsibility for *expressing* in action the will one *has*.

> **Second dimension of responsibility**: responsibility for *forming* and thus *having* the will one *expresses* in action.

To be responsible in this second dimension it must be that at least some time in one's life, when one acts responsibly and hence voluntarily and intentionally in the first dimension, it was also possible for one to have voluntarily and intentionally *done otherwise*, not by being forced or by accident but in a manner that would also have expressed the true quality of one's will and the self that one was at the time. To be responsible in this second dimension, in other words, it cannot be at all times in one's life that only one possible action is determined by, and expressive of, one's *already existing will*. Some choices or actions in one's life must be, as explained in Section 7, *will-setting*, and not already *will-settled*.

13 Compatibilist Responses I: Conditional Analyses

Compatibilists are not without further responses to the preceding arguments concerning free will and moral responsibility. Historically, compatibilists have in fact pursued a number of different strategies we have not yet discussed to show that freedom and moral responsibility are compatible with determinism The most common strategy attempting to show this employed by compatibilists in the modern era – from Hobbes and Locke in the 17th century to David Hume and John Stuart Mill in the 18th and 19th centuries, and well into the 20th century, is often called the "classical compatibilist strategy." It involves conceding that moral responsibility *does* require the freedom or power to do otherwise *in some sense*. But then it involves defending *conditional* or *hypothetical* interpretations of the freedom or power to do otherwise, according to which that power turns out to be compatible with determinism.

According to such classical compatibilist strategies, what we mean when we say that agents were "free or had the power to do otherwise," or "could have done otherwise," is that "*they would or might have done otherwise, if* the past (or the laws of nature) had been different in some way."

If, for example, persons had had different beliefs or desires, or had reasoned or chosen differently, or were in different circumstances, they would or might have acted differently. And saying persons would or might have acted differently, if the past or laws had been different in some way, these compatibilists then argue, is consistent with saying that the agents acting as they did was determined, given the past and the laws as they actually were.

I believe this standard compatibilist strategy is deeply flawed. Immanuel Kant, as is well-known, called it a "wretched subterfuge" and William James a "quagmire of evasion"; and I think they were right. A number of cogent objections have been made against such conditional interpretations of the freedom to do otherwise since the mid-20th century; and even many compatibilists today express doubts about such analyses. I believe they do so with good reason.

For it may be true that persons would or might have done otherwise, if the past or the laws had been different in some way. But the difficulty is that the actual past when they do act was not different in some way; it was as it was.

Likewise, the actual laws were not different; they were as they were. *Our freedom and responsibility must be exercised in the world that actually is, not in some hypothetical or merely possible world that might have been, but never actually was.* And if determinism is true of this actual world in which we live and act, then acting otherwise than we do *in the circumstances we actually find ourselves in* would always be causally impossible. It is not excusing to be told that persons would or might have acted otherwise in some merely hypothetical or possible worlds that never actually existed, if their acting otherwise in the actual world in which they do live and act was causally impossible.

Imagine a 16th-century incarnation of a modern classical compatibilist who took it upon himself to correct Luther when Luther said, "Here I stand. I can do no other." "You were mistaken, sir," this classical compatibilist might have said to Luther. "For all we mean when we say, 'I can now do other' is simply that in some possible worlds in which the past or the laws were different in some ways from the actual past and laws – in which, for example, you had had different beliefs or reasons or purposes – you would or might have done otherwise. And this may well have been true of you, sir" – this classical compatibilist might have said to Luther – "at the time you said, 'Here I stand. I can do no other.' So, you see, you were mistaken at that time to say that you 'could not have done otherwise' at that moment."

Luther would likely have replied, "Get thee gone, sophist! What I meant when I said, 'I can do no other' is that in the *actual world where I found myself at that moment* with all the beliefs, reasons, and purposes I had actually acquired in my long difficult journey to that point, my doing otherwise would have been impossible. What is it to me that I would or might have done otherwise in some merely possible world that did not actually exist at the time. Moreover, it was to some important degree the result *of my own past choices and actions* that the actual world that did exist and in which I acted at that moment was one in which I could not then have done other. For I had brought myself to that point in great part by my own past actions and choices. What you are claiming, therefore, not only distorts what I was saying. It devalues and insults my own contribution to making that actual world in which I was acting at that moment the kind of world in which I could not then have voluntarily and rationally done otherwise."

14   Compatibilist Responses II: Frankfurt-style Examples

Most traditional arguments for compatibilism, like the classical compatibilist one considered in Section 13, have conceded that the power to do otherwise *is* required for moral responsibility, but have argued that this power, properly understood, is compatible with determinism. Yet a different and more radical strategy has become especially popular in contemporary philosophy among compatibilists. It is to argue more directly that the power to do otherwise is not required at all for moral responsibility. The most widely discussed and sophisticated versions of this compatibilist strategy in recent philosophy involve appealing to so-called Frankfurt-style examples (FSEs), named for Harry Frankfurt who formulated the first of these influential examples in 1969.

Frankfurt's aim in formulating the first of these examples was to refute a principle he called:

> **The principle of alternative possibilities (PAP)**: agents are morally responsible for their actions, only if they could have avoided performing them or could have done otherwise when they performed them.

To refute this principle, Frankfurt imagined the following scenario:

> A controller, Black, has direct control over the brain of another man, Jones, and wants to allow Jones to do only what Black wants him to do. Black prefers, however, to allow Jones to act on his own whenever possible and so will only intervene if Jones is about to do something that he, Black, does not want.

Given this scenario, Frankfurt asks us to consider situations in which Jones is about to do what the controller Black wants, so that Black does not intervene. In such situations, Frankfurt argues, Jones could be morally responsible for acting as he does, since he would have acted on his own, from his own motives and for his own reasons, and nothing and no one (including Black) would have interfered with or prevented him from doing what he chose to do.

Yet Jones in such situations, Frankfurt argues, could not have done otherwise, for if he had given any indication of doing otherwise, Black would have prevented him from doing so. Thus, this principle of alternative possibilities (PAP), Frankfurt concluded, is false: it is *not* true that agents can be morally responsible for what they have done, *only* if they could have done otherwise. For such Frankfurt-controlled agents could be responsible for what they have done, if they did it on their own and the controller did not intervene, even though the agents could not have done otherwise, because the controller would have intervened and not let them do otherwise.

Now the first thing to be said about this line of argument is that it should not surprise us at this point that this PAP of Frankfurt's is false. For we have already seen from the discussion of the Luther example and other examples that agents can be morally responsible for actions that flow from their wills at the time they acted and such that they could not have done otherwise at that time. One can be responsible for "will-settled" actions like Luther's "Here I stand," even if one could not have done otherwise than perform them when they were performed. In other words, we don't need to appeal to unusual examples involving Frankfurt-style controllers to establish that Frankfurt's PAP is false.

But not all of our actions in our lifetimes could be determined or already will-settled in this way when we act, if we are ever to be responsible for our wills being set the way they are when we act. For this to be the case, we would have to, at some times in our lives, be capable of not merely will-settled but also will-setting or self-forming choices or actions that were not determined by our existing wills when we performed them and were such that we could have willingly done otherwise when we performed them. In other words, some, even many, morally responsible actions in the course of our lives may be such that, at the time we performed them, we could not then and there have willingly done otherwise, like Luther's act. But it does not follow that all our morally responsible actions could be like this, if we are ever to be morally responsible to any degree for the state or quality of our wills.

So such examples do show that Frankfurt's PAP is false: it is not true that agents can be morally responsible for their actions, only if they could have avoided performing them, or could have done otherwise, when they performed them. Frankfurt-style examples show this as well and so he and others are right in saying that these examples show that Frankfurt's PAP is false. But such Frankfurt-style examples fail to show the falsity of a more complex principle required for free will that might be stated as follows and that may be called:

> **Will-setting**: agents are ultimately responsible for having the wills (characters, motives, and purposes) they express in action, only if sometimes in their lives they willingly (voluntarily and intentionally) perform certain ("will-setting" or "self-forming") actions (SFAs) that it was causally possible at the time for them to have willingly avoided performing.

These results have more general implications for Frankfurt-style examples. For it can be shown that if all actions were under the control of Frankfurt controllers or mechanisms as in such examples, there could be no such self-forming choices or actions (SFAs) and hence no will-setting of the kind required for agents to be responsible for having the quality of wills they do have.

This is the case because, in all Frankfurt-style examples, including all the more sophisticated versions proposed since Frankfurt's original one, the one thing the Frankfurt controllers can never allow is the following: Frankfurt controllers can never allow the agents an opportunity to bring to completion "will-setting" or "self-forming" actions such that the agents are able to willingly perform the actions and are also able to willingly do otherwise. The controllers must always intervene in some way to prevent such will-setting actions from occurring so that *they* themselves, *the controllers and not the agents*, can *ensure* the agents always do what the controllers want them to do. For the essence of a will-setting or self-forming action is that *the agent, and no one or nothing else*, can determine how such a will-setting action will turn out when it is performed.

15 The Intelligibility Question

We arrive finally at the most common and powerful objection made against libertarian views of free will that require its being incompatible with determinism. This objection has been made in various forms throughout history and continues to be commonly made and widely accepted in the present age. It is the objection that a libertarian and incompatibilist free will requiring UR is not even *intelligible* or *possible*. It is *not* something we *could* have anyway.

The culprit here is not determinism, but indeterminism. For, as noted in Section 1, this objection is related to an ancient dilemma: if free will is not compatible with determinism, it does not seem to be compatible with *indeterminism* either. Arguments have been made since ancient times, as noted in Section 3, that undetermined events would occur spontaneously and hence could not be controlled by agents in the way that free and responsible actions would require. If a choice occurred by virtue of some undetermined events in one's brain, it would seem a fluke or accident rather than a responsible choice. Undetermined events occurring in brains or bodies, it is commonly argued, would not seem to enhance freedom and control over, or responsibility for, actions but rather to diminish freedom, control, and responsibility.

In response to such arguments, as also noted, libertarians about free will have often appealed throughout history to special and unusual forms of agency or causation to explain undetermined free actions. Libertarians have appealed to noumenal selves outside space and time, to immaterial minds, uncaused causes, nonevent agent causes, and the like, to account for an otherwise undetermined free will. And their critics have responded in turn that these appeals reinforce the critics' view that one cannot make sense of an undetermined free will without appealing to unusual forms of agency that have no place in the modern scientific picture of the world and of human beings.

These debates thus lead us to another central question concerning libertarian free will that must now be considered. It may be called:

> **The Intelligibility Question:** Is a libertarian free will requiring UR even *intelligible* or *possible*? Can one make sense of such a free will requiring indeterminism without reducing free will to mere *chance*, on the one hand, *or* to *mystery*, on the other, and can such a free will be reconciled with modern scientific views of the cosmos and of human beings?

16   Indeterminism: Empirical and Philosophical Questions

In approaching these questions, let us first be clear that it is an empirical and scientific question whether any indeterminism *is* there in nature in ways appropriate for free will – in the brain, for example. No purely philosophical theory alone can settle the matter. As the Epicurean philosophers said centuries ago, if the atoms don't "swerve" in undetermined ways, and in the right places, there would be no room in nature for free will. Christoph Koch is a distinguished neuroscientist and a tough-minded one at that. He argues that "there is no evidence that any components of the nervous system – a warm and wet tissue strongly coupled to its environment – display quantum entanglement" (2009: 40). But Koch goes on to say that "what cannot be ruled out," however, "is that tiny quantum fluctuations deep in the brain are amplified by deterministic chaos" so that they might have nonnegligible nondetermined effects on neural processing and thereby affect human decision-making (2009: 40). Koch does not endorse this idea, but says it cannot be ruled out, given what is currently known about the brain. And such a role for indeterminism is all that would be needed for the view to be presented here.

In the most recent edition of *The Oxford Handbook of Free Will* (2011), Robert Bishop agrees with Koch and cites a number of other neuroscientists and philosophers who have made similar suggestions. If minute quantum indeterminacies occurred at the intraneural or synaptic levels of the brain, affecting the timing of firing of individual neurons, Bishop argues, these indeterminacies, however minute, could be amplified, due to sensitivity to initial conditions, so that they had nonnegligible effects on neural processing in the form of neural noise. Bishop goes on to point out that one need not even appeal only to chaos to get these effects. For, as he notes: "the exquisite sensitivity needed for . . . the amplification of quantum effects is a general feature of nonlinear dynamics and is present whenever nonlinear effects are likely to make significant contributions to the dynamics of a system" (Bishop 2011: 91). And it is generally agreed, Bishop adds, that nonlinear dynamics is pervasive in the functioning of human brains.

A growing number of other scientists, not mentioned by Bishop, have also made suggestions about the possible role of indeterminism in the brain in recent years, including, interestingly, its potential evolutionary significance. They include neuroscientist, Peter Ulric Tse, who has made detailed and highly original suggestions about these topics in a recent book (2013), as well as neuroscientists Paul Glimcher (2005) and Michael Shadlen (2014), biologists Bjorn Brembs (2011) and Martin Heisenberg (2013), astrophysicist Robert Doyle (2011), physicists G.F.R. Ellis (2009), John Polkinghorne (2009), David Layzer (2022), and psychologist Dean Simonton (2004), among many others.[4] It remains an open scientific question, of course, whether indeterminism does function in the neural processing of the brain. But rather than being dismissed out of hand, as in the past, this possibility is now regarded as a serious one by these and other scientists.

Yet our question at present is a philosophical one that has boggled people's minds since the time of the ancient Stoics and Epicureans: What could one *do* with indeterminism, assuming it was there in nature in the right places, to make sense of free will as something other than mere chance or randomness and without appealing to mystery? If minute quantum indeterminacies in the firings of individual neurons were amplified so that they introduced some indeterminism into the larger-scale processing in deliberation and decision-making, how could this help to make sense of free choice as something other than mere chance? This is the Intelligibility Question, just defined, about an incompatibilist free will that we must now address.

17   Initial Pieces: Self-formation, Efforts, Willpower, Volitional Streams

Let us begin by recalling that indeterminism does not have to be involved in all actions done "of our own free wills." It need be involved only in those choices or acts by which we make ourselves into the kinds of persons we are, with the wills we have. These are the "will-setting" or "self-forming" actions (SFAs) of earlier sections.

I believe these SFAs would occur at those difficult times in life when we are torn between competing visions of what we should do or become; and they would be more common in everyday life than one may think. Perhaps we are torn between doing the moral thing or acting from ambition, or between present desires and long-term goals, or we are faced with difficult tasks for which we have aversions, or have to exert willpower to keep prior commitments and resolutions rather than break them. In all such cases and many others, we are faced with competing motivations and have to strive or make an effort or exert willpower to overcome the temptation to do something else we also strongly want.

At such times, the tension and uncertainty we feel about what to do, I suggest, would be reflected in some indeterminacy in our neural processes themselves – in the form of amplified background neural indeterminacy as described in Section 16 – neural indeterminacy that is "stirred up," one might say, by the conflicts in our wills. The uncertainty and inner tension we feel at such soul-searching moments of self-formation would thereby be reflected in some indeterminacy in our neural processes themselves. The experienced uncertainty would correspond physically to the opening of a window of opportunity that temporarily screens off complete determination by the past.

A further step would then involve noting that in such cases of self-formation, where we are faced with competing motivations, whichever choice is made will require an effort of will or exercise of willpower to overcome the temptations to make the alternative choice. I thus postulate, in such cases, that different goal-directed cognitive processes ("volitional streams," we might call them) might be involved in the brain, corresponding to these exertions of effort or willpower. These cognitive processes or efforts would have different goals corresponding to the different choices that might be made (e.g. a moral choice or a self-interested choice). But, importantly, it is not being claimed that these efforts or exercises of willpower aimed at different choices would be occurring at the same time during deliberation. Nor would they be occurring throughout the entire deliberation. Rather, different efforts or exertions of willpower may be initiated at different times depending on the course of the agent's reasoning.

To illustrate, consider a familiar example of Peter van Inwagen's (1983) of a would-be thief, call him John, who is deliberating about whether or not to steal from a church poor box. Suppose John is deeply torn because, on the one hand, he is desperately in need of money and knows that no one is usually in the church on weekday afternoons, so he can likely steal the money without being caught. On the other hand, he has moral qualms about doing so because he knows that the money in the poor box is used to help other people who are in need, some of whom may need it as much as, or more than, he does.

We might then imagine that in the course of John's deliberation, various thoughts, experiences, and memories come to mind, various preferences, desires, and possibilities are assessed and weighed, so that his considered reasons incline him to choose to steal the money rather than not to steal it. Of crucial importance, however, if this is a self-forming choice situation in the sense described in prior sections, we must say that the reasons motivating the choice to steal the money merely *incline* John to make that choice at this time rather than the alternative choice. These reasons do not determine he will do so. To use a traditional expression of Leibniz, his reasons "incline without necessitating." If a choice is thus to be made in accord with these inclinations, effort would have to be made or willpower exerted to overcome the resistance in his will. This resistance would be coming from his motives to make the contrary choice, which motives also remain important to him.

This is where indeterminism would enter the picture as well. For, in the manner described earlier in this section, this conflict in John's will would "stir up" indeterminism in the effort to make the choice to which he is currently inclined (to steal from the poor box), making it uncertain the effort will succeed in attaining its goal. If the effort to choose to steal from the poor box in terms of his presently inclining reasons does succeed, despite this indeterminism, the choice to steal to which John is presently inclined would be made and the deliberation would terminate.

Note that if this should happen, the choice to steal, *despite being undetermined*, would have been made *by John* purposefully and in accordance with his will. For it would have been the result of a goal-directed effort of will to make just this choice at this time rather than an alternative choice. Moreover, the choice would have been made for the reasons inclining him toward that choice rather than the alternative at the time. Thus, it wouldn't have been a mere accident that the choice occurred, *even though its occurrence was undetermined*. The choice would have been brought about voluntarily and on purpose, as a result of the goal-directed effort of the agent.

What would happen, however, if due to the indeterminism involved, the effort to choose to steal from the poor box did *not* succeed at that time and the choice had not been made? Many critics of a free will requiring indeterminism assume that if a choice is undetermined, the agent would be able to make a different choice (e.g. to steal or not to steal) given exactly the same deliberation leading up to moment of choice, including exactly the same desires, beliefs, thoughts, inclinations, and prior reasoning. And given this assumption, it would follow, these critics argue, that if John had failed to choose to steal from the poor box at the time he did choose, due to the indeterminism involved, he would instead have chosen *not* to steal from the poor box at that time instead. And this seems problematic, these critics argue, given that his deliberation would have been exactly the same leading up to the choice. What would explain the difference in choice?

But this commonly made assumption need not be made, nor is it made, in the account of self-forming choices being given here. It is not assumed, nor need it be assumed on this account, that if a choice is undetermined, the agent might make different choices (e.g. to steal or not to steal) given exactly the same deliberation, including exactly the same desires, beliefs, and reasoning, leading up to the choice. All that follows from the assumption that a self-forming choice or SFA is undetermined is that the effort to make it may succeed *or may fail* at a given time in overcoming the resistance in the will to making it. And from this, it does not follow that if the effort fails, an alternative choice would be made at that same time.

Failure is rather a signal to the agent not to choose too quickly in terms of the presently inclining reasons. Failure says in effect: think more about this. The resistant motives for the alternative choice (e.g. John's motives for *not* stealing from a poor box) *still matter to you and these resistant motives should not be dismissed too readily.* These resistant motives are the causal source of the indeterminism in the effort to choose to steal in the first place, making it uncertain that the effort will succeed here and now. The stronger these resistant motives are, the greater the probability the effort may fail, due to the indeterminism to which the resistant motives give rise.

In other words, a distinction needs to be made between John's *not choosing to steal* at a time and his choosing *not to steal* at that time. What is assumed, if John fails in his effort to choose to steal from the poor box at a time, due to the indeterminism involved, is not that he would have made the contrary choice, not to steal, at that same time, but rather that no choice at all would have been made at that time. The deliberation might continue until a potential reassessment of the motivating reasons that inclined to one choice or the other led to another later effort to make the choice to steal or a potential reassessment led to a later effort to make the choice not to steal. Or, the deliberation might terminate without any decision being made.

John, we may imagine, if he fails to overcome the resistance in his will to making the choice to steal at a time, might reconsider his motivating reasons. Then, moved by his moral qualms about stealing money from a poor box used to help other people, he may be inclined seconds or minutes later to choose *not* to steal and make an effort to choose in accord with that inclination. The success of this further effort would also be undetermined, but if it succeeded nonetheless, the choice not to steal would be made. Or, John may find on reconsidering that he really needs the money and makes a further effort at a time later to overcome his moral qualms. This effort may in turn fail as well, but if it succeeds despite the indeterminism, he would make the choice to steal at this later time. Or, the deliberation may terminate without any decision being made. John may leave the church planning to think more about it, perhaps berating himself for his indecisiveness.

Note that in any of these possible scenarios, if John does succeed at a time in an effort to make one or another of the choices to which he is inclined at that time, he will have brought about the choice made and will have done so voluntarily and intentionally and for the motivating reasons that inclined him toward that choice at that time. For he would have succeeded in an effort whose goal was to make that very choice for those inclining (though not necessitating) reasons; and this would be the case even though the choice were undetermined.

> **Indeterminism** would have been involved in the effort, but it would not be the cause of the choice, if the effort succeeds. For the effort would have succeeded, *despite* the indeterminism and not *because* of it. The cause of the choice would have been the *agent*, whose effort or exercise of willpower brought about the choice.

Note also that the indeterminism that is ingredient in the agent's effort to make the choice to which the agent is then inclined *is not an accidental feature of the situation*. It does not just *happen* to be present. The presence of the indeterminism is rather a consequence of the conflict in the agent's will and of the resistant motives that are a feature of that conflict – resistant motives that have to be overcome by effort, whichever choice is made. The stronger these resistant motives are, the greater the degree of indeterminism stirred up, and the greater the probability of failure of the effort.

The idea is thus to *think of the indeterminism involved in self-forming choices*, not as a cause *acting on its own*, but as an *ingredient* in larger *goal-directed* activities of the agent, in which the indeterminism functions as a *hindrance* or *interfering* element in the attainment of their goals. The choices that result would then be *achievements* brought about by the goal-directed activities (the efforts of will or exercises of willpower) of the agent, which might have failed since they were undetermined, but one or the other of which might succeed in its goal.

Moreover, if such processes aimed at different goals may occur at different times in the course of deliberation (in the conflicted circumstances of a self-forming choice), *whichever choice may be successfully made will have been brought about by the agent's volitional striving* (the effort) to make that particular choice rather than the other at that time, despite the possibility of failure due to the indeterminism.

18   Indeterminism and Responsibility

Another significant consequence of thinking of indeterminism in this way is the following: when indeterminism functions in this manner as an obstacle to the success of goal-directed activities, the *indeterminism does not undermine responsibility, if the activities succeed in attaining their goals*, despite the indeterminism.

Consider the example introduced in Section 6 of an assassin trying to kill a prime minister from a distance with a high-powered rifle when, owing to a nervous twitch in his arm, he fails to hit his target. Or consider another example of a husband arguing with his wife, who in anger swings his arm down on her favorite glass tabletop intending to break it. In each of these cases we could imagine that an element of genuine chance or indeterminism is involved. We might imagine that the nervous twitches in the arms of the assassin that lead to missing his target – or the reduced momentum in the swing of the husband's arm that might lead to his failing to break the tabletop – are the result of undetermined quantum events in their brains or nerve pathways.

Due to this indeterminism in their nerve pathways, they might fail to do what they were intending and trying to do. But suppose that, despite the indeterminism, the assassin *succeeds* in his goal of killing the prime minister and the husband in breaking the tabletop. In such cases, both the assassin and the husband would be fully responsible for their actions, because both would have succeeded in doing what they were intending and trying, and making efforts to do, despite the indeterminism involved.

It would be a poor excuse for the assassin to plead in the courtroom that he was not guilty of killing the prime minister because due to the indeterminism in his nerve pathways it was undetermined, and hence a matter of chance, that he succeeded in hitting his target. It would be equally absurd for the husband to offer the excuse to his wife that, since it was undetermined that his arm swing would break the tabletop, the breaking of the tabletop was a matter of chance *and so he was not responsible.* His wife would not be impressed – and for good reason.

For there was indeed a "chance" these agents would fail in doing what they were trying or making efforts to do. But if they succeeded, nonetheless, chance would not have been the *cause* of the prime minister's death or the table's breaking. *They*, the agents, would have been the causes, by virtue of the fact that they would have succeeded in doing what they were intending and trying, and making efforts, to do.

> When indeterminism thus functions as an obstacle to the success of goal-directed activities, the indeterminism does not preclude full responsibility, if the activities succeed in attaining their goals nonetheless.

This would be the case for self-forming choices or SFAs as well, but with an important difference. *Whichever choice the agents should make* in the course of a deliberation in a self-forming choice situation, the agents would have succeeded in doing what they were making an effort to do at that time, despite the indeterminism involved in their neural processing.

If John, for example, chooses to steal from the poor box at any time during his deliberation, it will be due to the success of his effort to make that choice at that time, thereby overcoming the resistance in his will to doing so. And if he chooses not to steal from the poor box at any other time in the deliberation, it will be due to the success of his effort to make that other choice not to steal at that time, thereby overcoming the resistance in his will to doing so. Whichever choice is made in such self-forming choice situations, the indeterminism involved would thus not be a cause acting on its own but an ingredient in a larger goal-directed cognitive activity of the agent that would have succeeded in attaining its goal, *despite* the indeterminism and not *because* of it. The agents would be responsible for the choice made since they would have succeeded in doing what they were intending and trying to do; and this would be the case whichever choice should be made in the course of the deliberation.

To sum up, I have been arguing that self-forming actions (SFAs) occur at those difficult times in life when we are torn between competing visions of what we should do or become. On such occasions of self-formation, agents are, as is often said, "of two minds." Yet they are not two separate persons. They are not dissociated from either of their conflicted states of mind.

Consider a young woman who is about to graduate with honors from a law school and who is deliberating about which of two attractive job offers to accept. One offer is with a large corporate law firm in a big city, the other a smaller, up-and-coming, but less prestigious, firm in a smaller city near where she grew up. She is torn because each firm has features that are deeply attractive to her. On the one hand, people at the smaller firm are more friendly and there is more of a chance of attaining an eventual partnership there. The smaller firm is also near to where she grew up and hence to her family and many friends. On the other hand, she is extremely ambitious and the chance to be part of this very prestigious firm in a large city is very attractive to her, despite the difficulties it may involve. She is a small town person with big time ambitions.

The young woman of this example is a complex creature, torn inside by different visions of who she is and what she wants to be, as we all are from time to time. But **this is the kind of complexity needed for genuine** *self-formation* and hence for *free will rather than merely freedom of action*. And when agents, like this young woman, decide in such circumstances, and the indeterminate efforts they are making become determinate choices, they *make* one set of competing reasons or motives prevail over the others then and there by deciding. They thereby **voluntarily and purposefully commit themselves to a particular pathway into the future; and this will be so, whichever choice they should succeed in making,** despite the indeterminism involved.

19 Initial Questions and Objections: Indeterminism and Chance

Many questions and potential objections naturally arise about this view as so far presented. Addressing them will allow us to bring out more features of the view, which is far from complete. Many of the most obvious objections people have to views of free will requiring indeterminism, including the view presented here, rest on intuitions they have that if choices are undetermined, they *must* happen merely by chance – and so must be "random," "capricious," "uncontrolled," "irrational," and all the other things usually charged. Such intuitions are deeply rooted. But if we are going to understand free will, I think we have to break habits of thought supporting such intuitions and learn to think in new ways.

The first step would be to question the intuitive connection in people's minds between "indeterminism's being involved in something" and "it's happening merely as a matter of chance or luck." "Chance" and "luck" are terms of ordinary language that imply "something's being out of one's control." So, using them already begs certain questions and may mislead us. Whereas:

"Indeterminism" is a technical term that merely *rules out deterministic causation, not causation altogether. Indeterminism is consistent with probabilistic forms of causation*, where outcomes are caused, but not inevitably. It is thus a mistake – one of the most common mistakes in the long history of debates about free will – to assume that "undetermined" must mean or imply "uncaused."

Another common source of misunderstanding is the following: suppose our young law graduate does decide to join the larger firm in the big city. If her decision is undetermined up to the moment when it occurs, one may have the image of her first making the effort to overcome the still strong motives to do otherwise (to join the smaller firm) and then at the last instant "chance takes over" and decides the issue for her. But this image is misleading. On the view presented, one cannot separate the indeterminism and the effort, so that *first* the effort occurs *followed by* chance or luck. Rather, the efforts or exertions of willpower are temporally extended goal-directed processes of the agent and the indeterminism is an ingredient in these larger processes, not something separate that occurs *after* or *before* them. The neural networks that realize the efforts in the brain are circulating impulses and there is some indeterminacy assumed in the timings of firings of individual neurons in these circulating impulses. But these processes as a whole are her efforts and they persist right up to the moment when the decision is made.

There is no point at which her effort stops and chance "takes over." She decides as a causal result of her effort, even though she might have failed due to the indeterminism ingredient in the effort. Likewise, the husband breaks the table as a causal result of his effort, even though he might have failed because of the indeterminacy. This is why his excuse "chance broke the table, not *me*" is so lame when he succeeds.

20 Further Questions and Objections: Phenomenology and Rationality[5]

Yet another frequently made objection is that we are not introspectively or consciously aware of making efforts and performing multiple cognitive tasks in self-forming choice situations. But it is not being claimed that agents must always be introspectively aware of making such efforts or exertions of will-power (though sometimes they might be when they are very conflicted). And importantly, as emphasized in Section 5, it is not being claimed that these efforts or exercises of willpower aimed at different choices would be occurring at the same time during deliberation. Nor will they be occurring throughout the entire deliberation. Rather, different efforts or exercises of willpower may be initiated at different times depending on the course of the agent's reasoning.

What persons are introspectively aware of in self-forming choice situations is that they are trying to decide about which of two competing options to choose and either choice is difficult because there are resistant motives pulling them in different directions, some of which will have to be overcome, whichever choice is made. In such introspective conditions, I am theorizing that what is going on underneath is complex processing in the brain that may involve, at various times in the course of deliberation, one or another goal-directed cognitive process whose goal is making a specific choice and thereby overcoming resistance in the will to making that choice.

There is a more general point here that I have often emphasized: *introspective evidence cannot give us the whole story about free will*. Stay on the conscious surface and libertarian free will is likely to appear obscure or mysterious, *as it so often has in history*. What is needed is a theory about what might be going on behind the scenes when we exercise such a free will, not merely a description of what we immediately experience. There is, in fact, a growing body of empirical evidence showing that in complex cognitive processes, such as practical reasoning, much of the processing that is going on occurs unconsciously.[6] Moreover, some of what occurs unconsciously may involve effort making or exercises of willpower (e.g. to access memories or associations or considerations that may have a bearing on a decision, to overcome temptations to suppress other information we may not want to think about, to resist strong inclinations, to avoid rationalizations or self-deception, and so on).

Another common objection is that it is irrational to make efforts to do incompatible things. I agree it would be irrational, if the efforts to make incompatible choices (say to steal or not to steal) were being made at the same time, given exactly the same reasoning up to that time. But this is not what is being assumed here in the case of self-forming choices. Rather one or another of these efforts or exercises of willpower may be initiated at different times, depending on the trajectory of the agent's reasoning up to that time. In particular, one such effort may be initiated when, in the course of deliberation, the agent's considered reasons at that point incline (without necessitating) the agent to make one of the choices rather than another. It is not irrational to make an effort to make a choice in such situations in terms of one's presently inclining reasons. Though it would be irrational to also make an effort to make an opposing choice at *this same* time, given these same inclining reasons.

It is important in this regard to recognize the uniqueness of such self-forming choice situations. For our normal intuitions about efforts are formed in everyday situations in which our wills are already "set one way" on doing something, where obstacles and resistance have to be overcome, if we are to succeed in doing it. We want to open a door which is jammed, so we have to make an effort to open it. Such ordinary situations are what were earlier called "will-settled situations," where our wills are already set or settled on doing what we are making efforts to do. I am making an effort to open a jammed closet door to get what is inside. There is no resistance in my will to doing so, no reasons to do otherwise: I need what is in the closet for my day's activities. The resistance that has to be overcome by effort thus has an external source, in the conditions of the door and the door frame. The resistance is not coming from my own will.

By contrast, self-forming choices or SFAs, as we have seen, are will-*setting*, not already will-*settled*. Our wills are *not* already settled on doing what we are making efforts to do. The resistance that has to be overcome by effort is thus not coming from an external source. It is coming from our own wills. We *set* our wills one way or the other only in the act of choosing itself, when an effort we are making succeeds in overcoming the resistance in our will to making the choice in question.

This feature of will-setting choices – that the resistance to making them is coming from our own will, not from an external source – is related in turn to the fact that the reasons motivating the efforts to make such will-setting or self-forming choices merely "incline" without necessitating. The reasons motivating an opposing choice, which still matter to the agent, must be overcome by effort, if the choice to which the agent is presently inclined is to be made. It is thus rational to make an effort in such circumstances in terms of one's presently inclining reasons, if the resistance in one's will is to be overcome. What would *not* be rational would be to make an effort to make a contrary choice at this same time, given these same inclining reasons.

It would also be irrational to make no effort at all to overcome the resistance in one's will to making the choice to which one is inclined, but rather to leave the outcome to "chance" and "hope" the choice to which one is inclined "wins" out.

> Self-forming choices are not a matter of certain motivations *winning out* over others *on their own*. Rather, self-forming choices involve the *agent bringing it about* that one set of motivations wins out over another, by making an effort to do so and succeeding in that effort.

Because most efforts in everyday life, such as the effort to open the jammed closet door, are made in will-settled situations where our wills are already set on doing what we are trying or making efforts to do, we tend to assimilate all effort-making to such situations. We thereby fail to consider the uniqueness of *will-setting*, which is of a piece, in my view, with the uniqueness of **free will**.

21　Micro- vs. Macro-control

Another common line of reasoning lying behind many objections to an undetermined free will is the following: Is it not the case, one might ask, on the view proposed that whether agents succeed in making a choice A in the circumstances of a self-forming choice (i) depends on whether certain neurons involved in their cognitive processing fire or not (perhaps within a certain time frame), is it not the case that (ii) whether or not these neurons fire is undetermined and hence a matter of chance, and hence that (iii) the agent does not have control over whether or not they fire? But if these claims are true, it seems to follow that the choice merely *happened* as a result of the chance firings of these neurons and so (iv) the agent would not have had control over whether the choice of A was made or failed to be made and (v) hence the agent would not be responsible for making the choice.

For many persons, this line of reasoning clinches the matter. It looks like the outcome *must* be merely a matter of chance or luck after all. Yet they reason too hastily. For the really astonishing thing is that even though agents do not have control over whether or not the undetermined neurons involved in their cognitive processing fire or not, it does not follow that the agents do not have sufficient control to be responsible for the choices ultimately made. This does not follow when the following three things are also true: (i) the choosing of A rather than B (or B rather than A, whichever occurs) was something the agent was striving or trying to bring about at the time, (ii) the indeterminism in the neuron firings involved in this striving or trying was a hindrance or obstacle to the achievement of that goal, and (iii) the agent's striving or trying nonetheless succeeded in achieving the goal despite the hindering effects of the indeterminism.

For, consider the husband swinging his arm down on the table. It is also true in his case that (i) whether or not his endeavoring or trying to break the table-top succeeds *depends* on whether certain neurons in his nervous system fire or do not fire. It is also true in his case that (ii) whether these neurons fire or not is undetermined and hence a matter of chance and is (iii) not under his control. Yet, even though we can say all this, it does not follow that (iv) the husband did not break the tabletop, and that (v) he is not responsible for breaking the tabletop, if his endeavoring or trying to do so succeeds. And, importantly, each of these things would be true in the case of a self-forming action, whichever choice should be made. Astonishing indeed! Yet this is the kind of surprising result one gets when indeterminism or chance plays an interfering or hindering role in larger goal-directed activities of agents that may succeed or fail.

It is well to meditate on this: we tend to reason that if an action (whether an overt action of breaking a table or a mental act of making a choice) depends on whether certain neurons fire or not (in the arm or in the brain), then the agent must be able to make those neurons fire or not, if the agent is to be responsible for the action. In other words, we think we have to crawl down to the place where the indeterminism originates in the individual neurons and makes them go one way or the other. We think we have to become originators at the micro-level and "tip the balance" that chance leaves untipped, if we (and not chance) are to be responsible for the outcome. And we realize we cannot do that. But we do not have to. It is the wrong place to look. We do not have to micromanage our individual neurons one by one to perform purposive actions and we do not have such *micro-control* over our neurons even when we perform ordinary free actions such as swinging an arm down on a table.

What is needed when we perform purposive activities, mental or physical, is *macro-control* of processes involving many neurons – processes that may succeed in achieving their goals despite the interfering or hindering effects of some recalcitrant neurons.

We do not have **micro-control** our each individual neuron or muscle that might be involved in our purposive activities. But that does not prevent us from having **macro-control** over these purposive activities themselves (whether they be mental activities such as practical reasoning, or physical activities, such as arm-swingings) and being responsible when those purposive activities attain their goals.

22   Control and Responsibility

But if indeterminism does not take away control altogether, does it not at least *diminish* the control agents have over their actions? Is it not the case that the assassin's control over whether the official is killed (his ability to realize his purposes or what he is trying to do) is lessened by the undetermined impulses in his arm – and so also for the husband and his breaking the table? Their control is indeed lessened. But a further surprising thing worth noting is that *diminished control in such circumstances does not entail diminished responsibility*, when agents *succeed* in doing what they are trying or making efforts to do. The assassin is not less guilty of killing the official if he did not have complete control over whether he would succeed because of the indeterminism; nor is the husband less guilty of breaking the table if he succeeds, despite the indeterminism involved.

Suppose there were three assassins, each of whom killed an official. Suppose one of them (an older assassin contemplating retirement) had a 50% chance of succeeding because of the indeterministic wavering of his arm, another had an 80% chance, and the third (a young stud) nearly a 100% chance. Is one of these assassins less guilty than the others, *if they all succeed*? It would be absurd to say that one assassin deserves a hundred years in jail, the other eighty years, and the third fifty years. The diminished control in the assassins who had an 80% or a 50% chance does not translate into diminished responsibility when they succeed.

There is an important further lesson here about free will in general. We should concede that indeterminism, wherever it occurs, does diminish control over what we are trying to do and is a hindrance or obstacle to the realization of our purposes. But recall the case of the young law graduate mentioned in Sections 18 and 19. The indeterminism that is admittedly diminishing her control over the choice she may be trying to make (to join one law firm or another) is coming from her own will. It is coming from the motives she has for making the opposing choice (to join the competing firm).

In each case, the indeterminism is functioning as a hindrance or obstacle to her realizing one of her purposes – a hindrance or obstacle in the form of resistance within her will which has to be overcome by effort. If there were no such hindrance – if there were no resistance in her will – she might indeed in a sense have "complete control" over one of her options. There would be no competing motives standing in the way of her choosing it and therefore no interfering indeterminism. But then also, she would not be free to *rationally* and *voluntarily* choose the other purpose (choose otherwise), because she would have no good competing reasons to do so. Thus:

> By being a hindrance to the realization of some of our purposes, indeterminism opens up the genuine possibility of pursuing other purposes – of choosing or doing otherwise in accordance with, rather than against, our wills. *To be genuinely self-forming agents (creators of ourselves) – to have free will – there must at times in life be obstacles and hindrances in our wills of this sort that we must overcome.* Free will is a gift, but it also involves struggle – and achievement.

23 Agency, Complexity, Disappearing Agents

Another question that has had a hypnotic effect on modern free will debates, reflecting deeply rooted intuitions, is the following: Do we not have to postulate an additional kind of "agent-causation" over and above causation by states and events to fully capture libertarian free choices, given that such choices must be undetermined by prior states and events? There is a residual fear underlying questions of this kind that the "agent" will somehow "disappear" from the scene if we describe its capacities and their exercise, including free will, in terms of causation by states and events alone involving the agent. I believe this fear to be ultimately misguided.

A continuing substance (e.g. an agent) does not absent the ontological stage because we describe its continuing existence – its life, if it is a living thing – including its capacities and their exercise, in terms of states, events, and processes involving it. One needs more reason than this *to think that agents do not cause things, only events cause things.* Human agents are continuing substances with both mental and physical properties. But it is not inconsistent to say this and to say that the *lives* of agents, their capacities, and the *exercise* of those capacities, including free will, must be spelled out in terms of states, processes, and events involving them. In short:

> One does not have to choose between **agent (or substance) causation** and **event causation** in describing freedom of choice and action. One can affirm both.

In the case of self-forming choices or SFAs, for example, it is true to say both that "the agent's deliberative activity, including their effort, caused or brought about the choice" and that "the agent caused or brought about the choice." Indeed the first claim *entails* the second. Such event descriptions are not meant to deny that agents, qua substances, cause their free choices and free actions. Rather, the event descriptions spell out in more detail *how* and *why* the agents did so. There is thus no reason to worry that the "agent" will somehow "disappear" from the scene if we describe its capacities and their exercise, including free will, in terms of causation by states and events involving the agent.

Relevant here to explaining the role of agents in the causation of action is a peculiarly modern scientific way of understanding this role that has roots in ancient views, such as that of Aristotle.

> **Agents**, according to this modern conception with ancient roots, are to be conceived as *information-responsive complex dynamical systems.* "An agent's causing an action" is to be understood as "an agent, conceived as such an information-responsive complex dynamical system, exercising *teleological guidance control,* over some of its own processes."

Complex dynamical systems are understood in this context in the manner of "dynamical systems theory." Such systems (now known to be ubiquitous in nature and which include living things) are systems in which emergent capacities arise as a result of greater complexity. When the emergent capacities arise, the systems as a whole impose novel constraints on the behavior of their parts.

Such complex systems exhibit **teleological guidance control (TGC)** when they tend through feedback loops and error correction mechanisms to converge on a goal (called an attractor) in the face of perturbations.

Such control, as neuroscientist Marius Usher argues (2006), *is necessary for any voluntary activity* and he interprets it in terms of dynamic systems theory, as I would as well. Neuroscientists E. Miller and J. Cohen (2001) argue that such cognitive (guidance) control in human agents stems from the active maintenance of patterns of activity in the prefrontal cortex that represent goals and the means to achieve them. These patterns provide signals to other brain structures, they argue, whose net effect is to guide the flow of activity along neural pathways that establish the proper mappings between inputs, internal states, and outputs (Miller and Cohen 2001: 403).

An important consequence of understanding the agent causation involved in free agency and free will in this way is that the causal role of the agent in intentional actions of the kind needed for free agency and free will is not *reducible* to causation by mental states of the agent alone, such as beliefs, desires, and intentions. That would leave out the added role of the agent, qua complex dynamical *system*, exercising teleological guidance control (TGC) over the process*s linking* mental states to actions. In the absence of this *systemic control* by the agent over the *manner* in which the mental states cause the resulting events, the causation by mental states might be "deviant" and the outcomes would not be intentional actions of the agent.

A further significant consequence of understanding causation of free actions in this way, as neuroscientist Usher (2006) points out, is that while the TGC of the kind required is compatible with determinism, it is also compatible with indeterminism. A complex dynamical system can exhibit TGC, tending through feedback loops and error correction to converge on a goal, even when, due to the presence of indeterminism, it is uncertain whether the goal will be attained. Such control is necessary for any voluntary activity, as noted, whether the voluntary activity is will-settled and determined or will-setting and not determined.

To sum up, one does not have to choose between agent (or substance) causation and event causation in accounting for free agency, libertarian or otherwise. You can, indeed you must, affirm both. And the agent or substance causation involved is not reducible to event causation by mental states alone for the reasons explained. There is thus no "disappearing agent problem" as well.

My view has often been called an event-causal (EC) libertarian view of free will to distinguish it from the two other familiar kinds of libertarian views, agent-causal (AC) and noncausal (NC). But I was never happy with this EC designation because of what has been said in this section, namely that an adequate libertarian theory of free will must appeal to both agent-causation and event-causation, and neither is reducible to the other. Thus, I now argue that we need to add to the three standard kinds of libertarian views (AC, EC, and NC) a fourth kind of view which I call AC/EC (if that doesn't sound too much like a rock group, as I noted when this title was first introduced), a view that requires both agent and event causation. My view, I argue, has always been of this AC/EC kind, which I now refer to as "a fourth way forward" in understanding libertarian free will.

24 Regress Objections: Responsibility and Character Development

Another common worry is that views of free will requiring UR lead to a vicious regress. To be ultimately responsible for a choice that issues from an agent's present will (character, motives, and purposes), the agent must be at least in part responsible by virtue of choices or actions voluntarily performed in the past (SFAs) for having the will he or she now has. But to be ultimately responsible for these earlier SFAs by which we formed our present wills, would we not have to be responsible in turn for the characters, motives, and purposes from which these earlier SFAs issued? And would this not require still earlier SFAs by which we formed these characters, motives, or purposes?

We would thus be led backwards to the earliest choices of childhood when the wills from which we chose were not formed by us at all but were entirely the product of influences outside ourselves: parents, social conditioning, heredity, genetic dispositions, and so on. It may thus appear that all responsibility for later choices in life would go back to the earliest choices of childhood when we seem to have far less freedom and responsibility than we have later in life, which is absurd.

The first response to make to this familiar worry is to note that UR for choices in later life need not have its source entirely in choices of childhood. This would be true only if we made no subsequent self-forming choices in later life. Whereas, by contrast, the account of self-forming choices given in Sections 4–7 implies that if self-forming choices are possible for agents at all, they would normally occur throughout our lives and more so as we mature and life becomes more complex. This is so because:

> It is the complexity of our lives, and of our wills and motivations, that gives rise to conflicts in our wills and to **self-forming actions (SFAs)** in the first place; *and this complexity does not abate, but normally grows, as we develop beyond childhood.* In making self-forming choices as we mature, we would be constantly forming and *reforming* our existing characters, motives, and purposes as we go along in ways that, while influenced by our prior characters, motives, and purposes, are not determined by our prior characters, motives, and purposes.

I argue therefore, in partial agreement with philosophers, such as Aristotle, who talk about the development of "character," that responsibility for our *wills* (characters, motives, and purposes) accumulates over time (Kane 1996). Putting the matter in terms of the present theory: by making many self-forming choices through a lifetime, we gradually form and reform our characters, motives, and purposes in ways not determined by our past. It would follow that with regard to most of the self-forming choices we make, our responsibility has a twofold source: first, in the self-forming choices themselves we make in the present between our conflicting motives and purposes and, second, in the conflicting motives and purposes themselves from which the choices are made, many of which had *their* source in earlier SFAs by which we gradually formed our present wills over time.

The only exceptions, of course, would be the very earliest SFAs of childhood when it *is* normally true, if we go back far enough, that the motivations among which we choose all come from sources outside ourselves, parents, society, upbringing, etc. I have discussed these first SFAs of childhood in a number of writings (e.g. Kane 2011) and have a distinctive view about them, which may be spelled out as follows.

In the earliest SFAs of childhood, our responsibility, so far from being the source of all later responsibility, *is* very limited, precisely because there is as yet no backlog of self-formed character. That is why we hold children less responsible the younger they are. I further argue that:

> **The earliest self-forming actions (SFAs) of childhood** have a probative (or probing or learning) character to them. Young children are often testing what they can get away with and what consequences their behavior will have on them and others (among the many reasons why child-rearing is so exhausting). Their character is thus slowly built up by how they respond to the responses to these earliest probes. *Character and purposes to which they commit themselves accumulate and they become more responsible for subsequent acts that flow not just from present efforts but from past formed character and purposes as well.*

If a three-year-old is told not to take more than his share of cookies, but tries to do so anyway the next time, resisting his conflicting motives not to disobey his parents, then the child is responsible. But he is not as responsible as when he does it a second, third or fourth time and it becomes a pattern of behavior. The wise parent will not punish him severely the first time, but may do so mildly, by withholding something he wants. *But the wise parent will also know that it is a mistake never to hold the child responsible at all for these earliest probes. For it is only by being so held responsible in however limited ways in our earliest years that we gradually become self-forming beings with wills of our own making.*

25 The Explanatory Luck Objection: Authors, Stories, Value Experiments, and *Liberum Arbitrium*

These reflections lead to one of the most common and powerful variants of the luck objection made against this view and many other libertarian theories during the past three decades. This objection, which has been called the "Explanatory Luck Objection," is stated in the following way by Alfred Mele (1998), one of its most astute and persistent defenders:

> **The Explanatory Luck Objection**: If different free choices could emerge from the same past of an agent, there would seem to be no explanation for why one choice was made rather than another in terms of the total prior character, motives, and purposes of the agent. The difference in choice (i.e. the agent's choosing one thing rather than another) would therefore be just a matter of luck.

This objection in various formulations is now so widely cited and affirmed by critics of libertarian views of free will that it is often referred to as *the* luck objection in the literature. And many philosophers assume it is decisive. I think they are mistaken. But I also think the objection has the power it has because it teaches us something important about free will.

The first obvious thing to be said in response to this luck objection is the following: in the case of self-forming choices as described here, it is not true to say, as the objection does, that "different free choices could emerge from the same past of an agent." This is not true, if it means the agent could make opposing choices (e.g. to steal or not to steal) given exactly the same prior reasoning leading up to the moment of choice. All that follows, as argued in Sections 5 and 6, from the fact that a self-forming choice is undetermined is that it might be made at a given time or might fail to be made at that time. It does *not* follow that the opposing choice (not to steal) would be made at that same time, given exactly the same reasoning leading up to the choice to steal. And this would be true whichever choice is made in a self-forming choice situation.

Moreover, for whichever choice should be made in a self-forming choice situation, (i) the agent would have caused or brought about that choice by succeeding in an effort to bring it about, thereby overcoming resistance in the will to doing so, (ii) the agent would have knowingly made that choice *rather than* the alternative, and (iii) the agent would have had the power to bring about the choice made and would have successfully exercised that power when it was made. This power was not unlimited since the effort through which it was exercised might have failed due to the indeterminism involved. But if the effort succeeded, the agent's power to make the choice would have been successfully exercised. (iv) The choice would have been made for reasons that inclined (without necessitating) the agent to make that choice at that time rather than the alternative – reasons that the agent then and there chose to act upon. (v) The agent would have made the choice rather than the alternative *voluntarily* (without being coerced against his or her will) and (vi) would have done so *intentionally* or on purpose, not merely by mistake, by succeeding in an effort aimed at making that very choice rather than the alternative.

If saying "the agent's choosing one thing rather than the another is just a matter of luck," as this explanatory luck objection also does, is meant to deny any of these things (i–vi) about such self-forming choices, then saying that the outcome was just a matter of luck seems to be the wrong conclusion to draw. And if one were to say that "just a matter of luck" is meant to be consistent with all of these things, the argument from luck would seem to lose much of its traction.

Ah, but not quite all traction; and this is where things get interesting. With powerful arguments in philosophy, it is not enough to show their conclusions do not necessarily follow from their premises. One needs also to show why they seem to have such power and seem irrefutable. The luck objection in this popular form does not show that libertarian free choices must be "just a matter of luck," if that entails denying any of the claims (i–vi). But it does show that there is something to the oft-repeated charge that such self-forming choices must be *arbitrary* in a certain sense.

A residual arbitrariness seems to remain in all self-forming choices (SFAs) because the agents cannot in principle have *sufficient* or *overriding* (*conclusive* or *decisive*) prior reasons for making one option and one set of reasons prevail over the other. Therein lies the truth in this explanatory luck objection: *an undetermined free choice cannot be completely explained by the entire past, including past causes or reasons*; and I think it is a truth that reveals something important about free will. I have argued elsewhere that such arbitrariness relative to prior reasons tells us that:

> **Every undetermined self-forming choice** is the initiation of a novel pathway into the future, whose justification lies in that future and is not fully explained by the past (Kane 1996: 145–146). In making such a choice we say, in effect, "I am opting for this pathway. It is not required by my past reasons, but is consistent with my past and is one branching pathway my life can now meaningfully take. Whether it is the right choice, time will tell. Meanwhile, I am willing to take responsibility for it one way or the other."

Of special interest here, as I have often noted, is that the term "arbitrary" comes from the Latin *arbitrium*, which means "judgment" – as in *liberum arbitrium voluntatis* ("free judgment of the will" – the medieval designation for free will). Imagine a writer in the middle of a novel. The novel's heroine faces a crisis and the writer has not yet developed her character in sufficient detail to say exactly how she will act. The author makes a "judgment" about this that is not determined by the heroine's already formed past, which does not give unique direction. In this sense, the judgment (*arbitrium*) of how she will react is "arbitrary," but not entirely so. It had input from the heroine's fictional past and in turn gave input to her projected future. In a similar way:

> Agents who exercise free will are both authors of and characters in their own stories at once. By virtue of "self-forming" judgments of the will (*arbitria voluntatis*) (SFAs), they are *"arbiters" of their own lives, "making themselves" out of a past that, if they are truly free, does not limit their future pathways to one.*

If we should charge them with not having sufficient or conclusive prior reasons for choosing as they did, they might reply:

> True enough. But I did have "good" reasons for choosing as I did, which I'm willing to endorse and take responsibility for. If they were not sufficient or conclusive reasons, that's because, like the heroine of the novel, I was not a fully formed person before I chose (and I still am not, for that matter). *Like the author of the novel, I am in the process of writing an unfinished story and forming an unfinished character who, in my case, is myself.*

26   Contrastive Explanations

Closely related to this explanatory luck objection is another objection concerning "contrastive explanation" that is frequently made against theories of free will requiring indeterminism. A contrastive explanation is an explanation for why one thing occurred *rather than* another. In the case of free choices, it would be an explanation in terms of an agent's prior character, reasons, or motives for why the agent made one choice rather than another.

The objection in this case is that if a self-forming choice (e.g. between A and B) is undetermined up to the moment when it is made, there could be no adequate contrastive explanation for why it was made rather than the alternative choice. For the fact that the choice was undetermined would mean that either choice (of A or of B) might have occurred, given the totality of the agent's traits of character, motives, and reasoning preceding the moment of choice. And there thus could not be an explanation for why one choice was made rather than the other at that moment in terms of the totality of the agent's character, motives, and reasoning prior to choice.

The first thing to be said in response to this familiar argument is similar to the first thing said in response to the explanatory luck objection: in the case of self-forming choices as understood here, it is not true to say, as this objection does, that either choice (of A or of B) might have occurred, "given the totality of the agent's traits of character, motives, and reasoning preceding the moment of choice." All that follows from the fact that a self-forming choice (e.g. the choice of A) is *undetermined* at a given time is that it might be made at that time or might *fail* to be made at that time. It does *not* follow that if the choice (of A) fails to be made at that time, the opposing choice – (of B) – would be made *at that same time*, given exactly the same reasoning that led to the choice of A.

But those who make this objection concerning contrastive explanation to views of free will requiring indeterminism usually have another assumption in mind that also needs to be addressed. They often assume that for an explanation of a free choice to be adequately contrastive in the sense they require, the following would have to be the case: if making the choice that was made during a deliberation rather than any alternative was the rational or reasonable thing to do, given the totality of the agent's reasons or motives, then making an alternative choice during that same deliberation, given the totality of the agent's reasons or motives, would *not* have been rational or reasonable. If making an alternative choice in the circumstances might also have been a rational or reasonable thing to do, we would not have an adequate contrastive explanation, in the sense these critics would require, for why one choice was made *rather than* another in terms of the agent's reasons and motives.

But if this is what contrastive explanations would require, there clearly could not be contrastive explanations in the sense these critics require of self-forming choices or SFAs. For it is an essential feature of self-forming choices that no *such* strong contrastive explanations could be given for them. The reason is that, in addition to being undetermined, self-forming choices must satisfy *plurality conditions* for free choice: the power to make them and the power to do otherwise, *either way*, voluntarily, intentionally, *and rationally*. And this rules out the requirement that any other choice that might have been made in the course of a deliberation, other than the choice actually made, would have been unreasonable or irrational.

Moreover, this feature is not a defect of self-forming choices, according to the account given of them, but it is a consequence of their power. For it is precisely because agents have the power to make such choices and the power to do otherwise, voluntarily, intentionally, and rationally either way that makes it possible for such choices to be *will-setting* rather than *will-settled*. And the power to make will-setting choices at some points in our lives is what makes it possible for us to be makers or creators to some degree of our own wills rather than to be always acting from wills already formed.

It is also important to emphasize, however, that while agents who make such will-setting or self-forming choices may not have conclusive or decisive reasons for making the choice that is made rather than any other, such agents do nonetheless have reasons for choosing as they do that are "good enough" to render the choices they do make reasonable and rational ones, given their total reason sets when they choose. Some mathematical decision theorists speak in this connection of:

> **Satisficing reasons:** reasons that are good enough to justify a choice or action even though they are not sufficient to render any possible alternative choice or action that might have been made in the circumstances unreasonable or irrational.

Reasons for will-setting or self-forming choices are satisficing reasons in this decision-theoretic sense.

Moreover, the fact that the reasons for self-forming choices (SFAs) are satisficing in this sense is related to something important about free will that was spelled out in Section 25. It is related to the fact that "every undetermined self-forming choice is the initiation of a novel pathway into the future, whose justification lies in that future and is not fully explained by the past." In making such a choice we say, in effect, "I am opting for this pathway. It is not *required* by my past reasons, but is consistent with my past and is one branching pathway my life can now meaningfully take."

This "narrative" conception of self-formation, as we might call it, is nicely captured in an important recent book by John Doris *Talking to Ourselves: Reflections, Ignorance, and Agency* (2015a). In a section of this book in which

Doris talks about my views of agency and responsibility, he notes that in my defense of libertarian free will, I "develop the intriguing suggestion that ambivalence" about what one's true values are "and its resolution in action" is not contrary to responsible agency, but is essential to responsible agency (Doris 2015a: 162). It is so at least at some points in our lives when we are torn between conflicting values.

At such times, Doris says, when on my view we are engaged in self-formation, it is possible that more than one path into the future could represent our "true values," and it would be "up to us" which path we will take. We decide then and there which of our *possible* true values our actions will express. If we were never ambivalent – ambi-valent, I would say – in this way, we could not be self-creating beings, since our choices and actions would always be expressing what we *already* were, the formed will we already had.

At the point in his book, where Doris references these views of mine on conflicting values and ambivalence, he also discusses the example of Huckleberry Finn – an example that has played such a prominent role in contemporary philosophical writings on agency and ethics. On one telling of the Huck story, Doris says, "Huck held values favoring *both* the conventional course of action," that he should turn his friend and companion Jim, a black man who had escaped from slave owners, over to the authorities and, on the other hand, "the course [Huck] actually followed," of not turning Jim over. In sum, Doris says, "Huck's values *conflicted* . . . he suffered a kind of *ambivalence*" (Doris 2015a: 161).

That, I believe, is how Mark Twain himself tells the story. As I would put it:

> Huck is growing and developing as a self or agent. In deciding not to turn Jim in, Huck is not merely *expressing* what sort of a self he already is; he is also *deciding* what sort of a self he is going to be by deciding from among the conflicting values he has, which ones he will follow. He is thereby not merely engaged in self-*expression*, but in self-*making*, of the kind I believe *freedom of will* and not mere *freedom of action* sometimes requires. Such conflicts in the will and their resolution or lack thereof (as my wife, a writer, continually reminded me) are the stuff of most great literature and drama, Huck Finn, Madame Bovary, Hamlet, Anna Karenina, you name it.

Further Reading

For a more advanced discussion of the issues considered in this chapter by various authors, see the collection of readings in two editions of Robert Kane (ed.), *The Oxford Handbook of Free Will* (Oxford, 2002, 2011). The libertarian view of free will presented in this chapter is further developed in the following books of mine: *Free Will and Values* (Paragon, 1985), *The Significance of Free Will* (Oxford, 1996), *A Contemporary Introduction to Free Will* (Oxford, 2005), and a new, as yet unpublished work, *The Complex Tapestry of Free Will: A Philosophical Odyssey* (Oxford, accepted for publication) as well as numerous articles. A festschrift involving ten authors discussing my views of free will and my responses is edited by David Palmer, *Libertarian Free Will: Contemporary Debates* (Oxford, 2014).

Other libertarian views of free will, AC, EC, or (NC), different in various ways from the AC/EC view defended here, include Peter van Inwagen, *An Essay on Free Will* (Oxford, 1983), Timothy O'Connor, *Persons and Causes* (Oxford, 2000), Randolph Clarke, *Libertarian Accounts of Free Will* (Oxford, 2003), Carl Ginet, *On Action* (Cambridge, 1990), Hugh McCann, *The Works of Agency* (Cornell, 1998), Mark Balaguer, *Free Will as an Open Scientific Problem* (MIT, 2010), Laura Ekstrom, *Free Will: A Philosophical Study* (Westview, 2000), Stewart Goetz, *Freedom, Teleology and Evil* (Continuum, 2008: 303–316), David Hodgson, *Rationality+Consciousness = Free Will* (Oxford, 2012), E.J. Lowe, *Personal Agency: The Metaphysics of Mind and Action* (Oxford, 2008), Helen Steward, *A Metaphysics of Agency* (Oxford, 2012), Robert Doyle, *Free Will: The Scandal of Philosophy* (I-Phi Press, 2011), Kevin Timpe, *Sourcehood and its Alternatives* (Continuum, 2008), James Felt, *Making Sense of Our Freedom* (Cornell, 1994), Thomas Pink, *Free Will: A Short Introduction* (Oxford, 2004), Tim Mawson, *Free Will: A Guide for the Perplexed* (Continuum, 2011), and Meghan Griffith, *Free Will: The Basics* (Routledge, 2013). Three authors developing unique libertarian views are Christopher Evan Franklin, *A Minimal Libertarianism: The Promise of Reduction* (Oxford, 2018), John Lemos, *A Pragmatic Approach to Libertarian Free Will* (Routledge, 2018) and *Free Will and Values: Criminal Justice, Pride and Love* (Routledge, 2023), and Ken Levy, *Free Will, Responsibility and Crime* (Routledge, 2020) and "On Three Arguments Against Metaphysical Libertarianism" (*Review of Metaphysics* 76(4), 2023: 725–748). Alfred Mele, in his book *Free Will and Luck* (Oxford, 2006) and other works, develops some original possible libertarian views, without endorsing any particular view.

Useful introductions to scientific views of complexity and complex systems include R. Lewin, *Complexity: Life at the Edge of Chaos* (MacMillan, 1992) and M. Mitchell Waldrop, *Complexity: The Emerging Science at the Edge of Chaos* (Simon and Schuster, 1992). Works that attempt to apply theories about complex systems to issues of action and agency include E. Thelen and R. B. Smith, *A Dynamic Systems Approach to the Development of Cognition and Action* (MIT, 1994) and Alicia Juarrero, *Dynamics in Action: Intentional Behavior as a Complex System* (MIT, 1999). Writings by scientists suggesting possible roles for indeterminism in the brain and behavior include, among others, neuroscientist Peter Ulric Tse, *The Neural Basis of Free Will* (MIT, 2013), neuroscientist Paul Glimcher, "Indeterminism in Brain and Behavior," *Annual Review of Psychology* 56: 25–56), neuroscientist Michael Schadlin, "Comments on Adina Roskies: Can Neuroscience Resolve

Issues about Free Will?" in *Moral Psychology: Volume 4*, ed. by Walter Sinnott Armstrong (MIT, 2014: 139–150), biologist Martin Heisenberg "The Origin of Freedom in Animal Behavior," in A. Suarez and P. Adams (eds.), *Is Science Compatible with Free Will?* (Springer, 2013), physicist G.F.R. Ellis, "Top-down Causation and the Human Brain," in N. Murphy, G.F.R. Ellis, and T. O'Connor (eds.), *Downwards Causation and the Neurobiology of Free Will* (Springer, 2009), astrophysicist David Layzer, *Why We are Free: Consciousness, Free Will and Creativity in a Unified Scientific Worldview* (I-Phi Press, 2021), John Park, "Decision-making and Quantum Mechanical Processes of Cognitive Processing," *Journal of Cognitive Science* (accepted for publication), J.R. Busemeyer and P.D. Bruza, *Quantum Models of Cognition and Decision* (Cambridge University Press, 2012), Antonella Corradini and Uwe Meixner (eds.), *Quantum Physics Meets Philosophy of Mind: New Essays on the Mind-Body Relation in Quantum Theoretical Perspective* (De Gruyter, 2014), and Antoine Suarez and Peter Adams (eds.), *Is Science Compatible with Free?: Exploring Free Will and Consciousness in the Light of Quantum Physics and Neuroscience* (Springer, 2013).

Notes

1. Libertarianism *about free will* should not be confused with political and economic doctrines of libertarianism. Libertarians about free will can, and do, hold differing views on political and economic matters.
2. I have addressed these issues in Kane (1985, 1996, 2005, 2007, 2011, 2014), among other writings.
3. Galen Strawson has made this case most forcefully with his "Basic Argument" (1986).
4. For example, Satinover (2001), Vasiri and Plenio (2010), Rolls (2012), Stapp (2007), Hameroff and Penrose (1996).
5. Objections addressed in this section and subsequent ones have been made in various forms by many critics of these features of libertarian views of free will, including Pereboom (2001), Clarke (2003), Mele (2006), Haji (2009), Levy (2011), Caruso (2012), among others. Other attempts to answer such objections have been made by defenders of libertarian views, including Balaguer (2010), Franklin (2018), Lemos (2018).
6. See, for example, Nichols (2015), Balaguer (2010), Jedlicka (2014), Usher (2006), Miller and Cohen (2001), Glimcher (2005), Shadlen (2014), and Brembs (2011).

2

Compatibilism

John Martin Fischer

There may be outward impediments even whilst [an agent] is deliberating, as a man deliberates whether he shall play at tennis, and at the same time [unbeknownst to him] the door of the tennis court is fast locked against him.

Bishop Bramhall, A Defense of True Liberty

1 Introduction

To begin, take "compatibilism" to be the view that both some central notion of freedom and genuine, robust moral responsibility are compatible with causal determinism. This scientific claim is that, among other things, every bit of human behavior is causally necessitated by events in the past together with the natural laws. Of course, compatibilism, as thus understood, does not in itself take any stand on whether causal determinism is true.

Compatibilism is appealing because it appears so obvious to us that we (most of us) are at least sometimes free and morally responsible, and yet we also realize that causal determinism could turn out to be true. That is, for all we know, it is true that all events (including human behavior) are the results of chains of necessitating causes that can be traced indefinitely into the past. Put slightly differently, I could imagine waking up some morning to the newspaper headline, "Causal Determinism is True!" I could imagine reading the article and subsequently becoming convinced that causal determinism is true: that the generalizations that

Four Views on Free Will, Second Edition. John Martin Fischer, Robert Kane, Derk Pereboom, and Manuel Vargas.

describe the relationships between complexes of past events and laws of nature, on the one hand, and subsequent events, on the other, are universal generalizations with 100% probabilities associated with them. I feel confident that this would not – nor should it – change my view of myself and others as free and robustly morally responsible agents, deeply different from other animals.

The fact that these generalizations or conditionals have 100% probabilities associated with them, rather than 99 or (say) 90%, would not and should not have any effect on my views about the existence of freedom and moral responsibility. My basic views of myself and others as free and responsible are and *should be* resilient with respect to such discoveries about the generalizations of physics. This of course is not to say that these basic views are resilient to *any* empirical discovery – just to *this sort* of discovery.

So, when I deliberate, I often take it that I am free in the sense that I have more than one option that is genuinely open to me. Since causal determinism might, for all we know, be true, compatibilism is attractive. Similarly, it is very natural to distinguish agents who are compelled to behave as they do from those who act freely; we make this distinction, and mark the two classes of individuals, in common sense and the law. If causal determinism turned out to be true, along with incompatibilism, all behavior would be put into one class, and the distinctions we naturally and intuitively draw in common sense and law would be in jeopardy of disappearing.

And yet there are deep problems with compatibilism. Perhaps these are what have led some philosophers to condemn it in such vigorous terms: "wretched subterfuge," (Kant), "quagmire of evasion" (James), and "the most flabbergasting instance of the fallacy of changing the subject to be encountered anywhere in the complete history of sophistry . . . [a ploy that] was intended to take in the vulgar, but which has beguiled the learned in our time" (Wallace Matson). Kant added, for good measure, that compatibilism offers us "the freedom of the turnspit." Yikes!

In this essay, I will start by highlighting the attractions of compatibilism, and sketching and motivating a version of traditional compatibilism. I shall then present a basic challenge to it. Given this challenge, I suggest an alternative version of compatibilism, which I call "semicompatibilism," and I elaborate its advantages. Finally, I consider objections to this specific version of compatibilism, as well as compatibilism in general. My goal will be to present the scaffolding of a defense of semicompatibilism (highlighting the main attractions), rather than a detailed elaboration or defense of the doctrine. In Section 2, I begin with "classical" or "traditional" compatibilism, then turn to semicompatibilism. Many, although not all, their virtues are shared.

Oscar Wilde wrote in *The Portrait of Dorian Gray* that, if an author tries to exhaust the subject, he is in danger of exhausting the audience. I will not do the former, and I hope that I will not have done the latter!

2 The Lure of Compatibilism

Often, it seems to me that I have more than one path open to me. The paths into the future branch out from the present, and they represent different ways I could proceed into the future. When I deliberate now about whether to go to the lecture or to the movies tonight, I think I genuinely *can* go to the lecture and I genuinely *can* go to the movies (but perhaps not both). I often have this view about the future as a "garden of forking paths" (in Borges's wonderful phrase). But I can also be brought to recognize that, for all I know, causal determinism is true; its truth would not necessarily manifest itself to me in my subjective experience. Compatibilism allows me to keep both the view that I often have more than one path genuinely open to me and that causal determinism may be true. I can keep both views in the same mental compartment, so to speak; they need not be compartmentalized into different mental slots or thought to apply to different realms or perspectives.

It is incredibly natural – almost inevitable – to think that I could either go to the movies or to the lecture tonight, that I could either continue working on this essay or take a coffee break, and so forth. It would be jarring to discover that, despite the appearance of the availability of these options, only one path into the future is genuinely available to me. A traditional compatibilist need not come to the one-path conclusion, in the event that theoretical physicists conclusively establish that the conditionals discussed above have 100% probabilities, rather than (say) 90%. A compatibilist can embrace the resiliency of this fundamental view of ourselves as agents who (help to) *select* the path the world takes into the future, among various paths it genuinely *could* take.

Similarly, it is natural for human beings to think of ourselves as morally accountable in a deep way for our choices and behavior. Typically, we think of ourselves as morally responsible precisely in virtue of exercising a distinctive kind of freedom or control; this freedom is traditionally conceived as exactly the sort of "selection" from among genuinely available alternative possibilities involved in deliberation about the future. When an agent is morally responsible for her behavior, we typically suppose that she could have (at some relevant time) done otherwise.

Think of moral responsibility broadly, to include *aptness to* (or, possibly, *fittingness of*, or *desert of*) the full range of "reactive attitudes" (using P.F. Strawson's 1962 term): moral blame, punishment, moral praise, and moral reward. So construed, moral responsibility is central to our lives, and, arguably, to our status as persons. At the very least, its constituents help to bind us together as friends, lovers, teams, social groups, nations, and so forth.

So far as we are morally responsible agents, we are fundamentally different from nonhuman animals in specific and important ways. We morally blame and punish other human beings, and they can be deserving targets of the reactive attitudes, such as resentment, indignation, and gratitude. Resentment and indignation involve moral anger, and punishment is (among other things) an expression of such anger. Although we can legitimately "condition" and negatively re-enforce a nonhuman animal's behavior, it would be inappropriate to morally blame or punish them (or, for that matter, to morally praise or reward them).

The assumption that we human beings are morally responsible agents is extremely important and pervasive. In fact, it is hard to imagine human life without it. At the least, such a life would be very different from our current ones – less richly textured and, arguably, less desirable. A compatibilist need not give up this assumption, even if, as above, she were to wake up to the headline, "Causal Determinism is True!" (and she were convinced of its truth, over time). The resilience of moral responsibility with respect to the truth of causal determinism is not just a *desideratum* but also a *truth-making* feature of compatibilism (Fischer, accepted for publication, a).

In ordinary life, and in our moral principles and legal system, we distinguish individuals who behave freely from those who do not. Sam is a "normal" adult human being, who grew up in favorable circumstances. She has no unusual neurophysiological or psychological anomalies or disorders, and she is not in a context in which she is manipulated, brainwashed, coerced, or otherwise "compelled" to do what she does. More specifically, no factors that uncontroversially function to undermine, distort, or thwart the normal human faculty of practical reasoning or execution of the outputs of such reasoning are present. She deliberates in the "normal way" about whether to withhold pertinent information on her income tax forms, and, although she knows it is morally wrong, she decides to withhold the information and cheat on her taxes anyway.

According to our commonsense way of looking at the world and even our more theoretical moral and legal perspectives, Sam freely chooses to cheat on her income taxes and freely implements this choice. It is plausible that, given the assumptions I have sketched, she was free just prior to her decision and action *not* to so decide and behave. Insofar as Sam selected her own path, she acted freely and can be held both morally and legally accountable for cheating on her taxes.

We tend to exempt *other* agents from *any* moral responsibility in virtue of their lacking even the *capacity* to control their choices and actions; we take it that such individuals are so impaired in their cognitive and/or executive capacities that they cannot *freely* select their path into the future. Such agents may have significant brain damage or neurological or psychological disorders in virtue of which they are not even capable of exercising the distinctive human capacity of control in any morally significant context. Other agents have the basic features that underwrite this capacity, but they nevertheless may be exempt from moral responsibility in specific circumstances (perhaps due to coercion).

On the commonsense view, agents who are brainwashed (without their consent), involuntarily subjected to hypnosis or subliminal advertising or other forms of behavioral conditioning, or even direct stimulation of the brain, are not morally responsible for the relevant behavior. These people may nevertheless be morally responsible for choices and actions that are not the result of these "stock" examples of freedom-undermining and thus responsibility-undermining factors.

There are difficult cases of significant coercion or pressure that fall short of genuine compulsion, or subliminal suggestion that is influential but not determinative, about which reasonable persons may disagree. Further, there is considerable controversy over the role and significance of early childhood experiences, deprivations, poverty, physical and psychological abuse, and so forth. Even though there are "hard cases," common sense, and our moral and legal frameworks, have it that there are clear cases of freedom (and responsibility), and clear cases of the lack of it.

A compatibilist can maintain this distinction, even if it turns out that the physicists convince us that the probabilities associated with the relevant conditionals linking the past and laws with the present have 100% probabilities. *This is a significant and attractive feature of compatibilism.* Incompatibilism would seem to lead to a collapse of the important distinction between agents such as Sam and thoroughly manipulated or brainwashed or coerced agents. A compatibilist need not deny what seems so obvious, even if the conditionals have probabilities of 100%: there is an important difference between agents such as Sam, who act freely and can be held morally responsible, and individuals who are completely or partially exempt from moral responsibility in virtue of *special* hindrances and disabilities that impair their functioning. Again, a compatibilist's view of human beings as both free and morally responsible agents is *resilient* to the particular empirical discovery that causal determinism is true. Wouldn't it be bizarre if our basic view of ourselves as free and morally responsible, and our distinction between responsible agents and those who are insane or literally unable to control their behavior, would hang on whether the probabilities of the conditionals in the ultimate theory in physics are 90 or 100%? These central aspects of our interpersonal framework would then hang on a thread. How could so much depend on so little, on *this* kind of issue?

3   A Compatibilist Account of Freedom

One might distinguish between the forward-looking aspects of agency, including practical reasoning, planning, and deliberation, and the backward-looking aspects, including accountability and moral (and legal) responsibility. I noted in Section 2 that it is extremely natural and plausible to think of ourselves as having more than one path branching into the future. This same assumption appears to frame both our deliberation and attributions of responsibility. I shall here take it that the possibilities in question are the *same* in both forward-looking and backward-looking aspects of agency: when we deliberate, we naturally presuppose that we have different paths into the future, and when we assign responsibility, we suppose that the relevant agent had a different path available.

In both forward-looking and backward-looking contexts, it is appealing to think that the relevant sort of possibility or freedom is analyzed as a certain sort of choice-dependence. That is, when I'm deliberating, it is plausible to suppose that I genuinely can do whatever it is that I would do, if I were to choose to so act: I can go to the movies later insofar as I would go to the movies, if I were to choose to do so, and I can go to the lecture insofar as I would go to the lecture, if I were to choose to do so, and so forth. On this view, I can do, in the relevant sense of "can," whatever is a (suitable) function of my "will" or choices: the scope of my deliberation about the future is the set of paths along which my behavior is a function of my choices. I do not deliberate about whether to jump to the moon, because (in part at least) I would not successfully jump to the moon, even if I were to choose to do so.

Similarly, given the assumption of the unity of forward-looking and backward-looking features of agency, the alternative possibilities pertinent to the attribution of responsibility are understood in terms of choice-dependence. On this approach, an agent is morally responsible for a certain action (or omission) only if she could have done otherwise, and she could have done otherwise just in case she would have done otherwise, if she had so chosen. We would never hold someone morally responsible for failing to jump to the moon or save a drowning child in Alaska (while living in California).

This compatibilist analysis of freedom (or the distinctive sort of possibility relevant to deliberation and responsibility) is called the "conditional analysis" because it suggests that our freedom can be understood in terms of certain conditionals ("if–then" statements). More specifically, the conditional analysis commends to us the view that an agent S's freedom to do X can be understood in terms of the truth of a statement such as, "If S were to choose (will, decide, and so forth) to do X, S would do X." The subjunctive conditional specifies the relevant notion of "dependence." The analysis seems to capture important elements of our intuitive picture of what is within the legitimate scope of our deliberation and planning for the future. It also helps to sort out cases in which agents are morally responsible for their behavior and to distinguish these from cases in which agents are not. If someone is kidnapped and chained, she is presumably not morally responsible for not helping someone in distress insofar as she would still be in chains (and thus would not succeed in helping), even if she were to choose (decide, will) to help. Note that the relevant conditionals can be true in the context of causal determinism. An agent's actual choice to X can be causally determined, while it is true that if she were to have chosen Y, she would have done Y. (In this case, the choice to do Y would have been determined.)

Despite its considerable attractions, the conditional analysis, as presented thus far, has significant problems that should be recognized, even by the compatibilist. First, note that it may be that some outcome is choice-dependent in the way specified by the conditional analysis, and yet there may be some factor that seems to impair or hinder the relevant agent's capacity for *choice* in the circumstances in question. This factor could render the agent powerless to choose and do otherwise (in the sense presumably relevant to moral responsibility), even though the outcome is choice-dependent.

To see this, consider the following example due to Keith Lehrer. As a boy, Thomas had a terrible and traumatic experience with a snake. He thus has a pathological aversion to snakes that renders him psychologically incapable of bringing himself to choose to touch a snake (much less pick one up), even as an adult. A snake is in a basket right in front of Thomas. Whereas it is arguably true that *if* Thomas were to choose to pick up the snake, he would do so, it seems that Thomas cannot choose to pick up the snake. Thomas cannot pick up the snake because he cannot choose to do so, and yet the conditional analysis would have it that he can pick up the snake. This is a problem that even a compatibilist should see as significant; the problem clearly does not come from causal determination *per se*. The general form of the problem is that the relevant subjunctive conditional can be true consistently with the actual operation of some factor that intuitively (and apart from any contentious views about the compatibility of causal determinism and freedom) seems to make the agent psychologically incapable of choosing the act in question and thus unable to perform the act. Factors that would seem to render an agent psychologically incapable of choice might include past trauma, phobias, subliminal advertising, aversive conditioning, hypnosis, and so forth.

Lehrer's snake example and similar ones involving various phobias, however, do not indisputably refute the conditional analysis. That's because it is plausible that Thomas's aversion to snakes makes it false that if he were to choose to pick up the snake, he would do so. That is, the phobia (or pathological aversion) might render him unable to *translate* his choice into action, but not unable to make the choice itself. Intuitively, Thomas cannot pick up the snake, and on this analysis of the situation, the relevant conditional is false. So it is unclear whether this sort of example shows the inadequacy of the conditional analysis.

We can, however, construct similar examples that are closer to decisive against the analysis. An individual could have his brain directly manipulated (without his consent) to choose X. This would presumably render it true that he cannot choose to do another act Y, even though it might well be the case that *if* he had chosen to do Y, he would have done Y. (Of course, if the individual were to choose Y, then he would not have been subject to the actual manipulation to which he had been subjected – manipulation that issues in his choosing X.) Think of a demonic (or even well-intentioned) neuroscientist who can manipulate parts of the brain by using (say) a laser. The neuroscientist knows the systematic workings of the brain so that she knows what sort of laser-induced manipulation is bound to produce a choice to do X. If she does manipulate the individual's brain in this way, it would seem ludicrous to suppose that he is free to do Y; and yet it may well be true that *if* he were to choose Y, the neuroscientist would not have intervened, and the individual would successfully do Y. The outcome is choice-dependent – the conditional is true – but the individual is clearly powerless (in the relevant sense).

Some compatibilists about freedom and causal determinism have given up on the conditional analysis in light of such difficulties. Others have sought to give a more refined conditional analysis. We might distinguish between the generally discredited "simple" conditional analysis, and the "refined" conditional analysis. Different philosophers have suggested ways of refining the simple analysis, but it is beyond the scope of this chapter to discuss these interesting refinements.

If I were a traditional compatibilist (which I'm not), I would first note (as in the case of Thomas and the snake) that the phobia cases do not indisputably show that the conditional analysis is inadequate. Further, I would insist that it is impossible as a conceptual matter to induce mental states via electronic stimulation of the brain (or similar interventions). This is a view held by many philosophers, based on the nature of mental states, which must stand in certain relationships to other mental states. These relationships, defined in terms of dependencies and "counterfactual conditionals," are not consistent with secret neurophysiological inculcation.

This is the simplest, cleanest, and most plausible way of defending the conditional analysis of freedom. Adopting this approach would sidestep a huge set of debates (and voluminous literature) on fixing up the conditional analysis, referred to as "the new dispositionalism." This is a friendly, but not too friendly, suggestion, because I am not convinced that mental states cannot be inculcated, and I think that a defense of an analysis of freedom would be significantly weakened by *reliance* on such a controversial assumption.

Despite the basic intuitive appeal of the conditional analysis, and the possibility of refinement to avoid the kind of counterexample discussed just above involving manipulation of the brain, the analysis implies that an agent whose choice is causally determined can still be free to choose and do otherwise. To some (including, of course, the incompatibilist), this implication is fatal.

The compatibilist, however, insists on a crucial point – that not all causal sequences are "created equal." The worry then is, at most, a "near-death experience."

More specifically, the compatibilist wishes to insist that not all causally deterministic sequences undermine freedom; a straightforward and "upfront" commitment of the compatibilist is that we can distinguish among causally deterministic sequences, and, more specifically, that we can distinguish those that involve "compulsion" (or some freedom- and responsibility-undermining factor) from those that do not. For example, a compatibilist will contend that there is an obvious and important difference between a bank teller who is held up at gunpoint and one who secretly steals money from the bank for his own financial benefit. The first bank teller might be *coerced* into handing over the money, whereas the second isn't. Assuming an irresistible desire to comply with the threat, the first bank teller is not free to do otherwise – to refrain from handing it over – but the second one is free to refrain from stealing the money from the bank. Crucially, this distinction is present, even if causal determinism obtains, according to the traditional compatibilist.

4 The Consequence Argument

It is indeed a basic commitment of the compatibilist that not all causally deterministic sequences undermine freedom equally. There is nevertheless an argument that presents a significant challenge to this commitment and to the commonsense idea that we can be confident in distinguishing cases of freedom and responsibility from cases where some freedom- and responsibility-undermining factor operates. This argument is a "skeptical argument," rather like the skeptical argument from the possibility of illusion to the conclusion that we don't know what we ordinarily take ourselves to know about the external world. The skeptical argument in epistemology employs basic ingredients of common sense to challenge other parts of it; it employs ordinary ideas about the possibility of illusion and the concept of knowledge to generate the intuitively jarring result that we don't know what we take ourselves to know about the external world.

Similarly, the skeptical argument about our freedom employs ordinary ideas about the fixity of the past and natural laws to generate the intuitively jarring result that we are never free, if causal determinism turns out to be true (something we can't rule out a priori). If this skeptical argument is sound, it calls into question *any* compatibilist analysis of freedom (freedom of the sort under consideration – involving the capacity for selection among open alternatives). If the argument is sound, then not only both the simple and any refined conditional analysis but *any* compatibilist analysis of the relevant sort of freedom must be rejected. It is thus an extremely powerful and disturbing argument. I think that any honest and serious discussion of compatibilism must address this argument, to which I now turn.

The skeptical argument has been around in one form or another for a very long time (Fischer 2016a). A structurally similar argument was originally presented thousands of years ago; then the worry was fatalism (the idea that the truth values of statements about the future are fixed and thus we lack freedom). In the Middle Ages, the worry stemmed from the doctrine of God's essential omniscience. In the Modern Era, our attention has focused primarily (although by no means exclusively) on the threat posed by science – more specifically, the possibility that causal determinism is true. We simply do not know whether causal determinism is true. If it turns out to be true, then all our behavior could in principle be deduced from a complete description of the past and laws of nature.

Here's the argument (very informally). Suppose that causal determinism is indeed true. Given the definition of causal determinism, it follows that my current choice to continue typing (and not take an admittedly much-needed coffee break) is entailed by true propositions about the past and laws of nature. Thus, if I were free (just prior to my actual choice) to choose and subsequently do otherwise, I must have been free so to behave that the past would have been different, or the natural laws would have been different. But, intuitively, the past is "fixed" and out of my control and so are the natural laws. I cannot now do anything that is such that, if I were to do it, the past would have been different (say, John F. Kennedy never would have been assassinated) or the natural laws would be different (say, some things would travel faster than the speed of light). It appears to follow that, despite the natural and almost ineluctable sense I have that I am frequently free to choose and do otherwise, I am *never* free in this way, if causal determinism obtains.

Although the compatibilist wishes to say that not all causally deterministic sequences equally threaten freedom, the Consequence Argument, so-called by Peter van Inwagen because under causal determinism all our behavior is the consequence of the past plus the laws of nature, appears to imply that causal determinism per se rules out the relevant sort of freedom. If the Consequence Argument is sound – and it relies on intuitively plausible ingredients, such as the fixity of the past and natural laws – the commonsense distinction between cases of "compulsion" and "ordinary" cases in which freedom is present would vanish, if causal determinism were true; and since we do not know that causal determinism is false, our basic views about ourselves (as free and morally responsible agents) would be called into question.

It is uncontroversial that I would not be morally responsible if I were subjected to clandestine (and unconsented-to) manipulation by a neuroscientist's laser beam. For a different choice to have occurred, the laser beam must not have connected the neurosurgeon with my actual choice. Similarly, if causal determinism were true, then the Consequence Argument brings out the fact that, even in the most "ordinary" circumstances, for a different choice to have occurred, the past or the natural laws would have had to have been different. The "line" connecting the past to my choice (via the laws) would have had to have been broken (or erased). The line posited by causal determination is like the laser beam.

Another way to look at the ingredients that go into the Consequence Argument is to consider the intuitive idea that, as Carl Ginet (1990) puts it, my freedom now is the power to add to the given past, holding fixed the laws of nature. In terms of our metaphor, my freedom (on this view) is the freedom to draw a line that *extends* the line that connects the actual past with the present (holding fixed the natural laws). The future may well be a garden of forking paths, but the forking paths all branch off a single line. The Consequence Argument throws into relief an intuitively jarring implication of compatibilism: the compatibilist cannot embrace the almost undeniable picture of our freedom as the power to add to the past, given the laws. Some have said that responsibility involves "making a connection" with values, or "tracking values" in a certain way, but there is even a more fundamental way in which our freedom and moral responsibility involve making a connection: we must be able to connect our current actions with the past (holding the natural laws fixed). In James Joyce's *The Portrait of the Artist as a Young Man*, Stephen Daedalus says, "The past is a nightmare from which I'm trying to awake." It's tough!

The Consequence Argument is a powerful and highly plausible argument. It does, however, fall short of being indisputably sound. Some compatibilists – multiple-pasts compatibilists – are willing to say that we can sometimes so act that the past would have been different from what it actually was; these compatibilists say that our freedom need not be construed as the freedom to extend the given past, holding the natural laws fixed. On such a view, I might have access to a possibility with a different past associated with it (say, a possible world with a different past from the actual past) insofar as there are no special "obstacles" in the actual course of events (or the actual world) that "block" such access. Other compatibilists – local-miracle compatibilists – are willing to say that we can sometimes so act that a natural law that actually obtains would not have obtained; some such compatibilists are also willing to countenance small changes in the past, as well as the laws. On this sort of view, I might have access to a possibility (or possible world) with slightly different natural laws from those that obtain actually, as long as these alternative scenarios do not involve widespread and big changes in the laws. This view is defended in a classic paper by David Lewis (1981) and more recent work by Kadri Vihvelin (2013).

There is thus room in philosophical space for compatibilism about causal determinism and the sort of freedom that involves genuine access to alternative possibilities, even in light of the Consequence Argument. Excellent philosophers have opted for compatibilist responses to the argument. I, however, find the Consequence Argument highly plausible. I thus think it is important to argue that there is an attractive kind of compatibilism that is consistent with accepting the conclusion of the Consequence Argument. The doctrine of semicompatibilism is the claim that causal determinism is compatible with moral responsibility, quite apart from whether it rules out the sort of freedom that involves access to alternative possibilities. Note that semicompatibilism does not take a stand on whether the Consequence Argument is sound; it is consistent with the acceptance or rejection of the Consequence Argument. My main goal is to defend semicompatibilism, although I am also inclined to accept the soundness of the Consequence Argument. The total package of views I am inclined to accept includes more than semicompatibilism, but semicompatibilism is the principle doctrine I seek to defend here.

5   Semicompatibilism and the Frankfurt-style Examples

Let's say you are driving your car and it is functioning normally. You want to go to the coffee house, so you guide the car to the right (into the parking lot for it). Your choice to go to the coffee house is based on your own reasons in the normal way, and the car's steering apparatus functions normally. (We assume that you, unlike me, are not a caffeine addict.) Here you have a certain distinctive kind of control of the car's movements – you have "guidance control" of the car's going to the right. This is more than mere causation or even causal determination; you might have causally determined the car's going to the right by sneezing (and thus jerking the steering wheel to the right) or having an epileptic seizure (and thus slumping over the wheel and causing it to turn to the right) without having exercised this specific and distinctive sort of *control*. Supposing that there are no "special" factors at work – no special psychological impairments, brain lesions, neurological disorders, and so forth – and imagining (as above) that the car's steering apparatus is not broken, you had it in your power (just prior to your actual decision to turn to the right) to continue going straight ahead, or to turn the car to the left, and so forth. That is, although you exercise guidance control in turning the car to the right, you presumably (and apart from special assumptions) possessed freedom to choose and do otherwise: you had "regulative control" over the car's movements. In the normal case, we assume that agents have both guidance and regulative control – a signature sort of control *of* the car's movements, as well as a characteristic kind of control *over* the car's movements. Here we are not assuming that causal determinism is true, since that would threaten our regulative control; in our ordinary reflection on moral responsibility, we do not presuppose the truth of causal determinism.

Whereas these two sorts of control are typically presumed to go together, they can be prized apart. Suppose everything is as above, but the steering apparatus of your car is broken in such a way that, if you had tried to guide the car in any direction other than the one in which you actually guided it, it would have gone to the right anyway – in just the trajectory it actually traveled. (A conspiracy of Starbucks employees?) The defect in the steering apparatus plays no role in the actual sequence of events, but it would have played a role in the alternative scenario (or range of such scenarios). Given this sort of "preemptive overdetermination," although you exhibit guidance control of the car's going to the right, you do *not* have regulative control over the car's movements: it would have gone in precisely the same way, no matter what you were to choose or try.

In this context you *do* possess *some* regulative control: you could have chosen otherwise, and you could have tried to guide the car in some other direction. This is reminiscent of Bishop Bramhall's example in the epigraph to this chapter, in which a person deliberates about whether to play tennis, even though, unbeknownst to the individual, the gate to the court is locked. Let's suppose he freely decides not to play tennis but could not have played. Similarly, in John Locke's famous example in his *Essay Concerning Human Understanding*, a man is transported into a room while he is asleep. When the man awakens, he considers leaving, but he decides to stay in the room for his own reasons. Locke says he voluntarily chooses to stay, and stays, in the room. (I would say he *freely* stays in the room.) Unbeknownst to this person, the door to the room is locked, and thus he could not have left the room. According to Locke, the man voluntarily stays in the room, although he does not have the power to leave the room. He exhibits a certain sort of control of his staying in the room ("guidance control"), even though he cannot do otherwise than stay in the room (and thus lacks regulative control over it). But note that, as in the second car example above, the man could have chosen to leave the room, and he could have tried to do so. Bramhall's tennis player could have chosen and tried to open the gate to the court. Thus, neither Bramhall nor Locke has expunged *all* alternative possibilities. (Note that Bramhall is an incompatibilist, whereas Locke is a compatibilist.)

Can structurally similar examples be given in which there is guidance control but *no* regulative control? This is where the "Frankfurt-style examples" come in (Frankfurt 1969). The contemporary philosopher Harry Frankfurt has sought to provide just such an example. One could say that he puts the locked gate/door inside the brain. In Locke's example, some factor (the locked door) plays no role in the individual's deliberations or choice, and yet its presence renders it true that the individual could not have done otherwise (could not have left the room). Frankfurt posits some factor that has a similar function in the context of the agent's brain: it plays no role in the agent's actual deliberations or choice, and yet its presence renders it true that the individual could not have chosen or done otherwise. If Frankfurt's examples work, then one could *entirely* prize apart guidance control from regulative control.

Here is my favorite version of a Frankfurt-style case. Jones has left his political decision until the last moment, just as some diners leave their decision about what to order at a restaurant to the moment when the waiter turns to them. In any case, Jones goes into the voting booth, deliberates in the "normal" way, and chooses to vote for the Democrat. Based on this choice, Jones votes for the Democrat. Unbeknownst to Jones, he has a chip in his brain that allows a neurosurgeon (Black) to monitor his brain. The neurosurgeon wants Jones to vote for the Democrat, and if she sees that Jones is about to choose to do so, she does not intervene in any way – she merely monitors the brain. If, on the other hand, the neurosurgeon sees that Jones is about to choose to vote for the Republican, she swings into action with her nifty electronic probe and stimulates Jones's brain in such a way as to ensure that he chooses to vote for the Democrat (and goes ahead and does so). Given the setup, it seems that Jones freely chooses to vote for the Democrat and freely votes for the Democrat, although he could not have chosen or done otherwise: Jones exhibits guidance control *of* his choice and vote, but he lacks regulative control *over* them. The neurosurgeon's chip and electronic device have brought Locke's locked door into the brain. Just as the locked door plays no role in Locke's man's choice or behavior but nevertheless renders it true that he could not have done otherwise, Black's setup plays no role in Jones's actual choice or behavior but renders it true that he could not have chosen or done otherwise.

How exactly does the neurosurgeon reliably know how Jones is about to vote? Frankfurt himself is vague about this point, but let us imagine that Jones's brain registers a certain neurological pattern if Jones is about to choose to vote for the Democrat and a different pattern if Jones is about to choose to vote Republican. The chip can subtly convey this information to the neurosurgeon, which she can then use to good effect. The mere possibility of exhibiting a certain neurological pattern is not sufficiently *robust* to ground ascriptions of moral responsibility, on the picture that requires access to alternative possibilities. That is, *if* moral responsibility requires the sort of control that involves selection from among various paths that are genuinely open to an agent, the mere possibility of involuntarily exhibiting a certain neurological pattern would not seem to count as the relevant sort of "selection." Put slightly differently, just as it is not enough to secure moral responsibility that a different choice could have *randomly* occurred, it is not enough to secure moral responsibility that a different neurological pattern could have been exhibited *involuntarily*. Such a trivial possibility is a mere "flicker of freedom" and not sufficiently robust to ground moral responsibility. How could something as important as moral responsibility come from something so thin and entirely involuntary?

It is tempting then to suppose that one could have a genuine kind of control, guidance control, without another, regulative control, and that such control is all the freedom required for moral responsibility. Even if the Consequence Argument were sound and thus all causally deterministic sequences were equally potent in ruling out the sort of control that requires access to alternative possibilities (regulative control), it would *not* follow that all causally deterministic sequences equally threaten guidance control and moral responsibility. If moral responsibility does not require the sort of control that involves access to alternative possibilities, this opens the possibility of defending a kind of compatibilism, even granting the soundness of the Consequence Argument. Even with the acceptance of the incompatibility of causal determinism and regulative control, the Frankfurt-style cases offer us a kind of metaphysical "soft landing."

Various philosophers – spoilsports! – have resisted the conclusion that one can expunge all vestiges of regulative control while at the same time preserving guidance control. They have pointed out that the *appearance* that Frankfurt-style cases help to separate guidance from (all) regulative control may be misleading. Perhaps the most illuminating way to put their argument is in terms of a dilemma first presented by Robert Kane (1985). The first horn assumes that indeterminism is true in the Frankfurt-style examples; in particular, it assumes that the relationship between the "prior sign" (read by Black) and Jones's subsequent choice is causally *indeterministic*. It follows that right up until the time Jones begins to choose, he can begin to choose otherwise; after all, the prior sign (together with other factors) falls short of causally determining the actual choice. Thus, there emerges a robust alternative possibility – the possibility of beginning to choose otherwise. This is no mere flicker of freedom; although it may be blocked or thwarted before it is completed or comes to fruition, it is nevertheless a voluntary episode – the initiation of a choice to do otherwise.

The second horn of the dilemma assumes that causal determinism is true in the examples. Given this assumption, it would appear to be straightforwardly question-begging to say that Jones is morally responsible for his choice and behavior (despite lacking genuine access to alternative possibilities). After all, the compatibility of causal determination and moral responsibility is precisely what is at issue!

The dilemma is powerful, but I am not convinced that it presents an insuperable objection to the employment of the Frankfurt-style examples as part of a general strategy of defending compatibilism. First, there have been various attempts at providing explicitly indeterministic versions of the Frankfurt-style cases, and some of them are promising. I don't think it is obvious that one could not construct a Frankfurt-style example under the explicit assumption of causal indeterminism in which there are *no* robust alternative possibilities. Recall that it is not enough for the proponent of the regulative control requirement to identify just *any* sort of alternative possibility; rather, she needs to find an alternative possibility that is sufficiently *robust* to ground attributions of moral responsibility, given the regulative control picture. If the ground of moral responsibility is a certain sort of *selection* from genuinely available paths into the future, then paths accidentally or inadvertently taken are irrelevant. To seek to get responsibility out of mere flickers of freedom is akin to alchemy. Here I agree with the distinguished philosopher Robert Kane, who ably defends libertarianism in this volume. He accepts the regulative control model and insists on the "dual voluntariness" constraint on moral responsibility. This is the idea that moral responsibility for a voluntary and free action requires an alternative possibility in which the agent acts voluntarily (and freely). He essentially denies that mere flickers of freedom are sufficiently robust to secure regulative control. Kumbaya!

On the second horn of the dilemma, causal determinism is assumed. I agree that it would be dialectically rash to conclude precipitously from mere consideration of the example presented above that Jones is morally responsible for his choice and vote. Rather, my approach would be more circumspect. First, I would note that the distinctive contribution of the Frankfurt-style examples is to suggest that, if Jones is not morally responsible for his choice and behavior, this is *not* because he lacks genuine access to (robust) alternative possibilities. After all, in the example Black's setup is sufficient for Jones's choosing and acting as he actually does, but intuitively irrelevant to Jones's moral responsibility. We can identify a factor – Black's elaborate setup – that is (perhaps in conjunction with other features of the example) sufficient for Jones's actual choice and behavior but plays no role in Jones's deliberations or actions. As Frankfurt noted, Black's setup could have been subtracted from the situation and the actual sequence would have flowed in exactly the way it did. When something is in this way irrelevant to what happens in the actual sequence issuing in an agent's choice and behavior, it would seem to be irrelevant to his moral responsibility.

The distinctive element added by the Frankfurt-style type examples, under the assumption of causal determinism, is this: if the relevant agent is not morally responsible, it is not because of his lack of regulative control. They show it is not the lack of genuine access to alternative possibilities (regulative control) *in itself* (and apart from pointing to other factors) that rules out moral responsibility. Now we can ask whether there is some other factor – some factor that plays a role in the actual sequence – that rules out moral responsibility, if causal determinism obtains. We will turn to a more thorough and careful consideration of such "actual-sequence factors" in Section 6. For now, I simply wish to note that there is nothing question-begging or dialectically inappropriate about how I have invoked the Frankfurt-style examples thus far, and their distinctive role is to call into question the relevance or importance of regulative control in grounding moral responsibility.

Taking stock, in Section 4, I presented the Consequence Argument. I did not officially endorse its conclusion, although I am inclined to believe that the argument is valid and, further, that its premises are based on extremely plausible ingredients. I suggested that it would be prudent to seek a defense of compatibilism that does not presuppose that the Consequence Argument is unsound. Here I have presented the rudimentary first steps toward just such a compatibilism. I have invoked the Frankfurt-style examples (the prototypes of which are in Bishop Bramhall and John Locke) to support the contention that moral responsibility does not require regulative control, but only guidance control. Further, I have suggested that (thus far at least) there is no reason to suppose that causal determinism is inconsistent with guidance control. Better: I have contended that even if causal determinism threatens regulative control, it does not thereby threaten guidance control. In Section 6, I will explore whether there are other reasons (apart from the lack of regulative control) why causal determinism is incompatible with moral responsibility.

6   Direct Incompatibilism

In Section 5, I sketched an argument for the conclusion that regulative control (and genuine access to alternative possibilities) is not required for moral responsibility. I suggested that alternative possibilities do not – in themselves and apart from indicating something else – ground ascriptions of moral responsibility. Note that if causal determinism is true and the Consequence Argument is sound, then there are *no* alternative possibilities available to agents – even mere flickers of freedom. One reason someone might insist on the importance of even insignificant possibilities – mere flickers of freedom – would be as *indicators* of something in the actual sequence: the lack of causal determination. Some philosophers have argued then that, even though access to alternative possibilities does not in itself explain or ground moral responsibility ascriptions, it is a necessary condition of them.

Why might one think that causal determinism rules out moral responsibility "directly," and not by closing off alternative pathways? As discussed in Section 4, suppose we represent causal determination as a line from features of the past to one's current choice (and behavior). Now we consider whether we as theorists must posit a broken or dotted line for it to be plausible that the agent is morally responsible. In terms of the metaphor, the question is about the significance of the gaps. Why must there be gaps or spaces between the dots, in order to make room for moral responsibility?

One reason it might have been supposed that we need to posit gaps or spaces is to allow for access to alternative possibilities. Here the gaps give rise to "elbow room" that provides the space to pursue alternative paths. To employ another metaphor with which I am, lamentably, well acquainted, living in Southern California: if traffic is proceeding on the freeway literally bumper to bumper, there are no gaps or spaces between the cars. Given this, no car after the first can exit the freeway or the lane in which it is traveling; the lack of space between cars renders it impossible for the drivers to change directions (although of course they can try). But the argumentation in Section 5 (pertaining to the Frankfurt-style examples) showed that the significance of the gaps or spaces in the actual sequence cannot be to make room for access to alternative possibilities. We must look for some other significance of the gaps.

Leaving aside elbow room for changes of direction, why might we insist on not being "scrunched up" in the indicated way? In this section, I shall explore views about the (intrinsic) importance of the gaps. First, it might be suggested that, without gaps, there is no room for "agents." Second, I consider the related idea that only with spaces can one have "activity," rather than mere passivity. Third, I evaluate the notion that if the line is entirely filled in, then the "source" of the relevant choices and behavior must be external to the agent in a way that rules out moral responsibility. I turn, finally, to a fourth strategy, much in vogue in contemporary discussions.

It is sometimes proclaimed that if causal determinism were true, there would be no room for "agency." It is, however, unclear what the claim amounts to. Here is one way of specifying it. If causal determinism is true, then individual agents – persons or selves – are entirely composed of events (construed broadly) that have deterministic causal interaction with each other and the external world. If we are just complexes of events related deterministically to our external and internal surroundings, there might not seem to be space for "selves" or "persons." The worry here appears to be that causal determinism entails a kind of "reductionism" about the self or agent alleged to be unattractive and implausible. If all there is is a bunch of events in a deterministic causal network, where, it might be asked, is the self or agent? The self is crowded out.

I find this worry hard to get a handle on. There are various versions of "reductionism" – about meaning, explanation, metaphysics, and so forth. This is not the place to address them, or their relationship to the doctrine of causal determinism. The main point I wish to make is that it is not clear that causal determinism entails *any* obviously problematic reductionism. One can be misled by looking in the wrong place. If you were to micro-miniaturize yourself and explore the human nervous system from inside the body, all you would see are cells bumping into each other. It does not follow that the human nervous system cannot support thought or consciousness.

If one were to take apart a television set and look at its inner workings, all one would see would be a bunch of physical components. I suppose one could be completely perplexed if one tried to find the tv at the level of the components. But it does not follow that the tv is not composed of a set of components, perhaps structurally and functionally related in the right ways. The tv is nothing more than these parts, structured and capable of functioning in certain characteristic ways; to look for the tv at the level of the parts, just as objects and apart from relationships and functioning, is to look in the wrong place. Similarly, it may well be that a self or agent is a set of events (broadly construed) within a deterministic causal network structured and capable of functioning in certain distinctive ways; to look for the self or agent at the level of the parts is to look in the wrong place. Further, it is not at all clear how simply breaking the line (representing causal determinism) and inserting spaces really helps us to find the self; if anything, it threatens to make matters worse. (It would obviously be unpromising to look for the tv set in the spaces between the components!) The self would disappear – lost in space(s).

There may well be something to the worry about causal determinism not leaving room for the self or agent, but it is not obvious. I have not proved the worry is not to be taken seriously; rather, I have simply suggested that it is not decisive (at least as thus far developed). The second worry is perhaps closely related to the first. An agent is not simply a coherent and separate individual or self – an agent must be "active" in a signature sense, rather than merely or wholly passive. The second concern then is that causal determinism rules out *activity* in the relevant sense – it would render us all completely passive. Harry Frankfurt, who many philosophers assume is a compatibilist, has expressed the worry that causal determinism might rule out activity; he thus concludes that we do not yet have a conclusive defense of compatibilism. In my terminology, Frankfurt's point is that, even if regulative control were not required for moral responsibility, it is not clear that we would have guidance control (and thus moral responsibility) in a causally deterministic world. This is because causal determination might crowd out being *active*.

The relevant notion of activity is difficult to put one's finger on, and its relationship to causal determinism is obscure. Not surprisingly, however, I am not convinced that determinism is inconsistent with the relevant notion of activity. Here I seek to present some considerations that render it plausible that causal determination is consistent with activity. I agree with Frankfurt that we don't have an entirely satisfactory grasp of the distinction between activity and passivity, but I hope to assuage some of the anxieties. I offer a philosophical tranquilizer.

Note first that there is an ordinary way of making the distinction between being active and being passive that is entirely irrelevant to issues pertaining to causal determinism; being active in this sense is in no way threatened by causal determination. So, for example, we characterize someone as "active" in a relationship insofar as she "takes the lead" in various ways: she typically and frequently makes suggestions about activities, projects, and ways of doing things, she anticipates potential problems and seeks to head them off, she does not defer to her partner's wishes or suggestions easily, and, in general, she "listens to her own voice" or perhaps "takes cues from herself." She is a leader, as opposed to a follower. On the other hand, someone is relatively passive insofar as he is deferential: he typically allows his partner to take the lead in setting policies and making suggestions, he tries to please her and often defers to her wishes, and he basically takes his cues from her, rather than listening to his own voice. Of course, this is all very rough, but it should be evident that nothing in the distinction between being "active" in the ordinary interpersonal sense and being passive requires the absence of causal determination: being on the look-out for new adventures and taking one's cues from within can be part of a caus-ally deterministic sequence.

Now someone might object that this "ordinary and commonplace" way of making the distinction is *not* what is at issue in the more refined reflection on moral responsibility in which we are currently engaged. Here (it is alleged) we can just see that the ordinary notion of activity is not enough, and in order to be active in the sense that is required for moral responsibility, one's choices, behavior, and the formation of one's character over time cannot be causally determined. This, however, is to abandon the idea that there is a widely shared and appealing notion of "being active," which is embedded in our common-sense ways of understanding ourselves and interpreting our behavior, by refer-ence to which we can see that causal determination would rule out moral responsibility. The relatively widely shared and appealing notion of "being active" is completely consistent with causal determinism. In contrast, the incompatibilist is invoking a rather *special* and *particular* notion of "being active," and it is unclear that *this* notion of activity is required for moral respon-sibility. Why, one might ask, demand this rarified sort of "activity" for moral responsibility?

It is almost as if the incompatibilist is in the grip of a certain metaphor – that of a row of dominos. Suppose you impart enough force to the first domino to cause (via a deterministic sequence) the rest of the dominos in the row to top-ple one by one. Each step along the way is causally determined. When the second domino falls, it deterministically causes the third domino to fall, and so forth. Clearly, the third domino is entirely passive. But it would be a mistake to suppose that all causally deterministic sequences are relevantly similar to this simple model of falling dominos! Note that the capacity for activity requires mental states, including "executive" states, such as volitions, decisions, and choices. A domino has no mental states and thus no executive states of the pertinent kind; a domino is not the *sort* of thing that can be active, quite apart from whether it is embedded in a causally deterministic sequence. The meta-phor is misleading: it is not causal determination that is the problem, but lack of executive mental states.

I now turn to the third worry mentioned above: that causal determinism would entail that an individual would not be the "source" of his choices and actions, in the sense of "sourcehood" required for moral responsibility. The idea that an individual must himself be the source of his behavior – or perhaps that the source must be "internal" to the individual – is arguably the idea that an agent must "initiate" his behavior. There is a widely shared and relatively uncontroversial view that moral responsibility requires that I be the initiator of my behavior – that I "start" the sequence that issues in certain consequences in the world. But, as with activity, there is a perfectly ordinary and commonplace notion of "initiation" that is orthogonal to issues pertaining to causal determinism; initiating something, in this sense, does not require the falsity of causal determinism. A boy may start a fire by lighting a match and throwing it in dry weeds, even in a causally deterministic world. Similarly, the Beatles (or perhaps the Dave Clark Five [or?]) started the so-called "British Invasion" of the United States involving rock bands in the 1960s, and to invoke a less-well-reported phenomenon (except in philosophy classes), Kant started the "transcendental turn" in philosophy, quite apart from whether or not causal determinism is true. We make perfectly reasonable attributions of initiation without bothering to consider whether causal determinism is true; and, upon reflection, it is not evident that we ought to retract the claims, even under the assumption of causal determinism. Lewis and Clark were pioneers along the Oregon Trail, whether or not determinism is true.

Now an incompatibilist might concede that there is a perfectly reasonable and "ordinary" notion of initiation that is not in fact threatened by causal determinism. But, as above, she might insist that this ordinary notion is not enough for moral responsibility; what is required, on this view, is a more rigorous kind of initiation that is inconsistent with causal determination. After all, it might seem that the boy does not "really" start the fire, if his choice was causally determined by previous events, and so forth. In reply, I would emphasize (as above) that the incompatibilist's strategy here abandons the idea that there is a widely shared and attractive notion of initiation that is appealing to both compatibilists and incompatibilists and is uncontroversially ruled out by causal determinism. The relatively widely shared and appealing notion is consistent with causal determinism. In contrast, the incompatibilist is identifying a *special* and *rarified* notion of initiation, and it is not at all clear or uncontroversial that *this* notion of initiation is required for moral responsibility. Note the similarity between the dialectic concerning being active and that of initiation.

There is thus a plausible notion of sourcehood that is consistent with causal determination. I wish now to explore some of the other reasons why philosophers have contended that causal determinism rules out sourcehood in the sense required by moral responsibility, and I wish to offer some plausibility-arguments against them. If causal determinism is true, then our behavior is the result of causally deterministic sequences that began well before we were even born. Since we are not responsible for initiating these sequences, and our decisions and behavior are the necessary results of them, we are not "ultimately" in control of our behavior. Saul Smilansky has a nice phrase for what he takes to be the responsibility-undermining characteristic of causal determination: the "mere unfolding of the given." Since our behavior under causal determinism would be the mere unfolding of the given, Smilansky concludes that compatibilism is "morally shallow." The locus of control would not be "internal" to us, in the required sense; from a perspective that considers the possibility of different beginnings of the sequences, which are out of our control, it is entirely arbitrary or a matter of pure luck that we behave as we actually do.

I suggest, however, that the incompatibilistic sourcehood requirement might come from a certain picture of agency. On this picture, the locus of control must be *entirely within* us, if we are to be morally responsible. When there is some factor that is external to us, over which we have no control, and upon which our behavior and even "the way we are" is (or might be) counterfactually dependent, the locus of control is not within us in the relevant way. It is as if the proponent of the incompatibilistic sourcehood constraint thinks of agents who are morally responsible as having "total control." An agent has total control when the locus of control is "within him" in a certain way. More specifically, an agent has total control over X only if, for any factor f which is a causal contributor to X and which is such that if f were not to occur, then X would (or might) not occur, then the agent has control over f.

Total control is a total fantasy – metaphysical megalomania, if anything is. The sun is shining (through the smog of Southern California), and its shining is a contributing causal factor to my continuing to exist, continuing to be an agent, and so forth. If the sun were to flicker out, I would not continue to exist, continue to be an agent, or engage in any behavior. So the sun's continuing to shine is a contributing cause of my behavior, is completely out of my control, and is such that, if it were not to occur, I would not even exist. Molly Bloom said in James Joyce's *Ulysses*, "The sun shines for you. . ."; and it is a good thing. The sun's continuing to shine is just one of an indefinitely large number of such factors: a huge meteorite's not hitting the United States, my not being hit by a lightning bolt, and so forth. I have no control of these factors, and thus lack total control, but this is surely irrelevant to the control required for moral responsibility.

The sun's continuing to shine is a (background) sustaining cause of my existence and agency. Consider now the fact that my parents did not seriously injure me when I was young and helpless. That they took good care of me was a contributing cause of my developing into an agent at all. Had they significantly abused and injured me, I would or at least might not have developed into an agent at all. And how my parents treated me when I was an infant was entirely out of my control. Clearly, my parents treating me in a gentle way is just one of an indefinitely large number of such factors: my not falling on my head and incurring a significant brain injury when I was young, my not having been born with a terrible neurological disorder, and so forth. (Note that a factor that is described negatively can be transformed easily into a positively described factor: my not being born with a neurological disorder is my being born with a normal central nervous system, and so forth.)

It is ludicrous to aspire to total control or to regret its absence. The locus of control is not ever wholly within us. Rather, we are thoroughly and pervasively subject to luck: actual causal factors entirely out of our control are such that if they were not to occur, things at least might be very different. Although it is perfectly reasonable to wish to be the source of one's choices and behavior, it is unreasonable to interpret the relevant notion of sourcehood in terms of total control. My suggestion is that once one sees that the picture favoring total control is inflated and illusory, one might have considerably less inclination to accept such a requirement for *any* reason.

Consider now what has recently become an influential reason to adopt the sourcehood requirement. On this view, if there is a condition or event in the past which, together with the laws of nature, entails that the agent makes a particular choice now, the source of the choice is external to the agent, and thus she is not morally responsible for the choice (and action). In general, if there is a deterministic cause of a choice, indisputably out of the agent's control, the source of it is external and the agent is not morally responsible for it. Sourcehood then requires lack of causal determination.

I find this understanding of the sourcehood requirement puzzling, especially within the dialectic context of an evaluation of compatibilism. It strikes one right off the bat that this version of the sourcehood requirement simply contends that if a choice is causally determined, the source is external to the agent and thus she is not morally responsible. This is question-begging. I am flummoxed when an incompatibilist invokes this requirement as if it settles the matter. Some take it as a conversation-stopper, but it can be, at best, a conversation-starter.

How might a proponent of the sourcehood requirement, so understood, defend its necessity for moral responsibility? To reiterate: without a defense it is question-begging. Maybe the background idea is that nonresponsibility is "transferred" from one thing to another by entailment. So: if an agent is not morally responsible for C and L (conditions in the past and the laws of nature), and C and L entails X, then the agent is not morally responsible for X (and, more specifically, her choice now).

I claim, however, that in evaluating this principle, it is crucial to keep in mind the distinction between regulative and guidance control. It is indeed plausible that if an individual lacks regulative control over (say) C and L, and C and L entails X, then she lacks regulative control over X. It does not, however, follow that if an individual lacks guidance control of (say) C and L, and C and L entails X, she lacks guidance control of X. We can see this by recalling our Frankfurt-style case discussed in Section 5. Jones lacks guidance control of the presence (and dispositions) of the counterfactual intervener, Black, and the presence (and dispositions) of Black entails that Jones chooses to (and does) vote for the Democrat. It does not, however, follow that Jones lacks guidance control of his choice to vote for the Democrat (and so acting). It is guidance, not regulative control, that is necessary for moral responsibility. We do not yet have any reason to accept an indeterministic sourcehood requirement.

Now a proponent of such a sourcehood condition might respond by pointing out an important difference between C and L, on the one hand, and Black and his setup, on the other. She may contend that, whereas C and L both entails and *explains* Jones's choice and action, Black and his setup entail but do not explain them. This distinction gives rise to an adjusted condition, according to which sourcehood is eliminated in the presence of an "explaining entailer" that is out of the agent's control: if an individual lacks guidance control of C and L, and C and L is an explaining entailer of X, then she lacks guidance control of X. Here the Frankfurt-style case is unhelpful as a counterexample, since Black and his set-up do not constitute an *explaining* entailer.

I would, however, resist this adjustment, absent further clarification. In the adjusted sourcehood condition and underlying principle, the notion of "explanation" is treated as if there is one explanation of an event or fact that is context-independent. This is, however, manifestly false; explanation is crucially context-dependent, and even within a particular context, there can be different explanations, in the presence of different interests, purposes, audiences, and so forth. Given the context- and purpose-relative nature of explanation, we would need a further clarification and specification of the incompatibilist's sourcehood condition, in order to evaluate it in a satisfactory way. To reiterate: the notion of explanation is extremely complex, and it would be a mistake to rest one's case on a principle that invokes it without further specification. Suppose, for instance, that X is "Jones chooses to vote for the Democrat." How does reference to a distribution of fundamental (or other) physical constituents in the distant past *explain* Jones's choice? And Black's setup *does* help to explain *the fact that Jones chooses to vote for the Democrat, one way or another*. Thus, the difference between a mere entailer and an explaining entailer is not applicable in an obvious way to help the proponent of the indeterministic source requirement, and we are left with no justification for the interpretation of it currently under consideration.

Imagine a beautiful dive. The diver may exhibit great skill and even courage. He may be commendable for his dive, even though he had no control over the building of the diving board, or the fact that it is not subtly cracked as a result of a lightning bolt during the previous evening, and so forth. He controls his dive, although he obviously does not control all the causally enabling conditions. His agency takes place literally on a platform that is not his own creation. Further, an agent who dives into a cold river to save a drowning child may control his choice and behavior, and be morally responsible for it, quite apart from issues pertaining to the creation or maintenance of the "platform" from which he leaps. Nietzsche (1954) famously wrote, "the *causa sui* is the best self-contradiction that has been conceived so far; it is a sort of rape and perversion of logic" (*Twilight of the Idols, or: How to Philosophize with a Hammer*, section 8, "The Four Great Errors"). To be the cause of oneself (in a stringent way) is surely an unreasonable aspiration, if coherent at all. Whereas some philosophers would claim (with Nietzsche) that being a *causa sui* is both ludicrous and part of common sense, I would urge that being the "initiator" or "source" of our choices and behavior is indeed part of common sense but is inchoate and undeveloped. We should not be quick to attribute a ludicrous and obviously self-contradictory notion to common sense. Rather, we should seek to capture the kernel of truth embedded in our ordinary conceptual scheme and articulate it in a more plausible, attractive way.

In this section, I have considered the possibility that causal determinism rules out moral responsibility "directly" (and not via threatening genuine access to alternative possibilities). If causal indeterminism issues in spaces or gaps, the question is, "What is the significance of the gaps for moral responsibility, given that what matters about the gaps is not that it provides elbow room for alternative possibilities or changes of direction?" The view that the gaps matter apart from providing such elbow room is typically called "source incompatibilism." Here I have considered various versions of this doctrine, and I hope to have shown how compatibilism of a certain sort – semicompatibilism – is left standing after the best punches of its opponents.

7 Why Be a Semicompatibilist?

I began with motivations for compatibilism. Especially because our most fundamental views of ourselves as free and morally responsible should not "hang on a thread" (should not depend on deliverances of theoretical physicists) there are strong attractions to compatibilism. But we have also looked at serious objections to it. First, we considered the Consequence Argument. This argument employs extremely plausible ingredients, such as the fixity of the past and natural laws, to derive the conclusion that if causal determinism were to obtain, then no one is free in the sense of having genuine access to alternative possibilities. I have suggested (in Section 5) that we distinguish two kinds of freedom or control: regulative control (which requires genuine access to alternative possibilities) and guidance control (which involves a distinctive kind of guidance but not necessarily access to alternative possibilities). We can now sidestep the difficulties presented by the Consequence Argument by noting that guidance control, not in any way threatened by the Consequence Argument, is the sort of freedom or control bound up with moral responsibility. Semicompatibilism contends that moral responsibility is compatible with causal determinism, quite apart from whether causal determinism threatens regulative control. Semicompatibilism is thus consistent with, although it does not in itself *require*, the acceptance of the soundness of the Consequence Argument. Further, I have argued (in Section 6) that the most influential versions of source incompatibilism are not persuasive. Given the considerable attractions of compatibilism (all of which are enjoyed by semicompatibilism), I believe that a careful evaluation of the dialectical situation should issue in an acceptance of semicompatibilism.

Why should one be a semicompatibilist rather than a traditional compatibilist? What exactly is the benefit of switching from a model that requires regulative control to one that only requires guidance control? Some philosophers have claimed that semicompatibilism is merely old wine in new bottles. They have stated that it seems to have a "scholastic air" to it (in Jay Wallace's phrase), and that no one really cares (or for that matter ever has cared) about a sort of freedom that holds all the past and laws fixed: regulative control (as I have conceived of it). One important compatibilist, Gary Watson, has pointed out that, given the definition of causal determinism, it is *blatantly obvious* that causal determinism would rule out any kind of freedom that required that all the past and natural laws be held fixed; Watson wonders why we should belabor this point, or why it should be in the least surprising. (This is reminiscent of my objection to one of the specifications of the sourcehood requirement above, although I believe Watson's objection to the Consequence Argument is, in the end, not as cogent.) For Watson and others, especially traditional compatibilists, semicompatibilism is not so much an innovation as something always presupposed by traditional compatibilists. Another influential compatibilist, Daniel Dennett (1984), has written that when we are interested in whether someone could have done otherwise, we are *never* interested in whether he could have extended the (entire) actual past, holding fixed the natural laws, "unless we are doing philosophy and confronting [the Consequence Argument]."

These remarks puzzle me for various reasons. It is quite natural to think that, in deliberating about the future, we are selecting from among various options that are genuinely metaphysically open to us, given the past. It is as if we are being guided, in the background, by a GPS that "updates," given what has just happened; we choose our path now as an extension of the path we've taken thus far.

I am perplexed by those who say that it is not natural or plausible that we often possess the freedom to choose and do otherwise, where this involves the power to extend the (entire) given past, holding fixed the laws of nature. Typically, of course, we are not in a position to know the entirety of the past or the complete statement of the laws of nature, so we do not seek to find out such things in our ordinary lives. When I deliberate, I don't check the totality of the past and the laws of nature. It does *not* follow that I don't *implicitly presuppose* that my freedom is the power to extend the actual past, whatever that is, holding fixed the natural laws, whatever they are. Our epistemic limitations imply that we do not worry about compatibility with the past and the laws when we plan for the future; additionally, it would be clunky and awkward (and beside the point) to do this in our practical reasoning. This is perfectly compatible with a background presupposition that whatever we can do must be connected to the past by a line (holding fixed the natural laws). Given the unity of deliberative and responsibility freedom, the latter sort of freedom must involve the fixity of the past and natural laws.

For thousands of years philosophers have wondered about whether we have such freedom – the freedom that involves power to select from options that are extensions of the past, holding fixed the natural laws – in light of such worries as the prior truth values of statements about the future ("fatalism") and God's existence and essential omniscience. The worries about prior truth values of statements about the future and God's omniscience, construed as foreknowledge, stem precisely from a deep concern we have about the relationship between the past and our freedom. More specifically, the classic debates that have dominated the discussion of free will for thousands of years assume that our freedom is the power to extend *all* the actual past. Some have pointed out that it is not clear that the *truth* of certain statements about the future is a fact about the past in the same way as paradigmatically fixed facts about the past, and others have said the same thing about God's beliefs about the future. These debates take place within the shared framework of an assumption that our freedom is the freedom to "get there from here" – to extend the actual past in its entirety. In James Joyce's novel *A Portrait of the Artist as a Young Man*, Stephen Dedalus says, "The past is a nightmare from which I'm trying to awake." It's tough!

To suggest that no one has ever seriously worried about whether we have regulative control (as I have conceived of it) seems to ignore great swaths of the history of philosophy. In the Modern Era, the debates have included worries that stem from science and the possibility of causal determinism, as well as logic and religion. Of course, I do not contend that everyone has agreed that we need regulative control for moral responsibility, or that such control needs to be analyzed in terms of stringent fixity of the past (or laws) constraints; reasonable people can disagree about these matters. That is not to say that the history of debates about free will has not been replete with disputes about precisely these matters, interpreted just as I have here!

Given the history of contentious and apparently intractable debates about the relationship between such doctrines as God's omniscience and regulative control, as well as causal determinism and regulative control, it would seem that it would clearly be a helpful (and substantial) step in the right direction to *sidestep* these debates by developing a defense of compatibilism that does not require their resolution. Indeed, my defense of semicompatiblism allows (although does not require) one to accept that we never have genuine metaphysical access to alternative possibilities, construed stringently.

My basic point is that it can help us make considerable dialectical progress in debates with those inclined toward incompatibilism to *allow* them their views about the fixity of the past and natural laws. Even if one does not care about possessing the sort of freedom that involves the power to extend the actual past (in its entirely), holding fixed the natural laws, others *do* care about precisely this sort of freedom. In my view, any compatibilist who ignores the natural attractiveness of the desire to have this sort of freedom vitiates her dialectical position significantly and, indeed, unnecessarily. Such a compatibilist risks being dismissed, or at least finding herself in an intractable dialectical stalemate. The most persuasive philosophers *engage* with their opponents sympathetically.

The strongest or most compelling feature in the incompatibilist's arsenal is the Consequence Argument. The ingredients that go into the Consequence Argument are considerably more gripping than the ingredients of source incompatibilism. Thus, semicompatibilism is able to embrace the most attractive features of incompatibilism without thereby having to accept its least attractive feature – that our freedom and moral responsibility "hangs on a thread," or, as in libertarianism, that we can know from our armchairs that causal determinism is false. We semicompatibilists can have our cake and eat it too.

My fundamental contention is that semicompatibilism can help by allowing us to sidestep traditionally intractable debates. If one can *grant* that there is an important kind of freedom that is (arguably, at least) ruled out by causal determinism – a notion that is typically and naturally associated with deliberation and moral responsibility – and still present a persuasive case for compatibilism, one is at a significant dialectic advantage. The traditional compatibilist has a much more difficult project: she must defeat the Consequence Argument as well as source incompatibilism. Why needlessly make your job more difficult than it already is? This would be an "unforced error."

Similarly, when a compatibilist argues that we typically care about what is dependent on our executive motivational states (say, our choices), given that there are no special impairments in our capacity for choice, I would agree. When I deliberate, I am typically not thinking about philosophical accounts of my activity. It does not follow that, upon reflection, I would reject the presupposition that my freedom is the power to extend the actual past, given the laws of nature. Even when one is engaging in theorizing or philosophical reflection, one might not always put together different views and assemble a comprehensive picture. One might find some version of choice-dependence or the conditional analysis of freedom attractive; but the Consequence Argument can help to bring to bear implications of compatibilism that go against other beliefs one has (about the fixity of the past and natural laws). Upon reflection, you might find the views about the fixity of the past and natural laws even more basic than one's attraction to a suitably refined conditional analysis of freedom.

I do *not* claim that we in fact have the sort of freedom typically presupposed in common sense and compatibilism. Rather, it is that this is precisely the sort of freedom that is *presupposed* and forms part of our implicit framework of practical reasoning. This makes life difficult for the compatibilist and provides motivation for semicompatibilism, which eases the compatibilist's pain. The semicompatibilist must engage in some conceptual re-engineering, conceiving of the requirement for moral responsibility in terms of guidance, rather than regulative control. Given the unity of the forward- and backward-facing aspects of agency, we would also need to rethink the vocabulary of practical reasoning, so to speak. Here the semicompatibilist contends that our deliberation considers "epistemically open" options: paths that are available to us, *for all we know*. Such options are not necessarily "metaphysically open," that is, extensions of the past, holding the laws fixed. We aim to choose the best option available, for all we know; but we can recognize that whatever we choose might have been the only one we could have. The move from metaphysical to epistemic options is not only theoretically necessary for the semicompatibilist but also faithful to our experience. Given that human deliberation operates in the space of epistemic possibilities, we can have an "actual-sequence" theory of *both* the forward- and backward-looking aspects of agency, thus honoring the deep unity of human agency.

Consider Gary Watson's contention that it is just obvious that a compatibilist must accept a notion of freedom that does not hold fixed the past and natural laws; after all, the definition of causal determinism straightforwardly implies this result. So why all the fuss about the Consequence Argument? Why suppose that it is somehow a deeply problematic revelation that the compatibilist must say that we (sometimes) have it in our power so to act that the past or the natural laws wouldn't be the same as they actually are? Watson's is the "Well, duh!" objection.

Note first that it is typically not thought to be a defect in an argument that it is short or simple! I would suggest that, as with most skeptical arguments, the Consequence Argument gets its grip by employing deeply appealing elements of common sense. As I pointed out in Section 4, a proponent of the Consequence Argument could be seen to be showing a compatibilist that he must consider our intuitive views *comprehensively*; one does not always put together views that one nevertheless is inclined to accept. Sometimes, an argument can bring out a troubling worry about a commitment by throwing it into relief in a new way, or even by associating it with a certain picture that renders its commitments salient.

It seems to me that our intuitive "picture" of the structure of possibility over time corresponds to a branching, treelike structure in which the various possible futures branch off a single line that can be traced back into the single actual past (a garden of forking paths). When I deliberate, I assume I have access to various possibilities that are connected to a single past; I do not assume that each possibility comes with its own past(s). To suppose that each future branch has its own past or set of pasts is to imagine a field overrun by weeds, and not an orderly garden. This picture is complex and inelegant. It is not clear we *have* such freedom involving access to different branches (regulative control), and the semicompatibilist claims we *need* not, but it seems to be a *presupposition* or part of our intuitive framework for practical reasoning. In reply to Watson, this is the point of the Consequence Argument: to bring out the tension between causal determinism and our ordinary and deeply entrenched views of ourselves.

Here is another suggestion about what I take to be a genuinely puzzling aspect of the dialectical situation. Often, compatibilists frame their discussions in terms of an attempt to give an "analysis" of the word "can," as it plays a certain role in discourse about free will and moral responsibility. This is a project that seeks to elucidate and regiment the meanings of our words. Similarly, sometimes the discussion is framed in terms of an attempt to articulate our inchoate "concept" of freedom (as it relates specifically to our concept of moral responsibility). These projects pertain to our language and our network of concepts. Here the "conditional analysis," perhaps suitably refined, is plausible. Maybe the notion of choice-dependence (where there are no impairments of the distinctive capacity to choose) captures nicely what we *ordinarily mean* by the relevant "can" or our *concept* of freedom (as it plays a specific role in our network of responsibility-concepts).

It is, however, well established that it can be one thing to articulate a meaning or concept, and quite another to specify the nature or "real essence" of something. The meaning of the term "water" and the ordinary concept "water" presumably do not contain anything about "H_2O." But arguably, the nature or real essence of water is H_2O. Similarly, the ordinary meaning of the term "can" and the ordinary concept of "freedom" may not contain anything about the possibility of extending the actual past, holding the natural laws fixed; but, arguably, the nature or real essence of our freedom includes these features. Manuel Vargas, one of the contributors to this volume, has written insightfully about these methodological and "metaphilosophical" matters.

I have for many years been intrigued by the fact that some philosophers find the Consequence Argument (in some form or another) absolutely and uncontroversially sound, whereas others dismiss it entirely. It is a weird feature of the discussions about free will and moral responsibility. One possible explanation of this puzzling phenomenon is that some philosophers are thoroughly focused on the issues about meanings and concepts, whereas others are attuned to the nature or real essence of freedom. My first suggestion was that we sometimes do not put together all our claims about a subject matter; this second suggestion could be taken as the view that the compartmentalization comes from a difference in the kinds of claims that are at issue.

The debates about whether the future is in fact a garden of forking paths, and whether we do in fact possess regulative control, are difficult and highly contentious. They have engaged serious and careful philosophers for millennia. The semicompatibilist, just as a semicompatibilist, takes no stand here; semicompatibilism is officially silent about whether (say) God's omniscience or causal determinism rules out regulative control. Rather, its distinctive claim is that causal determinism is compatible with the possession of a certain kind of control, guidance control, and thus moral responsibility, apart from whether causal determinism rules out regulative control. To someone who has absolutely no interest in a kind of freedom that involves the power to extend the past, holding fixed the laws of nature, someone not gripped at all by the ideas of the fixity of the past and natural laws (stringently construed), semicompatibilism will not be terribly interesting. It will simply be a different way of packaging views she already finds plausible. Of course, such an individual will likely *agree* with the basic thrust of semicompatibilism (that causal determinism is compatible with moral responsibility). In contrast, semicompatibilism will be most helpful within a dialectical context in which some participants are taken by the fundamental idea that our freedom is the power to add to the given past, holding fixed the laws of nature; it is important to see that a compatibilist about causal determinism and moral responsibility can *grant* a stringent interpretation of this idea. Given that millennia of debates have issued in a dialectical stalemate, semicompatibilism holds the promise of helping us to make real intellectual progress. If this is indeed old wine in new bottles, the possibility of progress in longstanding debates may be intoxicating!

Perhaps you remain unconvinced by the Frankfurt-style cases. For whatever reason – and there are respectable ones! – you do not accept that they show we can have guidance, without regulative control. I must concede that I am not totally shocked! I do not think there are knockdown arguments in any interesting area of philosophy, and this is no exception. When engaging someone who is not convinced by the examples, I would first note that various philosophers, including Harry Frankfurt (!), have argued that an actual-sequence model of moral responsibility (guidance without regulative control) can be motivated *without* invoking Frankfurt-style examples. Second, a compatibilist can always fall back on Plan B: traditional compatibilism. She can accept the Consequence Argument, given its stringent construal of the fixity of the past and laws, but contend that one (or more) "looser" analyses of regulative control are acceptable. Such accounts would include simple and modified conditional analyses, and others. The Consequence Argument does *not* show that freedom to do otherwise, so construed, is incompatible with moral responsibility.

Importantly, the traditional compatibilist must deny that the stringent interpretation of regulative control is the sort implicated in moral responsibility. She will accept that freedom to do otherwise is necessary for moral responsibility but deny that this freedom (and thus regulative control) is analyzed employing the fixity of the totality of the past and laws. This leads to compatibilism just as much as an actual-sequence approach. Traditional compatibilism has the virtues of resilience, the ability to countenance our ordinary distinctions between morally responsible agents and those who are not, and so forth. You do not need to be a semicompatibilist to enjoy most of the benefits of compatibilism. For the compatibilist, so much does *not* hang on so little! A benefit that is, however, unavailable to the traditional compatibilist is the opportunity to engage with the libertarian in a deeper way, by granting, for the sake of argument, the stringent notion of the fixity of the past and laws. This is an advantage of semicompatibilism.

8　An Account of Guidance Control

I have argued that moral responsibility does not require regulative, but only guidance, control. I have not here attempted to give an account of guidance control. This is not the place to develop such an account in depth; rather, I shall simply sketch the outlines in order to give the reader the flavor of an actual-sequence theory of moral responsibility – an approach that does not require an agent *ever* to have alternative possibilities with respect to choice, action, or even the formation of character.

Return to the Frankfurt-style example presented in Section 5 in which Jones votes for the Democrat on his own (for his own reasons and as a result of the normal human deliberative process). If Jones were about to choose to vote for the Republican, Black would intervene and cause (via direct electronic stimulation of the brain) Jones to choose to vote for the Democrat (and to go ahead and vote for the Democrat). The actual sequence and the alternative scenario involve intuitively *different kinds of mechanisms*: in the actual sequence, there is the normal operation of the human capacity for practical reasoning, whereas in the alternative scenario there is significant and direct electronic stimulation of the brain by the neurosurgeon. Even though it is difficult to provide a general account of mechanism individuation, it is intuitively clear that different kinds of mechanisms operate in the actual and alternative sequences of the Frankfurt-style cases. Further, it seems to me that what grounds the moral responsibility of the agent in such cases are features of the "actual-sequence mechanism" – properties of the path that actually leads to the behavior in question.

On my view, one relevant feature of the actual-sequence mechanism is responsiveness to reasons. Note that it is distinctive of the normal human capacity for deliberation that it is reasons-responsive. Even if the thorough electronic stimulation of Jones's brain (by Black) of the sort applied *in the alternative scenario* would issue in a choice to vote Republican, no matter what reasons there are for Jones to vote for the Democrat, Jones's actual-sequence mechanism is reasons-responsive. In ascertaining reasons-responsiveness, one must *hold fixed* the actual-sequence mechanism, which, in the Frankfurt-style case, is the normal human faculty of practical reasoning. Even if the agent (Jones) does not have genuine access to alternative possibilities (regulative control) in virtue of the existence of Black's setup, he may well exhibit guidance control of his choice and voting behavior; after all, Black's setup simply monitors the situation and does not play any role in Jones's choice and decision along the actual pathway. In the actual sequence, Jones exhibits guidance control and might be deemed morally responsible.

By "mechanism," I simply mean, roughly speaking, "way"; I do not mean to reify anything. We have intuitions about clear cases of "same mechanism" and "different mechanism." The actually operating mechanism (in a Frankfurt-style type case) – ordinary human practical reasoning, unimpaired by direct stimulation by neurosurgeons, and so forth – is in a clear sense responsive to reasons. Holding fixed that mechanism, the agent would presumably choose and act differently in a range of scenarios in which he is presented with good reasons to do so. In contrast, the "manipulation mechanism" in the alternative sequence is not responsive to reasons.

The above discussion suggests the rudiments of an account of guidance control of action. On this account, we hold fixed the kind of mechanism that actually issues in the choice and action, and we see whether the agent responds in a specific way to reasons (some of which are moral reasons). My account presupposes that the agent can recognize reasons, and, in particular, certain reasons as moral reasons. The account distinguishes between reasons-recognition (the ability to recognize the reasons that exist) and reasons-reactivity (the capacity to choose in accordance with reasons that are recognized as good and sufficient). The sort of reasons-responsiveness linked to moral responsibility, on my view, is "moderate reasons-responsiveness."

We can build up to the conditions for moderate reasons-responsiveness by starting with "strong reasons-responsiveness":

> Suppose that a certain kind K of mechanism actually issues in a choice and action. Strong reasons-responsiveness obtains under the following conditions: if K were to operate and there were sufficient reasons to do otherwise, the agent would *recognize* them and thus *choose* to do otherwise and *do* otherwise.

In the envisaged alternative scenario, the agent must *take* the relevant reasons to be sufficient, choose in accordance with this judgment, and act in accordance with this choice. There are various problems with strong reasons-responsiveness as necessary for guidance control and thus moral responsibility. I'll just mention one: the pesky problem of weakness of the will. An agent who freely acts against what she takes to be her best or sufficient reason is weak-willed. Suppose an individual intuitively acts freely in choosing to do, and doing, X based on what she deems her sufficient reason, *R1*. But she might also have a tendency toward weakness of the will, such that if she had deemed *R2* (that commends some other act *Y)* her best or sufficient reason, she still would have chosen *X* (and so acted). This agent *actually* acts freely, in accordance with what she takes to be her best reason, and yet she *would have acted* in a weak-willed way. Strong reasons-responsiveness would imply that this individual does not act freely, counter to our intuitive view. Strong reasons-responsiveness is too strong: it demands too close a connection between reasons and choice (and action) in actual and hypothetical contests. It is an *ideal*, but not necessary for moral responsibility.

In order to make room for the possibility of morally responsible action in an individual disposed toward weakness of the will, we might try "weak reasons-responsiveness":

> An agent is weakly reasons-responsive when a certain kind *K* of mechanism actually issues in action, and in at least *some* alternative circumstances in which *K* operates and there are sufficient reasons for her to do otherwise than she actually does, she would be receptive to these reasons, and would choose and do otherwise.

Note that, unlike the requirement of strong reasons-responsiveness, weak reasons-responsiveness gives the right result for a person who is weak-willed, either counterfactually (as above) or actually. All weak reasons-responsiveness requires is that there be *some* possible scenario in which the agent would recognize sufficient reasons to do otherwise and act accordingly.

In weak reasons-responsiveness, the required fit between sufficient reasons and choices (and action) is looser. But whereas strong reasons-responsiveness is too strong, weak reasons-responsiveness is too weak. One problem for weak reasons-responsiveness stems from agents who recognize "crazy" individual reasons or (significantly) internally inconsistent patterns of reasons. Consider, as one kind of example, an agent who recognizes bizarre *patterns* of reasons. Suppose Alyssa freely shoots the mayor. Imagine further that she would recognize a purple-checked shirt as a reason to do otherwise (i.e. not to shoot the mayor), but not a red-checked shirt, a green-striped shirt, but not a blue-striped shirt, and so forth. We ask her and she has no explanation for this pattern. Maybe Keisha, reflecting and acting from the normal mechanism of human practical reasoning, would recognize a cost of $100 as a reason not to order the lobster, but not recognize $120 as such a reason, recognize $140 as a reason not to order the lobster, but not recognize $200 as such a reason, and so forth. Given its apparent irrationality, we ask Keisha about it, and she has no explanation. Such bizarre patterns of reasons-recognition are consistent with weak reasons-responsiveness but not moral responsibility (intuitively).

Due to the inadequacies of both strong and weak reasons-responsiveness, let's consider "moderate reasons-responsiveness." Here we require "regular" reasons-receptivity – receptivity to a pattern of reasons understandable from a third-party perspective. It is as if a third party conducts an interview with the relevant agent, asking whether a range of reasons would count as good and sufficient reasons for action. The third party must be able to interpret the pattern as minimally coherent, both logically and "content-wise." As above, we require that the agent be able to recognize *moral* reasons (reasons that commend an action from a perspective broader than the agent's own). Of course, all this is highly schematic, but it will have to do for our discussion here. (My co-author and I develop and defend these elements of moderate reasons-responsiveness in Fischer and Ravizza, 1998; I elaborate in Fischer 2006 and 2012.)

Accordingly, we might offer this account:

> An agent is moderately reasons-responsive in performing an action when her actual-sequence mechanism K is regularly receptive to reasons and suitably reactive to them.

One could, however, exhibit the right sort of reasons-responsiveness as a result of (say) secret, unconsented-to electronic stimulation of the brain (or hypnosis, brainwashing, and so forth). So moderate reasons-responsiveness of the actual-sequence mechanism is necessary but not sufficient for guidance control and moral responsibility. I contend that there are two elements of guidance control: reasons-sensitivity of the appropriate sort and mechanism ownership. The mechanism that issues in the behavior must be the agent's *own*. When an individual is secretly manipulated through clandestine mind control, her practical reasoning is not *her own*.

I argue for a subjective approach to mechanism ownership. On this approach, a mechanism becomes one's own in virtue of one's having certain beliefs about its effects in the world (i.e. by seeing oneself, when acting from this mechanism, in a certain way). It is not simply a matter of *saying* certain things – one must *have* the relevant constellation of beliefs. On my view, an individual becomes morally responsible in part by "taking responsibility"; she makes her mechanism her own by taking responsibility for acting from that kind of mechanism. In a sense, then, one acquires control by taking control. It is important to my approach that in the case of responsibility-undermining manipulation, the agent has *not* taken responsibility for the "manipulation mechanism," even if she has taken responsibility for "ordinary practical reasoning. They are different mechanisms, and taking responsibility for one does not imply taking responsibility for the other.

More carefully, the conditions for taking responsibility for the mechanism M from which one acts are as follows:

(a) The individual must see herself, when acting from M, as an agent; she must see that her choices and actions are efficacious in the world. This condition includes the claim that the individual sees that if, when acting from M, she were to choose and act differently, different upshots would occur in the world.

(b) The individual must accept that, when acting from *M*, she is a fair target of the reactive attitudes (and other responsibility-responses, such as punishment).

(c) The individual's view of her actions from *M* specified in the first two conditions must be based, in an appropriate way, on the evidence.

The requirement in (c) that the agent's beliefs be connected to her evidence in an "appropriate" way rules out the secret manipulation of the agent's taking responsibility itself. (My co-author and I offer a suggestion about how to specify the notion of appropriateness in Fischer and Ravizza 1998.) Here I have simply gestured toward the two main ingredients of the account of guidance control. Although I have not offered detailed accounts of the relevant kinds of reasons-responsiveness and ownership, I contend that they can in fact be developed in a way that is both plausible and compatible with causal determinism (Fischer and Ravizza 1998; Fischer 2006, 2012).

My view then is that the "freedom-relevant" condition of moral responsibility is guidance control. (There is also a "knowledge" or "epistemic" component, but it is beyond the scope of this chapter.) One can have guidance control of behavior without also having regulative control over it. Although the two kinds of control typically go together, they can be analytically prized apart in contexts involving preemptive overdetermination (the Frankfurt-style cases). An agent exercises guidance control insofar as her behavior issues from her own, moderately reasons-responsive mechanism. I further contend that both mechanism-ownership and reasons-responsiveness are entirely compatible with causal determinism; thus, I hold that even if causal determination threatens regulative control, it is compatible with guidance control and moral responsibility.

What is important to moral responsibility is the actual history of the behavior under consideration. One looks at the properties of the actual-sequence mechanisms or processes that issue in behavior in assessing an agent's moral responsibility. On my view, these properties can be "modal" properties or sensitivities, such as reasons-responsiveness. It is crucial that some feature of the actual path to the behavior – some (possibly modal) property or properties of the way the behavior is *actually generated* –rather than access to alternative pathways, grounds moral responsibility. My approach, then, is an "actual-sequence" model of moral responsibility.

Compatibilists traditionally contend that not all causally deterministic sequences equally threaten freedom and responsibility. Whereas I am inclined to accept the conclusion of the Consequence Argument and thus the view that all causally deterministic sequences equally rule out regulative control, I hold that not all causally deterministic sequences pose problems for guidance control (and thus moral responsibility). Now some compatibilists are content (perhaps reluctantly) to posit a mere list of "responsibility-undermining" factors, such as direct electronic stimulation or physical manipulation of the brain, certain kinds of hypnosis, brainwashing, aversive conditioning, subliminal advertising, drug interventions, irresistible impulses, unavoidable phobias, and so forth. These compatibilists contend that mere causal determination does not rule out moral responsibility, but they also want to say that the special circumstances specified in the (possibly-to-be-expanded) list *do* rule out responsibility. This approach is obviously not ideal or entirely satisfactory. In contrast, I have attempted to offer a *general* account of guidance control – an account that helps to explain why the special factors typically on the list do indeed rule out moral responsibility. Whereas some philosophers quite legitimately worry that it will not be easy to distinguish certain cases of problematic manipulation or causal influence from cases in which we are inclined to countenance moral responsibility, I have offered a general account that has some hope of sorting and distinguishing the range of possible cases in an illuminating, nonarbitrary fashion.

I ended my 1982 paper "Responsibility and Control" by saying that we must "decode the information in the actual sequence" leading to behavior for which the agent can legitimately be held morally responsible and ascertain whether it is compatible with causal determination. The account of guidance control – with the two chief ingredients, moderate reasons-responsiveness and mechanism-ownership – identifies the ingredients that undergird moral responsibility in the actual sequence, and I have argued that they are entirely compatible with causal determination. I argue elsewhere that guidance control is also compatible with causal *indeterminism*; it is regrettably beyond the scope of this essay to go through the details. On my approach, then, moral responsibility is *resilient* with respect to the truth (or falsity) of causal determinism: our most fundamental attitudes toward ourselves and other persons *do not hang on a thread*. I thus defend what might be called, somewhat inelegantly, "supercompatibilistic semicompatibilism."

Further, I have elsewhere attempted to show we can build a *comprehensive* account of guidance control from an account of guidance control of *actions* (Fischer and Ravizza 1998). That is, we can develop an account of guidance control of omissions, consequence-particulars, states of affairs or facts, and perhaps even emotions and character traits, by invoking certain basic ingredients contained in the account of guidance control of actions. I argue that it is a point in favor of my account of moral responsibility that it can give a comprehensive account that builds on simple, basic ingredients. I concede that my construction of the comprehensive account from the simpler elements, as I have presented it thus far, is not entirely adequate (Clarke 2014; Sartorio 2016), but I stick to the view that it *can* be done. Stay tuned.

9   Conclusion: Making a Statement

John Perry has told me that I need a new name for the position, and I agree that "semicompatibilism" is not very exciting. (My only consolation is that the other names for positions in the free will debates are equally uninspiring; could you imagine going to the barricades for "hard incompatibilism"? [Sorry, Derk Pereboom, who ably defends this view in his contribution!]) What is important, however, is not what's in the name, but what's in the doctrine. In this essay, I have focused mainly (but not exclusively) on the appeal of this form of compatibilism. I have attempted to provide a *general* motivation for compatibilism, and an explanation of the appeal of *this specific form* of compatibilism, as opposed to traditional compatibilism.

One of the main virtues of compatibilism is that our deepest and most basic views about our agency – our freedom and moral responsibility – are not *held hostage* to views in theoretical physics. Resilience is the beating heart of compatibilism. A semicompatibilist, as a compatibilist, would not have to revise these beliefs in light of a future discovery of the truth of causal determinism. A libertarian, it seems, must claim that she knows from her armchair that causal determinism is false; but how could we know in advance such an empirical thesis? These are significant advantages to semicompatibilism. It is as if semicompatibilism is an insurance policy one can pull out of one's waistcoat pocket if causal determinism turns out to obtain. Our battle cry: free the libertarians!

Moral responsibility skepticism (of the sort defended by Pereboom) is also resilient with respect to whether causal determinism obtains: we are not morally responsible (in a basic sense), whether determinism obtains or not. Our responsibility and personhood would not hang on a thread, because it doesn't hang at all. A libertarian's self-conception is tenuous, and the skeptic's dreary. A semicompatibilist, in contrast, can sleep at night and wake up to a bright new day.

Semicompatibilism combines the best features of compatibilism and incompatibilism. My doctrine of semicompatibilism can accommodate the most compelling insights of the incompatibilist (as crystallized in the Consequence Argument) and also the basic appeal of compatibilism – that not all causally deterministic sequences equally rule out the sort of control that grounds moral responsibility. Thus, semicompatiblism allows us to track common sense (suitably conceptualized in moral and legal theory) in making distinctions between those factors that undermine responsibility and those that do not. And a semicompatibilist need not give up the idea that sometimes individuals robustly deserve punishment for their behavior, whereas on other occasions they robustly deserve moral commendation and reward. We need not etiolate or reconfigure the widespread and natural idea that individuals *morally deserve* to be treated harshly in certain circumstances, and kindly in others. We need not in any way damp down our revulsion at heinous deeds, or our admiration for human goodness and even heroism (Fischer, accepted for publication, b).

Semicompatibilism is both a conservative and a radical doctrine. It is conservative in that it need not in any way call for revisions in the concept of moral responsibility or our actual responsibility practices, and it preserves the traditional idea that moral responsibility is associated with freedom or control. It is radical in that it identifies guidance control, rather than regulative control, as the relevant sort of freedom. It thus departs significantly from traditional views in the *conditions* it posits for the application of the concept of moral responsibility (and thus the triggering of the responsibility-practices themselves). As mentioned in Section 1, some have accused compatibilists of "changing the subject." The subject, however, is still free will, but the semicompatibilist focuses on guidance, rather than regulative, control. She thereby *sharpens* the subject.

We care deeply about being robustly free and morally responsible, and it is not straightforward to reconfigure our ideas and practices to eliminate residual retributive components. It is not easy to do so without a sense of loss. Semicompatibilism keeps a robust and traditional notion of moral responsibility. But the traditional picture is that we are morally responsible in virtue of *selecting* a path from among various paths that are genuinely open to us; we *make a difference* to the world. The semicompatibilist denies that the value of our free agency – or the basis of our moral responsibility – is the power to make a difference. After all, it might turn out that we are mistaken in the intuitive view that we have more than one genuinely available path into the future.

It may be that, just as there is a single line that connects the past to the present, there is only a single line into the future: a single metaphysically available path that extends into the future. This is a pictorial representation of the deep unity of forward- and backward-facing aspects of human agency. What matters is how we proceed – how we walk down that path. There may be features that block access to alternative paths and alternative ways of walking down our single path, but that play no role along the actual pathway. Whatever precludes access to alternative paths may not threaten the features that render us robustly morally responsible. When we walk down the path of life with courage or compassion, we might not (for all we know) make a certain sort of difference. For the semicompatibilist, the basis of our moral responsibility is not selection in the garden of forking paths, but self-expression in writing the narrative of our lives. It is not that we make a difference, but that we make a statement. In freely writing sentences in the stories of our lives, we give our lives a signature kind of meaning. Even if the name is unexciting, the idea is beautiful.

Further Reading

My contribution above relies heavily on my own previous work, as well as that of others. The essay is supposed to explain in a relatively informal way the main ideas in my approach to free will and moral responsibility and their motivations. I have thus not included extensive footnotes or other citations. I hope the reader will understand that the nature of this book requires a less substantial scholarly apparatus than one might expect in another context. In this section, I make some very minimal suggestions for further reading, with an admittedly lamentable emphasis on my own more detailed elaboration of the ideas presented here.

I have presented and defended semicompatibilism in John Martin Fischer, *The Metaphysics of Free Will: An Essay on Control* (Oxford: Blackwell Publishers, 1994); John Martin Fischer and Mark Ravizza, *Responsibility and Control: A Theory of Moral Responsibility* (New York: Cambridge University Press, 1998); John Martin Fischer, *My Way: Essays on Moral Responsibility* (New York: Oxford University Press, 2006); and *Deep Control: Essays on Free Will and Value* (New York: Oxford University Press, 2012). *My Way* contains a more detailed discussion of my suggestion that the value of our free agency consists in a certain distinctive kind of self-expression. There is additional development of the idea that in acting freely we endow our lives with a signature sort of narrative value in John Martin Fischer, *Our Stories: Essays on Life, Death, and Free Will* (New York: Oxford University Press, 2009). I give an overview of the arguments for logical and theological fatalism, and their relationships to the Consequence Argument, in John Martin Fischer, *Our Fate Essays on God and Free Will* (New York: Oxford University Press, 2016). For a defense of the central philosophical motivation of semicompatibilism, see John Martin Fischer, "The Resilience of Moral Responsibility." In Taylor Cyr, Andrew Law, and Neal Tognazzini (eds.), *Freedom, Responsibility, and Value: Essays in Honor of John Martin Fischer* (New York: Routledge, accepted for publication).

A landmark collection that explores and elaborates compatibilist themes is: Gary Watson, *Agency and Answerability* (Oxford: Clarendon Press, 2004). One (but not the only!) important theme in Watson's work is the suggestion that moral responsibility be modeled on a kind of conversation. Michael McKenna develops and significantly deepens this idea in: *Conversation and Responsibility* (New York: Oxford University Press, 2012). For important critical discussions of traditional compatibilist accounts of freedom and their difficulties, as well as presentations of the Consequence Argument, see Peter Van Inwagen, *An Essay on Free Will* (Oxford: Clarendon Press, 1983); and Carl Ginet, *On Action* (Cambridge: Cambridge University Press, 1990). A classic paper developing the local-miracle compatibilism reply to the Consequence Argument is: David Lewis, "Are We Free to Break the Laws?" *Theoria* 47 (1981): 113–27. A more detailed and sustained development of this reply is: Kadri Vihvelin, *Causes, Laws, and Free Will*, (New York: Oxford University Press, 2013).

P.F. Strawson's "Freedom and Resentment" is a seminal account of moral responsibility in terms of what he terms, "the reactive attitudes", in the *Proceedings of the British Academy* 48 (1962): 1–25.

Harry Frankfurt's "Alternate Possibilities and Moral Responsibility," *Journal of Philosophy* 45; 829–839 (1969) is an important paper in which he presents the prototype of the "Frankfurt-style cases". Much of Harry Frankfurt's seminal work on these subjects is collected in: Harry G. Frankfurt (ed.), *The Importance of What We Care About* (Cambridge: Cambridge University Press, 1988). There are helpful discussions of various aspects of the Frankfurt-style examples in David Widerker and Michael McKenna (eds.), *Moral Responsibility and Alternative Possibilities: Essays on the Importance of Alternative Possibilities* (Aldershot: Ashgate, 2003). For a more recent comprehensive treatment, see: Justin Capes, *Moral Responsibility and the Flicker of Freedom* (New York: Oxford University Press, 2023). Also helpful is David Robb's article on the Frankfurt-style cases in the online *Stanford Encyclopedia of Philosophy*.

There are important discussions and defenses of source incompatibilism in Robert Kane, *The Significance of Free Will* (New York: Oxford University Press, 1996); and Derk Pereboom, *Living Without Free Will* (Cambridge: Cambridge University Press, 2001), *Free Will, Agency and Meaning in Life* (Oxford: Oxford University Press, 2014), and *Wrongdoing and the Moral Emotions* (Oxford: Oxford University Press, 2021). Kane and Pereboom have crystallized and summarized their views in their contributions to this volume. There is a helpful debate in which Kane and Carolina Sartorio discuss both Kane's libertarianism and her actual-sequence approach to moral responsibility in their *Do We Have Free Will?* (New York: Routledge, 2022). As in his contribution to this book, Pereboom's work contains insightful and influential suggestions about the possibility of eliminating the retributive elements of our ordinary notion of moral responsibility. For additional worries about our ordinary and "robust" notion of responsibility, see Galen Strawson, *Freedom and Belief* (Oxford: Clarendon Press, 1986); and Saul Smilansky, *Free Will and Illusion* (Oxford: Clarendon Press, 2000). I offer critical reflections on these views in my paper "Moral Responsibility Skepticism: A Critique," accepted for publication, b, *The Harvard Review of Philosophy*. Myisha Cherry argues for the importance of moral anger and rage in achieving social justice in: *The Case for Rage* (New York: Oxford University Press, 2021).

There is an alternative development of an approach to moral responsibility that (apparently) does not require regulative control and that invokes a general capacity for reasons-responsiveness in R. Jay Wallace, *Responsibility and the Moral Sentiments* (Cambridge, MA: Harvard University Press, 1994). Carolina Sartorio defends a version of semicompatibilism in which the relevant notion of reasons-responsiveness invokes only nonmodal features (in contrast to mine) in her book *Causation and Free Will* (Oxford: Oxford University Press, 2016).

For two penetrating and insightful critiques of my account of guidance control, see: Clarke (2014) and Sartorio (2016).

3

Hard Incompatibilism

Derk Pereboom

People believe themselves free because they are conscious of their actions, but are ignorant of the causes by which they are determined.

Spinoza, Ethics, 1677

1 Outline of Hard Incompatibilism

Spinoza (1677/1985: 440–414, 483–484, 496–497) maintained that, due to very general facts about the nature of the universe, we lack free will in the sense at issue in the traditional debate. I agree. More specifically, Spinoza argues that it is because of the truth of determinism that we lack this sort of free will; he is thus a "hard determinist." But given contemporary quantum physics, it's not settled whether determinism or some type of indeterminism is true. Still, I contend that in either case we would very likely lack the sort of free will at issue. It would be misleading to call this view hard *determinism* for the reason that it allows for the possibility of indeterminism. So I've used the terms "hard incompatibilism" or else "free will skepticism" instead.[1]

One concern to keep in mind in deciding whether we have free will of the sort at issue is that the term "free will" has a number of distinct senses. Let me highlight two. The first is that to have free will is to have more than one option (i.e. alternative possibilities) for decision and action. To simplify this discussion, we might think of decisions as a type of action, a mental type, in addition to

Four Views on Free Will, Second Edition. John Martin Fischer, Robert Kane, Derk Pereboom, and Manuel Vargas.

actions such as raising one's hand, which include mental and bodily features. This first sense of free will can then be defined as follows:

Free will AP (for "alternative possibilities"): free will is an agent's ability, at a given time, either to act or to refrain, that is if an agent acts with free will, then she instead could have refrained at that time from acting as she did.

In the traditional debate free will is tightly connected to moral responsibility. To be blameworthy for an action requires a certain type and degree of control in action. The second sense of free will makes this connection:

Free will MR (for "moral responsibility"): free will is an agent's ability to exercise the control in acting required to be morally responsible for the action.[2]

As we'll see, our moral practice features different notions of moral responsibility, and not all of them are at issue in the free will debate.

How do these senses of "free will" play out in the philosophical debate? A traditional concern for free will is the prospect of causal determinism:

Causal determinism: every event has causal antecedents that render it inevitable.

Two prominent versions of causal determinism are "theological determinism," on which the determining causal antecedent is the divine will, and "naturalistic determinism," on which the antecedents are past events that causally determine succeeding events in accord with the laws of nature. The contestants in the free will debate are traditionally divided with reference to whether causal determinism and free will are compatible, which gives rise to two positions:

Compatibilism: our having free will is compatible with causal determinism, with all of our actions being causally determined by factors beyond our control.

Incompatibilism: our having free will is not compatible with causal determinism, with all of our actions being causally determined by factors beyond our control.

Incompatibilists in turn divide into those who hold that determinism is false and that we have free will – the "libertarians," and those who hold that determinism is true and that we lack free will – the "hard determinists." Libertarians endorse:

Causal indeterminism: not every event has causal antecedents that render it inevitable.

Incompatibilists about free will AP hold that if causal determinism is true, we would lack this sort of free will. But there are compatibilists about free will AP, for example David Hume (1739/1978) and A.J. Ayer (1954), who maintain that even if an action is causally determined by factors beyond one's control, it still may be, at the time of the action, that one could have refrained from performing it. This is a serious controversy, and one reason why free will AP is an important sense for the free will debate.

Regarding free will MR, virtually everyone holds that causal determinism is compatible with our having the control in action required for morally responsibility in *some* sense, for example in a sense focused solely on forward-looking objectives such as the moral reform of a wrongdoer and reconciliation relationships (to be discussed). But participants in the debate disagree about whether causal determinism is compatible with our having the control in action required for moral responsibility in the sense involving a resolutely backward-looking notion of desert, specifically "basic desert":

> For an agent to be *morally responsible for an action in the basic desert sense* is for the action to be attributable to her such a way that if she was sensitive to its being morally wrong, she would deserve to be blamed or punished in a way that she would experience as painful or harmful, and if she was sensitive to its being morally exemplary, she would deserve to be praised or rewarded in a way that she would experience as pleasurable or beneficial. The desert at issue here is basic in the sense that the agent, to be morally responsible in this sense, would deserve the pain or harm, the pleasure or benefit, just by virtue of having performed the action with sensitivity to its moral status, and not, for example, by virtue of consequentialist or contractualist considerations. (Pereboom 2021a: 11–12; cf., Feinberg 1970)

We can add that the imposition of such basically deserved pain or harm, pleasure or benefit, is conceived as noninstrumentally good, since such imposition is not envisioned as good only insofar as it brings about a further good. Rather, it is conceived as good in itself (McKenna 2019).

Basic desert contrasts with nonbasic desert, which invokes further goods, such as good consequences, in the justification of desert claims. John Rawls (1955) presents a two-tiered theory in which lawyers, judges, and juries appeal only to backward-looking, desert-invoking reasons for punishment, while this judicial practice is itself justified on the forward-looking basis of its anticipated good consequences. In a similar vein, Manuel Vargas (2013, 2015) endorses a position on which justifications for blame and punishment in the broader practice of holding people morally responsible appeal to desert while that desert is nonbasic because at a higher level that practice is justified by its anticipated good consequences, especially by, as he puts it, building better beings (cf. Dennett 1984, 2003). On the account set out by Vargas, our desert-attributing practice should be retained because it secures the best overall consequences relative to any alternative practices.[3]

For many, the intuition that wrongdoers deserve to be blamed or punished in a way that imposes pain or harm concerns basic desert specifically, in contrast with its nonbasic relative. That this is so might be shown by a type of thought experiment about punishment that derives from Immanuel Kant (1797/2017), in which there is no instrumental good to which punishing a wrongdoer would contribute. Imagine that a person on an isolated island viciously murders everyone else on the island, and that he is not capable of moral reform due to ingrained hatred and rage. Thus, there is no longer a society on the island whose rules might be determined contractually, and there are no good consequences that the punishment might aim to realize. Many nonetheless have the intuition that this murderer deserves to be punished severely. The desert would be basic, since the specifics of the example eliminate nonbasic desert. The resulting version of free will MR does distinguish the parties in the debate.

I'll first focus on free will MR where the "MR" refers to the basic desert sense of moral responsibility. In subsequent sections, I turn to free will AP, with a focus on whether it is compatible with determinism, and whether it is required for moral responsibility.

Given our initial focus on free will MR in the basic desert sense, here are the three traditional positions:

Hard determinism: because causal determinism is true, we cannot have the sort of free will required for moral responsibility in the basic desert sense.

Compatibilism: even if causal determinism is true, we can have the sort of free will required for moral responsibility in the basic desert sense, and we do in fact have it.[4]

Libertarianism: because causal determinism is false, we can have the sort of free will required for moral responsibility in the basic desert sense, and we do in fact have it.

Features of our practice of holding people morally responsible that don't invoke deserved pain and harm, pleasure and benefit, have not been a source of conflict in the free will debate. But there are such features. Someone might be held morally responsible because his tendencies to act wrongly are apt to be modified or eliminated partly by blaming, and his dispositions to act rightly might be strengthened by praising (Schlick 1939; Nowell-Smith 1948; Smart 1961). Or someone might be held morally responsible by asking her questions such as: "Why did you decide to do that? Do you think it was the right thing to do?" because as a consequence she will come to appreciate the moral reasons for changing her behavior, resulting in moral reform and reconciliation in her personal relationships. This is known as the forward-looking *answerability* sense of moral responsibility (Scanlon 1998; Shoemaker 2011, 2015; Smith 2012), contrasting with the backward-looking *accountability* sense, conceived as justifying angry responses and the imposition of harmful sanctions (Watson 1996; Shoemaker 2011, 2015). Incompatibilists would not view the control required for answerability to be incompatible with causal determinism, and it is thus open to hard determinists to endorse this notion of moral responsibility. The accountability sense, when it is conceived specifically as invoking basically deserved pain or harm, is typically not viewed by incompatibilists as compatible with determinism, and is rejected by hard determinists.

As I noted at the outset, many contemporary skeptics about free will are not typically hard determinists, since they don't believe that we are in a position to ascertain that the universe is causally deterministic. Instead, they maintain that, whether or not the universe is causally deterministic, our having the controversial sort of free will MR is either highly unlikely (Pereboom 2001, 2014; Levy 2011) or impossible (Strawson 1986, 1994). As noted earlier, I call this position "hard incompatibilism." I contend, like Spinoza, that we would not be morally responsible in the basic desert sense if determinism were true, but also that we would lack such moral responsibility if indeterminism were true and the causes of our actions were exclusively states or events. If the causes of our actions were exclusively states or events, indeterministic causal histories of actions would be as threatening to basic desert moral responsibility as deterministic histories are. However, I think that if we were undetermined agent-causes – if we as substances had the power to cause decisions without being causally determined to cause them – we might well then have the sort of free will required for such moral responsibility. But I argue that although agent causation has not been ruled out as a coherent possibility, the claim that we are agent-causes is not credible given our best physical theories. Thus, we need to take seriously the prospect that we are not free in the sense required for basic desert moral responsibility.

In addition, as we shall see at the close of this discussion, I reject a type of incompatibilism according to which the availability of alternative possibilities, that is free will AP, is crucial to explaining moral responsibility in the basic desert sense, and indeed in any sense, and accept instead a type of incompatibilism that ascribes the more significant role to the actual causal source of the action (Frankfurt 1969; Fischer 1982, 1994). I thus opt for *source* as opposed to *leeway* position. Agent-causal libertarianism is typically conceived as an incompatibilist view according to which an agent can be the source of her action in the way required for moral responsibility, and thus such libertarians are most often "source incompatibilists." But one might also be a source incompatibilist and deny that we have the sort of free will required for moral responsibility (in the basic desert sense), and this is the stance I take.

2   Against Compatibilism

Justifying hard incompatibilism requires arguing against compatibilism and libertarianism, the rival positions. I'll take on compatibilism first. Compatibilists set out conditions for moral responsibility that do not require the falsity of determinism, and they argue that satisfying these conditions is sufficient for responsibility. Incompatibilists object that even if someone satisfies these compatibilists conditions, being causally determined by factors beyond her control rules out moral responsibility in the contested sense, in my view the one that invokes basic desert.

I think that the best way to argue against the compatibilist option begins with the intuition that in a case in which an agent is intentionally causally determined to act by, for instance, neuroscientists who manipulate her brain by optogenetic stimulation, she will not be morally responsible for that action in the basic desert sense even if the compatibilist conditions are met. I then argue that there are no differences relevant to basic desert moral responsibility between this case and a possible case that features an agent who is causally determined to act in an ordinary naturalistic way. The conclusion is that an agent is not morally responsible in the basic desert sense if she is causally determined to act by factors beyond her control even if she satisfies the compatibilist conditions (Taylor 1974: 45; Kane 1996: 65–69; Pereboom 1995: 22–26; 2001: 110–120; 2014: 71–103; Mele 2006: 186–194).

In my four-case version of this argument (Pereboom 1995, 2001: 110–127, 2014: 71–103), in each of four cases an agent commits a crime, murder, for self-interested reasons. The cases are designed so that the action satisfies the various prominent compatibilist conditions. For instance, the action satisfies the rationality condition advocated by John Fischer (1994; Fischer and Ravizza 1998): the agent's desires can be modified by, and some of them arise from, his rational consideration of his reasons, and if he understood that the bad consequences for himself that would result from the crime would be much more severe than they are actually likely to be, he would have refrained from the crime for that reason. The action also satisfies the compatibilist condition proposed by Harry Frankfurt (1971): the agent's effective desire (i.e. their will) conforms appropriately to their second-order desire for which effective desire they will have.

The manipulation cases indicate that it's possible for an agent who knowingly acts wrongly not to be morally responsible in the basic desert sense even if the compatibilist conditions are met, and that, as a result, these conditions are not sufficient for moral responsibility in this sense, contrary to what the compatibilist claims. Force is added to the argument by setting out three such manipulation cases, each of which is progressively more like a fourth, in which the action is causally determined in the ordinary naturalistic way. These cases are designed with the aim that there be no difference relevant to basic desert moral responsibility between any two adjacent cases. As a result, if it's agreed that the agent isn't morally responsible in the first case, this feature of the argument will make it difficult to affirm that he is responsible in the final, ordinary naturalistic case.

Here are the four cases:

Case 1: A team of neuroscientists has the ability to manipulate Professor Plum's neural states at any time by remote optogenetic neural stimulation. In this particular case, they do so by pressing a button just before he begins to reason about his situation, which they know will produce in him a neural state that realizes a strongly egoistic reasoning process, which they know will deterministically result in his decision to kill White. Plum would not have killed White had the neuroscientists not intervened, since his reasoning would then not have been sufficiently egoistic to produce this decision.

Case 2 Plum is just like an ordinary human being, except that a team of neuroscientists programmed him at the beginning of his life so that his reasoning is often but not always egoistic (just as it is in Case 1), and at times strongly so, with the intended consequence that in his current circumstances he will be causally determined to engage in the process of deliberation that results in his decision to kill White for egoistic reasons.

Case 3: Plum is an ordinary human being, except that the training practices of his community causally determined the nature of his deliberative reasoning processes so that they are frequently but not exclusively egoistic. The resulting deliberative process is exactly as it is in Cases 1 and 2: in his current circumstances he is causally determined to engage in the process of deliberation that results in his decision to kill White for egoistic reasons.

Case 4: Everything that happens in the universe is causally determined by virtue of its past states together with the laws of nature. Plum is an ordinary human being, raised in normal circumstances, but his reasoning processes are frequently but not exclusively egoistic, and sometimes strongly so (as in Cases 1–3). In his current circumstances, he is causally determined to engage in the process of deliberation that results in his decision to kill White for egoistic reasons.

Case 1 involves intentional manipulation that is local and causally determining. Of all the cases, it seems most likely to elicit a nonresponsibility intuition. Case 2 is like Case 1, except that the deterministic manipulation occurs at the beginning of the agent's life. Case 3 differs in that the deterministic manipulation results from community upbringing. Case 4 is the ordinary naturalistic case in which the causal determination is not intentional and results from previous events in accord with the laws of nature. Case 4 is the kind of case in which compatibilists attribute moral responsibility in the sense at issue despite the causal determination of the action by factors beyond the agent's control.

In Case 1, is Plum morally responsible in the basic desert sense for the crime? In this situation, it seems clear that Plum is a causally determined victim of the neuroscientists, and thus nonresponsible. Are there any differences between Cases 1 and 2 that can justify claiming that Plum is nonresponsible in Case 1 but is responsible in Case 2? My aim was set out the cases so that there are no such differences between any two adjacent cases. If I was successful, then if Plum was not responsible in Case 1, he wasn't in Cases 2, 3, and 4 either. I propose that the best explanation for Plum's nonresponsibility (and for our intuitions of nonresponsibility) in each case is that he is causally determined to act by factors beyond his control. This is the argument's anticompatibilist conclusion.

A further variety of compatibilism, developed by P.F. Strawson (1962), is also vulnerable to this sort of argument. He contends that the priority of practice – in this case the practice of holding people morally responsible – insulates attributions of moral responsibility from scientific or metaphysical challenges such as the one based on causal determinism. In my view, the best sort of argument against this position involves what R. Jay Wallace (1994) calls a generalization strategy – arguing from generally accepted excuses or exemptions to the conclusion that causal determinism rules out moral responsibility. The excuses and exemptions that form the basis of this sort of argument would have to be generally accepted (but perhaps not uncontested), so that they are plausibly features internal to the practice of holding people morally responsible. The kinds of excuses or exemptions that I exploit in my argument are due to deterministic manipulation, and it is a feature of our practice that we excuse or exempt agents from moral responsibility when they are manipulated in this way, as in Cases 1 and 2. It is also a feature of our practice that if no morally relevant difference can be found between agents in two situations, then if one agent is legitimately exempted from moral responsibility, so is the other. No morally relevant difference can be found between agents in the manipulation examples and agents in ordinary deterministic situations such as Case 4. Thus, it is the practice itself – in particular, rules governing the practice – that renders moral responsibility vulnerable to causal determinism after all.

A number of challenges to this argument have been raised.[5] A first claims that the difference between intentional manipulation by other agents and ordinary naturalistic causal determination is relevant to moral responsibility (e.g. Lycan 1987; Feltz 2013; Murray and Lombrozo 2017). A compatibilist might cite this to justify the claim that while Plum is not responsible in Cases 1 and 2, he is in the ordinary Case 4. This strategy might be tested by having subjects imagine further cases that are exactly the same as Case 1 or Case 2, except that the states at issue are instead produced unintentionally. Gunnar Björnsson sets out a case in which the compatibilist conditions on moral responsibility are satisfied but a cause that isn't an agent – an infection – gradually makes the agent in the example increasingly egoistic without bypassing or undermining his agential capacities. Björnsson predicted that if subjects were prompted to see the agent's behavior as dependent on this nonagential cause, attributions of responsibility would be undermined to the same extent as in cases of intentional manipulation. This turned out to be correct. In a study he conducted involving 416 subjects, the infection undermined attributions of free will and moral responsibility to the same extent as in cases of intentional manipulation (Björnsson and Pereboom 2016). Björnsson's study indicates that the strategy used in manipulation arguments can successfully be employed without intentional manipulation.

A second challenge is developed by John Fischer. He contends that Plum *is* morally responsible in Cases 1 and 2, and that our intuition that he is not morally responsible stems from the correct sense that he is not *blameworthy*. In his statement of the objection, "guidance control" refers to the rationality condition set out above:

> In my view, further conditions need to be added to mere guidance control to get to blameworthiness; these conditions may have to do with the circumstances under which one's values, beliefs, desires, and dispositions were created and sustained, one's physical and economic status, and so forth. Professor Plum, it seems to me, is not blameworthy, even though he is morally responsible. That he is not blameworthy is a function of the circumstances of the creation of his values, character, desires, and so forth. But there is no reason to suppose that anything like such unusual circumstances obtain merely in virtue of the truth of causal determinism. Thus, I see no impediment to saying that Plum can be blameworthy for killing Mrs. White in Case 4. Note that there is no difference with respect to the minimal control conditions for moral responsibility in Cases 1 through 4 – the threshold is achieved in all the cases. But there are . . . wide disparities in the conditions for blameworthiness. (Fischer 2004: 158)

I agree that there are cases in which an agent is morally responsible without being blameworthy – when she is praiseworthy for having performed a morally exemplary action, or when she performs an action that is morally indifferent. But could Plum, who acts wrongly, and is also sensitive to the fact that he does – this is a standard compatibilist condition on moral responsibility – be morally responsible in the sense at issue without being blameworthy? Recall that for an agent to be morally responsible for an action in the basic desert sense is for the action to be attributable to her in such a way that if she was sensitive to its being morally wrong, she would deserve to be blamed or punished in a way that she would experience as painful or harmful, and if she was sensitive to its being morally exemplary, she would deserve to be praised or rewarded in a way that she would experience as pleasurable or beneficial, and the desert is not derivative, for example, from consequentialist or contractualist considerations. An agent's being blameworthy for an action would appear to be entailed by his being morally responsible for it in the basic desert sense together with his sensitivity to its being morally wrong. Thus, it seems that Plum cannot be morally responsible for his action without also being blameworthy for it (Pereboom 2024: 89–91).

A third challenge has us first consider beginning our evaluation of the manipulation argument with our intuition about Plum's responsibility in Case 4, which is arguably that he is responsible and blameworthy, and then exploit the contention that there are no responsibility-relevant differences between adjacent cases, which I endorse, to generate the conclusion that Plum in Case 1 is morally responsible and blameworthy (George Sher, in conversation, circa 1989). If beginning with the intuition that Plum is responsible in Case 4 is indeed reasonable, the compatibilist and the incompatibilist would then seem to be at a standoff, rather than the incompatibilist prevailing. However, in this context, for the compatibilist to propose leading with the intuition that Plum is morally responsible in Case 4 would be out of line, since this is exactly what's at issue in the debate. With this in mind, Michael McKenna's (2008) variant on this objection proposes instead that an *agnostic* stance about Case 4 is initially reasonable, and that this agnostic stance carries backward to Case 1 due to the absence of responsibility-relevant differences between adjacent cases. McKenna contends that a neutral inquirer, who is undecided about whether determinism precludes moral responsibility, would initially agree that it's open that Plum is morally responsible in Case 4, and that it's open that he isn't, and that this adjudication traces back to Case 1. In this way, the intuition that Plum is not morally responsible and blameworthy in Case 1, which is essential to the incompatibilist's argument, can be cast into doubt.

I respond (Pereboom 2014: 91–99) that from the point of view of a neutral party, one not initially committed to compatibilism or to incompatibilism, it is initially rational not to believe that Plum in Case 4 is morally responsible, and not to believe that he isn't, but to be open to clarifying considerations that would make one or the other of these beliefs rational. This "neutral inquiring stance" differs from the "confirmed agnostic stance," in which it is not clear that the ordinary determined agent is morally responsible, and it is not clear that he isn't, but one considers further inquiry closed, and regards the issue as not open to clarifying considerations. But the confirmed agonist stance seems unreasonable. On the contrasting neutral inquiring stance, which is reasonable, manipulation cases themselves can function as clarifying considerations, and so, in proceeding backward from Case 4, the intuition that it's open that Plum is morally responsible may well not survive the clarifying considerations that the manipulation in Cases 1–3 supply.[6]

3   Against Libertarianism

The remaining general position to be confronted in defense of hard incompatibilism is libertarianism, which is also incompatibilist but rejects determinism
and claims that we have the free will required for moral responsibility in the
basic desert sense. The science and metaphysics of libertarianism face certain
challenges, and this has motivated three different varieties of this view. Here I
consider the two most prominent versions of libertarianism: the event-causal
and the agent-causal libertarian positions.[7] In event-causal libertarianism,
actions are caused solely by way of states or events, and some type of indeterminacy in the production of actions by appropriate states or events is held to be
a decisive requirement for moral responsibility (Kane 1996; Ekstrom 2000).
According to agent-causal libertarianism, free will of the sort required for
moral responsibility is accounted for by the existence of agents who possess a
causal power to make choices without being determined to do so. Here it is
crucial that the kind of causation involved in an agent's making a free choice is
not reducible to causation among states of the agent or events involving the
agent, but is instead irreducibly an instance of a substance causing a choice not
by way of states or events. The agent, fundamentally as a substance, has the
causal power to make choices without being causally determined to do so
(Chisholm 1976; O'Connor 2000; Clarke 2003). Let me note that these libertarian accounts can be viewed as aiming to secure not only free will MR, but
free will AP, the availability of alternative possibilities for action, as well.

One route to libertarianism involves claiming that we are at least partly nonphysical, as mind–body dualists maintain, and that this allows for the required
indeterminism. We will soon discuss an objection to dualistic agent-causal libertarianism. Another possibility is that the laws governing the physical world
are indeterministic. Before the 20th century, physicists typically conceived of
the fundamental laws of nature as deterministic. In the early 19th century,
mathematician and physicist Pierre-Simon Laplace provided a characterization of the universe that accords with this conception:

> We may regard the present state of the universe as the effect of its past and the
> cause of its future. An intellect which at a certain moment would know all forces
> that set nature in motion, and all positions of all items of which nature is com-
> posed, if this intellect were also vast enough to submit these data to analysis, it
> would embrace in a single formula the movements of the greatest bodies of the
> universe and those of the tiniest atom; for such an intellect nothing would be
> uncertain and the future just like the past would be present before its eyes.
> (Laplace 1814/1951: 4)

However, beginning in the 1920s, quantum mechanics was developed as the
fundamental science of the microphysical, and has enlivened the prospects of

an indeterministic physical universe. In one account of quantum mechanics, it is antirealist and instrumentalist – while it is a remarkably successful predictive tool, its role does not include informing us about the nature of microphysical reality (e.g. Healey 2012, 2017). Realist accounts which, by contrast, affirm that quantum mechanics may inform us about the nature of microphysical reality, are a distinct option. For our purposes, the pertinent issue in quantum mechanics is how to get from premeasurement quantum states in which particles have indeterminate superposition (e.g. a superposition corresponding to a particle being spin-up and deflected upward and spin-down and deflected downward) to well-defined outcomes subject to measurement. The wave-function equation that describes this process is probabilistic, and the question at hand is whether there is a realist metaphysical interpretation of this equation that is fundamentally probabilistic and thus metaphysically indeterministic.

Albert Einstein famously said of the metaphysics of quantum mechanics, "God does not play dice," and that thought inspired the realist and determinist interpretation of David Bohm (1952), according to which there are hidden factors or variables that render the universe deterministic despite the probabilistic nature of the wave-function equation. In "Bohmian mechanics," particles are fundamental in the sense that they do not reduce to waves, and the wave function together with initial particle positions deterministically fix specific particle positions at all times.

However, there is an alternative realist interpretation of quantum mechanics, developed by Giancarlo Ghirardi, Alberto Rimini, and Tullio Weber (1986), which is fundamentally indeterministic. The "GRW spontaneous-collapse theory" adds a probabilistic equation to the standard quantum dynamics developed by Erwin Schrödinger, with the result that every particle, which on this view is reducible to waves, has a small probability per unit time of undergoing a "hit," in which its state jumps to a state that is relatively localized, that is a "collapse." While the prior state of the system determines a probability distribution for the location of the particle, knowledge of the prior state does not facilitate the prediction of specific locations with certainty, since those locations are not causally determined in virtue of the prior states.

A third interpretation, the "many worlds theory" developed by Hugh Everett (1957), features neither hidden variables nor a supplemental equation that probabilistically predicts locations. Consider again a quantum state involving an electron in superposition corresponding to its being spin-up and deflected upward and spin-down and deflected downward. On Everett's position, this is both a state in which the electron in deflected upward and one in which it is deflected downward. However, these states are causally isolated from each other, and hence they are distinct, and might be thought of as occurring in different worlds. Everett's picture is deterministic, but reality appears indeterministic from the point of view of an observer restricted to a specific world. The relevant upshot of this discussion is that the metaphysics of quantum mechanics isn't settled, and it is epistemically open that the universe is indeterministic, but also that it's deterministic.[8]

But even if the indeterministic GRW spontaneous-collapse theory turns out to be true, this wouldn't all by itself settle whether we have free will of any significant type. Free decisions of the sort that underwrite basic desert moral responsibility would require the indeterminism to be suitably located, plausibly at the level of the neural constitution of decisions, while quantum indeterminacy would, in the first instance, be located at a microlevel more fundamental than the neural. It's likely that quantum micro-indeterminacies, on the supposition that they exist, are ordered with enough redundancy so that at the neural level indeterminacy all but vanishes. As a result of such redundancy, the design of roads and bridges, for example, can ignore any fundamental quantum indeterminacy. And if all of our actions turned out to be 99.9% probable on their causal antecedents, we would have free will to a degree that would make a practical difference relative to the contrasting deterministic picture.

For alternative possibilities to be significantly probable, there would have to be mechanisms that facilitate the "percolating up" of significant microlevel indeterminacies to the neural level, on the analogy of a Geiger counter that senses microlevel events and registers them at the level of the moving of a macrolevel indicator. This issue was addressed by physicist Roger Penrose (1989, 1994) and anesthesiologist Stuart Hameroff (1998), who suggested that free will and consciousness arise through the enhancement of quantum effects within microtubules, subcellular structures internal to neurons. This hypothesis has been debated, but remains very speculative (for a recent overview, see Atmanspacher 2020; for a biologically informed discussion, see Sapolsky 2023: 218–222).

On the event-causal version of libertarianism, prominently defended by Robert Kane (1996), actions are caused solely by states or events, and indeterminacy in the production of actions by states or events is a key requirement for moral responsibility. The ancient Epicureans maintained that the universe ultimately consists of atoms and the void, and that if universal causal determinism were true, the atoms would all be falling downward (Lucretius 50 BCE/1998). Arguably, to explain the interaction of atoms and also free will, they posited random swerves in the otherwise downward paths of atoms. A traditional question for this view is: Do agents plausibly control how and when an atom swerves in a way that can subserve free will of a significant sort?

This concern is often framed as the "luck objection" (e.g. Haji 2000; Latham 2004; Mele 2006; cf., van Inwagen 1983).[9] A famous instance of this objection is found in David Hume's *Treatise of Human Nature* (1739/1978: 411–412; cf. Hume 1748/2000), where he argues that if an action is not determined by factors involving the agent, its connection with the agent will be insufficient for her to be morally responsible for it. This concern can be developed in different ways, but here is my own favorite. For an agent to be morally responsible for an action (in the basic desert sense), she must have a certain kind of control in producing that action. Suppose that a decision is made in a deliberative context in which the relevant causation is event-causal and indeterministic, the agent's moral motivations favor deciding to A, her prudential motivations favor her deciding to not-A, and the strengths of these motivations are in equipoise. A and not-A are the options she is considering. The potentially causally relevant events thus render the occurrence of each of these decisions equiprobable. However, then, crucially, the potentially causally relevant events do not settle which decision occurs, that is whether the decision to A or the decision to not-A occurs. Moreover, since on the event-causal view only events are causally relevant, *nothing* settles which decision occurs. Given the complete causal role of these preceding events, it *remains open* whether action occurs. Thus, it can't be the agent or anything about the agent that settles which decision occurs, and accordingly she lacks the control required for moral responsibility, in the basic desert sense in particular, for it. Since the agent "disappears" at the crucial point in the production of the action – when its occurrence is to be settled – we can call this the "disappearing agent argument" (Pereboom 2004, 2014, 2017a; cf. O'Connor 2008).[10]

Libertarians agree that an action's resulting from a deterministic sequence of causes that traces back to factors beyond the agent's control would rule out her moral responsibility for it. The deeper point of this objection is that if this sort of causal determination rules out moral responsibility, then it is no remedy simply to provide slack in the causal net by making the causal history of actions indeterministic. Such a move would fulfill one requirement for moral responsibility – the absence of causal determinism for decision and action – but it would not satisfy another – sufficient control (Clarke 1997, 2003). In particular, it would not provide the capacity for an agent to be the source of her decisions and actions that, according to many incompatibilists, is ruled out by a deterministic framework.

The agent-causal libertarian's core response to objections of this kind is to specify a way in which the agent can indeed settle which of the options for action occurs. Their proposal is to recruit the agent as the cause of the action (or at least a cause), not merely as involved in events but instead fundamentally as a substance-cause. The agent-causal libertarian maintains that we possess a distinctive causal power, a power for an agent, fundamentally as a substance, to cause a decision without being causally determined to do so, and thereby to settle which options for action occurs.

One concern raised for the agent-causal libertarian picture is that it cannot be reconciled with our best scientific theories. Suppose we allow that agents are free in the way specified by agent-causal libertarianism, perhaps because they are nonphysical beings, but that our best science reveals that the physical world is governed by exceptionless deterministic laws. On the causal route that issues from an undetermined agent-caused action, changes in the physical world, for example in the agent's brain or in other parts of her body, result. However, at this point we would then expect to encounter physical occurrences that diverge from the deterministic laws. Alterations in the brain that result from the causally undetermined decisions would themselves not be causally determined, and they would not be governed by deterministic laws. The agent-causal libertarian might propose that the physical alterations that result from every free decision just happen to dovetail with what can be predicted on the basis of the past and the deterministic laws, and that nothing actually occurs that diverges from these laws. But this proposal would seem to involve coincidences too wild to be credible. Thus, it seems that agent-causal libertarianism is not reconcilable with the physical world's being governed by deterministic laws (Pereboom 1995, 2001: 79–81; 2014: 65–66).

This type of objection also arises on a picture in which physics is fundamentally indeterministic, as it would be on the GRW spontaneous-collapse interpretation of quantum mechanics. Could agent-causal libertarianism be reconciled with a physical world governed by exceptionless indeterministic laws? Consider the class of possible actions each of which has a physical component whose antecedent probability of occurring is approximately 0.32. It would not violate this indeterministic law in the sense of being logically incompatible with it if for a large number of instances the physical components in this class were not actually realized close to 32% of the time. Rather, the force of the law is that for a large number of instances it is correct to *expect* physical components in this class to be realized close to 32% of the time. Are free choices on the agent-causal libertarian picture compatible with what this law leads us to expect about them? If they were, then for a large enough number of instances the possible actions in our class would almost certainly be freely chosen close to 32% of the time. But if the occurrence of these physical components were settled by the choices of agent-causes, then actually being chosen close to 32% of the time would also amount to a wild coincidence. The proposal that agent-caused free choices do not diverge from what such indeterministic laws would predict for the physical components of our actions would conflict so sharply with what we should expect as to make it incredible (Pereboom 1995, 2001: 81–83; 2014: 66–68).[11]

The agent-causal libertarian might now propose that exercises of agent-causal libertarian freedom in fact do result in divergences from what we would expect given our best theories of the physical laws. The idea is that divergences from the deterministic or indeterministic laws do occur whenever we act freely, and they are located at the interface between the agent-cause and the brain. An objection to this proposal is that we currently lack any evidence that such divergences occur (Sapolsky 2023). Thus, agent-causal libertarianism is not reconcilable with our best theories of the laws of nature, whether they render these laws as deterministic or probabilistic, and we have no evidence that the divergences from the laws that this view would accordingly predict actually occur.

Randolph Clarke contends that: "If there can be substance causation at all, then it seems that there can be substance causation the propensities of the exercise of which conform with complete nondeterministic microlevel causal laws" (2003: 181). I think that Clarke is right about this. It is *possible* that the agent causation accords with probabilistic microlevel laws, for it might just happen that in the long run the exercise of agent-causal powers conforms to the probabilities that the indeterministic microlevel laws would assign in the absence of agent causation. But should one *expect* this conformity? Timothy O'Connor argues that if the antecedent events are conceived as shaping the agent-causal power, then it is reasonable to expect the actions of agent-causes to conform to the probabilities conferred by these antecedent events:

> Imagine that some conscious reasons-guided systems "magnify" microphysical indeterminacies in such a way that several significantly different outcomes are physically possible. Then further suppose that agent-causal power emerges when conscious reasons-guided systems achieve a requisite threshold of complexity. Such a power might be shaped by states (such as the agent's reasons for acting) that embody the magnified quantum indeterminacies, so that agent-causal actions would be expected to reflect the physical probabilities in the long run. (O'Connor 2003: 309; cf. Clarke 2003: 181)

However, to answer the disappearing agent objection, the causal power exercised by the agent must be of a different sort from that of the events that shape the agent-causal power, and on the occasion of a free decision, the exercise of these causal powers must be distinct from the exercise of the causal powers of the events. For the luck objection shows that causal powers of the events are not the sort that can provide the control needed for moral responsibility. The agent as substance, by virtue of her agent-causal power, is meant to provide this sort of control. Given this requirement, we would expect the decisions of the agent-cause to diverge, in the long run, from the frequency of choices that would be extremely likely on the basis of the events alone. If we nevertheless found conformity, we would have very good reason to believe that the agent-causal power was not of a different sort from the causal powers of the events after all, and that on the occasion of particular decisions, the exercise of these causal powers was not distinct from the exercise of the causal powers of the events. Accordingly, the shaping that O'Connor has in mind cannot be so radical as to undercut the independence of the agent-causal power from the causal powers of the events, and if it is not, then we would expect the divergences at issue.

It is sometimes claimed that we have significant phenomenological evidence for the broader thesis that we have libertarian free will. Perhaps, then, if we could have libertarian free will only if we were agent-causes, and if we were agent-causes there would exist the divergences at issue, then our phenomenological evidence counts in favor of the existence of these divergences. However, the Spinozan response to this claim, that we believe our decisions are free only because we are ignorant of their causes, has not been successfully countered. The lesson to draw from Spinoza is that the phenomenology apt to generate a belief that we have libertarian free will would be just the same if decisions were instead causally determined and we were ignorant of enough of their causes. For this reason, the phenomenological evidence for our having libertarian free will is not especially impressive. This consideration counts strongly against the proposal that such evidence gives us reason to believe that the divergences in question exist.

On the other hand, nothing we've said conclusively rules out the claim that because we are agent-causes, there exist such divergences. We do not have a complete understanding of the human neural system, and it may turn out that some human neural structures differ significantly from anything else in nature we understand, and that they serve to ground libertarian agent causation (but see Sapolsky 2023). In defense of libertarianism, Steven Horst (2011) points out that physics features no exceptionless laws when they are construed as describing actual motions. The law of gravity, for example, will only result in accurate predictions of motions if there are no other forces, such as electromagnetism, at play. The preferable view, according to Horst, is to interpret the laws as describing causal powers, which in the case of fundamental physics are forces. He contends that this conception of the laws is amenable to a libertarian conception of free will, since any law should be understood as in principle open to the existence of powers not described by that law. The libertarian agent-causal power may be the relevant sort of causal power, and in Horst's view, nothing in current physics rules this out. Still, on this conception the view remains speculative, since we lack substantial evidence of the operation of libertarian agent-causal libertarian causal powers.

Thus, all versions of libertarianism face serious difficulties. In Section 1, we raised problems for the leeway positions, and for compatibilism. Hence the only position in the free will debate for which problems have not been raised is the version of source incompatibilism that denies we have the sort of free will required for moral responsibility. This is a variety of hard incompatibilism. The concern for this view is not, I think, that there is significant empirical evidence that it is false, or that there is a good argument that it is somehow incoherent, and false for that reason. Rather, the questions it faces are practical: What would life be like if we believed it was true? Is this a sort of life that we can tolerate?

4 Hard Incompatibilism, Responsibility, and the Moral Emotions

One might argue that giving up our belief in the free will required for basic desert moral responsibility would have harmful consequences, so harmful that thinking and acting in accord with hard incompatibilism is not a feasible option. Thus, even if the claim that we are morally responsible in the basic desert sense turns out to be false, there may yet be weighty practical reasons for continuing to assume that it's true. Still, this option would have us imposing the harm and pain of blame and punishment, conceived as basically deserved, on agents when they do not in fact deserve it, which would then seem wrong. As Bruce Waller argues, if people are not morally responsible in this sense for immoral behavior, treating them as if they were would be unfair (Waller 1990: 130–135).

However, our practice of holding people morally responsible includes a range of options for addressing wrongdoing that do not invoke basic desert, and retaining and developing them would not be subject to this charge of unfairness. Crucially, rejecting basic desert allows for the retention of forward-looking components of our practice. As mentioned in Section 1, forward-looking, nondesert-based components of our practice are in the clear. We may ask wrongdoers, "Why did you decide to do that?" and "Do you think it was the right thing to do?" and if the reasons given in response are morally unsatisfactory, we may regard it as justified to invite them to evaluate critically what their actions indicate about their intentions and character, to demand an apology, or to request reform. Engaging in such interactions is reasonable in light of forward-looking considerations. A first is the right of those harmed or threatened to protect themselves from wrongful behavior and its consequences, thereby securing safety. Second, we might have a stake in reconciliation with wrongdoers, and calling them to account in this way can function as a step toward realizing this aim. Third, on a personal and societal level we have an interest in the moral formation of wrongdoers, and the interactions just described function as a stage in that process. Finally, the good of the recovery and restoration of victims harmed by wrongdoing are at issue, and such interactions may help serve to realize that objective. Such interactions may thus be grounded not in basic desert but in forward-looking, nondesert-invoking desiderata, such as protection, reconciliation, moral formation, and the recovery and restoration of victims.

One aspect of human life for which our having basic desert moral responsibility may be a crucial issue is the personal relationships that are an important source of meaning and fulfilment for us. Such relationships are sometimes challenged by wrongdoing, and in such contexts it's natural for us to react with moral anger in ways that impose harm and pain. Such personal relationships are often enhanced by morally exemplary behavior, and it's natural for us to react with gratitude in ways that confer benefits and pleasure. These emotional reactions – moral anger and gratitude – are designated by the term "reactive attitudes," made familiar by Peter F. Strawson in his "Freedom and Resentment" article (1962). There he contends that without such reactive attitudes, and without the legitimacy of expressing them, we would face the prospect of an "objectivity of attitude," a stance that precludes the personal relationships of love and mutual regard we value. Strawson proposes that moral responsibility in fact consists in the legitimate having and expressing of these reactive attitudes, and thus such personal relationships presuppose that the participants are morally responsible. Moral responsibility, in turn, plausibly requires the right sort of control in action, and thus entails free will MR, arguably of the basic desert sort. Could our personal relationships do without supposing basic desert free will MR? If they could not, then we might need, practically, to assume we have it, because we could not flourish without the personal relationships.

Of the reactive attitudes associated with moral responsibility, moral anger is arguably most closely connected with it. Moral anger can be divided into various types, including resentment, that is anger directed toward an agent due to a wrong he has done to oneself; and indignation, anger directed toward an agent because of a wrong he has done to a third party. These attitudes often come with the presupposition that their targets basically deserve the pain or harm that their expressions are apt to inflict (Honderich 1988; Pereboom 2001; Nussbaum 2016).

I resist the claim that moral anger of this sort is required for valuable personal relationship. First, there are other attitudes for addressing wrongdoing that do not presuppose basic desert (Pereboom 2001, 2014, 2021a). They include, most importantly, that stance of moral protest. Pamela Hieronymi (2001), Matthew Talbert (2012), and Angela Smith (2013) propose that blame indeed be understood as moral protest, and I endorse this proposal (Pereboom 2021a: 27–53). But while for them the negative reactive attitudes (resentment and indignation in particular) have an essential role in blaming as moral protest, I resist this aspect of their view, since moral protest need not feature these attitudes. As I see it, moral protest is a stance of opposition to an agent for having performed a specific immoral action, or for having a disposition to act immorally. It has the function in our moral practice of engaging wrongdoers by communicating opposition to their immoral behavior, together with moral reasons to refrain from it. Such moral protest may be accompanied by expression of sadness and sorrow, hurt and disappointment. It might be confrontational to varying degrees, but need not involve a presupposition of the basically deserved blame or punishment that imposes harm or pain.

If moral protest together with these other attitudes is to supplant resentment and indignation, these alternatives would need to be fostered and promoted.

One might object that resentment and indignation are largely beyond our power to alter. But this supposition might be contested. Shaun Nichols (2013) appeals to the distinction between narrow-profile emotional responses, immediate emotional reactions to situations, and wide-profile responses, which are not immediate and may involve rational control. We might expect to have limited success in altering narrow-profile, immediate resentment when we are seriously wronged in personal relationships. However, in wide-profile circumstances, we may well be able to reduce, or even eliminate, resentment, or what is crucial, to disavow it in the sense of rejecting any force it might be conceived to have in justifying the imposition of harm or pain.

A hard incompatibilist will call into question the role of moral anger in our practice of holding people morally responsible insofar as that anger features a presupposition that the wrongdoer basically deserves to be targeted by an expression of that anger that imposes harm or pain. Now cognitivists about the emotions maintain that emotions generally have presuppositions as components – they may be judgments, thoughts, appraisals, or, arguably, beliefs held with some degree of confidence, that is credences (e.g. Lazarus 1991; Nussbaum 1997). Such components count as cognitive because they can be true or false, by contrast, say, with taste sensations on typical accounts. On this view, fear tends to include a cognitive appraisal regarding the presence of danger, conceived as a threat to the subject's goals. Similarly, on the cognitivist account, moral anger may include the cognitive appraisal that its target basically deserves blame or punishment that imposes harm or pain.

Exactly how does this view issue in a challenge to moral anger? It might be argued that it's possible to be morally angry with a wrongdoer, and while that anger has the basic desert appraisal as a component, one may be morally angry while rejecting that appraisal. In Robert Roberts's (2003) cognitivist account of emotions, the cognitive element of an emotion is a "concerned construal," a perceptual take that represents its target as being a certain way that calls for a response. But a subject who has the emotion can avoid affirming that the target is correctly represented that way.[12] The emotion has a component that is an analogue to a judgment, which the subject of the emotion does not necessarily share, even if the subject does share it in typical cases. In one of Roberts's examples, someone who was raised in a strict religious household but has since become more worldly may feel guilty for going to the movie theatre, but not affirm that she has done something wrong, which is nonetheless a component of her emotion of guilt. On this account, one can be morally angry, and that anger have, as a component, the appraisal that its target basically deserves to be the recipient of a harmful or painful expression of that anger, while rejecting that appraisal. So moral anger may include a perspectival take that has a basic desert presupposition, but its subject might not endorse this presupposition. The hard incompatibilist would emphasize the importance of rejecting the claim that the anger justifies targeting the wrongdoer with a painful or harmful expression of that anger conceived as basically deserved. At the same time, even though moral anger so conceived may be in the clear for the hard incompatibilist, it's important to count its cost. For instance, such anger tends to issue in false and morally objectionable beliefs that illegitimately rationalize these attitudes, and this effect may persist even if one rejects the basic desert appraisal.[13] Adopting the stance of moral protest as an alternative has the potential to avoid such results.

Forgiveness is another attitude that Strawson (1962) cites, one that might seem to presuppose that those being forgiven are blameworthy in the sense that they basically deserve the pain or harm that being targeted by expressions of resentment and indignation involves, and if this is so, this attitude would also be undermined by hard incompatibilism. But forgiveness can instead be envisioned as the renunciation of moral protest that does not involve resentment or indignation. Imagine a friend has wronged you in some way a number of times by acting inconsiderately, and you find yourself resolved to end your friendship with him. You then challenge him in a moral conversation, protesting the wrong he has done and the threat to you that his disposition to behave in this way poses, but without resentment. In response, he is contrite, takes on a resolute disapproving stance toward that disposition, and commits himself to its elimination. You now withdraw and renounce your protest and agree to continue with the relationship. On Hieronymi's proposal, forgiveness is such a withdrawal of moral protest to a threat upon acknowledgment of the offender's change of heart (Hieronymi 2001: 554). Ratifying such a change of heart generally also involves renouncing the stance of moral protest against the wrongdoer for having committed the specific wrong that was the focus of the protest. This renunciation involves coming to believe that this stance is no longer appropriate, together with a commitment to cease engaging in overt moral protest for the wrong at issue (Pereboom 2021a).

One might argue that hard incompatibilism threatens the self-directed attitudes of guilt and repentance, and that this would be especially bad for relationships. Without guilt and repentance, we would not only be incapable of restoring relationships damaged because we have done wrong but also be kept from retaining our moral integrity. For without the attitudes of guilt and repentance, we would lack the psychological mechanisms that can play these roles. But note first that it is because guilt essentially involves a belief that one is blameworthy in the basic desert sense for something that one has done that this attitude would appear to be endangered by hard incompatibilism. It is for this reason that repentance would also seem to be (indirectly) threatened, for feeling guilty would appear to be required to motivate repentance. However, suppose that you behave immorally, but because you endorse hard incompatibilism, you deny that you are blameworthy in the basic desert sense. Instead, you acknowledge that you have done wrong, you take the stance of moral protest toward yourself for your action, you feel sad that you did wrong, and you regret what you have done (Waller 1990). Because you are committed to doing what is right and to your own moral improvement, you resolve to refrain from behavior of this kind in the future, and seek the help of others in sustaining your resolve. None of this is jeopardized by hard incompatibilism.

Gratitude would seem to presuppose that the person to whom one is grateful basically deserves for you to praise her in a way that confers benefit or pleasure, and hard incompatibilism would then threaten gratitude. However, certain aspects of this attitude would be unaffected, and these aspects have the function that gratitude as a whole has in good relationships. Gratitude includes, first of all, being thankful toward a person who has acted beneficially. True, being thankful toward someone may often involve the belief that she is praiseworthy in the basic desert sense for an action. Still, one can also be thankful to a small child for some kindness, without believing that he is praiseworthy in this sense. This aspect of thankfulness could be retained while rejecting basic desert. Often, gratitude also involves joy as a response to the beneficent act of another, which brings about a sense of mutual harmony and goodwill, and no feature of hard incompatibilism undermines being joyful and expressing joy when others are considerate or generous on one's behalf.

Is the kind of love that mature adults have for each other in good relationships imperiled by hard incompatibilism, as Strawson's (1962) line of argument suggests? Consider first whether for loving someone it is important that the person who is loved has and exercises free will in the sense required for basic desert moral responsibility. Parents love their children rarely, if ever, for the reason that they possess this sort of free will, or decide to do what is right by free will, or deserve to be loved due to freely willed choices. Moreover, when adults love each other, it is also very seldom, if at all, for these sorts of reasons. The reasons we love others are surely varied and complex. Besides moral character and behavior, features such as intelligence, appearance, style, and resemblance to certain others in one's personal history all might have a role. Suppose morally admirable qualities are particularly important in occasioning, enriching, and maintaining love. Even if there is an aspect of love that we often conceive as a basically deserved response to morally admirable qualities, it is unlikely that love would be undermined if we came to believe that these qualities are not produced or sustained by freely willed decisions. Morally admirable qualities are loveable, whether or not people basically deserve to be praised for having them.

One might contend that we want to be loved by others as a result of their free will. Against this, the love parents have for their children is most often generated independently of the parents' will altogether, and we don't think that this love is deficient. Kane recognizes this fact about parental love, and he agrees that romantic love is similar in this respect. But he contends that there is a kind of love we very much want that would not exist if all love were determined by factors beyond our control (Kane 1996: 88; cf. Strawson 1986: 309; Anglin 1991: 20). The plausibility of Kane's view might be enhanced by reflecting on how you would react if you discovered that someone you love was causally determined to love you by, say, a benevolent manipulator.

Setting aside *free* will for the moment, when does the will play any role at all in engendering love? When an intimate relationship is disintegrating, people will sometimes decide to try to restore the love they once had for one another. Or when a student finds herself at odds with a roommate from the outset, she may choose to take steps to make the relationship a good one. When a marriage is arranged, the partners may decide to do what they can to love each other. In such situations we might want others to make a decision that might produce or maintain love. But this is not to say that we would want that decision to be freely willed in the sense required for basic desert moral responsibility. For it is not clear that value would be added by the decision's being free in this sense. Moreover, although in some circumstances we might want others to make decisions of this sort, we would generally prefer love that did not require such choices. This is so not only for intimate romantic relationships – where it is quite obvious – but also for friendships and relationships between parents and children.

Suppose Kane's view could be defended, and we did want love that is freely willed in the sense required for basic desert moral responsibility. If we in fact desired love of this kind, then we would want a kind of love that would be impossible if hard incompatibilism were true. Still, the kinds of love not challenged by hard incompatibilism are plausibly sufficient for good relationships. If we can aspire to the kind of love parents typically have for their children, or the type romantic lovers share, or the sort had by friends who were immediately attracted to each other, and whose friendship became close through their interactions, then the possibility of fulfillment through interpersonal relationships remains intact (Pereboom 1995: 41; 2001: 202–224, 2014: 190–193; 2018, 2021a: 123–140).

Hard incompatibilism, therefore, does not yield a threat to interpersonal relationships, although it might challenge certain attitudes that often have a role in such relationships. But love – the attitude most essential to good interpersonal relationships – would not appear to be threatened by hard incompatibilism at all. Love of others involves, fundamentally, wishing for their good, taking on their aims and desires, and a desire to be together with them, and none of this is endangered by hard incompatibilism.

5   Hard Incompatibilism and the Treatment of Criminals

Does hard incompatibilism have resources adequate for addressing criminal behavior? Here it would appear to be at a disadvantage, and, if so, practical considerations might force us nevertheless to treat criminals as if they were morally responsible in the basic desert sense. If hard incompatibilism is true, a retributivist justification for criminal punishment is unavailable, for it assumes that the criminal basically deserves punishment that involves the imposition of pain or harm, while hard incompatibilism denies this. And retributivism is one of the most naturally compelling ways for justifying criminal punishment.

By contrast, a theory that justifies criminal punishment on the grounds that punishment educates criminals morally is not challenged by hard incompatibilism specifically. So one might propose that the hard incompatibilist could appeal to a view of this kind. But we lack significant empirical evidence that the punishment of criminals brings about moral education, and without such evidence, it would be wrong to punish them for the sake of achieving this goal. In general, it is wrong to harm someone in order to realize some good in the absence of significant evidence that the harm will produce the good. Moreover, even if we had good evidence that punishment was effective in morally educating criminals, we should prefer nonpunitive methods for achieving this result, if they are available – whether or not criminals are morally responsible.

Deterrence theories claim that criminal punishment is justified on the grounds that it deters future crime. The two most prominent deterrence theories – the utilitarian version and the one that grounds the right to punish on the right to self-defense – are not undercut by hard incompatibilism per se. However, they are questionable on other grounds. The utilitarian theory, which claims that punishment is justified because it maximizes utility (Bentham 1823/1948), faces well-known challenges. It would seem at times to demand punishing the innocent when doing so would maximize utility; in some circumstances it would appear to prescribe punishment that is unduly severe; and it would involve *manipulative use* (Tadros 2017), that is, harming people without their consent merely as a means to the well-being, in this case the safety, of others. The type of deterrence theory that founds the right to punish on the right of individuals to defend themselves against immediate threats (Farrell 1985: 38–60) is also objectionable. For when a criminal is sentenced he is typically not an immediate threat to anyone, and this fact about his circumstances distinguishes him from those who may legitimately be harmed on the basis of the right of self-defense.

But there is an intuitively legitimate theory of crime prevention that is not undermined by hard incompatibilism, or by other considerations. This view draws an analogy between the treatment of criminals and the treatment of carriers of dangerous diseases. Ferdinand Schoeman (1979) contends that if we have the right to quarantine carriers of severe communicable diseases to protect people, then for the same reason we also have the right to isolate the criminally dangerous. Quarantining someone can be justified when she is not morally responsible for being dangerous to others. If a child is infected with a deadly contagious virus passed on to her prior to birth, quarantine may nevertheless be legitimate. Now suppose that a serial killer continues to pose a grave danger to a community. Even if he is not morally responsible for his crimes, it would be as legitimate to incapacitate him by detention as it is to quarantine a nonresponsible carrier of a deadly communicable disease.

It would be morally wrong, however, to treat carriers of the communicable disease more severely than is required to guard against the resulting threat. Similarly, it would be wrong to treat criminals more harshly than is needed to neutralize the danger posed by them. Just as moderately dangerous diseases may only license measures less intrusive than quarantine, so moderately serious criminal tendencies may only justify responses less intrusive than detention. Shoplifting, for example, may warrant only some degree of monitoring. Furthermore, I suspect that a theory modeled on quarantine would not justify measures of the sort whose legitimacy is most in doubt, such as the death penalty or confinement in the worst prisons we have. Moreover, it would demand a degree of concern for the rehabilitation and well-being of the criminal that would decisively alter much of current practice. Just as society has a duty to seek to cure the diseased it quarantines, so it would have a duty to attempt to rehabilitate the criminals it detains. When rehabilitation is impossible, and if protection of society requires indefinite confinement, there would be no justification for making a criminal's life more miserable than the protection of society requires.

Gregg Caruso (2021) embeds such a view within a "public health model," and I endorse this move. A primary aim of the public health system is the prevention of disease. The public health approach to criminal behavior makes the prevention of crime a primary aim, shifting the focus to identifying and addressing the social determinants of crime, such as poverty, abuse, and mental illness. Note that just as quarantine is required only when the public health system fails to prevent dangerous communicable diseases, criminal incapacitation would be needed only when the system falls short of its primary preventative aim. Caruso argues that the social determinants of illness and of criminal behavior are interrelated, and that we should adopt a public health approach for each.

Plausibly, the state should not conceal the fact that it detains violent criminals on the grounds the public health quarantine model sets out, but instead make this information publicly available. So even though this theory is justified as deterring just criminals themselves, i.e., special deterrence, it, together with a publicity provision, would yield, as a side effect, general deterrence – it would deter others who are tempted to commit crimes. This general deterrent effect comes for free, so to speak, since it is a side effect of the state's satisfying a publicity provision on a legitimate policy of special deterrence. I call such general deterrent effects justified as special deterrence "free general deterrence" (Pereboom 2020, 2021a: 89–96).

Free general deterrence comes with a significant limitation on how much harm can legitimately be inflicted – again, only the minimum harm required to protect against an aggressor is licensed. One might propose, however, that the free sort isn't enough to protect against certain sorts of wrongdoing, such as the manipulation of financial markets, large-scale embezzlement, and the illegal use of political influence for gain in personal wealth and power. Those who commit such crimes are often adept at calculating risk, at weighing the probability of the wrongdoing being detected against the probability of significant personal gain. Free general deterrence would arguably involve the threat of the loss of one's professional or political position or, say, of a license to trade in financial instruments. The general deterrence in place in much of the world is already much stronger than what free general deterrence would allow, and yet the incidence of such financial and political wrongdoing is fairly high. Reducing the strength of the deterrents is likely to increase the incidence of such wrongdoing, and thus stronger general deterrents are plausibly required (Pereboom 2020).

At this point we might re-examine the prohibition against manipulative use and ask what grounds this prohibition. I propose that it is the right to life, liberty, and physical security of the person that has the key role in the use objection to general deterrence. Those rights are grounded in the more general right to a life in which one's capacity for flourishing is not compromised in the long term. There is a presumption against punishment as manipulative use, where that involves intentional killing, long-term confinement, and the infliction of severe physical or psychological harm. But consider monetary fines, when they don't hinder a life lived at a reasonable level of flourishing. General deterrence involving monetary fines may be in the clear. So suppose that an agent is guilty of insider trading in the stock market, and she knows that insider trading is illegal. Now add that while satisfying all of the prominent compatibilist conditions on moral responsibility, she is causally determined to act as she does. Suppose that a $50,000 fine would deter her and others from this sort of financial crime. My sense that it would be illegitimate to fine her is weaker than my intuition that it would be illegitimate to imprison her for the sake of general deterrence.

It's plausible that if manipulative use involving monetary fines is within bounds, so are short prison sentences, say of several months. Victor Tadros and Richard Arneson (in conversation) argue that the difference between the two is not significant, while short prison sentences are often especially effective deterrents, especially in combination with a high expectation of being caught (Kleiman 2009), so they should be treated in the same way. In support, one might contend that while a short prison term is a violation of the liberty right, it is only a moderately serious violation, and does not preclude a life lived at a reasonable level of flourishing in the way that long prison terms typically do.

This provision would also help with a problem Tadros (in conversation) raises: What if people refuse to pay the fines they've been assessed? Here it would be helpful to have a short prison sentence as a backup, especially given its effectiveness as a deterrent.

Thus, it is at least open that a justified and workable response to criminal behavior is possible without recourse to the controversial sort of free will MR, the variety that invokes basic desert.

6   Alternative Possibilities and Determinism

In Section 1 we noted that besides free will MR, free will AP, the availability of alternative possibilities for action, is a further focus of the free will debate. In Section 3 we in effect considered the prospects of free will AP as arising from indeterminism, an option endorsed by libertarian incompatibilists about free will AP. Let us now turn to compatibilism about free will AP: Could one ever have the ability, on some occasion, to act and to refrain, and more generally, to have free will AP, if causal determinism, or something close, is true? According to the Consequence Argument, naturalistic causal determinism, in particular, rules out such an ability to do otherwise (van Inwagen 1975, 1983; cf. Ginet 1966). The argument operates under the supposition that naturalistic causal determinism is true, that the facts about the remote past and the laws of nature entail the facts about one, unique future. It then assumes the fixity of the laws and the fixity of the past, that no one is free to act in such a way as to alter the laws of nature, and no one is free to act in such a way as to alter the facts about the remote past. Here, then, is a version of the Consequence Argument.

(1)   No one is free to act in such a way as to alter the facts about the remote past and the laws of nature.

(2)   The facts about the remote past and the laws of nature entail the facts about one, unique future.[14]

(3)   Therefore, no one is free to act in such a way as to alter the facts about that one, unique future.

The objective of the Consequence Argument is to establish that on the supposition of naturalistic causal determinism, no one has free will AP. Given its conclusion that under the supposition of that type of determinism, no one is free to act in such a way as to alter the facts about the one, unique future, then in any situation in which someone is considering options for action, there is a fact about which option she will select, and she is not free to act in such a way as to alter that fact.[15]

How might compatibilist defenders of free will AP respond? A tradition among compatibilists since the 17th century has been to maintain that being able to do otherwise is a *conditional* ability, which renders it consistent with causal determinism, contrary to the conclusion of the Consequence Argument. Thomas Hobbes (1654), John Locke (1690/1975), and David Hume (1748/2000) claimed that an agent can do otherwise just in case she would have done otherwise had she chosen or willed to do so. Elaborating on an example from Locke, suppose you are in a room and the door to the outside is unlocked. You stay in the room. Could you have done otherwise, supposing that determinism is true? Even supposing determinism, if you chose to leave the room, you would have left – after all, the door was unlocked. If you chose to stay, as you in fact did, you would have stayed. So, in accord with Hobbes's (1654) account, your conditional ability is *two-way*: both acting and refraining are possible options for action – each conditional on your choosing the option – even if determinism is true. Hume's formulation is explicitly two-way: "by liberty, then, we can only mean a power of acting or not acting according to the determinations of the will – that is, *if we choose to remain at rest, we may; if we choose to also move, we also may*" (Hume 1748/2000: Section 8). G. E. Moore (1912) endorsed a conditional analysis, arguing that to say that I could have acted otherwise is to claim that I would have acted otherwise *if I had so chosen*, and A. J. Ayer (1954) followed suit.

Such conditional analyses of "could have done otherwise" were criticized in the 1960s by Roderick Chisholm (1964) and Keith Lehrer (1968), using the following type of consideration. Suppose Brown does not at some time jump into the sea to save a drowning child, and we say:

(1) Brown could have jumped into the sea at t.

An advocate of the conditional analysis would propose that (1) is equivalent to:

(2) If Brown had chosen to jump into the sea at t, he would have jumped into the sea at t.

Suppose that the sea is very cold, and Brown knows it, and due to this it is psychologically impossible for him to choose to jump into the sea. Still, we might suppose that if he did choose to jump, he would actually jump. Then (2) would be true, and yet it is intuitive that (1) is false – Brown could not have jumped into the sea. The conclusion is that (2) is not a correct analysis of (1). This criticism resulted in the demise of the conditional analysis, and while once a standard fixture of compatibilism, current interest in this strategy is sporadic.

Bur further compatibilist strategies for safeguarding the ability to do otherwise on the supposition of determinism have been proposed. One such strategy begins by reflecting on ordinary attributions of the ability to do otherwise, with the aim of discerning whether they are sensitive to causal determination in the way the Consequence Argument prescribes (e.g. Lewis 1981; Perry 2004; Dorr 2016). Consider language-speaking abilities. Mario speaks both Italian and English. His abilities persist over time, and he retains them when he is not exercising them. Such abilities are referred to as *general* abilities. Now one might think that Mario has the ability to do otherwise whenever he is speaking English, for at that time he retains the general ability to speak Italian. However, if he lacks the opportunity to exercise his general ability to speak Italian, or English for that matter, for instance when his mouth is clamped open at the dentist's, he can't in fact exercise it. So, to have an ability to do otherwise with the use of a general ability, one would need, in addition to the general ability itself, the opportunity to exercise it.

Now suppose Mario and I are in New York, we're in an Italian restaurant, the menus are in both Italian and English, and our waiter has told us he's from Italy. Here Mario would seem to have the opportunity to order in Italian. But suppose he orders in English. I later say to him: "You could have ordered in Italian!" It seems intuitive that what I said is true. In some contexts, uses of "can" and its various forms attribute only a general ability, such as Mario's general ability to speak Italian, by contrast with a *local* ability to exercise such a general ability in a particular circumstance. But in this situation, I'm not merely attributing a general ability to speak Italian to Mario; that's not aptly remarked upon in this context. Instead, what I said implies that in these specific circumstances he could have exercised his general ability to speak Italian. However, if in assessing whether "You could have ordered in Italian!" is true, the entire past and all the laws of nature are held fixed, its truth is ruled out. So it seems right to loosen what's held fixed. Here we can follow Ann Whittle (2010) in differentiating between a *truly* local ability, which holds the entire past and the laws of nature fixed, from a *fairly* local ability, which loosens what's held fixed, either the past or the laws, or both, to a certain degree, but still holds fixed particular features of the current circumstances (Pereboom 2021a).

What is the upshot of this discussion for the Consequence Argument? To accommodate the truth of "You could have ordered in Italian!" some premise or reasoning step in that argument would need to be rejected. The possibilities include denying the fixity of the laws or the fixity of the past. The denial of the fixity of the past involves not holding the entire past fixed in assessing the truth of the claim about being able to do otherwise, and the denial of the fixity of the laws involves not holding all of the laws of nature fixed, and either option would accommodate the truth of "You could have ordered in Italian!"[16]

At this point, the incompatibilist may object that it's questionable whether we should rely on our ordinary intuitions about the truth of statements such as, "You could have ordered in Italian!" They may plausibly contend that these intuitions are not produced by careful consideration of the implications of causal determinism. They may claim that if they were, we would see that these statements are in fact false. A more conciliatory discussant might concede that "You could have ordered in Italian!" is true on the supposition of determinism, and in assessing this statement the entire past and all the laws should not be held fixed. But in contexts in which what's being considered is whether a wrongdoer basically deserves to be punished, causal determination by factors beyond his control becomes salient, and in such contexts the entire past and all the laws of nature should be held fixed. This conciliatory position is a kind of "contextualism" about what is to be held fixed, and thus about the fixity of the past or the fixity of the laws, or both.

So we might ask: Does free will MR, supposing moral responsibility in the basic desert sense, require free will AP, and should we affirm that at least in the context in which claims about basic desert are assessed, the Consequence Argument shows that causal determinism rules out the alternative possibilities at issue?[17] If so, we have another route, in addition to the manipulation argument, from causal determinism to hard incompatibilism. But as we shall now see, there is reason to deny that free will MR, supposing moral responsibility in the basic desert sense, requires free will AP.

7 Alternative Possibilities and Moral Responsibility

Let us now turn to the often–assumed connection between free will MR, in the basic desert sense specifically, and free will AP: for an agent to be morally blameworthy for an action in the basic desert sense, it must be that he could have refrained from performing it. If he's really blameworthy in this sense for the action, it seems crucial that he could have voluntarily done something to avoid being blameworthy. However, Harry Frankfurt, in 1969, using an intriguing type of example, argued that an agent's blameworthiness for an action, and his moral responsibility more generally, does not require that he could have refrained. Since then, there has been a lively and voluminous debate about this issue.

The intuition that blameworthiness for an action requires that the agent could have refrained from performing it is aptly expressed by what David Widerker calls the "*W-defense*." About Jones, an allegedly blameworthy promise-breaker who could not have refrained, he writes:

> [S]ince you, Frankfurt, wish to hold [Jones] blameworthy for his decision to break his promise, tell me *what, in your opinion, should he have done instead?* Now, you cannot claim that he should not have decided to break the promise, since this was something that was not in his power to do. Hence, I do not see how you can hold Jones blameworthy for his decision to break the promise. (Widerker 2000: 191)

To be blameworthy for an action, it seems that an agent must have had an *exempting* alternative possibility, one that, should he have availed himself of it, would have exempted him from blame (Moya 2006: 67; cf. Mele 1996; McKenna 1997). Correlatively, to be praiseworthy for an action, it seems that the agent must have been able to do something less admirable – although this is more controversial.[18] Accordingly, many participants in the debate have affirmed the "principle of alternative possibilities" (PAP): an action is free in the sense required for moral responsibility only if the agent could have done otherwise than what she actually did.

Frankfurt's challenge to PAP features an example in which an agent considers performing an immoral action, and a neuroscientist wants him to do this, but is concerned that the agent will lose his nerve. So if there is any indication that the agent might not perform the action, the neuroscientist would intervene and cause him to perform it by manipulating his brain in the right way. But as things actually go, the neuroscientist does not intervene because the agent performs the action on his own, and there is no indication that he might refrain.

Here is Carolina Sartorio's version of Frankfurt's original example:

> A neuroscientist wants Jones to perform a certain action. He is prepared to go to considerable lengths to get his way, but he prefers to avoid showing his hand unnecessarily. So he waits until Jones is about to make up his mind what to do, and he does nothing unless it is clear to him (he is an excellent judge of such things) that Jones is going to decide to do something other than what he wants him to do. If it were to become clear that Jones is going to decide to do something else, the neuroscientist would take effective steps to ensure that Jones decides to do what he wants him to do, by directly manipulating the relevant processes in Jones's brain. As it turns out, the neuroscientist never has to show his hand because Jones, for reasons of his own, decides to perform the very action the neuroscientist wants him to perform. (Sartorio 2017)

Although Jones could not have avoided acting as he did, it's intuitive that he is morally responsible, and blameworthy in particular, for the action – or at least so Frankfurt, and many others, think.

On Frankfurt's diagnosis, such examples show that we should distinguish between factors that cause or causally explain an action and factors that contribute to making the action inevitable even though they do not cause or causally explain it (Frankfurt 1969; Fischer 1982, 1994). The neuroscientist's intention to intervene makes Jones's action inevitable, but that intention does not cause or causally explain the action; it has no actual causal role. The factors that cause and causally explain the action are Jones's reasons and deliberation, like in any ordinary case in which someone is morally responsible. Frankfurt proposes that in the example he introduced it is these causal factors, and not those that make the action inevitable, that are relevant to Jones's moral responsibility.

Frankfurt's example suggests two insights about moral responsibility (McKenna and Pereboom 2016: 103–104). The first is that because it's intuitive that Jones is morally responsible while he lacks alternative possibilities, the availability of alternative possibilities is not necessary for moral responsibility. Second, what instead accounts for moral responsibility is the actual causal history of the action, specifically the deliberative process by which the agent discerns and weighs reasons for action and the responsiveness to these reasons that the process involves (Frankfurt 1969; cf. Fischer 1982, 1994; McKenna 2005, 2008; Sartorio 2016). Michael McKenna proposes a response to Widerker's W-defense that accords with Frankfurt's suggested insights: "A person's moral responsibility concerns what she does do and her basis for doing it, not what else she could have done" (McKenna 2008: 785).

John Fischer (1982, 1994) observes that examples of the sort Frankfurt devised do not challenge the incompatibilist's claim that moral responsibility for an action requires that it have an indeterministic causal history. Notice that the Frankfurt example does not specify that Jones's action is causally determined. If it did specify that Jones's action was causally determined, in particular causally deterministically by factors beyond his control, then for many the intuition that he is morally responsible would dissipate. This suggests a core component of the free will required for moral responsibility that contrasts with the PAP:

> **The source principle:** an action is free in the sense required for moral responsibility only if its causal history, and in particular its causal source, is of an appropriate sort.

Note that Frankfurt's own compatibilist account adheres to the source principle. On that account, to be morally responsible for an action, the agent must have willed it, and she must have wanted to will it (Frankfurt 1971). For Frankfurt, when an action has this causal history, the agent will be its source in the way that moral responsibility for it requires, and access to alternative possibilities is not also required.

Incompatibilists contend that moral responsibility for an action (in the basic desert sense) requires that its causal history be indeterministic. However, incompatibilists who defend the PAP typically affirm the indeterministic requirement only because they believe that it is needed to secure alternative possibilities (Ginet 1997, 2007; Palmer 2011; Franklin 2011). Incompatibilists who endorse the source principle by contrast with PAP (i.e. "source incompatibilists") claim that the role an indeterministic causal history has in explaining why an agent is morally responsible is independent of alternative possibilities. Instead, they maintain that an indeterministic history – of the right sort – allows one to be the source of one's actions in a way that secures the absence of causal determination by factors beyond one's control (Stump 1990, 1996; Zagzebski 1991, 2000; Pereboom 1995, 2001, 2014; Hunt 2000, 2005; Shabo 2010). Source incompatibilists may hold that alternative possibilities for acting are entailed by the actual causal history having these features (Della Rocca 1998; Pereboom 2001). Still, on any source incompatibilist account, the feature of action that has the crucial role in explaining moral responsibility is the actual causal history of the action, not the availability of alternative possibilities.

In response to the challenge from examples like Frankfurt's, defenders of PAP have set out several strategies. A first contends that despite initial impressions, the example does feature a relevant alternative possibility after all; this is known as the "flicker of freedom strategy" (Fischer 1982, 1994). It concedes the intuition that the agent in the example is morally responsible, but then claims that the example features an alternative possibility that explains the intuition. The core of the flicker of freedom strategy is this: Frankfurt examples must feature some event that the neuroscientist, or her device, is set up to detect that could have but does not actually occur, such as the agent's intending to do otherwise (e.g. van Inwagen 1983: 166–180; Fischer 1994: 134–147). But then, this "flicker of freedom" can serve as the alternative possibility that explains the agent's moral responsibility. It's indeed not implausible that an agent's intending to do otherwise can count as an alternative possibility that can play this explanatory role.

Fischer's response to the flicker of freedom strategy is to construct a Frankfurt-style example in which the trigger for the neuroscientist's intervention is an event that cannot play this explanatory role. In Fischer's example, Jones will decide to kill Smith only if Jones blushes beforehand, and the neuroscientist intervenes only if Jones fails to blush by a certain time (Fischer 1982, 1994). Jones's failure to blush by a certain time would then be the trigger for the neuroscientist's intervention that would cause him to kill Smith. But, as things actually happen, Jones acts on his own, without an intervention, and we have the intuition that he is blameworthy. Fischer's example does feature an alternative possibility: Jones could have failed to blush. But Fischer argues that this alternative is too "flimsy and exiguous" and "insufficiently robust" to explain Jones's moral responsibility.

At this point we may ask: What is it for an alternative possibility to be robust, and why would the robustness of an alternative possibility be crucial to explaining an agent's moral responsibility? First, as we've noted, the intuition that supports the alternative-possibility requirement for moral responsibility is that if one is to be blameworthy for an action, one must have voluntary access to an exempting alternative. That is, as a result of voluntarily accessing that alternative possibility instead, one would thereby have avoided the blameworthiness one actually has for the action. In Fischer's example, Jones's failure to blush is not robust, since by failing to blush Jones would not thereby have avoided responsibility for killing Smith. What's more, failing to blush is not plausibly voluntary.

Robustness also has an epistemic aspect, which turns out to be highly significant. Suppose that Joe decides to take an illegal deduction on his tax form and that he is blameworthy for his decision. But just before beginning to work on his taxes the day he makes that blameworthy decision, Joe went to the coffee shop next door with a friend and ordered one cup of coffee, and then a second. Unbeknownst to him, the barista, having overheard Joe discuss his objectives for the day and making dismissive remarks about the tax laws, laces the second cup with a drug that induces compliance with the tax code for 24 hours. But as things turn out, Joe does not take a sip from the second cup, and leaves it on a table at the coffee shop before returning home to work on his taxes. Here Joe could have behaved voluntarily so as to preclude the decision to take the illegal tax deduction, as a result of which he would not have been blameworthy. But whether he could have voluntarily taken a sip from the second cup is irrelevant to explaining why or whether he is blameworthy for his actual decision, for he does not understand, nor could he reasonably be expected to have understood, that taking that sip would have made him blameless. Thus, if an agent is blameworthy because an alternative possibility is available to him, it must be that he understood, at least at some level, that or how it was available to him.

Here is an account of robustness that accommodates these reflections:

Robustness: For an agent to have a robust alternative to her immoral action A, that is, an alternative relevant per se to explaining why she is blameworthy for performing A, it must be that

(i) she instead could have voluntarily acted or refrained from acting as a result of which she would be blameless, and

(ii) for at least one such exempting acting or refraining, she understood, at some level, that she could so voluntarily act or refrain, and that if she voluntarily so acted or refrained, she would then be, or would likely be, blameless. (Pereboom 2014: 13)

With this account in mind, the response to the flicker of freedom strategy is that Frankfurt-examples can be constructed which, whilst featuring alternative possibilities, feature only alternative possibilities that are not robust, and thus cannot explain the agent's moral responsibility for her action. The resulting source view opposes, specifically, the following version of PAP:

PAP-robust: an action is free in the sense required for moral responsibility only if the agent has access to a robust alternative to that action.

A further objection to the argument from Frankfurt examples, the "dilemma defense," was initially suggested by Robert Kane, and subsequently set out as follows by David Widerker (Kane 1985: 51; 1996: 142–144, 191–192; Widerker 1995: 247–261). The objection is raised from the point of view of a libertarian, thus incompatibilist, defender of free will AP as a necessary condition of free will MR. For any Frankfurt-style example, if determinism is assumed to hold in the sequence of causes that results in the action, then a libertarian cannot be expected to have the intuition that the agent is morally responsible. Libertarians are, after all, committed to the claim that (basic desert) moral responsibility and causal determination are incompatible. This is the dilemma's first horn. The second horn is that if indeterminism in the actual sequence is assumed, the example will not secure Frankfurt's objectives, because then it will fall to a further dilemma. Frankfurt examples feature a prior sign, such as Jones blushing in Fischer's example, that allows the neuroscientist to predict that his intervention is not required. If this sign causally determined the action, or if it were associated with some factor that did, the neuroscientist's predictive ability could be explained. However, then the libertarian, given her incompatibilism, should not be expected to have the intuition that Jones is morally responsible. But if the relation between the prior sign and the action is not causally deterministic, then it's open that Jones could have done otherwise despite the occurrence of the prior sign, and his moral responsibility could then be explained by the availability to him of an alternative possibility. Either way, PAP, and PAP-robust, emerge unscathed.

David Hunt and I have proposed a type of Frankfurt-style example, referred to as a "buffer example", designed to be immune to the dilemma defense (Pereboom 2000, 2001: 18–22; 2014: 14–29; Hunt 2000, 2005).[19] The distinguishing features of the "tax evasion example" I set out are as follows: the cue for the neuroscientist's intervention is a *necessary condition for the agent's accessing any robust alternative possibility* (without the intervener's device in place), while that cue is not at the same time a robust alternative possibility, and the nonoccurrence at any specific time of the cue for intervention in no sense causally determines the action the agent performs:

> **Tax evasion**: Joe is considering claiming a tax deduction for the registration fee that he paid when he bought a house. He knows that claiming this deduction is illegal, but that he probably won't be caught, and that if he were, he could convincingly plead ignorance. Suppose he has a strong but not always overriding desire to advance his self-interest regardless of its cost to others and even if it involves illegal activity. In addition, the only way that in this situation he could fail to choose to evade taxes is for moral reasons, of which he is aware. He could not, for example, fail to choose to evade taxes for no reason or simply on a whim. Moreover, it is causally necessary for his failing to choose to evade taxes in this situation that he attain a certain level of attentiveness to moral reasons. Joe can

secure this level of attentiveness voluntarily. However, his attaining this level of attentiveness is not causally sufficient for his failing to choose to evade taxes. If he were to attain this level of attentiveness, he could, exercising his libertarian free will, either choose to evade taxes or refrain from so choosing (without the intervener's device in place). But to ensure that he will choose to evade taxes, a neuroscientist has, unbeknownst to Joe, implanted a device in his brain, which, were it to sense the requisite level of attentiveness, would stimulate the right neural centers so as to inevitably result in his making this choice. As it happens, Joe does not attain this level of attentiveness to his moral reasons, and he chooses to evade taxes on his own, while the device remains idle. (Pereboom 2014: 15)

Joe is intuitively blameworthy for deciding to evade taxes, even though he does not have access to a robust alternative possibility.[20]

The tax evasion example does feature alternative possibilities – flickers of freedom – accessible to him (i.e. achieving higher levels of attentiveness to moral reasons). This fact about the example suggests the objection that by voluntarily reaching the higher level of attentiveness, Joe would have voluntarily done something as a result of which he would have avoided the blameworthiness he actually incurred. For had he voluntarily reached that level of attentiveness, the intervention would have occurred, whereupon Joe would have decided to evade taxes, but not in such a way that he would have been blameworthy for that decision. However, this alternative possibility is not robust. Joe has no understanding at all of the fact that by voluntarily attaining that level of attentiveness he would not be (or would likely not be) blameworthy. Instead, he believes that attaining this level of attentiveness is compatible with his freely deciding to evade taxes (which would be true without the intervener's device in place), and he has no reason to think differently. We can even specify that Joe believes that if he did reach this level of attentiveness, he would still be highly likely to decide to evade taxes.

Despite lacking a robust alternative, it's intuitive that Joe is blameworthy for his decision, and this vindicates Frankfurt's argument against both the flicker and dilemma defenses. At this point, I'll let this discussion rest. There have been many attempts to push back against this and similar examples, and the reader may decide whether they succeed.[21]

Even if basic desert moral responsibility does not require the availability of alternative possibilities for action, the manipulation argument nonetheless indicates that responsibility of this sort is not compatible with determinism, with the causal determination of our actions by factors beyond our control. This is because the manipulation argument addresses moral responsibility of this sort directly, and not by way of targeting alternative possibilities. And even if it turns out that alternative possibilities for action are compatible with determinism, as discussed in Section 6, moral responsibility of the basic desert sort is not thereby vindicated. For again, the manipulation argument addresses responsibility of this sort directly, and our having alternative possibilities despite the truth of determinism would be irrelevant to its conclusion.

Further Reading

The ideas in this chapter are presented and discussed in greater detail in my *Living Without Free Will* (Cambridge: Cambridge University Press, 2001), *Free Will, Agency, and Meaning in Life* (Oxford: Oxford University Press, 2014), and *Wrongdoing and the Moral Emotions* (Oxford: Oxford University Press, 2021). Neil Levy defends a similar position in *Hard Luck: How Luck Undermines Free Will and Moral Responsibility* (Oxford: Oxford University Press, 2011). The position on treatment of criminals that I discuss is elaborated by Gregg Caruso in his *Rejecting Retributivism: Free Will, Punishment, and Criminal Justice* (Cambridge: Cambridge University Press, 2021). Caruso and I set out the hard incompatibilist position on moral responsibility in *Moral Responsibility Reconsidered* (Cambridge: Cambridge University Press, 2022).

As mentioned in the chapter, Spinoza argues for hard determinism in his *Ethics*, first published just after his death in 1677; the current standard translation is in *The Collected Works of Spinoza*, ed. and tr. Edwin Curley, volume 1 (Princeton, NJ: Princeton University Press, 1985). About a century later hard determinism is defended by Baron Paul d'Holbach in his *Système de la Nature* (Amsterdam, 1770), and by Joseph Priestley (who also made important contributions to modern chemistry) in *A Free Discussion of the Doctrines of Materialism and Philosophical Necessity, In a Correspondence between Dr. Price and Dr. Priestley* (1788), reprinted in Joseph Priestley, *Priestley's Writings on Philosophy, Science, and Politics*, ed. John Passmore (New York: Collier, 1965). Robert Sapolsky, in his recent *Determined: A Science of Life without Free Will*, sets out the case for determinism about human behavior and the absence of free will from a biological perspective.

The view that morally responsibility is in fact impossible – whether determinism or indeterminism is true – is defended by Galen Strawson in *Freedom and Belief* (Oxford: Oxford University Press, 1986), and in a number of more recent articles, including "The Impossibility of Moral Responsibility," *Philosophical Studies* 75 (1994), 5–24. Saul Smilansky, in *Free Will and Illusion* (Oxford: Oxford University Press, 2000), endorses an argument of the sort that Strawson advocates, but goes on to contend that for us to believe that we lack the sort of free will required for moral responsibility would be harmful, and thus it would be best to maintain the illusion that we have this kind of free will. Detailed versions of hard determinism or hard incompatibilism have been presented by Ted Honderich in *A Theory of Determinism* (Oxford: Oxford University Press, 1988), and by Bruce Waller in *Freedom Without Responsibility* (Philadelphia: Temple University Press, 1990).

Richard Double, in *The Non-reality of Free Will* (New York: Oxford University Press, 1991), and in *Metaphilosophy and Free Will* (New York: Oxford University Press, 1996), argues that the claim that we have the free will required for moral responsibility cannot be true for the reason that the very concept of free will is internally incoherent if it is construed in a realist, nonsubjectivist way.

Notes

1. Skeptics about free will in the history of philosophy include Śāntideva (700/1995), Spinoza (1677/1985), Paul d'Holbach (1770), Joseph Priestley (1788/1965), Arthur Schopenhauer (1818/1961), Friedrich Nietzsche (1954), and, in more recent times, Galen Strawson (1986, 1994), Ted Honderich (1988), Bruce Waller (1990, 2011, 2015), Michael Slote (1990), Derk Pereboom (1995, 2001, 2014), Saul Smilansky (2000), Daniel Wegner (2002), Gideon Rosen (2003, 2004), Joshua Greene and Jonathan Cohen (2004), Benjamin Vilhauer (2004, 2008, 2012), Shaun Nichols (2007, 2013), Tamler Sommers (2007, 2012), Brian Leiter (2007), Thomas Nadelhoffer (2011), Neil Levy (2011), Sam Harris (2012), Gregg Caruso (2012, 2021), 'Trick Slattery (2014), Per-Erik Milam (2016), Robert Sapolsky (2017, 2023), Stephen Morris (2018), Elizabeth Shaw (2019), and Farah Focquaert (2019). For an overview, see Caruso (2018).

2. I set out these characterizations in Pereboom (2022a).

3. Others advocates of nonbasic desert, such as James Lenman (2006) and Ben Vilhauer (2009a), ground desert in social contractualist considerations.

4. There is a broader sense of compatibilism on which one might be a compatibilist and deny that we have free will of the sort specified (G. Strawson 1986: 6). For example, one might believe that this sort of free will is compatible with determinism, but since our actions are never produced by conscious willing, we lack such free will.

5. Objections to manipulation arguments have been raised by William Lycan (1987), Ishtiyaque Haji (1998), John Fischer (2004), Al Mele (2006), Lynne Baker (2006), Michael McKenna (2008, 2014), Kristin Demetriou (2010), Dana Nelkin (2011: 52–60), Stephen Kearns (2012), Chandra Sripada (2012), Dan Haas (2013), Adam Feltz (2013), Justin Capes (2013) Hannah Tierney (2013, 2014), Adam Khoury (2014), Dylan Murray and Tania Lombrozo (2017), Carolina Sartorio (2016: 156–170), Kadri Vihvelin (2016: 148–155), Oisín Deery and Eddy Nahmias (2017), Maria Sekatskaya (2019), Sofia Jeppsson (2020), Marius Usher (2020), Daniel Dennett (Caruso and Dennett 2021), and David Brink (2021). Defenses of manipulation arguments are advanced by Derk Pereboom (2001: 117–120; 2008; 2014: 71–103), Alfred Mele (2006, 2008), and Patrick Todd (2011), Ben Matheson (2016), Gunnar Björnsson and Derk Pereboom (2016), Hannah Tierney and David Glick (2020), Gregg Caruso in Caruso and Dennett (2021) and in Caruso (2021: Chapter 2), and Derk Pereboom and Michael McKenna (2022).

6. See Daniel Haas (2013) and Maria Sekatskaya (2019) for defenses of McKenna on this point, and Pereboom (2014) for a reply to Haas.

7. A third type is noncausal libertarianism, whose distinctive claim is that basic actions, such as decisions, for which agents are morally responsible, are undetermined and uncaused events. Noncausal theories have been advocated by Henri Bergson (1889/1910), Carl Ginet (1997, 2007), Hugh McCann (1998), Stewart Goetz (2008), Mark Balaguer (2014), and David Palmer (2021).

8. This discussion is indebted to Peter Lewis's (2016) *Quantum Ontology*. See this book for a clear and thorough account of the metaphysics of quantum mechanics.

9. For responses to the luck objection, see Kane (2007), Balaguer (2014), and Hartman (2016).

10. Objections to this argument are set out by Mele (2017) and Clarke (2019); for replies to these objections see Pereboom (2017a).

11. Replies to this argument include those set out by O'Connor (2008); for defenses of the argument see Pereboom (2014: 68–69).

12. Roberts (1988, 2003, 2013). Patricia Greenspan (1988) and R. Jay Wallace (1994: 45–46) also affirm that a subject of an emotion may not accept its content.

13. For the tendency of moral anger to issue false beliefs that rationalize these attitudes, see Goldberg, Lerner, and Tetlock (1999) and Alicke (2000).

14. Here "entail" signifies necessary implication, so F entails G just in case: necessarily, F implies G, that is in all possible worlds F implies G.

15. The argument crucially assumes that the powerlessness we have over the facts about the past and the laws transfers across the entailment in (2), which is an instance of the following general principle:

> **Transfer:** if no one is free to act in such a way as to alter facts F, and facts F entail facts G, then no one is free to act in such a way as to alter facts G.

There has been a lively debate about the best version of a transfer principle, but there is a consensus that this is the best one. This is transfer principle "beta-box," defended by David Widerker (1987), Kadri Vihvelin (1988), and Alicia Finch and Ted Warfield (1998) in response to problems pointed out for Peter van Inwagen's transfer principle "beta," which is, in essence:

> If facts F imply facts G, and no one is free to act in such a way as to alter the fact that facts F imply facts G, then no one is free to act in such a way as to alter facts G.

See McKenna and Pereboom (2016), Chapter 4, for an overview.

16. On the fixity of the laws, David Lewis (1981) argued that the compatibilist can agree that we are not free to act so as to *cause* laws of nature to be altered, but need only affirm a weaker claim: that if one had acted otherwise, a law of nature would have been (slightly) different from what it actually is. If the compatibilist instead wanted to contest the fixity of the past, she can agree that that no one is free to act so as to cause facts about the remote past to be altered, but she can still affirm that if one had acted otherwise, the past would have been (slightly) different from how it actually was (Perry 2004; Dorr 2016).

17. Patrick Todd (2017) develops a manipulation argument that directly targets the ability to do otherwise, by contrast with directly targeting basic desert moral responsibility.

18. Susan Wolf (1980, 1990) and Dana Nelkin (2008, 2011) accept the alternative possibilities requirement for blameworthiness but not for praiseworthiness.

19. Seth Shabo (2010) has proposed valuable refinements.

20. Frankfurt-style examples proposed prior to the formulation of the dilemma defense, such as Fischer's blush example, also feature a necessary condition for doing otherwise. In Fischer's case, that necessary condition is the blush not ever occurring. So the distinctive characteristic of the tax evasion example is not the presence of a necessary condition for doing otherwise, but a necessary condition for doing otherwise the absence of which at any specific time does not causally determine the agent to perform the action. This feature of the example ensures that at no specific time is the agent in the example causally determined to perform the action, and this facilitates a requirement for moral responsibility to which the libertarian is committed. In the tax evasion example, the necessary condition for Joe's not deciding to evade taxes, his having the specified level of attentiveness to the moral reasons, is the appropriate sort, because its absence at any one particular time does not causally determine his deciding to evade taxes. At any one time at which the level of attentiveness is absent, Joe could still make it occur at a later time, and so he is not causally determined to decide to evade taxes by its absence at the previous time.

21. For a recent overview of this debate see Pereboom (2022b).

4
Revisionism

Manuel Vargas

1   Changing Our Minds

We haven't always seen the world as we do now. There was a time when people thought water was one of the four basic, indivisible substances of the universe. Virtually no one thinks that now. For large parts of the 19th and early 20th century, many people educated in Europe and the US were convinced that race was a biological category. Today, perhaps the standard view is that race is mostly a social category only loosely linked, if at all, to biology. For centuries and perhaps millennia, many people thought whales were fish. Today, we know that whales are mammals and not fish. Some will go on to add that, anyway, the category of fish is, itself, something of a mess.

Science is full of examples of relatively radical transformations in our understanding of things, but this isn't just a scientific phenomenon. For example, philosophers have sometimes found plausible broadly revisionary accounts of psychological attitudes, personal identity, and gender. Nor is this phenomenon restricted to academics. Some people used to insist – and some still do – that marriage is a sacramental relationship between a man and a woman (and God, perhaps). However, ordinary usage, the historical record, and in many places, even the laws, now operate with a very different understanding of marriage. In short, we – scientists, theorists, and laypersons alike – have changed our minds about the nature of a lot of things.

Four Views on Free Will, Second Edition. John Martin Fischer, Robert Kane, Derk Pereboom, and Manuel Vargas.
© 2024 John Wiley & Sons Ltd. Published 2024 by John Wiley & Sons Ltd.

This chapter defends the view that, with respect to free will, we are as people once were with water, race, and marriage. We have a familiar, widely recognized way of thinking about free will that admits of more and less elaborate theories. Yet, even our best theories tend to encounter oddly recalcitrant intuitions and conflicting convictions. In some moods, free will seems to require powers that appear extraordinary, given what we know about the rest of the world. At other times, it can seem obvious people have free will. When we deliberate about what to do, it seems that we must assume we are free; when we have been wronged by anyone of normal ability and maturity, we tend to think they acted freely and culpably, unless they advance some excuse. Yet at other times, it seems unclear why we use the concept at all. Perhaps it is a relic of a fading religious framework, or an illusion generated by a deceitful psychology that encourages us to see the world as filled with magic.

There is no shortage of proposals for how to explain these puzzles, tensions, and challenges. If you've been reading this book, you have already seen three of the very best proposals for how to understand free will. Each chapter represents a rich tradition of efforts at unravelling the puzzle of free will. Yet, for all the centuries (millennia, really) invested in resolving the problem, none of the standard views has secured anything like a consensus. A conjecture I explore in this chapter is that an important difficulty we have in theorizing about free will is rooted in the shared assumption that the target of our theorizing must be free will as we have tended to conceive of it. On the standard approach, to produce a theory of free will, we must thus first identify its conceptual essence. Yet, this effort seems entangled in the persistence of the debate: most disputants are sure that the free will at stake is the free will we imagine ourselves to have, but there is robust disagreement about what exactly that free will comes to.

One way out of this quagmire is to resist hanging the success of our theory on identifying a conceptually nonnegotiable essence that shows up in all the diverse ways we think and talk about free will. That effort to identify essences is fated to founder on the fact that our everyday intuitions don't admit of a unified, coherent story. Our ordinary concept (or, if you prefer, our cluster of sometimes tacit commitments about the nature of free will) is too disordered and tendentious to admit of an elegant resolution in a theory wedded to its details. Free will matters for our practical and social lives, but a satisfying theory of it cannot vindicate the tangle of convictions that have, over the centuries, sprung up around our thought and talk about free will. A satisfactory theory of free will is going to require a new understanding of free will, one that captures many central elements of what is at stake in our concern for it, while abandoning other elements that, on reflection, are less important than they have seemed in our ordinary thinking about free will and its stakes. I call this picture "revisionism about free will."

The version I defend holds that free will exists, it is compatible with the possibility of determinism, and its distinctive features are a function of its mediating various practical and social interests. It falls short of the metaphysical aspirations some of us have for free will, but it nevertheless explains why what we have is free will worth the name.

2   Kinds of Theories

Consider the distinction between how we do, in fact, think about a target concept – whether "fish" or "foul" or "free will" – and how we ought to think about it. In aiming to capture how we do think about the nature of a thing, we are giving a *diagnostic* account. In aiming to defend an all-things-considered judgment about how we should be thinking of this thing, we are giving a *prescriptive* account.

To see why this difference matters, imagine Athena is one of the first chemists, in an era where people tend to hold that water is one of four basic and indivisible substances. Athena's proposal is that water is H_2O, something composed of hydrogen and oxygen. In that time and place, her theory would be revisionary because it conflicts with then-ordinary views about water. Suppose, though, that she wanted to anticipate how much resistance her theory would meet. To do that, she would need to know the widespread (if confused) thoughts about water had by her community. For that task, she would need a different kind of a theory, a theory about people's ordinary understanding of water. This latter thing is something we can call a "diagnostic theory" of water. A diagnostic theory won't tell us what, all things considered, we ought to think about water. Still, diagnostic theories can be useful for understanding why people say and do the things they do. For example, an accurate diagnostic account can help us predict why and on what basis people might resist the new chemical theory of water.

Having an accurate diagnosis of ordinary thought is sometimes vital. Suppose that someone named Barrows rejects biological theories of race but is regarded by people in her time as being a member of a biological race that is held to be dangerous, unpredictable, and morally inferior. It might well be a matter of life and death that she has an accurate model of how people around her think about race, even if she regards it as a bad theory of race. Barrows would have the burden of needing what W.E.B. Du Bois (2017) called "double consciousness" – a good model of other people's values, beliefs, and habits of interpretation, even if she repudiates some or all that picture. This is what a diagnostic theory provides. Yet, neither Barrows nor Athena needs to think that an accurate diagnostic theory constrains the best theory of race, water, or, for that matter, free will.

Some theorists reject the need, appeal, or even the possibility of revisionist theorizing, at least in some contexts. They are often motivated by the presumption that a conflict with ordinary beliefs is evidence the theory has gone wrong, that it is changing the topic, or that it has incurred a significant theoretical drawback in departing from ordinary convictions. Nonrevisionists favor *conventional* theories, or theories that do not conflict with ordinary convictions about some topic. A conventional account of something will have more bells and whistles than layperson views, but those details are intended as coherent developments of the basic architecture of everyday commitments about that thing. Unlike revisionary theories, conventional theories tend to have very little daylight between their diagnostic and prescriptive accounts. Most accounts of free will are conventional theories.

What of free will skeptics or eliminativists? They hold that we lack the things required by our diagnostic theory of free will, so we lack free will. (I will treat 'eliminativism' and 'skepticism' as interchangeable. Some use 'skepticism' to refer to views that are only dubious about free will, reserving 'eliminativism' for views that reject free will, holding that we ought not employ it in our truth-seeking talk about the world.) Skeptical views are typically conventional theories in the relevant sense: they hold that a satisfactory or correct theory of free will (even a theory that concludes that we do not have it) must cohere with the commonsense features of our diagnostic accounts.

Revisionary theories in any domain are often born of the insight that we are not limited to the verdicts of our diagnostic theories. If philosophical or scientific study reveals that we lack some feature that figures in our thinking about free will (or water, or marriage, or race, or . . .), this does not necessarily doom the possibility that we have that thing. If there is a successful positive prescriptive proposal, one that explains what free will is in a way that is illuminating and sufficiently continuous with enough of our relevant thought and talk about free will, then we can insist that we have free will.

Until relatively recently, the possibility of revisionism has been mostly overlooked in scholarly discussions of free will. Yet, a revisionary theory of free will is not just an abstract possibility. It is an especially powerful approach for explaining both what is appealing about standard theories and why, despite their venerable pedigrees, none of those more familiar theoretical approaches has succeeded in producing the kind of convergence of scholarly opinion we expect from successful theories.

If I am right that no standard account of free will can coherently capture all the conflicting aspects of everyday thinking about free will, then there is a trivial sense in which every account of free will is tacitly revisionary. However, a theory of free will is explicitly revisionary if it proposes an account of free will that takes itself to conflict with commonsense views about free will; such a theory proposes abandonment of some element in ordinary, widespread convictions about free will. Going forward, I employ this explicit sense of revisionism about free will. A credible revisionary theory requires an explanation for why revision is called for. It needs an account of why the proposed revision(s) to our thought, talk, and/or practices constitute an improvement or advance over alternatives, including those that reject the existence of free will.

There are many ways to be a free will revisionist, and concrete proposals need to be evaluated in all the usual ways. That is, revisionary theorizing is still subject to evaluation in terms of explanatory power, parsimony, theoretical fit with our best understanding of the world and of free will's apparent importance within it. At the same time, the free will revisionist must justify the theory's departures from common sense. The revisionist's not-so-secret hope is to contribute to a transformed understanding of the subject, so that what is initially reviewed as a revisionary picture eventually comes to be regarded as the new default understanding of that thing (at least among theorists, if not always among laypersons). In the end, how radical the proposal is partly depends on the context. If the proposed revision is only a modest departure from the convictions of a few, the revision is minor. If it is a significant departure from the convictions of many, it is a major revision. For any account, it is ultimately an empirical question how revisionary it is.

My account is revisionary about the concept of free will because I think important strands of ordinary thought are as libertarians have said. A variety of considerations – including the power of philosophical arguments in the vein of the Consequence Argument, experimental findings about people's conceptual commitments, and the long arc of our cultural history – suggest that many of us are at least sometimes committed to a form of agency that requires indeterminism. To put my cards on the table, I think many people – maybe most – have an earnestly held picture of free will according to which metaphysically robust notions of sourcehood and leeway are required of free will, at least sometimes and in some contexts, and they think we have these powers. By "metaphysically robust," I mean that these notions require things like nondeterministic causation, perhaps grounded in some nonreductive, emergent feature of agents according to which the action isn't entirely explained by features of the world existing prior to and external to the agent's deliberation or choice-making. Crudely: wide swaths of folk beliefs are libertarian.

There are, of course, many ways philosophers have tried to vindicate those convictions. A common strategy is to speculate that perhaps ordinary physical things, when arranged in the right ways, produce novel causal powers that do not reduce to their components. Free will leverages the happy accident of human beings having such powers. A different strategy attempts to explain how humans might harness existing physical indeterminism in a way that doesn't require positing a novel form of causation. Kane's account in Chapter 1 is often thought of as the most promising instance of these strategies. It relies on the idea of neural quantum amplification, holding that the brain can be in a state that makes it sensitive to quantum effects. A still further strategy holds that perhaps there is an order of things outside the physical, causally ordered world that can act upon the physical, causal order, and that is where free will is located. Immaterial souls and Kantian noumenal selves are accounts in this vein. Nothing in what follows depends on choosing between these regimentations, for that is what I think they are. Libertarian philosophical theories are attempts to make sense of everyday convictions that are oftentimes inchoate or unelaborated, but sufficiently contentful to exert pressure on what we regard as a satisfying account of free will.

On standard approaches to free will, we try to construct an account of free will by looking for its essence. We start with some supposedly neutral demarcation of the subject matter (e.g. "the ability to do otherwise," "the control condition on moral responsibility," ". . .in the basic desert sense"). We then elaborate on the general idea. On this picture, the conceptual work is front-loaded. We test the contours of our ordinary convictions by considering thought experiments, building arguments that rely on intuitively appealing principles, and checking for the fit of our verdicts with ordinary thought and talk. If a proposal runs afoul of our antecedent sense of the meaning or nature of free will, that's a cost to the theory. Finally, we check for fit with the world. We might find we are free and responsible, or that our belief in our freedom was in error, or that we are trapped in an inescapable but real illusion about our powers, and so on. The whole project, though, depends on that first step of accurately identifying some conceptual essence that is taken to set the constraints on theorizing.

The approach pursued in this chapter doesn't try to identify some essential conceptual content had by all free will thought and talk. Instead, it looks for the cognitive and/or social function of free will. As with any bit of theorizing, it first requires some coarse-grained demarcation of what we are looking for. However, unlike the alternative approach, it puts to the side questions of what is conceptually essential. Instead, it focuses on identifying what free will thought and talk *does* for us (i.e. how it functions in our cognitive and social lives). This can include normative functions like grounding justified blame.

With an account of free will's function(s), we then look to the phenomena of the world. We ask whether there are things in the world that produce, rely upon, or have similar functions as those we associate with free will. If we find none, we join eliminativists in asserting that free will does not exist. However, if most or all the identified functions can be found in the world in a relatively unified way, then we conclude that we have found what we are looking for, even if it lacks some of the features that figure in our everyday thinking. On this picture, locating the doings or functionings is the crucial step. That step doesn't require the identification of the full content of our naive convictions.

Putting things this way can make it look like the deck is stacked for success. However, prioritizing the identification of functions over conceptual essences provides no guarantee that we will find what we are looking for. We might find only partial or fragmented bits of functioning that do not constitute a relatively unified thing. Or we might find nothing at all. Our current understanding of the world is one stripped of sorcerers, absolute time, and the divine right of kings. For these things there are no good candidates with comparable functioning that fit with our best understanding of the world. So, we might yet conclude that free will cannot earn a place in our understanding of the world, even if we are prepared to take seriously the possibility that our best understanding of it may be a revisionary one.

When we stop looking for essences and start looking for functions, the result is a happy one. Put one way, this is entirely unsurprising. To borrow a phrase from Kant, much of our modern understanding of the starry heavens above and the moral law within has come about precisely because we moved away from focusing on *whats* in favor of identifying *hows*. So it goes for free will, too. When we go looking for how we would need free will to function and what in the world functions in that way, we discover a real power that makes sense of free will's importance and role in our life. Even better, it fits with a broadly scientific picture of the world. The result is a deepened understanding of free will, one that gets us what we were looking for while simultaneously showing how we were able to talk meaningfully about it, despite stubbornly false beliefs about its nature.

3   Diagnostic Remarks

In Section 2, I claimed that (i) ordinary or "folk" thinking about free will has libertarian elements to it that cannot be vindicated and (ii) that my positive account will not attempt to rescue those elements of ordinary thought. Given that the distinctive mark of a revisionary theory is its putative conflict with ordinary convictions, one might reasonably press the question of why we should think that folk thinking has libertarian elements.

Here, I appeal to the standard arguments advanced by incompatibilists, including those canvassed in Chapter 1–3 of this volume. Elsewhere, I have made my own case for "folk libertarianism," but there are no knockdown arguments to be had by anyone. Still, all my account requires is that a significant number of people have earnestly held commitments about the nature of free will that are most naturally interpreted as incompatibilist. The extent to which these commitments are widespread among us, where the "us" is, minimally, most members of Western, educated, industrial, rich, and quasi-democratic nations, is an empirical question. Still, libertarians are on to something. They are picking up on a real element of widespread self-understanding. For some, these commitments may be superficial and readily excised; for others, though, they may be so deeply entrenched that no theory of free will can seem adequate without them.

Why adopt a revisionary theory of free will, one that proposes an account that conflicts with our broadly libertarian commitments? There are three interlocking considerations in favor of revisionism: (i) the implausibility of folk commitments; (ii) their gratuitousness with respect to what is properly central to our thought, talk, and practices bound up with free will; and (iii) the overall advantages of the revisionary alternative. That is, although there are libertarian strands in ordinary thinking about free will, it turns out there is a compelling basis for abandoning them. The powers central to our practical concerns are what we really ought to have in mind when we talk about free will. Importantly, this is a discovery that comes from looking at the actual roles played by free will thought, talk, and practice, and not by armchair reflections on free will's meaning and intuitive metaphysics.

As it was with marriage, race, and many other concepts, we can learn important things about them by looking carefully at what such thought, talk, and involved practices *do* in our lives. For free will, I argue that at the end of that process, what we find is that even though many people believe it is transparently obvious that free will requires powers characteristic of libertarian accounts, those intuitions – powerful as they are – have no more authoritative role in formulating our best theory of free will than our, uh, fishy former convictions about whales. This turns out to be a good thing, as even the best libertarian accounts face serious challenges.

Even if I am mistaken about there being widespread strands of incompatibilist thinking in everyday thought and talk about free will, there is still reason to consider the positive proposal about free will advanced in this chapter. If the positive account proves to be more illuminating or plausible than alternative accounts, there would be reason to accept it even if I am wrong that swaths of ordinary thinking about free will are libertarian. Of course, I do think ordinary thought about free will, and related notions like moral responsibility tend to have incompatibilist strands woven into them. I also think recognizing this fact is important for explaining the persistent difficulty philosophers have had in resolving the debate. It also matters for avoiding objections that have been standardly advanced against accounts that do not think of themselves as revisionary, and that thereby tend to leave undiscussed the special burdens of proposing a revision in our concept and, perhaps, our practices.

As I have said, my theory is intended to be revisionary. A successful case for a revisionary theory of free will must do at least three things.

First, it must provide a new, positive, or prescriptive account of free will, of how we *ought* to understand what it is. A case for revision – as opposed to the elimination or flat rejection of free will – depends on there being a sufficiently appealing alternative to the difficulties of our pre-revised convictions. That alternative needs to be robust enough to allow us to see how things might look with a reformulated picture of free will, and to consider its account of the roles that free will plays in our lives.

Second, we need to understand why the proposed account of free will counts as a theory of free will, as opposed to a verbal trick or a change in topic. We don't make progress in understanding water or marriage or anything else by simply stipulating that we are going to use the words and their associated sounds to pick out something entirely disconnected from what we had been talking about.

Third, there must be some reason to favor the revisionary proposal. If it does no better than our existing concept, there is little reason to undertake what will inevitably be a slow, effortful reshaping of our thought, talk, and practices.

In what follows, I argue that free will exists, that we often have it, that it plays important roles in our lives, and that it can be further investigated, including with a range of empirical and philosophical tools. What makes the account revisionary is that it conflicts with some important aspects of common, although perhaps not universal, ways of understanding free will. To motivate this picture, I'll focus on what may initially seem like largely tangential considerations about our social practices. If I am right, though, these considerations turn out to be relatively central to finding our way to a better theory of free will, one that explains why it seems to matter whether we have it, and why there is so much disagreement about what it consists of. I'll then conclude with a discussion of why this account, or one like it, does better than conventional or nonrevisionary theories of free will.

4   Anger

Here are some truisms about free will: free will has something to do with deliberation about what to do; it involves the ability to act; it is the kind of thing that sets us apart from most of the rest of the natural order, including many or all animals; and our having free will is what makes sense of the idea that we can be morally faulted for what we do, at least some of the time. We can get a theory of free will that does all of this, but the best way to get there is to postpone questions about what kind of concept or essential properties can do all that, and instead, to consider some interesting features of our social and emotional lives.

Famously, many people have thought our emotions are in some way fundamentally at odds with rationality. Strongly felt emotions tend to make people fixate on the source of the emotion, often distorting their judgments about that thing. Anger, especially, motivates people to seek retaliation or the imposition of the loss of some value on the offending party, often at great cost to the one seeking it. Sometimes that cost is even greater than the initial harm or loss that motivated the anger. In those cases, even if the lost good is recovered there is still a net loss. Thus, strongly felt anger can seem like a fundamentally irrational way of responding to the world. If the emotions are so detrimental to rational calculations, and to our securing the goodies that enable us to live and to live well, how did anger and other strong emotions come to be part of our psychological repertoire?

A collection of psychologists, anthropologists, and behavioral economists have converged upon an illuminating answer: anger and other strongly felt emotions are often useful over time and in groups *because* of their disposition for motivating costly action. Imagine a society of people who are frequently self-interested but never prone to anger or other strongly held emotions. In such a society, if I know you are a purely rational deliberator, not disposed to anger, then I know I can steal from you, break contracts, or otherwise cheat you, just so long as I am confident that it is more costly for you to recover the goods than to let me go. After all, it is going to cost you if you must shut down your shop to chase me or if you might have to hire other people fast enough to chase me down. Unless the chance of recovery is sufficiently high and the value of what I cheated you of was substantial, spending resources to go after me would be to risk throwing good money after bad. Given that you and I are both rational, I know that you won't go after me if I make stopping me just risky or costly enough to you. So, we both know I can and will exploit you with some regularity. I can come by every day and do the same thing, repeatedly, and every day you won't expend the effort to stop me because it is never rational to do so in any serious way.

Notice, too, that in a society where everyone shares this psychology, trust is hard to come by. Agreements aren't worth the paper they are written on and what coordination and cooperation there will be is going to be a matter of whether there is enough overlapping immediate self-interest to make it work before the risk/benefit ratio of defecting from cooperation shifts.

Let's change the story, though. Suppose that as you are restocking an item I (again) stole from you the day before, you bang your head and lose consciousness. Upon waking you find that you now experience strong feelings about a wide range of things. One of those feelings is anger. Reflecting on the way I've systematically taken advantage of you day after day, you feel the flush of something you will later identify as rage. You feel a strong need to do something about my mistreatment of you. You promise yourself that things will change.

The next time I come into the shop, you are ready for me. You've hired a security guard. He costs you more than the value of what I steal over time. Still, you now think that maybe you need to stand up for your interests. After all, your dignity and self-respect have value, too. The next time I come around for some low-key theft I see the guard and barely make it out of there. That turns out to be a prelude to something even more unexpected. Normally, once I make it out of your store, I can be confident that it is irrational for you to chase me down when there has been minimal loss. Normally, I can break into a quick run for a few seconds and then you give up. This time, though, the guard keeps following. Even more surprisingly, you leave the store and start shouting to anyone that will listen that you will pay an absurdly large bounty for anyone to get me. My formerly very rational theft has become way more trouble than I bargained for.

The injection of anger-capable psychologies changes the risk/reward calculus in a dramatic way. A society with members generally disposed to anger at offenses isn't just a society inclined to a strong emotion, or a set of strong emotions. It is also one where agreements and elaborate forms of longer-term social cooperation become possible in a way that wasn't available for nonangry, self-interested agents. It isn't that it is impossible for the balance of self-interested reasons to favor breaking social norms. However, the possibility of anger-motivated confrontation and the demand that its targets suffer some loss of goods or interests (whether rights, privileges, or well-being) give social norms a much more powerful basis than local arrangements of nonangry rational self-interest.

Importantly, anger doesn't only do its work in the case of being angry at someone who directly harmed me. Perceived harms directed at my family, clan, or community can stir me to anger on their behalf, even if I don't witness the harm, and even if I am unclear about the identity of its perpetrator. In addition to this complexification of our outward-oriented psychology, there is an inward-oriented change, too. If I fail to live up to norms I accept, I can become angry at myself, and I can think it appropriate that I suffer a setback of some of my interests. What all these forms of anger share is that they are agent-directed responses to wrongdoing. Getting mad at the sky for ruining your day with rain does little to alter how the sky treats you, but getting mad and withholding offerings to the sky god might. In short, we have pressures for having anger that is a response to perceived wrongdoing of other agents, and that anger motivates us to either seek confrontation or to impose costs in response to that action.

This is obviously a toy example. We almost certainly didn't get emotions by bumping our heads. Moreover, the story as it tends to be told by some of its proponents tends to be evolutionary. On that approach, the acquisition or development of retributive emotions (i.e. "backward-looking" or "for the record" reactions according to which wrongdoing merits the imposition of a cost or loss of interest on the wrongdoer) was a product of natural selection, an outgrowth of more basic reactions that turned out to be beneficial for the survival of those with this trait. It is a picture supported by its continuity with animal psychologies, and various formal models suggest advantages for communities that have "costly" norm enforcement of the sort implied by retributive anger.

What my account requires is that we have these attitudes, and that they tend to produce these effects. Nothing depends on their having evolutionary origins. The issue is how our social psychologies function at scale, as part of a wider system of processes. There can be many individual cases of anger or other reactive emotions that don't produce the relevant result so long as we get the right results overall. This is an important feature of systemic functional explanations more generally. If your lungs fail to function in a specific instance – as when the wind is knocked out of you, or when you get a lung infection – this does not speak against the truth of one's lungs having the systemic function of helping you breathe. Similarly, that retributive anger might have the function of bolstering norm enforcement, and relatedly, enabling stable forms of cooperation and coordination, is compatible with there being many cases where it fails to do so. Moreover, that people are not aware of the function, nor have it in mind when they are so functioning, is no argument against the truth of a functionalist account. People can be entirely unaware that they have lungs, or what the lungs are doing, all while enjoying the benefits of functioning lungs.

Anger doesn't preclude the possibility of all wrongdoing, but it does make it more costly. It enables people to have greater confidence in widely known expectations, rules, and norms because everyone knows that others are disposed to enforce those rules, even at high cost to themselves. The stability of those rules encourages social trust, and it enables more complex forms of coordination and cooperation, which in turn facilitates longer-term planning, which in turn secures certain kinds of personal goods (such as becoming good at a team sport) and collective goods that require scale and time (for example: aqueducts, sewage, and organized food safety measures). In short, we have a first idea: agent-directed anger contributes to the stability of coordination and cooperation.

5 The Control Rule

A second and independent idea can help us appreciate how some subtle conceptual and social innovations can improve life in a social world that is shaped by anger and related emotions, or what P.F. Strawson (1962) called "the reactive attitudes." Let's return to our fictional world, wherein the advent of angry agents changes the incentives to engage in exploitation and cheating. Living in a world of relatively bare-bones angry retaliators has a new cost, though: everyone is chronically at risk of triggering other people's wrath. Anger raises the cost of violating norms and agreements, but it also makes us vulnerable to anger-motivated retaliation.

What produces this new cost is the coarse-grained nature of the bare disposition to strike back in anger against some source of harm. It produces what is sometimes called a system of *strict liability*, where penalties are insensitive to the transgressor's reasons or intent. In a strict liability or strike-back-based system of anger, if Amalia's chinchillas destroy your epazote patch, you'll be mad at her even if she took every reasonable measure to keep them away from your epazote. Similarly, if Michael violates our local dance norms by stepping on Taylor's toe during the village dance-off, that he did so unintentionally makes no difference to strict liability punishers.

Plausibly, there have been communities where anger practices have been, and perhaps sometimes continue to be, indifferent to the reasons, motives, or degree of control of offenders. But there is a threefold cost to organizing social practices around our coarse-grained emotional dispositions to automatically seek retaliation for any violation of agreements, norms, or expectations.

First, our lives become unpredictable, subject to seemingly capricious setbacks to our interests. It simply doesn't matter whether I did what I did unknowingly or by accident, or, for example, whether there was some even worse fate lurking if I didn't so act. It is therefore exceptionally difficult for us to anticipate and avoid the risk of angry retaliation for norm violations.

Second, in a world of bare-bones anger-as-commitment-device, there is no in-principle basis for determining when an offender has paid enough. Bare anger's systemic magic is that it is relatively indifferent to other value trade-offs, and apart from exhaustion, there isn't obviously a principled stopping point at which angry retaliation becomes too costly or inappropriate to pursue. Recall the wrath of Achilles for Hector's killing Patroclus: Achilles re-enters the Trojan War, knowingly forfeiting his immortality to seek not just the death of Hector but also to give expression to his grief and rage in the exaggerated desecration of Hector's body in front of the Trojan host.

Third, there is the cost of interpretive disagreement. Even when we have a relatively robust awareness of what the relevant norms, agreements, and expectations are, we might still disagree whether they apply in this case. The upshot – reciprocal violence – is familiar from history and literature: if a Capulet retaliates against a Montague for violating some norm, but the Montague disagrees that he violated that norm, then the Montague will seek to retaliate for that unjust retaliation by the Capulet, and so on.

To sum up, in a world structured by bare anger at perceived wrongs, we get to enjoy the otherwise surprising possibility of stable cooperation, enhanced coordination, and the possibility of longer-term planning. Yet these goods are vulnerable to the volatility of the emotions involved. Liability is unpredictable, anger can be unconstrained, and interpretive disagreements threaten our access to the collective goods of cooperation and social coordination. We can close the gap between a practice like that and our more familiar understanding of a system of responsibility, culpability, and norm enforcement by introducing something we can call a "control rule."

The issue is this: we have an independent, self-standing interest in controlling our exposure to having our interests set back. In this context, that means we're interested in managing our liability for violating a norm, even unknowingly. One way to do this is to agree on a new rule: *don't retaliate against wrongdoing if the wrongdoing was not in the wrongdoer's control.* This new rule gives us a way to manage our exposure to the risk of liability. If Ariel does something by accident, or if she was unaware that she was violating the rule, or there was some special consideration that made the rule violation the right thing to do all things considered, then Ariel doesn't have to be worried about whether she is going to be subject to retaliation because of her inadvertent violation of the norm.

Incorporating a control rule in our retributive, norm-enforcement practices unlocks many of the key features of our contemporary understanding of moral responsibility, including excuses, restricted targets, and various refinements to our system of holding one another responsible. First, consider how adoption of a control rule brings with it the possibility of an excuse. Recall that the control norm precludes retaliation where things weren't in the wrongdoer's control. Where you lack control, you cannot rightly be subject to the angry reactions that would otherwise follow. This is an excuse. An excuse blocks culpability for some piece of wrongdoing, and it is an important feature of our contemporary responsibility practices.

(Perhaps excuses can be arrived at without a control rule, but having a control rule ensures we have some notion of excuse. Again, the point here isn't to tell the actual history of how our practices developed, but to identify important ways our responsibility system functions.)

On this picture, the notion of excuse is the complementary shadow cast by control – or, perhaps, control is excuse's complement. Either way, it is in this reciprocal relationship between control and excuse that we begin to zero in on free will, including what it is and why it matters. I'll come back to that in a bit. First, though, I want to draw your attention to a general framework for thinking about control, something we might think of as an *ecological* approach to control. On this picture, there are at least three crucial elements of an individual agent's control: the ability to recognize considerations that bear on the agent's aims, the ability to guide one's behavior in accord with the considerations that bear on those aims, and the presence of situational circumstances conducive to so acting.

If I cannot see that there is a crocodile coming to eat my daughter, my lack of knowledge precludes my having control over whether she is going to be eaten. If I see there is a crocodile, but I am gripped by seizures as I try to save her, or I am unknowingly paralyzed by something I ate for lunch, then I lack the ability to control whether my child is going to be eaten. If I see there is a crocodile, and I have control over my body, but I am separated from my daughter by some impediment like quicksand, or an insurmountable barrier, then the environment precludes my having control. Each of these constitutes a different possible source of excuses. We might think of these as cognitive impairments, volitional impairments, and situational impairments, respectively. If one faces sufficient impairment along any of these axes, then we may recognize an excuse.

On this picture, it is a mistake to think we can say all that we want about agency, or the ability to act, without thinking about how an agent's abilities interact with an environment. Two agents with identical physical configurations might face very different challenges if their environments differ. My having poor vision is mostly immaterial given how our physical, material world is now arranged. My myopia would have been a very serious issue on the savannah of our ancient ancestors. For creatures like us, control is always ecological in the sense that it is a function of the powers of agents in circumstances.

Some of those circumstances are sociohistorical. Plausibly, communities differ about what counts as an impairment sufficient for excuse. Perhaps some communities do without excuses along one of these axes, or only recognize excuses in especially extraordinary situations. Depending on what considerations and varieties of control we emphasize, we might cultivate both *people* and *environments* so that they have widely variant capacities for meeting those standards. Twenty-first-century Silicon Valley is likely to demand, and to train, configurations of cognitive, volitional, and environmental control that are distinct from those of Carthage in the third century BCE. Even so, both communities will have an interest in fostering people who are sensitive to considerations of harm and to the importance of social norms, and who are responsive to the general conditions of cooperation in everyday social life.

So, a control rule gives us a notion of excuse. A control rule also enables a second feature characteristic of our contemporary system of moral responsibility: target selectivity, or some notion of being an apt or proper target. To see the importance of this idea, recall that in a simple system of anger-motivated retaliation, you might be able to get decent levels of norm enforcement from retaliating against a range of possible targets. I might deter your future norm violations by retaliating against your family or your clan. In a more narrowly control-responsive system of responsibility, though, there is new pressure to restrict the anger to offending agents. After all, it defeats the purpose of a control-responsive practice if you are unexpectedly on the hook for something someone else did. The foregoing thoughts tend to bring into sharper relief a question that might lurk from the outset of any responsibility practice: to whom do responsibility practices apply?

Today, we tend to think young children, those afflicted by various infirmities, and nonhuman animals aren't suitable targets for the full range of ordinary anger-propelled attitudes. Yet, different groups have had different views. For example, restricting our attention to the European tradition, it may help to know that *mens rea*, or the "guilty mind," requirement that we think of as central to contemporary criminal law came into existence in the 12th century. And, as late as the 18th century, animals were put on trial in European criminal proceedings. Although the history of the criminal law is not the same thing as the history of responsibility practices and norm enforcement more generally, it is not unrelated either. That history serves as a reminder of different ways communities have settled the question of proper targets, or conversely, who is exempt from responsibility practices.

Here's the form of a general answer to the boundaries question, though: we restrict our norm violation reactions to those suitably able to recognize and respond to norms, or to those who recognize the reasons reflected or expressed in those norms. This might seem only to postpone the hard question. What counts as a suitable ability to recognize and respond to norms and their underlying reasons? There are different answers one can give here. For example, one might appeal to the bare susceptibility to any improvement in control, sensitivity to moral considerations, or dispositions for prosocial cooperation. On that picture, if you can or could come to be positively affected by angry blame practices, you count as a proper subject of angry norm enforcement. A worry, though, is that this forfeits the virtues of prediction and control that were the point of moving away from a coarse-grained strict liability approach. Young children or animals might not apprehend the norms at all but might still be moved in the right ways by angry blame practices.

A different account, and one that I prefer, locates the answer in the connection between a person's interests in being held responsible and the interest we have in holding that person responsible. Ordinarily, we have a reason to be seen as competent at navigating the normative demands of our communities, including demands on how we conduct ourselves, reason about things, and so on. We want to enjoy the statuses and privileges of those who are regarded as fully mature, sufficiently competent members of a community that depends on relatively complex norms of cooperation and coordination. So, any failure to adhere to those norms creates a problem for managing one's reputation.

We solve the reputation-management problem by giving some strong signal of our competence with those demands even when we fail to meet them. In short, we acknowledge the normative failure and accept responsibility. The details of this can vary depending on the norm and the perceived harm. However, in accepting fault, we recognize the suitability of negative judgments and our potential liability for repair and apology, precisely because we share in the judgment that our control was good enough for those norms to apply to us. The otherwise curious phenomenon of our willingness to take the blame for our errors is thus explained by our commitment to the norms, the communities for whom these norms matter, and our standing interest in being regarded as competent at respecting those norms and their reasons.

On this picture, then, suitable control is, roughly, control sufficient to sustain some default level of coordination and cooperation in societies that have responsibility norms at all. In different times and places, we might draw the line for suitable control in distinct places. Still, something like a Goldilocks principle seems right. It can't be so demanding that no one satisfies it, because then we lose the benefits of having a responsibility system in the first place. Yet, it can't be so undemanding that everyone satisfies it, or else we lose the predictability of being vulnerable to blame that was the appeal of a control-sensitive practice.

6   Adjusting the Rules

The advent of a control rule gives us a picture of excuses and generates some pressure to provide an account of the scope of responsibility practices. It also points to a third way further innovations can take shape in our practices, over and above the simple picture of bare anger. Once a community recognizes the possibility that it can institute rules about when it is apt or permissible to express and act on anger, it can continue to adjust those rules. Excuses might be regarded as a matter of degree, and we might develop nuanced pictures about the varieties of different mental states and their implications for culpable wrongdoing.

We might, for example, decide that running a risk of violating a norm (recklessness) is not as bad as intentionally violating a norm. We might also expand the ways one can avoid liability to anger by, for example, introducing ideas that certain kinds of choices can be unreasonably difficult to resist (coercion and/or duress). Along a different dimension, we might narrow the way excuses work, seeking to block strategic claims of ignorance about vital matters by introducing the thought that there are things any competent member of our community ought to be sensitive to, regardless of whether it springs to mind (so, a negligence rule).

This picture suggests two other advances that are worth mentioning. Recall the general problem of volatility that besets a system of bare anger. Beyond the fact of unpredictability, which is relatively directly addressed by a control rule, there are two other recurring sources of volatility in an anger-based practice of norm enforcement: unconstrained retaliation and interpretive disagreement. Both phenomena create the risk of unremitting reciprocal violence, where Capulets relentlessly retaliate against Montagues for a harm that the former think is profound but the latter reject as mistaken or minor.

We might, however, exploit a feature of the control rule to establish a kind of constraint on expressions of anger and its disposition to fuel confrontation and retaliation. The operative idea is to limit the degree or kinds of expressions of anger (including sanctions or other ways of imposing losses to one's interests) by the degree of both wrongfulness and control exhibited in the offending act. This is the idea of proportionality. Our response to wrongdoing is apt only up to the point to which it reflects something about the moral quality of the wrongdoing. A great wrong that was not culpably done (because of excuse or exemption) does not license great retaliation. A great wrong without excuse or exemption (or some explanation of why it was the right thing to do) can license a proportionately great deal of angry norm enforcement.

A norm of proportionality, even in conjunction with a control rule, would leave a fair amount of volatility in this newer, more sophisticated social practice of angry norm enforcement. The reason is immediately recognizable: even if we agree about the necessity of control and the principle of proportionality, we might disagree about the nature of the wrong and what counts as proportional. The form of a solution is equally familiar: some mechanism of independent adjudication. Some forms of adjudication can be institutional, with relatively defined roles for resolving conflicts (such as duels and judicial proceedings). However, interpretive disagreements can also be solved in nonformal but deeply social ways. We appeal to a friend or a mentor to get perspective on our interpretation of events. Sometimes, we even appeal to a wider, entirely impersonal group of strangers to assess matters – plaintively asking in the frank language of this era: AITA?

Communities aren't just passive bystanders, springing to action only when asked. When there is convergence about the meaning of actions and norms of proportionality, it seems likely that individuals and groups will be proactive, for example, endorsing one or another interpretation of some act, or insisting that some instance of blame, retaliation, or punishment has gone too far. Conversely, there might be calls that a victim of the initial wrongdoing has not stood up to some offender. Woe to bad interpreters if they are unresponsive to the collective judgment of their communities.

Thus far, the account has focused on the social dimensions of the practice, and the general pressures that operate on it. Yet practices do not operate untethered from our psychologies. Those practices both express our underlying attitudes, and they also give shape to them. Even if it is not available to us to entirely abandon retributive anger, as some have thought, this does not mean that we cannot come to regiment the nature of its expression and our attitudes to it. There is some reason to think that constraints on *expressing* anger might lead to widespread pressure to disfavor *having* anger when the wrongdoing is excused or justified.

Here's one argument for thinking a community might be inclined to disfavor not just the expression but the having of anger in cases where there is an excuse or justification. Given that (i) being angry increases the likelihood of expressing anger, and given that (ii) expressions of anger toward those offenders with an excuse or justification for their wrongdoing will be regarded as itself a violation of the new norm, then (iii) there will be some reason to view one's own experiencing of anger in such cases as inapt, and thus (iv) individuals will have some reason to acquire methods for suppressing or controlling the experience and intensity of inapt anger. Over time, these pressures would presumably come to affect the way members of that community might educate and train the moral dispositions of the young. To the extent to which such psychology-shaping efforts succeed, those adjustments would make it easier to live in accord with the operative social norms concerning the propriety of anger.

To sum up: having a system of angry responses to norm violations enables forms of coordination, cooperation, and long-term planning that would otherwise be unstable or impossible to sustain over time. However, a simple system of bare, angry responses to any norm violation is subject to considerable volatility. A solution to this problem is to introduce a cognitively demanding innovation, a control rule that calibrates our risk of liability and the degree of that liability in a way responsive to our control over the resultant norm violation. There are different ways that calibration can go, but the centrality of it emerges when we think about its multidimensional significance. A notion of control gives communities with angry norm-enforcing practices a principled and effective way of mediating between (i) collective interests in the goods of angry norm enforcement, (ii) individual interests in demonstrating that one is competent at local norms and a good cooperator, and (iii) ongoing interests in mitigating one's exposure to liability. Finally, we've seen why a practice with this feature would give us reason to shape the sensibilities of those subject to such a practice, treating as a matter of important socialization the identification of various norms about what is important, how norm violations are to be responded to, when anger is apt and inapt, and ways of adjudicating disagreements when they arise.

Again, the aim in this section has not been the One, True, accounting of how we came to have our specific configuration of morally and psychologically nuanced practices of social regulation. Those details are interesting but mostly beside the point for present purposes. Instead, the ambition has been to call attention to an interlocking set of psychological and social functioning that we already enjoy. In focusing on them, we can see how those things create a demand for a kind of control that involves recognizing and responding to normative considerations that matter for complex forms of coordination and cooperation.

That is, the overarching logic or functional structure of the responsibility system depends upon – and is systematically entangled with – the nature of our emotions, the persistence of our interests in the goods of sociality, and the pressures to cultivate the powers distinctive of human agency. These considerations interlock with our interests in prediction and in avoiding setbacks of our interests. Jointly this collection of considerations create pressure for a practically useful form of control, the shape of which is given by those practices, the entwined psychology, and our interests in the goods of complex forms of cooperation and coordination.

7 What About Free Will?

One might worry that something has gone wrong, for free will has not yet made its appearance. But free will, at least how we ought to understand it, is just what I've been discussing. Free will is, for us, the ability or capacity for norm-sensitive control suitable for life in a community of creatures engaged in complex forms of coordination and cooperation. This is a higher-order capacity, supported or constituted by a collection of finer-grained recognitional and volitional capacities that enable us to meet the relevant normative demands. That higher-level capacity for recognizing and responding to norms and their reasons – which can be very diverse at the more granular level of the interaction of brains, bodies, and environments – has an identifiable general functional structure involving reasons-responsiveness in particular contexts. So, adding a bit more nuance, we can say that *free will is the situational ability to suitably recognize and appropriately respond to relevant normative considerations.*

Each major functional component of free will (the recognition element, the volitional element, and the situational element) might be realized in diverse ways. For example, your ability to recognize that a loved one is experiencing stress might rely on sensitivity to tone of voice, the posture of a body, the ability to imagine or compare past episodes to the present one, and so on. The ways in which agents might avoid acting on bad reasons might involve distraction in this case, focus on some other good in another case, and in yet another, massively culturally scaffolded efforts at habituation.

With respect to the partitioning of situations (i.e. when is something a similar situation for the assessment of control?), things are similarly flexible. The relevant distinctions presumably start as a matter of local practice sensitive to common contexts and general values. This yields a picture where we with these norms partition relevantly similar situations this way, even if you people do it that way. As groups interact, and the advantages for shared norms relevant to cooperation and coordination do their work, pressures to converge emerge. If a society or group of societies come to recognize that initially distinct-seeming situations share relevantly similar features, they can come to conclude that two putatively distinct situations are a species of the same general situation. They might draw similar conclusions if two situations realize or frustrate values in the same way or are best navigated by people with similar agent-level features.

There are several ways this picture can be developed. One might construe free will in terms of sensitivity to normative considerations, full stop. Or one might restrict it to those considerations that matter for coordination and cooperation. Yet another approach anchors free will in the idea of sensitivity to specifically moral considerations. This last version of free will yields a somewhat narrower band of powers, those organized around the specific role that morality plays in our life. So, for clarity, we might distinguish between wider and narrower senses of free will.

I am inclined to privilege a wider sense, although it isn't unreasonable to privilege or even exclusively employ a narrower one focused on morality, especially considering the central role that concerns for blameworthiness and responsibility have for free will. However, the rational, norm-sensitive contextual capacities implicated in those practices turn out to matter across a wide range of domains, including in attributions of credit and blame in contexts as diverse as art, sports, and epistemic endeavors. What unifies these things is the relevance of "oughts," or normative considerations more generally. Once we have an interest in the oughts required for social coordination and cooperation, there is some pressure to think the relevant kind of control involves any oughts that bear on deciding what to do. So, I favor a very wide notion of free will.

Even if it turned out there was a sense in which the origins of our concept and its role was exclusively rooted in specifically moral practices, this is compatible with our current interest being more capacious than that. Undoubtedly, some exercises of our distinctive, norm-sensitive capacities can have moral significance in some of those otherwise nonmoral contexts. Still, it isn't obvious that every choice in those contexts must be marked by moral significance. If so, that's a reason for favoring a wider notion of free will over a narrower one, even if a diversity of approaches is compatible with the general approach.

What about determinism, indeterminism, reductionism, and all the other "metaphysicalisms" that threaten freedom? On this approach, free will's metaphysics – like many other relatively high-level phenomena – has a functional characterization defined by a cluster of social interests and practices, but a realization given in the physical states that enable that functioning. Consequently, free will is relatively insulated from the particulars of how those functions are realized. The place to look for free will (and felonies, world-class forwards, and fair social arrangements) is at the level of human interests and practices. Only with an account of their functioning in hand does it make sense to see what arrangement of physical things produce those functions. Neuroscience, chemistry, and physics can help us fill in the details of how that functioning works. Yet, whatever the general facts are about the causal microstructure of our high-level functioning, those are details that explain how and not whether we have free will.

This picture is compatible with the idea that free will has a special causal role, despite its being realized in an open-ended set of lower-level physical processes. Suppose everything is linked in a complex but ultimately deterministic chain, where one can trace causes all the way back to some initial event. For creatures like us, with interests like ours, it is nevertheless often important to be able to identify special places in that chain. Speaking metaphorically, we want to know where the hinge points are, whether different kinds of inputs produce varied (even if potentially deterministic) outputs. We have reason to care about those places where we can intervene, places where the causal powers are distinctive, or where certain kinds of information or arrangements of the world can shape which way the hinges are pointing.

To get a sense of why this matters, even in deterministic systems, consider a video game. The typical video game is set up to function as an entirely deterministic system. Even the random elements are themselves often only random-seeming products of a deterministic algorithmic process. Still, as players in the game, we can be deeply invested in whether we are triggering this or that deterministic process. Will that monster be distracted if you put food in its path? Can it be distracted by in-game noise? If so, the monster has hinges. If the monster automatically goes after you no matter what else is happening, then it doesn't have a hinge.

One might protest that if determinism is true, it is also true that our attention and interests are, in part, functions of prior states of the world, whether we realize it or not. Fair enough. This doesn't undermine the significance of hinges, though. When we deliberate about what to do, it is vitally important to us (at least, given that we are hoping to be successful at playing the game) to be clear about which combination of button or keypresses produce which result, determinism or not. The point is that even when we know something is deterministic (as in most video games), we still have a live interest in figuring out how that system works. That knowledge allows us to intervene on the world in ways that are more responsive to our (perhaps deterministically produced) desires, values, and ambitions.

On this picture, free will – that situational capacity to recognize and respond to normative considerations – is itself a crucial human hinge point. It is the place in the causal chain where distinctive kinds of information make a difference in people's behavior and the (at least epistemic) possibilities for how people relate to that information. If creatures have the right kinds of hinges, we can relate to them in the complex, norm-sensitive ways that we expect of ordinary, mature agents. If they lack these things, we don't. (Unless, of course, they culpably made themselves that way.) Free will matters, in part, because it is a central hinge for distinctively human ways of relating.

Why then have so many of us come to think that free will requires something more than some form of competence with normative considerations? There may be no single or simple answer. It may be a byproduct of an easy-to-make cognitive mistake, perhaps involving a too-hasty interpretation of our phenomenology, or a tempting but unmotivated shift in the kinds of explanatory demands we put on instances of action. Or perhaps it is a product of later cultural accretions whose effects linger long after the impetus for adding them disappeared. This is a matter for further inquiry. In the absence of some compelling reason for thinking we need a more demanding notion of responsibility, though, the reality of free will is secured by the fact of our ability to navigate often complex normative demands.

8   Abilities

Here one might protest that this is still too quick, for even on the present account, free will is a kind of capacity or ability. Yet, one way determinism challenges free will is by showing that there is something suspect about the idea of abilities. Perhaps what determinism shows is that the only thing that can happen is what does, in fact, happen. If that's your thought, then because my proposal relies on some construal of capacity, ability, or the idea of "can," you might worry this account is an elaborate cheat, distracting us from the core problem for free will.

In reply, I agree that we can specify modal notions (i.e. a notion that involves the idea of possibility or necessity) such as "can," "ability," or "capacity" so that if determinism is true, we can't do anything other than what we do. That's not the issue, though. Every day we make use of a wide range of more and less demanding conceptions of the idea of "can." For example, if we want to know whether someone can speak a language, catch a ball, or tell whether someone else is sad, we don't need to know whether the underlying features of the agent are deterministic. We just need to know something about the relevant dispositions they have, and whether and how those things function in the range of relevantly similar circumstances at stake in the question.

We make these distinctions in nuanced and scalar ways, reflecting a range of intersecting interests. An alcohol-impaired dancer may be in less control of what he's doing than a sober one, but an impaired concert pianist might have a greater ability to play a passage of Schumann's "Concerto in A minor" than a beginning pianist. Whether Satya speaks Japanese might be something we settle in different ways depending on the context. Competence sufficient to navigate everyday social situations is different than competence at live translation in an academic context. Pinning down the precise specification of any modal notion is difficult. Even so, in everyday life we manage to navigate these distinctions, often with great nuance.

Given the foregoing, the issue (whether determinism means we lack the normative capacity at stake in the proposal of this chapter) depends on whether our having the relevant capacities requires the falsity of determinism. There is decisive reason to think it does not. To see why, consider the idea of abilities that depend on the interaction of the physical features of the agent with the roles defined by a practice. Judges can have the ability to settle a legal case, but the bailiff doesn't; that ability can be disrupted if the judge is sick or not at work. A given athlete might be comparatively capable of scoring in a basketball game because of her skill and knowledge of the rules, but she might be a bad bet in a kabaddi match on account of both her ignorance about the rules and her lack of relevant skills. For these everyday notions of ability, metaphysical truths about determinism are simply orthogonal to whether people have these abilities – at least, in the ordinary, everyday sense.

Even philosophers who believe determinism undermines free will tend to acknowledge that determinism does not undermine the point of deliberation (i.e. settling what to think or do, given the fact of "for all we know" possibilities), that we make choices, that we form intentions about what to do, that we sometimes act for reasons, and that there is a meaningful sense in which people's capacities can vary. The substantive issue that separates their views from the one on offer is whether these everyday notions are sufficient for making sense of our free will thought and talk. The argument of this chapter is that a situational capacity for recognizing and responding to normative considerations is indeed sufficient.

Whether determinism is true or not, everyday distinctions about capacities carve important parts of our lives at their socially significant joints, in part because the powers that matter are those in some sense defined by or dependent on features *internal* to a relevant practice. The question of who deserves to be fined for driving 35 miles an hour is a matter of rules internal to legal practices. Even if there is a standpoint available to us external to this practice, or even one external to all our human practices, it doesn't mean that claims about practice-dependent abilities aren't true, or that they lack authority. We might have reasons to wonder whether we want a given practice, and correspondingly, whether we care about the abilities specified by the practice. However, those thoughts are *external* to the practice, and would need to be anchored in our interests and reasons just as much as anything else. The fact that such a standpoint may be available to us does not vitiate the fact that we can and do have practice-specified abilities and interests.

This is not to deny that practice-dependent notions of 'can' interact, or that practice-dependent abilities can rely on yet other notions for some purposes. For example, we might think that, with respect to a given practice, only goalkeepers can use their hands. We might also think that *this* goalkeeper lacks the ability in *this* game because she just came back from getting surgery on both her hands. Again, these kinds of claims are obviously true and important for our everyday life, and again, the status of determinism has no bearing on them.

What then of the modal notion(s) involved in free will? The argument of this chapter has been that there is an important, practice-dependent role to be played by a notion of ability that is responsive to normative demands, that involves recognizing and responding to considerations, that is paradigmatically involved in deliberations about what to do, and that makes sense of the distinctiveness of human beings and the basis of culpability practices. Elsewhere, I've offered a detailed account of what that comes to (Vargas 2013). You don't have to call it free will, full stop, if you don't want to. (My coercive powers over you are minimal.) Still, this notion captures the functions we noncontroversially want out of free will, and it does so in a way that illuminates how and why free will matters, and how and why we can come to have false beliefs and persistent disagreements about the nature of free will. That's good enough for revisionism about free will, though. For those who want more from a theory of free will, the burden is on them to explain what further valuable work is done by their more demanding picture of free will.

Again, this account is compatible with a further interest in highly specified, very demanding versions of "can" questions. We may want to know whether, holding fixed the entire history of the universe and any governing laws, an agent could do otherwise. That we can specify a power that is that metaphysically demanding doesn't show that this is what free will must be; that such a power would be desirable doesn't show that it is necessary. The considerations advanced in this chapter show that the notion of capacity we need for free will is a much looser or flexible one, one that functions in the right way for shared, cooperative life. It is a less demanding picture than our intuitions and default conceptual content about free will tend to suggest.

9   Normative Authority

On the present proposal, free will exists, it is compatible with the possibility of determinism, and it has a functional structure that depends on its role in mediating various practical and social interests. Its metaphysics might seem less glorious than many of us prefer, given its reliance on merely psychological and social phenomena. However, revisionism about free will is not intended to capture the full contents of our collective imaginations about what free will is like.

Still, one might think that something has gone wrong in this account in a different way. Even if we grant that it identifies a cluster of agential powers that rightly figure in our everyday practices, even if it grounds a web of recognizable statuses and bases for differences in interpersonal assessment and reaction, and even if we allow that it employs a defensible conception of abilities, we might still think that the account is the wrong kind of account of free will. That is, it provides us with various pragmatic considerations for having free will thought and talk, but it doesn't really touch the morally serious core of our interest in it. There are lots of things that are instrumentally useful to us (e.g. pants, passports, and paychecks) that we do not think of as generating the robust normative authority (or the "oughtiness," as the philosopher John Doris has said), that somehow seems implicated in our having free will. So, one might think, something has gone wrong.

Although some people think that morality is just about considerations of cooperation and coordination among creatures with psychologies like ours, I agree that we want free will to do more than support social regulation. We want it to support moral and perhaps other robust forms of normative authority. Having free will is not like being genteel, having a terrific fashion sense, or being adept at platformer video games. The significance of those things is mostly a matter of personal preference. Instead, free will is a power that is intertwined in our collective moral lives and in our own self-regard. It is the kind of thing that seems to ground fault-finding and demands that one account for one's behavior, in a way that is more than a contingent form of social organization. Is there a way to explain that aspect of free will's significance for us?

Yes. Here's the idea: pressures for social regulation give us reason to identify the kind of control at stake in free will, but once we have that idea it turns out to have a further, distinctively moral significance: it is a morally valuable form of agency, one we have reason to cultivate. Recall that the situationally relevant power to recognize and respond to normative considerations is central to a practice of coordination and cooperation. An important subset of normative considerations are moral considerations, considerations that are grounded in what moral reasons there are. (I won't try to say anything about the content of those reasons – that's the subject matter of normative ethics.) The important thought is this: our having free will, and thus our being able to recognize and respond to moral considerations, is a way of having a distinctive and morally valuable form of agency.

We don't get that agency for free. A good deal of childrearing is about the shaping of values and concerns. This tends to be done by identifying for children the ways in which conduct makes one liable for moral praise and blame. We feign blame to teach children when and where they will be genuinely blameworthy when their baseline abilities to recognize and respond to moral considerations is sophisticated enough to meet default expectations required for mature members of the community. The development and eventual achievement of a free will that is sensitive to moral considerations, and that can anticipate and avoid liability for norm violations, is the centerpiece of how we shape our agency. On this "agency cultivation model" of responsibility, free will is at the center. Our participating in responsibility practices is our way of shaping our agency in morally valuable ways. That is, moral values anchor this form of instrumentalism about responsibility. Suppose we get to free will by social regulation pressures. Even so, once we have it, it turns out to be of tremendous moral significance in ways that go beyond its utility for social cooperation.

So, cooperative pressures give us a notion of control that in turn specifies the abilities that constitute free will. However, once we have such a notion, it turns out to matter morally, because it provides a basis for responsibility practices. When those control-sensitive responsibility practices are justified (i.e. they do sufficiently well at producing beings with sensitivity to moral considerations), they fix the truth conditions for culpability, blameworthiness, and desert.

Alas, there is no guarantee that fully justified practices are the ones that are operative in a given community. Indeed, we can predict that communities can do better and worse at tracking what moral considerations there are. Thus, that we have free will doesn't guarantee that we do a good job of tracking blameworthiness in everyday life. Still, free will is at the center of that web of practices that make us into morally sensitive agents we have reason to be. So, free will matters morally, and not just as a tool for social regulation.

10   Realism

The present account of free will, with its somewhat socially dependent nature, might raise the worry that it lacks the objectivity or realism that some might expect of free will.

As I will use the terms, a realist about X thinks there are facts about X that hold independent of us, our reactions, or our attitudes about that thing. So, a moral realist holds that there are facts about morality, and that they are independent of us in some important way. For the moral realist, morality has a nature independent of our thoughts and feelings. In contrast, the moral antirealist thinks that what facts there are about morality (if there are any) depend on how we think about morality, or on our psychological dispositions for responding to things. So, if one holds that a divine being sets up the moral facts about the world before there are any humans or other sentient beings, that's a realist picture of morality. In contrast, a paradigmatic antirealist picture holds that what facts there are about morality are at bottom a matter of how our psychological dispositions and feelings tend to converge into ways of seeing and feeling. For the antirealist, morality is not a matter of our tracking something independent of our psychologies.

My account appears to be antirealist about free will and/or related notions like responsibility, deservingness, and so on. It holds that free will is the kind of thing whose features are partly dependent on human interests and social practices. Undoubtedly, the most natural reading of this account is antirealist. It holds that free will is a bundle of capacities that realize a particular social role (or set of social roles). On this account, free will's nature and significance is emmeshed in a web of statuses and interests that are "post-social," or products of human social lives and our relationship to it. (Post-social does not mean post-institutional; we can have sociality without institutionality.) The account does not invoke some human attitude- or practice-independent notion of freedom, control, desert, and the like. This can seem troubling, though, if one thinks that a theory of free will should hold that free will is independent of our social attitudes and practices, or if one thinks free will requires realist normative phenomena.

Although the account is most naturally read as antirealist, I do not think that it requires antirealism about free will, responsibility, morality – or antirealism about normative and evaluative properties more generally. First, there is the possibility of overdetermination: perhaps there are separate practice-dependent and practice-independent (realist) bases for free will. Second, one could think that a realist notion of free will partly grounds or explains the practice that produces the notion of free will I have identified. Recall that my account requires that our social practices direct our concern toward a bundle of capacities that can perform specific social roles, and it holds that those considerations are sufficient for identifying a set of properties adequate for the various roles imposed by the practice. One might hold that a fuller explanation reveals that the capacities around which our practices have come to gravitate were already there. That we already had abilities with that general shape partly explains why our practices are what they are.

Such a view would not be without challenges. Were one's realist picture of free will to invoke significantly different powers than the account I have offered, one might think that we ought to adjust our practice-dependent notion in the direction of the realist notion. Still, this suggests that this account is compatible with some versions of realism. A third possibility is this: we could conclude that thought and talk about free will are ambiguous, picking out two distinct things, each independently sufficient to justify free will thought and talk. So, accepting revisionary antirealism about one sense of free will need not conflict with a potentially more ambitious further realist sense of free will.

I find this fourth possibility appealing: even if inclined to moral realism, one needn't be a realist about all aspects of morality. One can be a *patchy* realist, accepting realism about some values and not others, or about some but not all normative notions (e.g. aretaic qualities, valuable states of affairs, deontic notions, fairness, etc.). Some normative and evaluative notions may be foundational, with others derivative or dependent on those foundational notions.

As a conceptual matter, responsibility and attendant notions do not seem foundational to morality. We can conceive of a system of morality, as such, without responsibility, culpability, and desert. (Pereboom, at least, agrees.) In contrast, other normative or evaluative notions (including, perhaps well-being, better and worse, and fairness) seem more foundational to the possibility of morality at all. In sum, despite its antirealist appearance, the present proposal is compatible with a range of possible normative realisms. Even if we accept antirealism about responsibility, it's compatible with realism about morality.

Last, notice the account I have offered has an answer to a version of what is sometimes called the "Euthyphro dilemma" for normative realisms. The dilemma is this: either the response-independent thing is somehow suitably connected to us, our natures, and our interests, or it is hard to see why that thing generates reasons for us that aren't capricious or arbitrary. (The dilemma is named for the take-home lesson of a challenge Socrates raised for Euthyphro's claim about piety being what is dear to the gods: there must be something that explains or grounds what is dear to them, on pain of piety being grounded in something arbitrary or without reason.) My account grounds free will in our nature and interests, answering the dilemma without requiring some wider form of metaphysical or normative antirealism. This seems a virtue.

11 Topic Continuity

I favor a form of revisionism about free will that is primarily concerned with how we represent or understand free will. Yet, this sort of change – conceptual change – can also entail changes in the practices that involve that thing. Revisions to our concept of whales, water, marriage, and so on were entwined with a wide range of more or less central changes to practices that appealed to these concepts. On this chapter's proposal, free will is a natural, genuinely robust phenomenon. Yet, it has important limitations. It is a function of how individuals are built, both by nature and enculturation, and it is further con-strained by circumstances or opportunities. So, on this picture, free will is a kind of achievement that can be lost, undermined, or only intermittently avail-able, depending on what happens to people and their ecologies of action. I take it that this picture is importantly at odds with some ways of thinking about free will, especially those that treat it as a power that makes its possessors radically independent of the rest of the causal, physical universe. Such a critic might wonder if my revisionary account is still talking about free will.

As noted at the outset, a persistent challenge for any revisionary proposal is to show that it retains topic continuity (or the sameness of topic). If a revision is too radical, it runs the risk of changing what philosophers of language call the refer-ent or target of our thought and talk. When we revised our concept of water, we were still talking about that liquid stuff in rivers and streams. The evidence for topic continuity is that the revisionary proposal captures a wide swath of ordinary thought and talk, it explains how that talk could be true, and it also informatively explains a web of phenomena surrounding that thought and talk. Moreover, it seems to be *true* in a distinctive way, fitting together with other things we know about the world. Similar things can be said of other cases of revision.

The case for topic continuity about free will has a structure parallel to the case for water: in both pre- and post-concept revision, we continue to refer to a distinctive ability or power that enables us to navigate complex normative situations, the possession of which makes our conduct subject to evaluative regard. While there might be some contexts where employment of a revisionary account of free will would constitute a topic change, the proposed account delivers on our central concerns: (i) it captures a wide swath of ordinary thought and talk (i.e. it makes good on the truisms), (ii) it explains how these things could be true, (iii) it informatively explains a web of phenomena surrounding that thought and talk, and (iv) it seems to be true, given everything we know about the world.

No revisionary theory is immune to every objection regarding topic continuity. Consider, again, an old timey theory of water. Suppose members of the Philosophy Club are discussing Empedocles's theory of water because they are interested in understanding the mechanics of an ontology of four basic substances. Suppose someone interrupted the discussion to insist that because water is both hydrogen and oxygen, Empedocles's ontology requires at least five basic substances. The rest of the conversationalists wouldn't be wrong to think that that introduction of the chemical theory of water was a topic change. If one's interest in water is downstream, so to speak, from its being metaphysically basic, then even the (true) chemical theory of water would be a topic change.

Again, the parallel holds. Our topic is what free will really is, in a way that can capture claims like, "You did it of your own free will" or, "It was her free choice to ignore the warning." If, however, someone stipulates a different interest in the term, or a significantly different conceptual role for it, then my proposal may fail to preserve topic continuity.

This account is silent on at least one thing some people have wanted from a theory of free will. If one wants a theory of free will to explain why God is not a jerk for knowingly creating a universe in which infants are stricken with painful incurable diseases, this account comes up short. Or, if one wants a theory of free will to explain why one's wrongdoing in this world might justify eternal damnation, then the present account cannot do that for you. That my account cannot explain why people deserve to burn for an eternity does not seem to me a defect, regardless of whether one is religious.

Let's distinguish between a general theory of free will, whose principal burdens are recognizable across a wide range of usage, and a conception of free will that is intended to serve a particular set of theological commitments. Revisionism about free will is intended as an instance of the former, as an account of what could realize the kind of thing that figures in our ordinary thought and talk about free will. Religious concerns are widespread, and they can impose distinctive burdens on what one wants out of a theory of free will. Yet one can have an interest in free will without being religious. Moreover, given that the religious and nonreligious person can together meaningfully discuss the merits of different proposals about free will, everyone needs a general or nonsectarian theory of free will.

There is a parallel here with marriage. A general theory of marriage must explain a wide range of formal human mating arrangements across times and cultures. A particular religious community might want an "in-house" theory of marriage to do further work, specifying, say, sacramental elements that appeal to a relationship to the divine. Those requirements might be important and proper to their practice of marriage. However, that narrower, sectarian conception of marriage doesn't help us identify the wider range of marriage practices around the world. Thus, a specifically religious conception of marriage needn't be in conceptual conflict or competition with a more general proposal for how to understand marriage as such.

Undoubtedly, many people have reasons to be interested in articulating a religious conception of free will in the same way in which they can have reason to articulate a religious conception of marriage. Nothing here denies the urgency of that project. Yet, from the standpoint of accounting for a nonsectarian notion of free will we need not, and ought not, try to capture the distinctively religious functions that some have asked free will to support.

12   Reconsidering Alternative Positive Views

With a revisionary account in hand, it may be useful to reconsider some of the alternatives. This section focuses on libertarianism and compatibilism; the next on hard incompatibilism.

Many of the thought experiments and arguments standardly offered by incompatibilists have force precisely because they capture real, robust, and relatively widespread features of common sense. Those elements are part of our collective understanding about free will, and they partly explain why there is any philosophical puzzle about free will at all. Yet, there are also widespread aspects of thinking about agency, deliberation, and freedom that lend themselves to compatibilist theorizing. Debates about free will get a lot of mileage out of alternately playing up or disparaging each set of convictions. Effective philosophical presentations tend to encourage their audience to privilege one set of intuitions over others in a process that amounts to a pruning of alternative convictions. In time, those alternative pictures begin to appear increasingly mysterious, disingenuous, or confused. (Perhaps that has happened to you, as you have read this volume?)

If that is right, and if many of us start with libertarian intuitions, at least some of the time, why *not* libertarianism? I see no promising way to vindicate libertarianism in the face of its standard criticisms, even in ingenious and scientifically oriented accounts like Robert Kane's. For all its intuitive virtues, the powers required by libertarianism are metaphysically problematic and normatively gratuitous.

First, it isn't enough to say that a given libertarian picture is *compatible* with the findings of contemporary science. Science doesn't rule out the possibility that ectoplasmic miasmas influence decisions, either. We don't take it seriously as a hypothesis, though, because there is no independent reason to think that such phenomena occur when we decide what to do. Nor do we need it to explain any known feature of decision-making. Absent such considerations, an ectoplasmic theory of decisions is entirely ad hoc. The same is true, it seems to me, of the role of indeterminism in standard libertarian accounts of free will.

Second, and relatedly, libertarianism's scientific credentials are highly speculative. When I put quantum amplification proposals to working neuroscientists, I'm told that contemporary biology doesn't make much use of quantum amplification effects, and anyway, we haven't yet seen these sorts of effects at the temperature that neurons operate. I'm also consistently told that nothing in mainstream neuroscience independently suggests that we have Kane-like amplification of quantum indeterminacy. Parallel concerns arise for versions of libertarianism that invoke distinctive forms of causation, or whose adoption requires that standard pictures of causation are deeply in error.

One might reply that this is philosophy, and not yet science. Future discoveries might yet yield things undreamt of in our philosophies. But the stakes are too high to be indifferent about the epistemic credentials of our practices. We blame, punish, and even kill people on the putative basis that they act with free will. It is manifestly wrongful to punish offenders in the hope that libertarianism is vindicated by future science. This is true whether one appeals to quantum amplification, agent causation, noumenal selves, or anything else so speculative.

In contrast, the kind of power that figures in the present account – the power to situationally recognize and respond to normative considerations – is a readily recognizable feature of our lives. Few seriously doubt that we have it. The free will debate has been persistent in part because we wrongly believe free will must be more than that. The argument of this chapter is that careful attention to the demands of our practical lives and the exigencies of the world show that the power we often have can indeed do what work we want from free will.

Given the foregoing, one might wonder whether we would do better to be conventional compatibilists, or perhaps, semicompatibilists of the sort articulated by John Fischer. What compatibilists get right is that we can identify workable, less metaphysically tendentious notions of freedom that, with some finessing, seem to offer promising bases for organizing our thought and talk about free will, along with related notions like deservingness, culpability, and responsibility. Here, my complaints are less about plausibility than about theoretical significance and burdens.

Conventional compatibilist theories remain in the grips of efforts to respect our theoretical convictions as we find them. Because of the broadly non- or even antirevisionary presumptions of the historical debate, compatibilists find themselves insisting that their proposals aren't in conflict with important strands of common sense, that all they offer are accounts of what we mean ("of all we mean," as P.F. Strawson said) by 'free will' and related notions. These are not accounts that intend to offer a revisionary theory, and their proponents make no effort to address the special burdens of revisionary accounts, including responding to concerns about topic continuity. However, to those with broadly incompatibilist commitments, conventional compatibilists are, at best, trying to solve the free will problem with a cheat code. At worst, they are engaged in philosophical gaslighting, denying the force of the intuitions that create the very problem.

Unwillingness to recognize the revisionary nature of conventional compatibilism – perhaps because of earnest beliefs that it is not revisionary – has meant that compatibilists have left unaddressed questions about the basis of the proposed revisions and the grounds for thinking it isn't a topic change. Yet these are precisely the grounds for much of the snark directed at compatibilism, a view that has been described as a "wretched subterfuge," "petty word-jugglery" (Kant), and a "quagmire of evasion" (William James). Unable to recognize revision for what it is, compatibilists have not seen fit to address its burdens. In contrast, an explicitly revisionary approach may be wretched, but it is not a subterfuge. It is an account of what we *should* mean, what perhaps we would have meant, given a better understanding of things.

What about John Fischer's distinguished account of semicompatibilism? It allows that free will *may* be incompatible with determinism, but that responsibility is compatible with determinism. I am more sanguine about the possibility and reality of free will than is Fischer, although we are both unpersuaded by existing forms of libertarianism. One difference between our views is that I think the free will we have is different from the free will we imagine ourselves to have, as I think we have false beliefs about what free will is.

On the matter of the abilities we possess, Fischer and I are in broad agreement. The abilities I have identified constitute free will in the sense that matters; Fischer is less committed to that thought. Elsewhere, I have tried to spell out how I think about moral considerations sensitive agency in much fuller detail, and elements of it have figured in the present account. Unlike Fischer, I tend to think that the kind of "reasons-responsiveness" that matters is at the level of agents, not subagential mechanisms. I have also emphasized a broadly ecological picture of agency, where these powers are indexed to circumstances, and where the degree of responsiveness required might vary by type of consideration and by local concerns. Fischer's commitments on these issues are unclear to me.

Methodologically, our accounts come from different places. I have largely eschewed the conceptualist path of testing intuitions and abstract cases, focusing instead on the functioning of our practices and psychologies as they operate in the context of our ongoing scientific accounts of them. My metaphysics of free will derive from an analysis of our psychologies and the demands of our social practices. For Fischer, the direction of explanation mostly seems to go the other way.

That we come to a similar place is perhaps a point in favor of both accounts. (Or, at least, it is good news for me to be in his distinguished company!) Still, this points to a wider difference in orientation; beyond fit with everyday thought and talk, my account seeks to identify why the powers specified by the account ground the practical and normative authority of our concern for free will and associated practices of accountability. This is, I take it, a less central concern of Fischer's account. Even so, presumably his account could be supplemented in ways that would more directly address normative concerns.

13   Free Will Eliminativism

Here, I turn to hard incompatibilism. I begin with some general reflections on eliminativist views in philosophy. Then, I consider two elements of Pereboom's groundbreaking and insightful account: first, the methodology, which purports to fix the terms of the debate by stipulating conceptual content that is supposedly neutral, and second, the content of that stipulation. I argue it is insufficient to rule out the revisionary alternative I have offered.

Eliminativisms in many philosophical domains have faced some common challenges, including the existence of revisionist alternatives and the high costs of error theories. In evaluating the appeal of hard incompatibilism, it may be useful to keep in mind two wider lessons of other philosophical eliminativisms.

First, we now know that in many cases the impossibility of satisfying an armchair concept doesn't tend to entail that that thing doesn't exist. (Remember, the world can be different from what we think.) In many cases, we can accept most or even all the premises that animate the eliminativist without accepting the eliminativist conclusion. We can't justify eliminativism by identifying a merely conceptual defect, or even a failure of the world to vindicate our concepts. So, what the eliminativist owes us is a still further argument, some reason to think there isn't and can't be an adequate revisionary alternative. Absent that, eliminativisms are suspiciously close to being a hasty inference that begs the question against revisionism. Of course, if the revisionism doesn't work, then and only then does eliminativism go live. The upshot is that hard incompatibilism is, at best, a position of last resort.

A second general challenge for eliminativisms concerns the location of the error. Eliminativisms are typically error theories, in that they hold that we are systematically in error about something. For example, the hard incompatibilist thinks that ordinary ascriptions of free will and responsibility are in systematic error. The problem is that the bigger and more sweeping the error claimed by the theorist, the more plausible it is that it is the theorist, rather than the other competent users of the term, who errs.

Still, not all error theories are on a par. Free will revisionism asserts that our convictions have a comparatively modest kind of error, concerning beliefs about the nature of free will. Thus, the revisionist's call for conceptual housekeeping is less dramatic than the eliminativist's or skeptic's call to radically transform our moral psychologies and social practices. That's because the revisionist's diagnosis of error about *what X* is is typically less sweeping and problematic than the eliminativist's diagnosis that we have made an error in thinking *X* exists at all.

Partly because of these pressures, contemporary philosophy has witnessed a now-familiar trajectory of eliminativist views on topics as diverse as race, propositional attitudes, and the moral virtues. On those topics, as the theoretical options came into better focus, eliminativists tended to retreat from the more ambitious versions of those claims, gradually transforming into revisionists. In short, initially enthusiastic eliminativisms tend to give way to a more sober revisionism.

None of this shows that the free will eliminativist is fated to become a revisionist. Still, the underlying logic across all these cases is that the conceptual troubles that motivate eliminativisms tend to be captured by revisionisms, with less costly consequences for thought and talk. Still, there are no short cuts in weighing out the theoretical alternatives. Some surprising conclusions end up being true. Even if there are general reasons to regard hard incompatibilism with modest skepticism, it deserves to be considered on its own merits. Let's turn to that now.

Recall that, at the outset, I proposed that we understand the nature of free will and debates about free will in terms of what free will talk, thought, and practices do for us. The contrast is an approach that tries to identify some essential content to the idea of free will that any account must satisfy. I take it that Pereboom's approach is an instance of the latter, a broadly conceptualist approach that endeavors to identify some essential feature of free will ("the basic desert sense") that we can use as a basis for conceptual precisification and elucidation. I rejected that approach because it risks building into our accounts contested and erroneous features about the nature of free will. While Pereboom and I agree that there are incompatibilist elements in ordinary thinking about free will and moral responsibility, we disagree about whether an adequate theory of free will needs to be beholden to those elements.

Pereboom's approach for fixing the subject matter of the debate, and for blocking the risk of topic change, centers on the idea of what he calls "the basic desert" sense of responsibility. As he puts it in Chapter 3, "The desert at issue here is basic in the sense that the agent, to be morally responsible in this sense, would deserve the pain or harm, the pleasure or benefit, just by virtue of having performed the action with sensitivity to its moral status, and not, for example, by virtue of consequentialist or contractualist considerations." So, his target notion of free will is something required to make sense of responsibility with that notion of desert.

By my lights, this is the wrong way to set the terms of the debate. Even if we agree to fix our theoretical target by its relationship to moral responsibility, this approach runs afoul of the injunction to avoid trying to identify essences, to avoid potentially building into our account false beliefs about the nature of free will, responsibility, or desert. (Note: if this chapter is right, our having false beliefs about free will is actual, not merely possible.) In contrast, my functional-ist methodology makes no stipulation about the essence or nature of the desert that figures in our practices. On this approach, the proper theoretical target is not a philosopher's armchair construction of some sense of desert, conjured from one's intuitions and sense of fit with language. Instead, the relevant target is whatever sense of desert is minimally required to make sense of responsibility practices like these (i.e. the ones we find in the real world), that is *the stuff of actual praising and blaming practices*. That might turn out to be Pereboom's notion of basic desert, but it might not be.

A quartet of methodological matters merits mention. First, it isn't clear what the rules of the game are for characterizing basic desert. Since he first intro-duced the idea, Pereboom's characterization of it has grown more elaborate over time, adding a variety of additional conditions and exclusions (including the rejection of some bases of justification, the emphasis on pain or harm as opposed to having one's interests set back, and the idea that the imposition of that deserved harm being noninstrumentally good). Theoretical positions rightly respond to pressures to refinement over time. Still, it isn't clear why it isn't enough that the relevant notion of desert at stake in ordinary practices meets only some of these features, as opposed to all.

Second, there is a tradeoff between the degree of specificity in some notion and our ability to assess whether it is indeed the notion that figures in our thought and talk. The more elaborate the account of desert is – and it is now more rather than less elaborate – the less clear it is that this and not some other notion is the best fit with our explanatory ambitions.

Third, it is particularly problematic for Pereboom's project that we can successfully identify an obtainable notion of desert – nonbasic desert – that makes sense of our existing practices. Consider the nature of penalties in social practices like sports. Typically, a system of penalties is justified by forward-looking considerations, including protecting the health of the players, preserving enjoyment of the game, and creating constraints for innovation within the play of the game. Yet, whether and when something is really, truly a foul is an entirely backward-looking thing, a matter of what happened and what the rules are.

Were we to look to the systematic justification of fouls to assess whether something is a foul, we would fail to apply the rules governing when something is a foul. Of course, we might have all-things-considered reasons to not call some fouls (e.g. if an all-powerful being threatens to end life as we know it if we call a foul) or more pedestrian pragmatic reasons for ignoring the foul call rules (e.g. it is the end of the game, the outcome is settled, and everyone just wants to go home). Strictly speaking, though, whether something *is* a foul (its truth conditions, as philosophers sometimes say) is settled by what the rules say, and not by whether calling the foul in that case contributes to the health of the players, the enjoyment of the fans, or the development of strategic play. In a straightforward and recognizable sense, you only deserve to have a foul called on you if you in fact committed a foul as specified by the rules. Whether we have reason to adopt different rules or all-thing-considered reasons to not call the foul is something above and beyond whether that thing is a foul.

This basic explanatory structure generalizes to a wide range of practices, including the law and parts of morality. Recall the picture I've offered: responsibility practices are norm-enforcement practices that enable coordination and cooperation, whose moral authority, when it obtains, derives from its systemic effects on cultivating people's moral agency over time. The justification of responsibility norms is instrumentalist or forward looking, but the statuses within a practice thus defined are mostly backward looking. That is, the truth conditions about whether someone deserves blame is, within the practice, settled by backward-looking conditions. The content of the rules, and their truth conditions, make no reference to the system-level justification.

The significance of this is easy to miss. Because there are some contexts in which there is no loss of goods if one fails to distinguish between truth conditions and justification, philosophers sometimes run together the issues of the question of truth conditions (when does someone deserve blame?) and the basis for having those truth conditions (what makes those and not some other truth conditions the relevant ones?). A collapse of those questions – sometimes characterized as "tiers" or "levels" (the level of truth conditions; the level of justification) – isn't especially plausible for responsibility. Crucially, a system of responsibility grounded on predictability, information management, the reduction of free-riding, and the cultivation of moral sensibilities *only gets these goods by keeping first-order questions of truth status separate from systemic justification.*

The foregoing thought is about the normative logic, but it is buttressed by our psychologies. Our ability to fluidly engage in responsibility practices depends on our not always needing to ask about whether blaming or punishing will produce the right effects. How would we accurately decide such things on the fly? This is why we do better to internalize relatively coarse-grained norms that are sensitive to apparent control, thereby making characteristic ways of seeing and responding to norm violations a matter of enculturated habit.

A technical aside: Pereboom's characterization of basic desert curiously blends a characterization of desert's truth conditions (that something is deserved because of the nature of the agent and the moral quality of the act) with a set of constraints about the justification of those truth conditions (that they turn on neither consequentialist nor contractualist considerations, which means their effects or significance for hypothetical contracts don't count as relevant to justifying desert). The curiosity is that truth conditions and the basis of their justification are conceptually independent issues; they do not collapse in the context of responsibility. In the context of foundational normative ethics or practical reasoning as such, the truth conditions more plausibly collapse into questions of justification. That's why people have worried about tier collapse for rule utilitarianism, which holds that right action is that which conforms to a rule that would have the best effects overall. However, nonfoundational normative/evaluative practices needn't collapse in that way when the systemic good is secured precisely by having statuses internal to the practice that detach from the systemic justification. That's the lesson of the foul call case. Why then unify these things in a single notion of desert?

Here is a fourth and (for now) final concern. It seems that hard incompatibilism comes to nothing if implementing it leaves our moral practices intact. So, Pereboom's position requires that there be no basis for desert-entailing moral anger. Yet, my proposal identifies such a basis, albeit one that appeals to nonbasic desert. In reply, Pereboom has pointed to Kant's test as proof that this is not enough. If we cannot say that someone deserves blame or punishment even if there is no one else around to administer the punishment, then we do not have the kind of desert at stake in responsibility practices. This constraint is not unreasonable. It identifies a notion of desert without trying to specify its conceptual essence. Tellingly, my nonbasic desert picture readily satisfies it.

Recall that whether someone deserves blame is a function of whether they culpably violated a justified normative rule. (Why have a rule that we blame that violation? Answer: it enables cooperation and builds better beings.) So, suppose someone kills another person. Suppose, too, that everyone on earth besides the offender disappears six seconds after the murder, but before anyone can react to it. On this picture of responsibility, it would still be *true* that the murderer would deserve blame and punishment, even if no one was around to administer it and even if there were no positive effects in doing so. Like foul calls and criminal statuses, one can truly deserve these things even if no one is around to administer them and even if so administering them doesn't produce its customary effect.

The foregoing means that Kant's test of retributive desert can be passed by a nonbasic desert theory. To be sure, this is not a "presocial," from the "standpoint of the universe independent of human life" sense of desert. At best, it is a non-obvious, even surprising alternative basis for retaining our practices. Still, to the extent to which Kant's intuition is the idea that Pereboom is trying to capture with his notion of basic desert, and to the extent to which this is the stakes of his concern in debates about free will, then it seems that by Pereboom's own lights, a nonbasic desert theory of free will gives us what we need to reject hard incompatibilism.

14   Free Will and Back Again

The free will we were looking for wasn't the free will we needed. Like love, marriage, water, and all the rest, sometimes the world doesn't match our expectations. The animating idea of this chapter is that it isn't the precise content of free will that matters. Trying to achieve convergence about the full and specific content of the idea of free will is what has made it so difficult to resolve debates about free will. However, by focusing on the roles that free will thought, talk, and practices play in our practical deliberative lives we can locate a picture of free will that is informative and that leaves room for the possibility that we have erroneous but nonfatal errors in our thinking about free will.

We can agree that an adequate theory of free will should aspire to capture most of our coarse-grained truisms about free will. That's what this account attempts to do, and I have argued that we can capture the relevant truisms: free will has something to do with deliberation about what to do; it involves the ability to act; it is the kind of thing that sets us apart from most of the rest of the natural order, including many or all animals; our having free will is what makes sense of the idea that we can be culpable for what we do, at least some of the time; and free will matters morally. The picture on offer vindicates all these thoughts, without invoking the libertarian powers to which our imaginations direct us.

This revisionary picture comes at a necessary but acceptable cost: it conflicts with elements of common sense, including the idea that we are ultimate sources of what we do, perhaps with metaphysically robust alternative possibilities sometimes available to us. Still, our having free will marks us out as a distinctive part of nature, albeit one not radically separate from it. If things go right – if our biology and social conditions permit it – we often come to develop the distinctive normative powers that serve to mediate between the competing demands of sociality and self-interest. This is a good thing. These powers help us resolve deliberative challenges small and large. Although these powers are defined by a web of practical and normative functions, they are plausibly realized or built up out of thoroughly physical systems.

The foregoing means that we can make discoveries about the underlying physical structures involved in free will, in much the same way we have made discoveries about the composition of water, the diversity of marriage practices, and all the rest. For example, we could learn that other beings have this power in some or another form. Perhaps a few nonhuman animals have the requisite cognitive power to respond to moral considerations in the right ways. Alternately, we might learn that some human pathologies are more disruptive to free will than we thought if, for example, the disorder disrupts the ability to recognize or suitably respond to normative considerations.

It is part of the power of this approach that free will becomes a more tractable empirical matter, something whose contours we might come to understand by engagement with the relevant sciences. We needn't settle those particulars here. It is enough that we have an account that allows us to begin investigating things in those ways. That we can see how they might be answered suggests that we have made real progress.

Further Reading

Despite lingering disagreement about how to regiment labels, a variety of recent accounts have articulated broadly revisionary or potentially revisionary views about free will and moral responsibility. These include McGeer (2015, 2019), Doris (2015a), Nichols (2015), Deery (2021), and McCormick (2022). McCormick (2016) and Vargas (2023) provide general overviews of the literature and the main issues.

This chapter retains the general orientation of the view presented in the first edition (Vargas 2007), but it also contains numerous, sometimes substantial, transformations of my earlier views. The fullest statement of my version of revisionism, including of responsibility-relevant abilities and the agency cultivation model, is in Vargas (2013), with important updates in Vargas (2021). In Vargas (2015), owing to work by McKenna (2009), Pereboom (2014), and especially Doris (2015b), I changed my mind about how to think about desert, thereby abandoning significant elements of my earlier accounts (Vargas 2009, 2013). Wang (2021) has led me to be more explicit about the diversity of social and normative functions of responsibility; work by Brink (2021) and Nelkin (2016) has influenced me throughout.

I've argued for a two-tiered (2007, 2013), desert-invoking (2009, 2013) view of the justification of responsibility practices. Rawls (1955) and Hart (1961) provide the classic articulations of the idea of backward-looking rules justified by forward-looking considerations. Caruso and Pereboom (2022, pp. 9–10) have attributed discussions of desert and two-tiered justifications of responsibility practices to Dennett's monographs (1984, 2003), but I find explicit discussions of those things in those texts difficult to locate. In explaining when "tier collapse" isn't a threat, I've drawn from ideas in Hooker (2000) and Enoch, Fisher, and Spectre (2021).

Forerunners of contemporary free will revisionisms include Smart (1961), Bennett (1980), Walter (2001), Singer (2002), and Arneson (2003). Jackson (1998) self-identifies as a compatibilist but glosses it in revisionary way. Early Dennett (1984, 2003) is sometimes read as a revisionist, although the interpretive issues are complex (see Vargas 2005).

Overviews of recent efforts to study ordinary thinking about free will can be found in Björnsson (2022) and Nadelhoffer and Monroe (2022). For an intriguing, broadly functionalist proposal for explaining the shape of core puzzles, see Björnsson and Persson (2012). Citations to the wider literature on incompatibilism, libertarianism, reasons-responsiveness, and free will skepticism can be found in the prior chapters. Deployments of broadly ecological accounts of normative agency can be found in Morton (2011), Hurley (2013), Vargas (2013, 2017, 2018), and Nelkin and Vargas (forthcoming).

The *locus classicus* of the adaptive picture according to which retributive emotions enable cooperation include Frank (1988) and Fehr and Gächter (2002). For more recent overviews and complexifications, see Nichols (2015, Chapter 6), Cushman (2015), and O'Connor (2022). Many contemporary philosophers are interested in the intersection of naturalistic norm-sensitive agency and dispositions for cooperation, although not always with a focus on evolutionary explanation. Among the many works in that spirit, see McGeer (2012), Zawidzki (2013), Doris (2015a), Bicchieri (2017), Bratman (2022), Kelly (2022), Nichols (2022), and Madigan (forthcoming). My deployment of the idea of causal "hinges" draws from interventionist approaches to free will employed by Roskies (2012) and Deery and Nahmias (2017). For an instructive set of discussion between philosophers and neuroscientists, see Maoz and Sinnott-Armstrong (2022).

Nietzsche's *Genealogy of Morality* is the classic account of responsibility's genealogy. For a recent effort in that spirit, see Pettit (2018); for some challenges, see Plunkett (2016) and Vargas (forthcoming). Sommers (2022) discusses the diversity of responsibility practices. For a model of society-based justified norms, see Copp (1995). For the history of *mens rea* in English criminal law, see Chesney (1939). On animal trials, see Carson (1917) and Cohen (1986). For a contemporary overview of agency in animals, see Monsó and Andrews (2022). Miller (2020) argues that fish are not a well-ordered kind.

Since the first edition of this book, many of the issues that arise for revisionary theories of free will have been explored in an independent but parallel literature, under the guise of "conceptual engineering" and "conceptual ethics" (e.g. Burgess, Cappelen, and Plunkett (2020).

5

Response to Fischer, Pereboom, and Vargas

Robert Kane

1   Response to Fischer

John Fischer is a very astute and influential defender of what he calls a "semi-compatibilist" view in debates about free will and moral responsibility. He concedes that the *freedom to do otherwise* may not be compatible with determinism, a concession he makes, among other reasons, because he is well aware of the intuitive appeal of Borges's "garden of forking paths" image of our freedom. When we make free choices, it is like being in a garden of forking paths in which we must choose which of several possible paths to take. (Indeed, Fischer is responsible for introducing Borges's image of forking paths into current free will debates.) Fischer admits that it is extremely natural and plausible to think of ourselves (sometimes at least) as having more than one branching path into the future (i.e. having "alternative possibilities") and our freedom would involve "settling" which of these paths we will take by choosing.

What is unique and surprising, however, about Fischer's "semi-compatibilist" view is that he *denies* that "moral responsibility" *also* requires the freedom to do otherwise or having forking paths to choose from in this sense. On this topic, in my opening essay, I argued to the contrary for the plausibility of the well-known legal theorist H.L.A. Hart's "fair opportunity" criterion for holding persons responsible in legal contexts, which other philosophers, such as David Brink and Dana Nelkin (2013), have persuasively argued holds for ascriptions of responsibility in both moral and legal contexts: Hart's criterion says that

Four Views on Free Will, Second Edition. John Martin Fischer, Robert Kane, Derk Pereboom, and Manuel Vargas.
© 2024 John Wiley & Sons Ltd. Published 2024 by John Wiley & Sons Ltd.

"to be held responsible for acting in a certain way, one must have had a *fair opportunity for doing otherwise than acting in that way.*" In other words, one must have had some "alternative possibilities," so one could have avoided doing what one has done. This makes perfect sense to me and to many other philosophers and ordinary persons, as I argued in relation to the man on trial for raping a young woman in our neighborhood and other examples.

Fischer himself agrees that "it is extremely natural and plausible to think of ourselves as having more than one path branching into the future. This same assumption appears to frame both our deliberation and attributions of responsibility." Why then does he believe that being morally responsible does not require this assumption of having the power to do otherwise or having alternative possibilities? He rightly rejects all simpler traditional compatibilist responses to this question, such as the so-called conditional analysis. The conditional analysis, he argues, commends to us the view that an agent's freedom to do otherwise can be understood in terms of the truth of a conditional statement of the form, "If the agent were to have chosen or willed or decided to do otherwise, the agent would have done otherwise." As he nicely shows, such conditional analyses simply lead us to ask further questions such as, "Could the agent have chosen or willed or decided to do otherwise?" and so on, which brings alternative possibilities back into the picture.

Why then does he believe that moral responsibility does not require the freedom to do otherwise or having alternative possibilities? His arguments are characteristically subtle on this issue. The main argument appeals to what have come to be known as Frankfurt-style examples, which have played an influential role in contemporary debates about moral responsibility. Here is Fischer's Frankfurt-style example:

> Jones goes into the voting booth, deliberates in the "normal" way, and chooses to vote for the Democrat. Based on this choice, Jones votes for the Democrat. Unbeknownst to Jones, he has a chip in his brain that allows a neurosurgeon (Black) to monitor his brain. The neurosurgeon wants Jones to vote for the Democrat, and if she sees that Jones is about to choose to do so, she does not intervene in any way – she merely monitors the brain. If, on the other hand, the neurosurgeon sees that Jones is about to choose to vote for the Republican, she swings into action with her nifty electronic probe and stimulates Jones's brain in such a way as to ensure that he chooses to vote for the Democrat (and goes ahead and does so). Given the setup, it seems that Jones freely chooses to vote for the Democrat and freely votes for the Democrat, although he could not have chosen or done otherwise.

Jones, it is assumed, is morally responsible for his vote, *even though he couldn't have done otherwise* because the Frankfurt controller would not have allowed him to do otherwise if the monitor in his brain suggested to his controller that he was going to do otherwise. But since Jones acted on his own in the imagined case, and the controller stayed out of it, Jones could have been morally responsible for voting the way he did even though he couldn't have done otherwise because the controller would not have let him.

At this point in his discussion of Frankfurt-style examples, Fischer also introduces a distinction, which is crucial to his argument, between two kinds of control we might have over our actions, "guidance control" and "regulative control." Guidance control means simply the ability to guide your behavior toward a certain end, which is something you do when you perform any action, such as driving your car to the coffee shop. Regulative control requires more: the ability to guide your behavior toward a certain end, and also to do otherwise – to avoid guiding it to this end or to guide your behavior toward some other end. Regulative control, in other words, involves the power to act, and also the power to act otherwise. Fischer argues that normally we assume we have both kinds of control when we act. But Frankfurt-style examples, and many other examples, show the two kinds of control can be prized apart. When an agent like Jones acts on his own in a Frankfurt case, and the controller does not intervene, the agent exercises *guidance control* over his action. But he doesn't have *regulative control* because the controller would not have let him do otherwise.

The takeaway of such Frankfurt examples, for Fischer, can now be stated: guidance control is sufficient for moral responsibility. But having regulative control is not required. If Jones acts *on his own* in voting Democratic (exercises guidance control) and the controller does not intervene, Jones can be morally responsible for doing so, even though he could not have done otherwise (because the controller would not have let him). That is to say, he could be morally responsible for doing it even though he lacked regulative control over his action, the ability to perform it and the ability to do otherwise. Fischer generalizes this result: *guidance control over one's action is sufficient for moral responsibility. Regulative control, and the ability to have done otherwise, are not required.*

This allows him to say that moral responsibility is *compatible with determinism*, even if it *might* turn out that determinism is *in*compatible with the freedom to do otherwise. This is Fischer's *semi*-compatibilism. If you did something and you did it on your own, and you satisfied compatibilist criteria such as reasons-responsiveness, absence of coercion, addiction, control by others, etc., that is good enough to say you were morally responsible for it, *even if it turns out that you were determined to do what you did.* I find this result difficult to accept, and you may think so as well. If determinism were to turn out to be true then all of our *morally responsible* actions, good and bad, might have been *determined*, so that we could not have done otherwise than perform them.

Fischer's subtle arguments for these conclusions are based largely on his appeal to Frankfurt-style examples. But as I argued in my opening statement, while Frankfurt examples have important lessons to convey, they don't necessarily have these extreme conclusions. They do show, as Frankfurt rightly argues, that what he calls his "principle of alternative possibilities" (PAP) is false: it is not true that to be morally responsible for an action one must have been able to do otherwise than perform it or that it must have been undetermined. One can be responsible for many, what I called, "will-settled" actions, like Luther's "Here I stand," even if one could not have done otherwise than perform them when they were performed and even if they are determined when they are performed. Frankfurt examples are not the only examples that show this.

But, I went on to argue that not all of the actions in our lifetimes could be determined or already will-settled in this way when we act, *if we are ever to be responsible for our wills being set the way they are when we act.* For this to be the case, we would have to, at *some* times in our lives, be capable of not merely "will-settled" but also "will-setting" or "self-forming" choices or actions (SFAs), that were *not* determined by our existing wills when we performed them and were such that we could have willingly done otherwise when we performed them. In other words, some, even many, morally responsible actions in the course of our lives may be such that, at the time we performed them, we could not then and there have *willingly* done otherwise, like Luther's act. But it does not follow that *all* our morally responsible actions could be like this, *if we are ever to be morally responsible* to any degree *for the state or quality of our wills.*

Frankfurt examples, I argued, therefore do not refute a stronger principle, which I called "will-setting": agents are ultimately responsible for *having* the *wills* (characters, motives, and purposes) they *express* in action, only if at some times in their lives they willingly (voluntarily and intentionally) perform certain ("will-setting" or "self-forming") actions that it was causally possible at the time for them to have willingly avoided performing. In short, agents must have *regulative control* over such SFAs as well as guidance control.

It can be shown, as I further argued, that if all actions were under the control of Frankfurt controllers or mechanisms as in such examples, there could be no such self-forming choices and other self-forming actions (SFAs) and hence no will-setting of the kind required for agents to be responsible for having the quality of wills they do have. This must be so if *the controllers* themselves, *and not the agents*, are to *ensure* that the agents always do what the controllers want them to do. For the essence of a will-setting or self-forming action is that *the agent, and no one or nothing else*, can determine how such a will-setting action will turn out when it is performed. If a controller stayed out of it and let an agent make an undetermined self-forming action on his or her own, the controller could not be sure the agent would choose as the controller wanted.

These points are connected to some important distinctions I made in my opening statement that I believe are crucial for understanding issues about free will and moral responsibility. The first is the distinction between *two dimensions of responsibility*. The first dimension of responsibility is:

Responsibility for *expressing* the *will one has* in action.

The second dimension is:

Responsibility for *forming* and thus *having* the will one *expresses* in action.

The first dimension of responsibility corresponds to *freedom of action*, whereas the second dimension corresponds to *freedom of will*. Compatibilists about free will give us accounts of freedom of action. But freedom of will, I argue, is not just being able to do *what* you will (that's freedom of action). It is also the ability to form or shape the will that you express in action.

And the essence of a will-setting or self-forming is that the agent, and no one or nothing else, can determine how such a will-setting or self-forming actions will turn out when they are performed. Such will-forming or self-forming actions must be incompatible with determinism even if many other morally responsible actions that flow from a will already formed might be determined.

One final point involves another concession to Fischer. Will-setting or self-forming actions – which, on my account, are needed at some points in our lives if we are to have free will and ultimate responsibility for being the kinds of persons we are – must be free actions, albeit of a special kind. This means they must also satisfy the best compatibilist conditions of action, as well as further incompatibilist conditions, such as indeterminism, for being self-forming. They must be reasons-responsive, and reasons-reactive, they must be uncoerced and not controlled by others, they must not be determined by addictions, and other internal constraints, and so on. Fischer has been one of most perceptive and influential compatibilists in formulating these "compatibilist" conditions for free actions, as one can see from reading his opening statement in this debate.

Since freedom of will on my view is a kind of freedom of action, it must also require the best available compatibilist criteria for freedom of action, many of which Fischer has cogently described. But freedom *of will*, I believe, requires more – it also requires that sometimes in our lives we must also be capable of forming or shaping the will from which we act (through self-forming actions) in a way that is *not determined* by our past.

2   Response to Pereboom

According to free will skepticism, we lack the kind of free will required for moral responsibility of the kind that is at issue in debates about free will. That kind of moral responsibility is called by Derk Pereboom, a leading contemporary free will skeptic, moral responsibility in the "basic desert sense." He says that such desert "is basic in the sense that the agent, to be morally responsible, would deserve blame or credit just because [the agent] performed the action, given sensitivity to its moral status, and not merely by virtue of consequentialist or contractualist considerations." The free will that is necessary for such basic desert moral responsibility, according to free will skeptics such as Pereboom, is incompatible with determinism. Compatibilist views, he argues, thus fail to capture it.

I will not discuss here his arguments against compatibilism. I tend to agree with many of them. I will focus on his arguments against libertarianism and argue that they fail against the version of libertarianism I defend in my opening statement.

To make his case against libertarian views of free will, Pereboom critically examines what he takes to be the two major versions of libertarianism, "event-causal" (EC) and "agent-causal" (AC) libertarian views. Against EC versions of libertarianism, he offers the following objection.

> For an agent to be morally responsible for an action (in the basic desert sense), she must have a certain kind of control in producing that action. Suppose that a decision is made in a deliberative context in which the relevant causation is event-causal and indeterministic, the agent's moral motivations favor deciding to A, her prudential motivations favor her deciding to not-A, and the strengths of these motivations are in equipoise. A and not-A are the options she is considering. The potentially causally relevant events thus render the occurrence of each of these decisions equiprobable. However, then, crucially, the potentially causally relevant events do not settle which decision occurs, that is whether the decision to A or the decision to not-A occurs. Moreover, since on the event-causal view only events are causally relevant, *nothing* settles which decision occurs. Given the complete causal role of these preceding events, it *remains open* whether action occurs. Thus, it can't be the agent or anything about the agent that settles which decision occurs, and accordingly she lacks the control required for moral responsibility, in the basic desert sense in particular, for it. Since the agent "disappears" at the crucial point in the production of the action – when its occurrence is to be settled – we can call this the "disappearing agent argument"

In response, I want to now argue that this "disappearing agent objection" no longer applies to the revised view of free will presented in my recent writings, which are summarized in my opening statement, and will be further described here.

According to this revised view, one does not have to choose between agent (or substance) causation and event causation in describing freedom of choice and action. One can affirm both. In the case of self-forming choices or SFAs, for example, it is true to say both that "the agent's deliberative activity, including her effort, caused or brought about the choice," and that "the agent caused or brought about the choice." Indeed, the first claim entails the second. Such event descriptions are not meant to deny that agents, qua substances, cause their free choices and actions. Rather, the event descriptions spell out in more detail how and why the agents did so.

We must note, however, that if EC descriptions are to have these implications, the event causes they describe must be "agent-involving" in a special manner. Relevant to explaining this special manner, I argued, is a peculiarly modern scientific way of understanding human agency and causation by agents. Agents, according to this modern conception, are to be conceived as *information-responsive complex dynamical systems*. "An agent's causing an action" is to be understood as "an agent, conceived as such an information-responsive complex dynamical system, exercising *teleological guidance control*, over some of its own processes."

Complex dynamical systems are understood in this context in the manner of "dynamical systems theory." Such systems (now known to be ubiquitous in nature and which include living things) are systems in which emergent capacities arise as a result of greater complexity. When the emergent capacities arise, the systems as a whole or various subsystems of them impose novel constraints on the behavior of their parts. Alicia Juarrero whose informative book on the nature and significance of complex dynamical systems in the sciences, *Dynamics in Action* (MIT, 1999), calls these emergent novel constraints on the behavior of parts of the system "context-sensitive constraints."

Such complex systems exhibit "teleological guidance control" (TGC) when they tend through feedback loops and error correction mechanisms to converge on a goal (called an attractor) in the face of perturbations. Such control, as neuroscientist Marius Usher argues (2006), *is necessary for any voluntary activity* and he interprets it in terms of dynamic systems theory. Neuroscientists E. Miller and J. Cohen (2001) argue that such cognitive (guidance) control in human agents stems from the active maintenance of patterns of activity in the prefrontal cortex that represent goals and the means to achieve them. These patterns provide signals to other brain structures whose net effect, as Miller and Cohen describe it, is to guide the flow of activity along neural pathways that establish the proper mappings between inputs, internal states, and outputs.

An important consequence of understanding the agent causation involved in free agency and free will in this way is that the causal role of the agent in intentional actions of the kind needed for free agency and will is not *reducible* to causation by mental states of the agent alone. That would leave out the added role of the *agent*, qua *complex dynamical system, exercising TGC* over the processes *causally linking* mental states and events to actions.

The significance of this requirement can be shown by considering examples of "deviant causation" by mental states, such as desires and beliefs, in debates about action and free will. Consider Donald Davidson's (1963) well-known example of such causal deviance. The example is of a mountain climber who lets go of his rope, allowing his companion to fall. The climber *desires* to save his own life and *believes* he can do so in the present situation by letting go of his rope. But in the example, he does not *willingly* or intentionally let go of the rope. Rather, this desire and belief so unnerve him when he thinks of their consequences that they cause him to *accidentally* let go of the rope.

What is lacking in such examples of deviant causation is the agent, understood as a dynamical system, exercising *teleological guidance control* over the *manner* in which the mental states cause the resulting events. In the absence of this "systemic control" by the agent, qua information responsive dynamical system, over the manner in which the mental states cause the resulting events, the causation by mental states would be "deviant" and the outcomes would not be intentional actions of the agent, but accidental occurrences.

A further significant consequence of understanding causation of free actions in this way, as Usher (2006) points out, is that, while teleological guidance control (TGC) of the kind required for voluntary action is compatible with determinism, it is also compatible with indeterminism. A complex dynamical system can exhibit TGC, tending through feedback loops and error correction to converge on a goal, even when, due to the presence of indeterminism, it is uncertain whether the goal will be attained. Such TGC is thus available to libertarian theories of free will as well as to compatibilist ones.

To sum up, one does not have to choose between agent (or substance) causation and event causation in accounting for free agency, libertarian or otherwise. You can, indeed you must, affirm both. And the agent or substance causation involved is not reducible to event causation by mental states and events alone for the reasons given. There is thus no "disappearing agent problem."

As a consequence of these additions, the libertarian view of free will developed in my opening statement differs from traditional *agent-causal (AC)* and *noncausal (NC)* views of libertarian free will. But *it also differs from what are usually designated event causal (EC) views in the current literature.* It differs from what are usually designated EC views in rejecting claims that libertarian free actions can be adequately explained merely by claiming they are indeterministically caused in appropriate ways by beliefs, desires, intentions, and other mental states of agents. It turns out that the "appropriate ways" must bring in references to agents, qua substances, understood as complex dynamical systems, exercising TGC over some of their own processes, thereby allowing us to say that the agents *brought about* the action *for* these motivating mental states. And such references are not reducible to mere causation by mental states or events of agents alone, *which otherwise might be deviant.*

The view assumed here also differs from traditional AC libertarian views in the following ways: it does not involve a *sui generis* or "metaphysically primitive" notion of causation by an agent or substance. Nor does it require a notion of causation by agents that is not also required by compatibilist accounts of free agency, nor one whose *exercise* does not essentially involve causation by states, processes, and events. Nor does the view developed here require postulating a special kind of causation by an agent or substance that is, in principle, incapable of being itself caused by prior events, nor a special kind of causation by an agent that is not subject to or governed by laws of nature of the natural sciences; nor one that requires appeals to immaterial substances, noumenal selves, transempirical power centers, uncaused causes, or other examples of what P.F. Strawson called the "panicky metaphysics" of libertarianism.

To avoid these misunderstandings, it now seems appropriate, as suggested in my opening statement, to distinguish four kinds of contemporary libertarian views rather than three and to insist that my own view is of this fourth, agent-causal/event-causal (AC/EC) kind. In *The Significance of Free Will* and other writings (Kane 1996), I also referred to this fourth kind of view as a "teleological intelligibility" or TI view, and that title also remains appropriate for reasons explained here, according to which "an agent's causing an action" is to be understood as "an agent, conceived as an information-responsive complex dynamical system, exercising *teleological guidance* over some of its own processes."

The objections to my libertarian view spelled out by Pereboom in his opening statement do not apply to this revised AC/EC view. To show this we might consider how undetermined *self-forming actions* would be conceived, given the preceding reflections. Consider a familiar example of van Inwagen's of a would-be thief, call him John, deliberating about whether or not to steal from a church poor box. Suppose John is deeply torn because he is desperately in need of money and knows that no one is usually in the church on weekday afternoons, so he can likely steal without being caught. On the other hand, he has serious moral qualms about doing so, because he knows the money in the poor box is used to help other people who are also in need.

We might then imagine that in the course of John's deliberation, various thoughts, experiences, and memories come to mind, various thoughts, desires, and possibilities are assessed, so that his considered reasons incline him to choose to steal the money rather than not to steal it. Of crucial importance, however, is that if this is a self-forming choice we must say that the reasons motivating the choice to steal the money merely *incline* John to make that choice at this time rather than the alternative. These reasons are not *decisive* or *conclusive*, nor do they determine he will do so. To use a traditional expression of Leibniz, his reasons "incline without necessitating." If a choice is thus to be made in accord with these inclinations, effort would have to be made to overcome the still-existing resistance in his will. This resistance would be coming from his motives to make the contrary choice, which motives also remain important to him.

Though the reasons merely incline and are not decisive or conclusive, nonetheless when it is the case that the agent judges that they incline to one choice to a degree that might justify making that choice at the time, an effort would be initiated to make that choice and thereby to overcome the still-existent resistant motives in the will. This is where indeterminism would enter the picture as well. For, the conflict in John's will would "stir up" indeterminism in the effort to make the choice to which he is currently inclined, making it uncertain the effort will succeed in attaining its goal. If the effort to choose to steal does succeed, despite this indeterminism, the choice to steal to which John is presently inclined would be made and the deliberation would terminate.

Note that if this should happen, the choice to steal would have been made by John on purpose and in accordance with his will since it would have been the result of a goal-directed cognitive process (the effort or exertion of willpower) to make just this choice at this time rather than an alternative. Moreover, the choice would have been made for the reasons inclining him towards that choice at the time rather than the alternative. Thus, it wouldn't have been a mere accident that the choice occurred, *even though its occurrence was undetermined.* The choice would have been brought about voluntarily and on purpose as a result of the success of the goal-directed effort of the agent that might have failed due to the indeterminism, but did not fail.

But what if, due to the indeterminism involved, the effort to choose to steal from the poor box did *not* succeed at that time and the choice had not been made? Many critics of a free will requiring indeterminism assume that if a choice is undetermined, the agent would be able to make a different choice (e.g. to steal or not to steal), given exactly the same deliberation leading up to the moment of choice, including exactly the same desires, beliefs, thoughts, and prior reasoning. Given this assumption, it would follow that if John failed in his effort to choose to steal from the poor box at this time, due to the indeterminism involved, he would instead have chosen *not* to steal from the poor box at that same time instead. And this is problematic, these critics argue, given that his deliberation would have been exactly the same leading up to the different choices. What would explain the difference in choice?

This commonly made assumption, however, is *not* made in the account of self-forming choices in my opening statement. It is not assumed that if a choice is undetermined, the agent might make different choices (e.g. to steal or not to steal), given exactly the same deliberation, leading up to the choice. All that follows on this present account from the assumption that a self-forming choice or SFA is undetermined is that the effort to make it may succeed *or may fail* at a given time in overcoming the resistance in the will to making it. And from this, it does *not* follow that if the effort fails, an alternative choice would be made at that same time instead.

Failure would rather be a signal to the agent not to choose too hastily in terms of the presently inclining reasons. Failure would say in effect: think more about this. The resistant motives for the alternative choice still matter to you and they should not be dismissed too readily. These resistant motives are the causal source of the indeterminism in the effort to choose to steal in the first place, making it uncertain that the effort will succeed here and now. The stronger these resistant motives are, the greater the probability the effort may fail, due to the indeterminism to which the resistant motives give rise.

In sum, a distinction needs to be made between John's *not choosing to steal* at a time and his choosing *not to steal* at that time. What is assumed if, due to the indeterminism, John fails in his effort to choose to steal at the time is not that he would have made the contrary choice, not to steal, but rather that no choice at all would have been made at that time. The deliberation would either continue until a potential reassessment of the motivating reasons led to another later effort to make the choice to steal or a potential reassessment led to a later effort to make the choice not to steal. Or, the deliberation might terminate without any decision being made, if this is possible in the circumstances and the agent is so inclined.

Note that in any of these possible scenarios, if John does succeed at a time in an effort to make whatever choice he is inclined to make at that time, he will have brought about that choice and will have done so voluntarily and intentionally and for the motivating reasons that inclined him towards that choice at the time. For he would have succeeded in an effort whose goal was to make that very choice *rather than* the alternative *for* those inclining reasons; and this would be the case *even though the occurrence of the choice, if he succeeds, would have been undetermined.*

The indeterminism required by libertarian free will would then not undermine freedom of will, but would make possible the plural voluntary control required for free will at some times in our lives when we engage in self-formation. Is this manner, I believe an incompatibilist free will requiring indeterminism at certain points in our lives is possible, contrary to the subtle arguments of free will skeptics like Pereboom who argue against its possibility.

3   Response to Vargas

Manuel Vargas is a leading defender of a revisionist view of free will and moral responsibility. Revisionists concede that our ordinary understanding of free will and responsibility has some genuine incompatibilist strands as well as compatibilist strands. But revisionists are critical of the incompatibilist or libertarian strands in ordinary thinking about free will and moral responsibility, suggesting they cannot be realized. Revisionists argue as a consequence that what we should do is *revise* our ordinary thinking about free will and moral responsibility in a *compatibilist* direction, expunging all elements that imply or seem to imply the necessity of incompatibilist or libertarian views.

Vargas arguments for such a revisionism proceed in several steps. The first step is to argue that, contrary to the assumptions of conventional compatibilists and semicompatibilists, like Fischer, there are incompatibilist and libertarian intuitions embedded in our common sense that are not the results of mere confusions or errors. He says:

> I think important strands of ordinary thought are as libertarians have said. A variety of considerations – including the power of philosophical arguments in the vein of the Consequence Argument, experimental findings about people's conceptual commitments, and the long arc of our cultural history – suggest that many of us are at least sometimes committed to a form of agency that requires indeterminism. To put my cards on the table, I think many people – maybe most – have an earnestly held picture of free will according to which metaphysically robust notions of sourcehood and leeway are required of free will, at least sometimes and in some contexts, and they think we have these powers.

Despite the initial plausibility of such inclinations toward incompatibilist or libertarian views of free will and responsibility, however, Vargas offers several lines of argument to show why he believes such views that require indeterminism should be rejected. The first is that *indeterminism* adds nothing essential to the *control* agents must have over their free and responsible actions. Indeed, he argues, indeterminism would diminish, rather than enhance, that control, which suggests it is not necessary for either free will or moral responsibility.

Second, he offers us a complex view of how free will functions in our practical lives, arguing that it does not require the falsity of determinism. Free will, he argues, is the "situational capacity to recognize and respond to normative considerations" – that is situations concerning how we should act and relate to others in social situations. In focusing on such considerations, we can see how they "create a demand for a kind of control that involves recognizing and responding to normative considerations that matter for complex forms of coordination and cooperation." Such a kind of control that is needed to coordinate and cooperate with others, he argues, is what we mean by *free will* and it is necessary for a responsibility system that is systematically entangled with, the nature of our emotions, the persistence of our interests in the goods of sociality, and the pressures to cultivate the powers distinctive of human agency. What free will is and what responsibility demands are therefore practical matters, he concludes, that can be understood without getting into deep and insoluble *metaphysical* issues about whether they are or are not compatible with determinism, or require indeterminism, that have been at the center of traditional debates about free will and moral responsibility.

I agree with much of what Vargas says about the practical dimensions of recognizing and responding to normative considerations in everyday life that he describes. These practical dimensions must be accommodated by any adequate libertarian theory as well. But I don't believe these practical dimensions settle all that we need to know about free will and moral responsibility, as he has often put it "without getting into deep and insoluble 'metaphysical' issues about determinism that have been at the center of traditional debates about free will and moral responsibility." To the contrary, I agree with many distinguished philosophers in recent times, including prominently Bernard Williams and Thomas Nagel, who contend that while these "practical" dimensions of free will and moral responsibility are important, there is also a "metaphysical" dimension to debates about free will and moral responsibility that is critically important as well and cannot be dismissed so readily, as it often is by compatibilists, semicompatibilists, and revisionists.

I have described this metaphysical dimension of free will issues in prior writings by appeal to the origins of the term "metaphysics" in the history of philosophy: when ancient scholars organized Aristotle's large corpus of writings on philosophy and science, they placed what came to be called his treatise on metaphysics "after" (*meta*) his book on physics. Hence the origin of the term "metaphysics." In that treatise (placed after his book on physics), Aristotle says its subject matter is to understand the "ultimate causes and reasons" (*archai kai aitiae*) of all things. In earlier writings, I have argued that the free will issue has a metaphysical dimension in this ancient sense, since it seeks to understand the ultimate causes and reasons *of some things in the universe of particular concern to us, namely our human wills and actions.* Are the ultimate causes and reasons of our wills and actions to any degree "up to us," or were those ultimate causes and reasons for why we have the wills we do and act the way we do to be located entirely in features of the universe beyond our control as determinism would imply?

To understand what motivates us libertarians about free will, we want to know what the ultimate causes and reasons are for our being the kinds of persons we are with the *wills* we have that account for what we do and how we act. Are any of these ultimate causes and reasons for being what we are and acting as we do in us or are they all completely determined by other things over which we lack control? If all these ultimate causes and reasons were determined by other things over which we lacked control, it would always have been causally impossible for us to have done anything differently in the course of our lives *to have made ourselves any different than we in fact are,* though we may have *believed* otherwise when we acted.

I find this an unpalatable conclusion, not only with regard to my own life, but for all other humans – the good ones, who may inspire admiration and love, and the bad ones, who may have acted cruelly or harmfully to others, including, at worse, evil dictators and exploiters of other persons and groups. If determinism were true, it would never have been causally possible for any of them, good or bad, to have done anything differently in the course of their lives to have made themselves any different than they are. These are strong motivations for libertarian views of free will and moral responsibility.

But they bring us back to Vargas's other criticisms of libertarian views. The first was that *indeterminism* adds nothing essential to the *control* agents must have over their free and responsible actions. Like many others, including compatibilists and free will skeptics, he argues that indeterminism would diminish, rather than enhance, any control we might have over our actions, which suggests it is not necessary for either free will or moral responsibility. I addressed such an objection at length in my opening statement and in my response just given to Pereboom. The first point to make is that the indeterminism involved in acts of free will that are *self-forming* on my AC/EC view *is not an accidental feature of the situation*. It does not just *happen* to be present. The presence of the indeterminism is rather a consequence of the conflict in the agent's will and of the resistant motives that are a feature of that conflict – resistant motives that have to be overcome by effort, whichever choice is made.

The idea is thus to think of the indeterminism involved in self-forming choices, not as a cause *acting on its own*, but as an *ingredient* in larger *goal-directed* activities of the agent, in which the indeterminism functions as a *hindrance* or *interfering* element in the attainment of their goals. The choices that result would then be *achievements* brought about by the goal-directed activities (the efforts of will or exercises of willpower) of the agent, which might have failed since they were undetermined, but one or the other of which might succeed in its goal. Moreover, if such processes aimed at different goals may occur at different times in the course of deliberation (in the conflicted circumstances of a self-forming choice), whichever choice may be successfully made will have been brought about by the agent's volitional striving (the effort) to make that particular choice rather than the other at that time, despite the possibility of failure due to the indeterminism stirred up by the contrary motives in the agent's will.

Thus, while diminishing, without eliminating, one kind of control (teleological guidance control, or TGC) agents might have over their SFAs the presence of indeterminism would make possible another kind of control, plural voluntary control (PVC), the power at some times to make one choice or a different choice, voluntarily, intentionally, and rationally, whichever choice should be made. In this way, indeterminism would enhance the exercise of free will, allowing agents at some points in their lives to engage in self- and will-formation in a way that is not *determined* by their past. Indeterminism would thus open up a window that allows them to make themselves one way or another without being determined by what they already are. It allows persons to be responsible for being *the kinds of agents they are with the wills they have* as well as being responsible for what they do and how they act.

This brings us to Vargas's second major criticism of libertarian views of free will. He says "libertarianism's scientific credentials are highly speculative." "I'm also consistently told," he says, "that nothing in mainstream neuroscience independently suggests that we have . . . amplification of quantum indeterminacy" of the kind that would be involved in libertarian views like those Kane suggests. In response, I would note that while there is disagreement on this topic among neuroscientists and other scientists, there are a growing number of physicists, neuroscientists, and other scientists in the past several decades who have argued that such amplification of quantum indeterminism in the brain is a distinct possibility and how it might operate in human decision-making.

I cited many such figures in my opening statement and in the further readings accompanying that section which suggest as much. I've also encountered many other physicists and neuroscientists in the past 20 years who take seriously the possibility of quantum influences in human reasoning and decision-making, in conferences involving philosophers and scientists discussing issues of free will – in the US and many other countries of the world. The proceedings of many of these conferences in which I participated are collected in various volumes noted in my suggested readings, including, to take several examples, *Quantum Physics Meets the Philosophy of Mind* (Corradini and Meixner 2014), *Streit um die Freiheit* (Von Stosch et al. 2019), and *Is Science Compatible with Free Will?* (Suarez and Adams 2013). This new work in the neuro- and other sciences does not prove that amplified quantum indeterminacies play a role in cognitive and mental processing. But it does counter Vargas's claim that "nothing in mainstream neuroscience . . . suggests that we have . . . amplification of quantum indeterminacy" of the kind that might be involved in libertarian views. And many neuroscientists I've cited suggest ways in which this might occur. As a consequence, what much of this research shows, as Mark Balaguer (2010) suggests, is that whether a libertarian view of free will requiring indeterminism could exist in the natural world remains an "open scientific question."

In facing this question, compatibilists, semicompatibilists, and revisionists, like Fischer and Vargas, argue that since libertarian free will is impossible, both empirically and theoretically, we should abandon hope of a free will supporting moral responsibility that is incompatible with determinism. And we should develop and accept in its place notions of free will and/or moral responsibility that *are* compatible with determinism.

My strategy is quite different. If determinism were true, it would never have been causally possible for anyone to exercise their capacities of acting and willing in the course of their lives in ways that were any different from how they actually exercise them. As a consequence, it would never have been causally possible for any of us to have made ourselves and our wills any different than they in fact are. Yet this is what I believe freedom *of will* would require over and above freedom of action. So, I have set out to show here and in other writings that such a free will requiring indeterminism at certain points in our lives is coherent and intelligible by answering the many objections against it and showing that it is both conceptually and empirically possible. This would not demonstrate that such a free will exists, but it would allow one to rationally believe in such a free will until such time as it was definitively shown to be conceptually or empirically impossible.

In the original edition of this book, *Four Views of Free Will* (2007), John Fischer put the following challenge to me. Suppose a headline saying that "SCIENTISTS HAVE DISCOVERED THAT DETERMINISM IS TRUE" were to appear in a distant future newspaper and should turn out to be true. Then, he said, his view (as well as the views of Pereboom and Vargas) would not be threatened. But Kane would have to give up his libertarian view. I responded as follows.

> Future scientific research into the cosmos and the brain could indeed show a view such as mine might be false. But that doesn't mean as a libertarian I am prepared to jump over to one of these other views, which I regard as pallid substitutes (if not subterfuges) for free will, or no free will at all. I prefer to wait, thank you, till science does prove that determinism is true or that the brain operates on strictly determinist processes, or at least till a good deal more evidence on these matters is in. If I do ever read Fischer's headline and it is true, I would have to give up my libertarian view and perhaps go over to one of these other views. I think empirical evidence matters. But I don't know which of these other views I'd go to. For someone with libertarian intuitions like me, it would be like being asked whether I wanted to live in desert or in the middle of a jungle or at the South Pole. Well, I don't like any of the options. Do I have to choose *now*? Can I spend a few weeks in Hawaii while I think about it? (Kane 2007: 181)

One final concession must be made to Vargas, however: if I did ever have to give up my view and accept one of these other views or some other, the view that I accepted would in his sense *be* revisionist from my point of view.

6

Response to Kane, Pereboom, and Vargas

John Martin Fischer

1   Response to Kane

Let us begin by distinguishing various components of Kane's version of the doctrine of libertarianism. A central claim is that freedom to will and do otherwise (regulative control, in my terminology) is required for moral responsibility. (This view is not held by all libertarians; some are "source incompatibilists," who maintain that, although regulative control is not required for moral responsibility, indeterminism in the actual sequence is.) Kane's second key claim is that the required freedom (regulative control) is incompatible with causal determinism (based on the Consequence Argument). Finally, Kane contends (with other libertarians) that causal *indeterminism* is compatible with willing and acting with the freedom implicated in moral responsibility. Acceptance of the conjunction of the first two claims makes him an incompatibilist. The third assertion is the "indeterminist freedom" claim. A libertarian will also insist that we do in fact have such freedom (and thus causal determinism does not obtain in our world).

I disagree with the first two claims (where the alternative-possibilities freedom is interpreted "strictly," i.e. holding all the past and laws fixed), but Kane and I have an important point of agreement. We both accept the indeterminist freedom claim. As I argued in my initial piece, guidance control and moral

Four Views on Free Will, Second Edition. John Martin Fischer, Robert Kane, Derk Pereboom, and Manuel Vargas.

responsibility are entirely consistent with causal indeterminism. If that were not the case, our moral responsibility would indeed hang by a thread. Kane's defense of the possibility of willing and choosing voluntarily, intentionally, and freely in an indeterministic world is persuasive – and welcome!

Kane helpfully distinguishes two requirements for free will of the sort required by moral responsibility: the "alternative possibilities" (AP) requirement and the condition of "ultimate responsibility" (UR). He believes that UR is the fundamental worry for compatibilists, and that it is even more important than AP. Further, Kane contends that although UR "does not require that we could have done otherwise for *every* act done 'of our own free wills . . . [it] does require that we could have done otherwise with respect to *some* acts in our past life histories by which we formed our present characters." Kane applies this idea to cases such as Martin Luther, who alleged that he literally couldn't have done otherwise (than break with the Church in Rome). Kane says that we can (and, indeed, must) trace Luther's moral responsibility to past acts to which there were genuine alternative possibilities open to him. He contends that if there were never alternative possibilities open to us (at *any* points in our lives), then "there [would be] *nothing we could have ever done differently in our entire lifetimes to make ourselves different than we are*" and thus we would not satisfy UR.

I agree with Kane that we can distinguish an alternative possibilities and sourcehood condition on moral responsibility. But I do not see why a suitable sourcehood condition should entail any sort of AP condition (even a "tracing" condition – a condition that reaches back into the past). Kane seeks to argue that UR entails a version of AP. The argument is that UR entails the existence of "will-setting" actions at some points in our lives, which in turn implies that some of our actions satisfy the "plurality conditions." The plurality conditions entail alternative possibilities at some points in our lives. It is to Kane's credit that he seeks to *argue* for the putative connection between UR and some version of AP, but I am unconvinced. I do not see why "will-setting" should be any different from ordinary action with respect to the requirement of alternative possibilities. For example, why can't one have Frankfurt-style examples at the stage of "will-setting"? After all, it is plausible that there are indeterministic Frankfurt-style cases. (A recipe for one kind of such cases is given by Pereboom in his essay, and others have offered purported indeterministic Frankfurt-style cases.)

I believe that it is better to insist on a sharp distinction between the sourcehood condition and the alternative possibilities condition. When one acts freely, one must be the source of one's action in some suitable sense. It is contentious whether sourcehood is consistent with causal determination. On my view, if Luther were indeed morally responsible for breaking with the Roman Church, his moral responsibility for doing so could indeed be traced to previous free actions: it could be traced to past instances of exercises of guidance control in choosing and acting freely. One can explain the "Luther examples" via this sort of tracing approach (in which one reaches into the past to find instances of acting freely or guidance control), just as one can explain moral responsibility for the consequences of drunk driving or behavior under the influence of drugs. One need not trace back to instances of regulative control.

Similarly, there is no need to abandon the guidance-control framework in light of the Brink and Nelkin (2013) "fair opportunity to avoid" approach or Kane's analysis of fair judgments in criminal trials. Regarding the fair opportunity to avoid model, we'd need to know what such an opportunity is. If, holding fixed all the past and laws, we never would will/choose or act differently, does one have a "fair opportunity to avoid" willing, choosing, or acting as we do?

I reject an AP analysis of the control required for moral responsibility, of which "fair opportunity to avoid" is an instance. I reject it in part based on the Frankfurt-style cases, although (as in my initial piece), I do not think they are the *only* road to an actual-sequence approach. Further, we can analyze the phenomena pertaining to moral responsibility in terms of choosing/acting freely (guidance control), *just as well as with fair opportunity to avoid*. This is important. As the pressures mount, an individual has less and less of a fair opportunity to avoid her actual choice and behavior. Similarly, as the pressures mount, it is more and more difficult for her to choose and act freely. At some point things have got so bad that she lacks a fair opportunity to avoid her actual choice and action; at the same point, presumably, she would have lost her capacity to act freely. In acting in this sort of situation, the agent would not be acting freely (exhibiting guidance control).

There is thus *no advantage* to invoking fair opportunity to avoid, rather than guidance control. Why prefer a guidance, rather than a regulative control approach to the freedom requirement for moral responsibility? As in my initial contribution, a big plus is that we can thereby sidestep the very old and contentious debates about the relationship between causal determinism and alternative possibilities. This is a considerable advantage of an actual-sequence model of moral responsibility.

Same with fair judgments in criminal trials. We observe the horrible acts of the criminal, and we are filled with revulsion and the desire that justice be done. Kane contends that, as we learn more about the terrible formative circumstances of the criminal, our attitudes toward him are tempered to the degree we recognize how difficult it would have been for him to avoid making his heinous choices and acting on them. Kane would withdraw any negative attitudes or attributions of moral responsibility if he were to come to believe it literally causally impossible for the criminal to have avoided committing the crimes. I do not, however, agree with this analysis of our very reasonable tendencies to adjust our judgments and attitudes toward an offender, given information about his circumstances and background.

Again, there is no need to abandon the guidance-control framework. I do not think we *have* to suppose that in evaluating the individual's formative and current circumstances, we are trying to figure out whether it was causally impossible for him to will and do otherwise. Rather, we can just as easily interpret the project as trying to figure out whether, given everything, the offender has indeed acted freely (exhibited guidance control). If not, then no moral responsibility. We can analyze Kane's perfectly reasonable empathy with the criminal, while also continuing to reap the metaphysical benefits of an actual-sequence model of moral responsibility.

Kane and I have another important point of agreement: we both deny Peter Strawson's (1962) "insulation thesis," according to which we can insulate our moral responsibility attributions from metaphysical questions about free will. Strawson held that no "metaphysical proposition" had to be true of an individual who can legitimately be held morally responsible. I agree that the individual need not have indeterministic freedom, as opposed to Kane. But I do hold that must exhibit actual-sequence freedom – guidance control. We can thus insulate our status as morally responsible agents from the intractable philosophical debates about the relationship between causal determinism and regulative control, as well as the deliverances of the theoretic physicists – all without abandoning the association of responsibility and control. If Strawson's metaphysical proposition is about guidance control, the proposition asserting a connection with moral responsibility must be true.

Strawson called "agent-causation" (irreducible to event-causation) a "pitiful intellectual trinket." This is an element of some, though not Kane's, versions of libertarianism. I do not think Strawson's amusing epithet is fair, and, further, I wish to note that my account of guidance control is consistent with a framework that involves agent-causation, either to the exclusion of, or in combination with, event causation. It is even compatible (adjusted suitably) with a noncausal view of the relationship between reasons, choices, and actions. Compatibilism, including semicompatibilism, is a big tent.

Some compatibilists have contended that causal determinism is not only consistent with free will and moral responsibility but also *required* for it. This claim is not, however, essential to compatibilism, and I do not accept it. The proponents of the necessity of determinism for freedom are held hostage to the scientists in a different, but just as troublesome a, way: the discovery of indeterminism would now spoil the party.

Kane argues that it is empirically plausible that the brain works in a particular indeterministic way and points out that the possibility of indeterminism in the brain is now taken seriously by neuroscientists. This is indeed true, but some reject it, holding that the brain works deterministically, and the jury is out at this point. For Kane's theory to be acceptable, the brain must not only work indeterministically but also in certain specific ways (involving the magnification of quantum events through chaotic processes). It is problematic that the very fundamental view of ourselves as morally responsible – as persons – should depend on this sort of empirical fact. If the neuroscientists had a press conference in which they were to announce whether they've established whether the brain works in this specific way, would you be on the edge of your seat? Should you be? I don't think so. We shouldn't conceptualize the freedom condition for moral responsibility so as to render us hostages to the neuroscientists.

2   Response to Pereboom

One of the challenges for compatibilism I highlighted in my initial chapter is to distinguish responsibility-undermining manipulation from "normal" and (arguably) unproblematic causal determination. Do they pose the same difficulty? I do not think so, but Pereboom's Four Case Argument nicely brings out the challenge of explaining the difference. He presents a series of four cases in which, he claims, the adjacent ones are indistinguishable with respect to moral responsibility. Further, he contends that, in the first case, the agent – Professor Plum – is not morally responsible for his heinous deed, and thus he concludes that in the fourth case, Plum is also not morally responsible for it. But the fourth case simply involves "ordinary" causal determination. So far as the compatibilist is unable to distinguish an uncontroversial case of lack of moral responsibility from a case involving ordinary causal determination, compatibilism must be rejected (according to Pereboom).

Over the years, I've struggled with how best to reply. He refers to one of these attempts, in which I argue that Professor Plum is morally responsible in all four cases, but not blameworthy in Cases 1 and 2, in virtue of the manipulative interventions in these cases. I then maintain that Plum is morally responsible and blameworthy in Cases 3 and 4 and thereby defend compatibilism. With my strategy here, all four cases involve moral responsibility, but we might be confused because the first two do not involve blameworthiness. Pereboom dismisses this response because he contends that it is impossible to be morally responsible, but not blameworthy, for a wrong action. It is indeed true that this follows from his definition of moral responsibility (in the "basic-desert sense"), but the definition is not obviously correct.

Recall a part of his definition:

> For an agent to be *morally responsible for an action in the basic desert sense* is for the action to be attributable to her in such a way that if she was sensitive to its being morally wrong, she would deserve to be blamed or punished. . .

I prefer:

> For an agent to be *morally responsible for an action in the basic desert sense* is for the action to be attributable to her in such a way that if she was sensitive to its being morally wrong, she would *prima facie* deserve to be blamed or punished. . .

On my version, one can indeed be morally responsible for doing something wrong, but not (all-things-considered) deserve to be blamed for it. Guidance control is the freedom component of moral responsibility, and moral responsibility is the "gateway" to (say) deserved blame. Someone who is morally responsible for a wrong action may not be (all-things-considered) deserving of blame because of the causal history of his action. (One such causal history is Professor Plum's in the first case, and another in the second.)

An individual who exhibits guidance control in doing something wrong is *eligible* for blame: she is *apt for* basic-desert blame. But it does not follow that she indeed basic-deserves blame, all things considered. A separate but related point: even if someone does in fact all things considered deserve basic-blame, it does *not* follow that it is justified, all things considered, to blame her; "desert" does not exhaust the reasons for justifiably blaming someone. "Apt for desert of blame" is only *part* of "desert of blame," and "deserves to be blamed" is only *part* of "ought, all things considered, to be blamed."

So I do not accept Pereboom's critique of this response to the Four Case Argument. I see no reason to accept Pereboom's definition of moral responsibility in the basic desert sense for acting wrongly, rather than mine. Upon careful reflection, I hold that mine is the more plausible account – more faithful to the complex phenomena pertinent to moral responsibility, blameworthiness, and blame. An important data point is that it allows for moral responsibility, but not blameworthiness, for a wrong action; I believe this is intuitively correct.

It is helpful to consider an additional response. It is always good to have a Plan B. My definition of guidance control has two elements: reasons-responsiveness and ownership. An agent exhibits guidance control (and thus the freedom component of moral responsibility) insofar as she acts from her own, moderately reasons-responsive mechanism. In Pereboom's discussion he leaves out the ownership condition, but this is absolutely crucial to my analysis of manipulation arguments in general, and the Four Case Argument, in particular. In this strategy of response to the argument, I would contend that Plum is *not* morally responsible in Cases 1 and 2, because the mechanisms that issue in his actions are not *his own*. This is intuitively the case, and it also follows from my account of ownership. Recall that an agent makes a mechanism her own by taking responsibility for it; she takes (or perhaps acquires) control by taking responsibility. Plum has *not* taken responsibility for the manipulation-mechanisms in the first two cases, but I would argue that he *has* taken responsibility for the action-producing mechanisms in the third and fourth. Thus, it is open for me to contend that the four adjacent cases are *not* indistinguishable. Case 3 is different from Case 2, and thus we need not assimilate Cases 1 and 4.

Here and elsewhere, I have offered a general strategy for responding to manipulation arguments, not just Pereboom's: either the manipulation removes ownership or reasons-responsiveness (Fischer 2016b, 2021). In either case the intended assimilation of responsibility-undermining and responsibility-conferring causal sequences is unsuccessful. In his important book, *Elbow Room*, Daniel Dennett (1984) described the various manipulation scenarios as "intuition-pumps" that are designed to scare us into accepting a spurious assimilation of them to causal determination per se. He suggested we needn't take the nefarious neurosurgeons, secret puppet-masters, etc., seriously. Although I agree with Dennett's resistance to the problematic assimilation, I *do* take the hypothetical examples seriously and seek an explanation of the differences between the "bugbear" examples (in Dennett's term) and ordinary causal determination. Guidance control, with its two elements (ownership and reasons-responsiveness), figures centrally in this explanation.

Allow me to step back and sketch a picture of the overall dialectic. I argued in my initial essay that there are considerable advantages of compatibilism. I think they establish a strong prima facie case for compatibilism, and, indeed, my particular version of it: semicompatibilism. This is my offense, but I also have to play defense, and this involves addressing legitimate and pressing objections. Pereboom has sharpened one of the traditional worries for compatibilism stemming from manipulation, and he deserves kudos for this. I believe, however, that my defense has been strong enough to keep compatibilism in the game, so to speak. After all, if the argument for a doctrine is strong, then all the defense has to do is produce a stalemate.

The Four Case Argument is a puzzle. Puzzles challenge us, and often help us to sharpen our views. Sometimes we think we have discovered a solution, and in other cases we might conclude there is none (or, at least, not yet). But are we really going to give up a powerfully appealing theory of freedom and responsibility based on a puzzle? Is it not necessary to engage directly with the arguments *for* compatibilism, showing why its proponents fall short of offering persuasive considerations in its favor? It is as though Pereboom and some proponents of similar views take it that the central and most (if not only) important issue in the evaluation of compatibilism is what exactly one wants to say about the Four Case Argument, but this is surely a distortion of the dialectic.

Pereboom's hard incompatibilism implies that causal determinism is incompatible with "basic-desert responsibility," and indeterminism most probably is as well. Thus, in his view, we almost certainly do not have basic-desert moral responsibility. We therefore must eliminate the retributive and punitive elements of our responsibility practices, including both our attitudes and our behavior in interpersonal relationships and our treatment of criminals (even the most heinous and cruel). He adopts a certain kind of "forward-looking" theory of moral responsibility: a public heath quarantine model, also defended by Gregg Caruso (Caruso 2021; Dennett and Caruso 2021).

The idea that we lack genuine free will and thus also robust moral responsibility, incorporating retributive elements, is not new, but Pereboom's argumentation is resourceful and ingenious. I am not, however, convinced. As indicated by the arguments in my initial chapter laying out and defending compatibilism, I am unpersuaded that we cannot reconcile either causal determinism or indeterminism (or both) with the freedom implicated in moral responsibility: guidance control. I do not suppose my arguments are knockdown, and reasonable people can, and do, disagree with my conclusions. (See some of the arguments of my interlocutors in this book!) But I hold that I've provided a strong prima facie case for compatibilism (and, indeed, semicompatibilism). On my view, there is no need to give up robust, basic-desert moral responsibility. That's my story, and I'm sticking to it.

In discussing Pereboom's replacements for desert-based attitudes and practices, I'll focus on our treatment of criminals, rather than the role of indignation, resentment, and moral anger (as well as gratitude, respect, and love) in interpersonal relationships more generally. Simply put: I find the public-health quarantine model unappealing and intuitively jarring. There is a legitimate and, indeed, crucial role for moral anger and retributive punishment. Although Pereboom's forward-looking model is aimed in part at preventing further crimes, it does not give sufficient and appropriate attention to those who have already been victimized. The fact is that victims and their families are typically horrified by the crimes in question, and frequently harbor lifelong anger and resentment. They often attend – every day – long trials of the offenders. They wait years and even decades for justice (as they see it) to be done and hold firmly that they cannot achieve "closure" until this is accomplished. I seriously doubt that they (most of them) accept the idea that this justice involves only quarantine and other nonpunitive measures.

The anger, pain, and resentment can in some instances diminish or even flicker out entirely, but for many, this is not so. It is plausible that their anger has a basic-desert presupposition: they believe the offender basic-deserves the anger and associated punishment. I claim their reactions are not just natural but also morally unobjectionable.

Consider also, just for one example of too many horrifying events in our troubled nation, the parents and families of the students killed at Sandy Hook. Recall that, in addition to the unspeakable loss of their beloved children, the Sandy Hook parents have had to endure the hateful diatribes of the radical right-wing demagogue Alex Jones and his many followers. *Stop and think empathetically about them and their deep sorrow.*

Would you think (or rehearse silently in your mind), "I get it – we are human beings and it is natural to want to 'strike back.' But I implore you, or at least invite you, to forswear your anger and take a more enlightened, humane attitude. The murderers will be quarantined. Alex Jones will be fined heavily, and significant sums of money will be extracted from him, if they can be found. The purpose of our punishment will not be to inflict any sort of suffering (*he doesn't basic-deserve that*), but to protect all of us and perhaps achieve moral improvement." Could you really think these things, even if you didn't articulate them? Yet, as far as I can see, Pereboom's approach to moral responsibility implies just these sorts of thoughts.

Although it might at first seem more humane than a basic-desert-based retributive approach, the public-health quarantine model is only asymmetrically humane: the criminal's interests are attended to, but not the victim's. How is this humane or progressive? Thinking carefully about victims, and perhaps reading their victim-impact statements, can reveal a significant empathy gap in the Pereboom/Caruso model. Given that many, if not most, of the victims of violent crimes are poor and members of racial and ethnic groups that have experienced significant injustice in our society, it is *not progressive* either. In standing up for the victim, we speak truth to power. Further, moral anger and even rage might well be the only, or best, way to fight social injustice (Cherry 2021).

Pereboom's theory also implies that, for example, Vladimir Putin does not basic-deserve to be blamed and punished extremely harshly for what he has done: Putin does not deserve to be blamed and punished, simply in virtue of what he has done freely while capable of grasping the wrongness of his actions. If Hitler had been captured, he could not legitimately have been blamed and punished (in backward-looking senses) for what he had done. This result, which applies quite generally, and not just to the most heinous moral monsters, is jarring and a very big problem, in my view.

In a fanciful and extremely improbable hypothetical scenario in which we were fully convinced that a sequestered Putin has realized the horrendous wrongness and monstrous nature of his prior behavior and we are similarly convinced he will never do it again, he would have to be released! At least I don't see anything in the public-health quarantine model that would preclude this. Same, of course, retrospectively with Hitler, or, again, any other heinous (or even just bad) criminal.

These implications are, in my view, defeaters. There is, nevertheless, much – a very great deal – in Pereboom's work, and, in particular, his forward-looking approach to punishment, that is illuminating and appealing. He shows how such an approach to punishment, and more generally to the attitudes involved in interpersonal relationships, can capture almost all of what we care about, while leaving behind the "dark" side of human nature (as some of the proponents of this sort of view would put it). Although many throughout history have dismissed this kind of view without much thought, Pereboom has performed the philosophical miracle of convincing all of us to take it seriously. It is a significant accomplishment.

3   Response to Vargas

Manuel Vargas has, more than anyone else, explored the methodological issues surrounding the contemporary (and traditional) debates about free will and moral responsibility. He has thus helped to provide illumination of otherwise intractable theoretical conflicts, leading to potential progress.

One might distinguish a *first-order* theory of such phenomena as free will and moral responsibility from a *metaphilosophical* thesis, such as "revisionism." I am in substantial agreement with Vargas at both the first-order and meta-levels. Let's start with the meta-level thesis of revisionism. As it is important, I will reproduce part of a paragraph from Vargas's initial essay:

> If I am right that no standard account of free will can coherently capture all the conflicting aspects of everyday thinking about free will, then there is a trivial sense in which every account of free will is tacitly revisionary. However, a theory of moral responsibility is explicitly revisionary if it proposes an account of free will that takes itself to conflict with commonsense views about free will; such a theory proposes abandonment of some element in ordinary, widespread convictions about free will.

He goes on to write:

> My account is revisionary about the concept of free will because I think important strands of ordinary thought are as libertarians have said.

Vargas maintains that much of common sense about free will contains libertarian views about the importance of free will in the sense of freedom to do otherwise (regulative control) to moral responsibility, the fixed past and laws conception of such freedom (as encoded in the Consequence Argument), an indeterministic sourcehood requirement for moral responsibility, etc. His account is revisionary in that he thinks these views are false, and he develops a compatibilist account of free will (and moral responsibility) based on their functions, not their essences.

On Vargas's definition, my theory of the central ideas – free will and moral responsibility – is explicitly revisionary. Nice to be in the club! I concede that the "garden of forking paths" model of moral responsibility, according to which it requires freedom to do otherwise (regulative control), is pervasive and a deep part of our way of conceptualizing both the forward-looking and the backward-looking aspects of agency: practical reasoning and moral responsibility. Nonetheless, I argue that the Frankfurt-style cases at least *point us* in a different direction, according to which we do *not* need regulative control for practical reasoning or moral responsibility. Even if they are not part of a *decisive* argument for an actual-sequence model of responsibility, I contend they provide a strong prima facie case and they can be supplemented by additional considerations on behalf of such a model. It is appealing and plausible that moral responsibility is a matter of how we walk down our path, not whether there are other paths available to us.

My theory of moral responsibility holds that the required freedom is guidance, not regulative, control. I thus explicitly depart from a central view of commonsense and even more refined theorizing and thus count as an explicit revisionist. I do not, however, depart entirely from our ordinary analytical framework for freedom and responsibility. I am willing to take seriously, and am inclined to accept, the Consequence Argument, with its fixed past and fixed laws constraint. I am confident we are morally responsible agents (but for special impairments), and this significant status should not hang on a thread – should not depend on the deliverances of the theoretical physicists.

I suppose I'm a "conservative explicit revisionist," rather than a revolutionary one. My approach is to construct an overall theory that gives *both* the central libertarian and compatibilist intuitions their place. I distinguish regulative from guidance control, and argue that it is not unreasonable to understand regulative control as the power to add to the past, holding the laws of nature fixed. I thereby am open to accepting a central libertarian tenet. But I argue that guidance control, the freedom implicated in moral responsibility, does not require regulative control, and, further, it embodies an owned reasons-responsiveness consistent with causal determinism.

In my framework, I do not reject or explain away our libertarian views, but "find a place" for both these and our compatibilist views. They are not in fact in conflict. In contrast to Vargas, who seems to me more of a revolutionary revisionist, I contend that our libertarian and compatibilist views are true in their respective places. I thus do not have to "throw out" what Vargas refers to as "vast swaths" of folk thinking about freedom and responsibility. Here's a google-map of this philosophical terrain, Free Will Land: Robert is a conservative, I'm a conservative explicit revisionist, Manuel a revolutionary explicit revisionist, and Derk is, well, an emigrant.

Turning to the first-order account of moral responsibility, we both hold that moral responsibility consists, in large part, in a kind of reasons-responsiveness with two components: the capacity to recognize relevant reasons, and to react to such reasons. Further, we both hold that such capacities are compatible with causal determinism. I should note that Vargas's "meta" views about the purposes of attributions of moral responsibility and holding ourselves and others responsible are entirely consistent with my guidance control model. They are both insightful and a potentially helpful supplementation to the intuition-based methodology on which I largely rely. Vargas also agrees with me about the central role of moral anger in moral responsibility, and he provides a sophisticated explanation and defense of it. Again, his thoughtful and penetrating discussion provides a helpful supplement to my intuition-based approach.

Vargas writes, "I think the free will we have is different from the free will we imagine ourselves to have, as I think we have false beliefs about what free will is." He takes this view to differentiate him from me, but we need to parse the claim carefully. I take "free will" to be a term used in different ways in different contexts. It might be called an "umbrella term," with lots under the umbrella. I think it is useful to think of free will as the freedom required for moral responsibility, but there are two conceptions of such freedom: regulative and guidance control. I think we generally have true beliefs about regulative control (it requires an extension of the actual past, holding the natural laws fixed, and it is plausible to think it is incompatible with causal determinism), but some false beliefs about guidance control (it requires regulative control and indeterministic sourcehood). So I *do* believe that at least *some* important commonsense views about free will are false, while maintaining that many are true in their proper domains.

He writes, "Unlike Fischer, I tend to think that the kind of 'reasons-responsiveness' that matters is at the level of agents, not subagential mechanisms." There is a thriving philosophical "industry" maintaining that my mechanism-based approach is to be jettisoned on behalf of an agent-based reasons-responsiveness model. I think the debate is much ado about, well, not very much. This is because one can go back and forth between considering reasons-responsiveness of the agent and of the mechanism. For example, one can say that an *agent* is reasons-responsive *in virtue of* acting from her own reasons-responsive mechanism. We can do the translation without changing the implications of the resulting views.

Observe that we often attribute a property to an individual in virtue of a part of the individual's having that very property (or a related one). On a certain sort of account of knowledge, we say a person knows that p so far as her belief-producing mechanism is "evidence-sensitive." We might also say that the individual herself is evidence-sensitive, in virtue of her belief-producing mechanism having that property. There is no bar to saying that a person is reasons-responsive so far as her own choice/action-producing mechanism is, if one wishes to speak the language of agents, rather than mechanisms. The bottom line for me is that at the level of one's theory (and its claims about compatibilism, incompatibilism, etc.), the two languages are mere notational variants.

7

Response to Kane, Fischer, and Vargas

Derk Pereboom

1   Response to Kane

Let me begin by examining Robert Kane's response to the disappearing agent objection to event-causal libertarianism. I contend that it allows us to see the problem for event-causal libertarianism most directly. This objection can be successful in showing why event-causal libertarianism cannot secure responsibility-conferring control. Consider Anne, the businesswoman, who in Kane's (1996) example can either decide to stop and help the assault victim or can refrain from so deciding. The relevant causal conditions antecedent to this decision – agent-involving events or, alternatively, states of the agent – would leave it open whether this decision will occur, and she has no further causal role in determining whether it does. I contend that with the causal role of the antecedent conditions already given, whether the decision occurs is not then settled by anything about the agent – whether it be states or events in which the agent is involved or the agent herself. This fact provides a strong reason to conclude that the agent lacks the control required for being morally responsible for the decision.

   I argue that agent-causal libertarianism can be conceived as a satisfactory response to the disappearing agent objection. Agents as substance-causes can supply what is missing in event-causal libertarianism. If Anne, as substance, causes her action to stop and help, the agent is no longer missing, and an important necessary condition for basic desert moral responsibility has been met.

Four Views on Free Will, Second Edition. John Martin Fischer, Robert Kane, Derk Pereboom, and Manuel Vargas.
© 2024 John Wiley & Sons Ltd. Published 2024 by John Wiley & Sons Ltd.

Now, Kane argues (in Chapters 1 and 5) that agents are complex dynamic systems that exhibit teleological guidance control when they, through feedback loops and error correction mechanisms, converge on a goal in the face of perturbations. Such control stems from the maintenance of patterns of activity in the prefrontal cortex that represent these goals and the means to achieve them. As a result, agents, as complex dynamical systems, exercise teleological guidance control in acting. Kane views this as causation by agents, as substances, "not reducible to event causation by mental states and events alone" (Ch. 5), and that "there is thus no 'disappearing agent' problem."

I agree with Kane that on this theory as he describes it there is no disappearing agent problem. An agent-causal view of this type, he points out, might be deterministic or indeterministic. If it's deterministic, then on the basis of the manipulation argument I'd contend that free will of the sort required for basic desert moral responsibility is ruled out. If it's indeterministic, then if the theory is true, an important necessary condition for this sort of responsibility is satisfied. But for it to be true, then, as I argue in Chapter 3, the indeterminacies must exist and must be of the right sort and at the right level, and for this, barriers remain.

Still, the indeterministic version of Kane's proposed teleologically guided agent causation remains speculative. Mechanisms must exist that facilitate the "percolating up" of significant microlevel indeterminacies to the neural level. As I pointed out in Chapter 3, this issue was addressed by physicist Roger Penrose (1989, 1994) and anesthesiologist Stuart Hameroff (1998), who suggested that free will and consciousness arise through the enhancement of quantum effects within microtubules, subcellular structures internal to neurons. But this proposal is only speculative (Atmanspacher 2020), and Robert Sapolsky (2023: 218–222) makes a case against it. And as long as it remains speculative and not established, treating wrongdoers as if they have free will in the sense required for ultimate and basic desert moral responsibility, as basically deserving of the harm and pain of blame and punishment, is not justified. Justification for inflicting pain or harm must meet a high epistemic standard. If a key component of a justification for harming another is not established, then treating wrongdoings in this way is prima facie wrong (Pereboom 2001: 161; 2014: 158; Vilhauer 2009b, 2013; Caruso 2020). If indeterministic teleological agent causation is not established, then justifications of this sort are too weak for practical application.

Kane responds to Frankfurt cases, which I defend, by arguing that while agents in such cases may be morally responsible, their actions are not will-setting or self-forming choices; they are actions "that were *not* determined by our existing wills when we performed them and were such that we could have willingly done otherwise when we performed them." Frankfurt examples, he contends, do not refute the will-setting principle: agents are ultimately responsible for having the wills they express in action, only if at some times in their lives, they willingly perform certain will-setting or self-forming actions that it was causally possible at the time for them to have willingly avoided performing. But we can test Kane's proposal by imagining an agent (Ben) who has the indeterministic teleological agent causal power Kane describes, and who satisfies the will-setting principle by performing will-setting and self-forming actions at key points in his life. Let's agree that Ben would count as ultimately responsible, and basic desert responsible for many of his actions. Crucially, there are no Frankfurt setups in Ben's life. But imagine Ben 2, whose life is an exact replica of Ben's except that all of Ben's self-forming actions are now, in Ben 2's case, embedded in Frankfurt setups. The devices in these setups are never actually activated, since the necessary conditions for doing otherwise that would trigger these activations are never satisfied. Ben 2's life is exactly like Ben's from the inside, and all of Ben 2's teleologically agent-caused decisions are exactly like Ben's in their actual causal profile. Ben 2's actions differ from Ben's only counterfactually since the interventions in Ben 2's case (which are not possible in Ben's case due to the absence of Frankfurt setups) never actually occur. Is it plausible that while Ben is ultimately responsible for many of his actions, Ben 2 is ultimately responsible for none of them? Here the initial plausibility of Frankfurt's argument, I think, remains in force.

2   Response to Fischer

Fischer contends that incompatibilist conditions on moral responsibility would be difficult or impossible to satisfy, and that it makes sense to prefer a compatibilist account whose conditons are clearly satisfied. My response begins with the intuitive claim that if an action is produced by way of a deterministic process that traces back to causal factors beyond the agent's control, then she will not be morally responsible for it in the basic desert sense. If an agent decides to commit a crime, but this decision is produced in this deterministic way, it is strongly intuitive that she is not basically deserving of painful blame or punishment for this decision. To be sure, one should regard this intuition just as a starting point, and as potentially defeasible. However, the four-case manipulation argument (Pereboom 1995, 2001: 110–127, 2014: 71–103) strengthens the force of this intuition, and my justification for denying compatibilism is based on this argument. The incompatibilist conditions on agency are indeed very difficult to meet. Arguably, we would need to be agent-causes – we would require the power, as substances, to cause decisions without being causally determined to cause them – and the likelihood that we have this power is far from established. But it is the arguments that lead us to such a requirement, and I don't think that we should be strongly motivated to reject it simply by the unattractiveness of the result in skepticism about moral responsibility. At the same time, I have tried to show that this position is not nearly as unattractive as it might initially appear to be.

I see the plausibility of incompatibilism as tied to the success of the manipulation argument. In Fischer's (2004) objection to this argument he contends that Plum in Case 2 is morally responsible, but not blameworthy. In his response, he embellishes the claim that judgments of moral responsibility and judgments of blameworthiness and praiseworthiness are connected but distinct − "two separate but obviously related moments in our evaluation of behavior." Fischer's idea is that if an agent is legitimately judged morally responsible, he is then *eligible* to be judged blameworthy, but further considerations must be brought to bear before a judgment of blameworthiness is legitimate. I agree: once it is settled that an agent is morally responsible, it then needs to be determined whether what he did was wrong, and whether he understood that it was wrong, and if he did not, whether he could have or should have understood that it was. But if it is settled that he is morally responsible for the action in the sense at issue in the debate, and that it was wrong and he understood that it was, then I claim that it is entailed that he is blameworthy for it (Pereboom 2014: 89–91).

I contend that, in general, an agent's being blameworthy for an action is entailed by his being morally responsible for it in the sense at issue in the debate, together with his understanding that the action was in fact morally wrong. This is because for an agent to be morally responsible for an action in the sense at issue is for the action to be attributable to her in such a way that if she were sensitive to its being morally wrong, she would deserve to be blamed or punished in a way that she would experience as painful or harmful, and if she were sensitive to its being morally exemplary, she would deserve to be praised or rewarded in a way that she would experience as pleasurable or beneficial. The desert at issue here is basic in the sense that the agent, to be morally responsible in this sense, would deserve the pain or harm, the pleasure or benefit, just by virtue of having performed the action with sensitivity to its moral status, and not, for example, by virtue of consequentialist or contractualist considerations. Assuming this characterization, and Plum's understanding that killing White is morally wrong, he could not be morally responsible for committing this murder without also being blameworthy for it.

Let me reiterate that there are other senses of "moral responsibility," and the thought that an agent be morally responsible for an action, understand that what he did was wrong, and yet not be blameworthy could be understood with reference to one of these senses. An agent could be morally responsible in the forward-looking sense I endorse; it would then be legitimate to expect him to respond to such questions as: "Why did you decide to do that?" and "Do you think it was the right thing to do?" and to evaluate critically what his decisions and actions indicate about his moral character with a view to its future formation. An intuition that Plum can be morally responsible without being blameworthy might be explained by his being responsible in this sense while not being blameworthy. But while this may be a bona fide notion of moral responsibility, it is not the one at issue in the free will debate. For incompatibilists would not find our being morally responsible in this sense to be even prima facie incompatible with determinism. The notion that incompatibilists do believe to be incompatible with determinism is rather the one defined in terms of basic desert. If one wanted to pursue Fischer's strategy, one would need to specify a sense of moral responsibility that is plausibly the one at issue in the debate, and that allows for Plum not to be blameworthy while he is morally responsible and understands that his action is morally wrong.

The four-case manipulation argument serves to draw attention to the deterministic causes of action that would be present if determinism were true, but which would nonetheless typically be hidden from us. Spinoza observed "people believe themselves free because they are conscious of their actions, but are ignorant of the causes by which they are determined" (Spinoza 1667/1985: 440). In his response, Fischer (2007) contends that we can make a distinction between two kinds of hidden causes, the first of which impairs responsibility, while the second does not. The first kind interferes with the normal functioning of mechanisms, while the second "is simply the set of constituents of the overt properties – these are the more specific or concrete ways in which the overt properties are instantiated." So, plausibly, our beliefs, desires, efforts of will, and decisions are instantiated in the neural structure of the brain. Fischer would contend that if the brain is functioning properly, the neural instantiation of properly reasons-responsive deliberation and action will not threaten our intuitive judgments of moral responsibility, even if the neural structure were governed by deterministic laws.

Fischer's key claim is that hidden causes of the second sort pose no threat to moral responsibility even if they are governed by deterministic laws. I disagree, and I base this judgment on the manipulation argument, and, more generally, my case against compatibilism rests on the strength of that argument. If the objection Fischer advances indicates that this argument is in fact unsound, I would agree that hidden causes of the second sort fail to imperil moral responsibility.

All of that said, I think that the forward-looking sense of moral responsibility can be retained, and that it may well be that Fischer's notion of guidance control, developed in terms of reasons-responsiveness, yields the most promising account of this sort of responsibility. The ability to do otherwise would not explain how an agent might be morally responsible in this sense. What would explain it is the agent's capacity to appreciate the reasons for action that are present in the situation, and her ability to act in accord with these reasons.

Causal determinism, and I suspect, any sort of indeterminism that is likely to be true, are compatible with our being morally responsible in this sense. So I can agree with Fischer on the following claim: his theory of moral responsibility – guidance control spelled out in terms of reasons-responsiveness – provides the most promising account of what might be the most significant sense of moral responsibility that can be retained given the best philosophical arguments and the best scientific theories we have about the physical world.

Against the antiretributivism about treatment of criminals that I defend, Fischer cites the strength of retributive intuitions, specifically those of victims and those who sympathize with them, in favor of harsh treatment in cases of egregious wrongdoing. One objection to this type of justification is that the retributivist sentiments invoked may well have an origin in vengeful desires, and if so, retribution may inherit a concern for vengeance as a reason for punishing (Pereboom 2001: 160–161; 2014: 158–159). Vengeful desires do not aim at a good other than the pleasure of their satisfaction. In this respect, such desires are like the desires of bullies and sadists to inflict pain. Such desires also, in themselves, aim at no good other than the pleasure of their satisfaction, and for this reason acting on them is at least prima facie wrong. Vengeful desires do not seem relevantly different from such desires, and so acting on them would also be prima facie wrong.

Another objection derives from the limited justifiable purview of the state. Would that role include inflicting on criminals basically deserved pain or harm? The legitimate functions of the state are generally agreed to include protection from harm and providing a framework for constructive human interaction. These functions support a treatment of criminals justified by the aim of the prevention of crime. But they have no direct connection to the objective of apportioning punishment in accord with basic desert. In addition, what if, by analogy, the state set up institutions devoted to fairly distributing rewards on the grounds of basic desert? Wouldn't retributivism generalize so that the state would have as much reason to reward morally impressive behavior as to punish criminal behavior (Pereboom 2014: 159–160; 2021a: 82; 2024)?

Against harsh treatment justified retributivistically, I've argued against Fischer that disagreement among retributivists about the strength of retributivist reasons places a limit on the severity of punishment that can be justified in this way (Pereboom 2024). Michael Moore (1987) is an example of a retributivist who maintains that retributive reasons for punishment are very strong. He has argued for what David Brink (2021) calls "pure retributivism," according to which retributive reasons are necessary and sufficient for punishment whose severity is proportional to the severity of the crime. If someone has committed a crime and is aware that what he did was wrong, retributive reasons are sufficient to justify punishing him in proportion to his wrongdoing, and also necessary, so that in absence of retributive reasons, punishment would not be justified. But for Michael McKenna, Shaun Nichols, Tim Scanlon, and Dana Nelkin retributive reasons exist but are considerably weaker.

McKenna (2020, 2021) cites the need to meet the high epistemic standard demanded by justifications of harming in the face of arguments for free will skepticism, the concern that many criminals are mentally ill, and the countervailing value of compassion. His conception of the strength of retributive reasons differs from Moore's in that for him retributive reasons are typically not sufficient to justify proportional punishment, while they yet justify some punishment. Nichols (2013) considers the fact that retribution faces a competing consideration: "*ceteris paribus*, it's wrong to harm others," which for him is sufficient to rule out applying retributive reasons in support of the serious harming involved in criminal incarceration or the death penalty. For Scanlon (2013), retributive reasons are even weaker. While there is basic desert for wrongdoing, the most it can justify is the withdrawal of good will. For Nelkin (2019), retributive reasons are never sufficient on their own to justify punishing wrongdoers. Rather, they can alone provide a supplement to other reasons for punishment. The state's proper function in criminal justice includes deterring crime, but punishment justified on general deterrence grounds is subject to the manipulative use objection. Yet as long as criminals basically deserve punishment of a particular severity, in Nelkin's view it may be legitimate to recruit that punishment to the service of general deterrence.

Accordingly, an impressive number of prominent retributivists advocate a conception that tends toward the minimal. This variation among defenders of retributive reasons indicates that it is not clear how strong these reasons would be as reasons for punishment. At this point we can again point to the high epistemic standard for justifying harm, this time under the supposition that retributivism is defensible. Punishment inflicts harm, and justification for harm must meet a high epistemic standard. If it is a serious open question whether one's justification for harming another is unsound, then there is a strong reason for regarding that behavior as wrong, and for refraining from engaging in it. With this variation regarding strength of retributivist reasons among retributivists themselves, the epistemic standard counsels that in applying retributivism to criminal justice we should count those reasons as weak. Views on which they are strong, and justify harsh treatment, do not meet the standard.

3   Response to Vargas

Manuel Vargas has us turn our attention to what in our ordinary conception of free will and moral responsibility should be revised, and what should be retained – a recommendation that yields a valuable perspective on the debate. His diagnosis is that our ordinary conception of free will has a significant incompatibilist component, and his advice, in effect, is that this component should be revised to make it compatibilist. I would endorse this advice if it were specified that our conception of moral responsibility, which in my view has the basic desert sense as a significant component, were revised to eliminate it in favor of a forward-looking notion with objectives such as moral formation, reconciliation in relationships, and protection against wrongdoing. Vargas emphasizes that the desert component of our conception can be retained if it were revised or specified as nonbasic desert, where the desert claims are more fundamentally justified by forward-looking goals. I am more skeptical than he is that nonbasic desert provides the best way to achieve the forward-looking goals.

As I explain in Chapter 3, I think there are two main controversies in historical free will debate: first, whether we have free will MR, where the moral responsibility at issue is the basic desert sense, and whether it is compatible with determinism and with the indeterministic ways the universe may turn out to be; and second, whether we have free will AP, the availability of alternative possibilities, the ability to do otherwise, and whether it is compatible with causal determinism. As I point out elsewhere (Pereboom 2022a), there are yet other notions of free will in the historical debate, such as free will in the sense of the ability to act rationally, or in such a way as to be responsive to reasons. But whether we have free will in that sense has never been controversial. I don't think that one can discern these notions of free will by conceptual analysis, but rather by examining the historical debate. My aim in characterizing free will has been to secure the notions of free will whose existence people have in fact been debating.

Vargas has a different approach: to find the notion of free will that we actually have and that has the functional role that "free will" has in the relevant human practice. More specifically, "(i) it captures a wide swath of ordinary thought and talk (i.e. it makes good on the truiss), (ii) it explains how these things could be true, (iii) it informatively explains a web of phenomena surrounding that thought and talk, and (iv) it seems to be true, given everything we know about the world." I agree that this is a valuable approach. He then proposes that free will is "the situational ability to suitably recognize and appropriately respond to relevant normative considerations." Note that whether we have free will in this sense is not in dispute. What emerges from my own view is that the ability we actually have with that functional role is the control in action required to be morally responsible in the forward-looking sense, I endorse. Here, Vargas and I are in close agreement, although, I'm skeptical that nonbasic desert should have the prominent place that Vargas specifies (Pereboom 2021b).

Vargas writes that "it is particularly problematic for Pereboom's project that we can successfully identify an obtainable notion of desert – nonbasic desert – that makes sense of our existing practices." Vargas (2015; cf. 2013) advocates a view according to which the practice-level justifications for blame and punishment invoke backward-looking considerations of desert, while that desert is not basic because at a higher level the practice is justified by the anticipated consequences, in his case with a focus on fostering and refining the ability to recognize and respond to moral considerations. Vargas writes, "I can allow that first-order desert claims are justified retrospectively while maintaining that, at the level of the practice, these kinds of desert claims are prospectively justified" (Vargas 2015: 2666). On this two-tier account, our practice of holding agents morally responsible in a desert sense should be retained because doing so would have the best overall consequences relative to alternative practices. Against understanding our practice in terms of basic desert, He argues that "desert judgments embedded in ordinary responsibility ascriptions are metaphysically silent on questions of whether there is a consequentialist or contractualist basis for making desert judgments. Moreover, what conceptual content they have is focused on the propriety of the responsibility-characteristic response in light of the violation of responsibility norms" (Vargas 2015: 2663; for further discussion, see Vargas 2013: 249–256).

While, as I indicate in Chapter 3, I do believe that attributions of basic desert are not compatible with determinism and certain varieties of indeterminism, I do not have a similar issue with nonbasic desert. On Vargas's conception, nonbasic desert is fundamentally grounded in forward-looking considerations that I fully endorse. Moreover, we clearly invoke nonbasic desert in our actual practices. As he points out, in various sports "a system of penalties is justified by forward-looking considerations, including protecting the health of the players, preserving enjoyment of the game, and creating constraints for innovation within the play of the game." At the same time, we correctly think of those penalties as deserved.

My hesitation about Vargas's nonbasic desert (Pereboom 2021b) is rather that it comes with a two-tier system, which, at the level of our moral psychology, insulates practitioners from the ultimate forward-looking justifications of the practice. Rules about what penalties people deserve are of necessity coarse-grained, which works well in the context of sport, but less well in the context of, for example, personal relationships. Here a sensitivity to the forward-looking aims of the practice of holding people morally responsible is best always to be kept in mind so that responses prescribed by general rules can be modified by those considerations. Accordingly, I've set out a view on which our ground-level practice of holding people morally responsible is directly sensitive to forward-looking aims such as moral formation and reconciliation and is not subject to a barrier between tiers (Pereboom 2021b). On this proposal, forward-looking considerations can also more readily motivate substantial revisions, notably to the aspects of the practice engaged to disempower and dominate others, and which enlist the angry emotions to advance that objective.

Vargas makes a strong case that his proposal for what free will is has as much continuity with previous conceptions as in certain scientific cases. I would argue, however, that the free will case, and more generally cases of philosophical notions that are hotly contested, cannot, or at least for now should not be assimilated to scientific cases. Once chemistry became established and it was determined that water was the compound H_2O, there were very quickly no seriously competing conceptions. But as the debate in this volume indicates, current participants in the free will debate are not generally ready to accept that we are debating whether we have the situational ability to suitably recognize and appropriately respond to relevant normative considerations. My guess is that we'll be debating whether we have the ability to do otherwise and the control in action for a weighty sense of moral responsibility for some time into the future. While this debate lasts, we can't think of free will solely in the way Vargas proposes, and instead we'll have to continue to extract senses of "free will" from the debate as it stands and as it develops.

Here we might draw analogies to the other two members of Kant's famous triad of concepts of practical reason: "God, freedom, and immortality." On God, it's been proposed that on a scientifically respectable conception, God is a nonsupernatural process that pervades all of reality. Suppose this conception of God captures a wide swath of ordinary thought and talk, explains how all of this could be true, informatively explains a web of phenomena surrounding that thought and talk, and seems to be true, given everything we know about the world. Suppose that in view of this "God" refers to such a process. Still, although process theology has been prominent for at least a century, it wouldn't work in contemporary debates about whether God exists to specify that "God" refers to such a process. It's still much too controversial. Similarly, one might propose that what best plays the functional role of immortality is being widely remembered. But here again, in philosophical and theological debates about immortality, specifying this conception of immortality wouldn't function well.

The diagnosis is that the role of the concepts "God," "free will," and "immortality" in contemporary philosophical debates differs from the role of the concept "water" in science. Since the 16th century, the physical sciences have developed methodologies that have led to rapid widespread agreement on a massive range of specific topics. Not so for the debates that are the purview of philosophy. We participants in those debates may have our views, for which we vigorously argue, but in those debates we're not yet at a stage to specify conceptual recommendations that are tailored to just one specific contender in the debate.

Vargas's account is revisionist in the sense that while there are incompatibilist elements in our ordinary beliefs and attitudes about free will, it recommends that we revise our concepts to eliminate these elements and replace them with compatibilist alternatives. I advocate a position that in certain respects is more strongly revisionist about our attitudes and practices than the one Vargas defends. It would, for example, result in a radical change in how we assess the reactive attitudes of resentment and indignation, subjecting them to more revision than ordinary practice would have it. True, our control over these reactive attitudes in the heat of an argument, or at the time one is personally wronged, is limited, and so in practice there might be little revision at this stage. Yet we have significant control over our expressions of these attitudes, and so here revision is practically possible. We also have the relevant sort of control when we are deciding whether to adopt a system of criminal treatment that is justifiable only on retributivist grounds, or else one that can be justified in ways consistent with hard incompatibilism.

Is my view less revisionist about folk theory than Vargas's? If folk theory is incompatibilist in the sense that I specify, then in this respect my position is not revisionist at all, while Vargas's is. But what of the proposal that we come instead to think of free will as the control condition for moral responsibility in the forward-looking sense I endorse? That might be fine, but with a caveat. I suspect that the attitudes that presuppose basic desert – retributive sentiments, for example – will always be a feature of our psychology. I maintain that we need to retain concepts that allow us to think that these attitudes may have false presuppositions, and I would oppose any revisionism that proposes to dispense with these conceptual resources. More generally, when deciding how to revise, we need to retain concepts that facilitate our thinking that some of our attitudes and beliefs may lack justification. For this reason, we require concepts that apply to moral responsibility in the basic desert sense, and the control required for it, and to the sort of control condition required for this sort of moral responsibility, even if these concepts do not correctly apply to anything real.

8

Response to Kane, Fischer, and Pereboom

Manuel Vargas

Revisionism about free will is the view that our best theory of free will, the theory we ought to accept, conflicts with elements of everyday thinking about free will. The revisionist account I favor is one that takes its cue from an idea sometimes associated with P.F. Strawson's view of responsibility, namely that our responsibility practices and our ways of thinking and talking about them are bound up in our social psychology. My account departs from his in many of the particulars, for example in emphasizing the social pressures for enabling coordination and cooperation, in emphasizing our independent interest in some control over our exposure to the risk of having our interests set back, and in the value of responsibility for shaping our agency. Unlike traditional compatibilists, including Strawson, Frankfurt, and many others, I do think that there really are – at least sometimes and among some people – genuinely libertarian elements to ordinary thinking about free will. In this, my account is closer to the convictions of libertarians.

Yet, it is a mistake to be satisfied with the thought that libertarianism could be true. Too much hinges on the thin reed of hope that future science will show that indeterminism appears in this or that felicitous place, shaped in exactly and only the ways that the libertarian needs. In the time you have been reading this volume, there are people who have been blamed, stigmatized, punished, and even condemned to death on the basis of their being free and responsible. As I will argue below, it is a deeply compromised position to hold that these practices depend on libertarianism, and that we can therefore permissibly

Four Views on Free Will, Second Edition. John Martin Fischer, Robert Kane, Derk Pereboom, and Manuel Vargas.
© 2024 John Wiley & Sons Ltd. Published 2024 by John Wiley & Sons Ltd.

continue to participate in such practices on the grounds that someday we might have evidence that vindicates our convictions. Were that our situation, rather than continue on as before, we ought to suspend our culpability-dependent practices until we have the relevant evidence.

If we are going to continue to embrace and engage in practices that presume we have free will, we need more than the hope that future science will show we were right all along. That gets us to the other prong of my revisionary proposal. Whether we should retain or abandon those practices depends on whether there is an adequate basis of justification for retaining them. On this point, I find common cause with compatibilists because I think there are theoretically and practically sound conceptions of free will that are compatible with determinism. Although they don't accurately capture the full contents of ordinary thinking about our agency, the right account of this sort gives us what we need to justify responsibility practices. It thereby earns its place as a new theoretical understanding for organizing our theories and practical lives going forward.

Unlike conventional compatibilists, though, I don't view this as an account that coheres with our everyday convictions, but as an upgrade to or replacement of our ordinary picture of free will. In putting libertarianism behind us, we do give up an important part of our self-image. To be sure, there might well be some limiting cases in which the resources afforded to us by our revisionary picture do not precisely capture all the libertarian would confidently assert regarding responsibility. Still, if the account I have offered is correct, it provides a secure foundation for the bulk of our responsibility practices and it provides an explanation of how most of ordinary thought and talk about free will and responsibility can turn out to be true, even if not in exactly the way our libertarian impulses have implied. This is enough, I insist, to allow us to resist the pressures that have driven too many to free will skepticism.

The structure of this chapter is as follows. First, I begin with some reflection on the general contours of the debate and on the way seemingly small differences in how the debate is framed or understood have far-reaching consequences for the persistence of debates about free will and the kinds of theories philosophers have produced. Second, I offer some replies to my coauthors, sometimes to make objections, sometimes to identify ongoing disagreements, and sometimes to point to places of actual or potential convergence. Last, I take up a handful of lingering general issues.

1 The Free Will Debates

Nietzsche once remarked that a philosophical system is "the personal confession of its author and a kind of involuntary and unconscious memoir" (Nietzsche 2000, BGE 6). I suppose that my convictions about free will comport with the spirit of his remarks. In part, I got to revisionism about free will after first trying out the more traditional views. However, the other part of the story for me was that I spent graduate school in two places. The first was a place where philosophers tended to think incompatibilism was not just true but *obviously* true. The second was a place where philosophers tended to think that compatibilism was obviously true, and where incompatibilism was regarded as vaguely mysterious, unmotivated, or just plain bizarre.

Philosophers disagree all the time. In this case, though, it felt like the disagreements had a different shape than many philosophical debates. Eventually, I came to think that there were differing accounts of what is at stake in this debate – that is competing accounts of both the theoretical problem itself – and differing views about how to evaluate putative solutions to the problem(s). Decades later, I am as convinced as ever that much of the apparent intractability of debates about free will is a byproduct of unarticulated presumptions about the nature of the problem, tacit but distinct convictions about methodology, and mostly submerged disagreements about what constitutes a good solution to the problem of free will.

Where many philosophers have thought it obvious that we are engaged in a single debate with mostly agreed-upon topics and stakes, I've been inclined to see this as more aspirational than actual. There are ways to regiment things so as to capture most of the central themes and concerns in the relevant philosophical literature. However, I also think that philosophical (and, for that matter, more popular) discussions of free will are littered by innocuous-seeming differences in presumptions about the framing of the issues that turn out to have significant consequences for how we have come to understand the disagreements and the theoretical options. In what follows, I try to motivate this thought.

Consider this question: What is the free will debate about? Do the authors of this volume agree on how to answer that question? There is some reason to think we do not.

In Chapter 1, Robert Kane presents the debate as one centered on whether what we do is "up to us" and whether the ultimate sources of our actions are within us. What is core to his position is the idea that "there is at least one kind of freedom that is also worth wanting and is not compatible with determinism," which he understands as "the power to be the ultimate source and sustainer to some degree of one's own ends or purposes." We need this, he thinks, to have what he calls "ultimate responsibility."

First, notice that everyone could, at least in principle, accept that the stakes involve some notion of "up-to-us-ness." Compatibilists and incompatibilists will disagree about what that notion requires, but they might agree about this as the general characterization of at least part of what is at stake. Second, notice that, as Kane frames it, our interest in this broadly metaphysical/explanatory issue is not purely theoretical. He thinks it gets a good deal of its philosophical oomph, so to speak, from its entanglement with questions of moral responsibility. This is where things begin to get a little more elusive. Consider, again, his characterization of the core of his position in terms of one-kind-of-freedom-worth-wanting, a kind not compatible with determinism. It is not obvious why compatibilists need to disagree with this sort of claim. The compatibilist could allow that there is some (by compatibilist lights, extravagant) form of freedom worth wanting and incompatible with determinism, but it is not the kind of freedom at stake in our everyday practices or that is at stake when we fight about free will and determinism.

Of course, Kane thinks that ordinary practices do implicate ultimate responsibility and the kind of freedom he defends. But that's not actually required by the way he frames his account. In light of that, two modest observations about his picture are worth highlighting: (i) on Kane's account, free will is entangled in responsibility, and (ii) we theorists can define notions of freedom and responsibility from the armchair that, at least in principle, might turn out to depart from whatever notions of responsibility are at play in our everyday practices. That we characterize something as "ultimate," "genuine," "deep," or what have you is typically a stipulative matter, and it carries the implication that this is in some or another form the proper stakes of some dispute. However, whether the stipulation latches on to our everyday interests or ordinary practices is a further issue, not one settled by substantive armchair characterizations. One can accept the value of some substantive but stipulative notion without thereby agreeing that it aptly characterizes our actual practice.

In Chapter 2, John Fischer characterizes compatibilism in terms of "some central notion of freedom" linked to "genuine, robust moral responsibility" that is compatible with causal determinism. In many ways, this way of framing the issues accords well with Kane's. Again, though, it produces a puzzle that parallels the one facing Kane's framing. That there is a form of freedom connected to our centrally shared convictions and that we do, in fact, enjoy is perfectly compatible with there being some other form of freedom, equally or even more centrally at home in our shared convictions, that we, unfortunately or not, simply lack. That is, suppose we have a genuine, robust form of moral responsibility, one that is compatible with determinism. That fact could be compatible with a discovery that we lack some other genuine, robust form of moral responsibility, perhaps one significantly implicated in our practices.

In Chapter 3, Derk Pereboom regards the debate as about whether we have the kind of free will required for responsibility that requires a specific, technical notion of desert that he calls "basic desert." He thinks we lack it, and this grounds his hard incompatibilism. In Chapter 4, I argued that Pereboom's claims about our failing to meet the conditions for basic desert responsibility are compatible with it also being true that our everyday notion of desert is either not basic or can be replaced with a nonbasic desert conception that leaves our practices unchanged in all but theoretical understanding. The big point is, again, that there seems to be slippage between the different ways the different proposals frame the debate. That slippage shapes the theoretical alternatives and it alters how we understand the relationship between everyday thought, talk, and practices of freedom and responsibility.

Of course, my distinguished coauthors could rule out the "perverse" possibilities I've identified that violate the spirit of their formulations by tightening up the letter of their respective formulations. They would undoubtedly want to reject the suggestion that their individual accounts do decouple in this way from the nature, reality, and the stakes of our practices as we find them. Even Pereboom, our representative hard incompatibilist, presumably thinks that our ordinary practices do depend in some significant way on basic desert assessments, even if the formulation of his view doesn't strictly require that it does.

The main point to which I am calling your attention, though, is the striking fact that the actual formulation of the stakes employed in those presentations seem to permit a decoupling of philosophical interests from the everyday, on-the-ground facts of our practical lives. A better strategy, one might think, is to build into the stakes of the debate our ordinary, everyday thought, talk, and practices surrounding free will and responsibility, including assessments of fault and credit, and whether we are justified in retaining them. These, one might think, are the best candidates for the stakes of the debate. On this framing, the stakes of the debate are not some stipulative notion or armchair definition, but instead the comparatively concrete question of whether we have the kind of agency or power that grounds everyday responsibility practices and their apparent authority for us. This is – surprise! – the framing I prefer and that I endorsed in Chapter 4. My proposed framing allows us to regiment the concerns of all the parties, leaves us with a substantive issue about which there are more than verbal disagreements, and makes clear the tangible stakes of the disagreement.

Over the next few sections, we'll see how some of the puzzles about framing ramify across the particulars of different accounts of free will.

2   Kane's Libertarianism

There is a lot to like about Kane's defense of libertarianism. He's thoughtful about the history of these debates and the way they connect to diverse concerns we have, and he's especially sensitive to how pictures of free will connect to our interests in self-making. Although I'm sympathetic to the intuitions that animate Kane's view, I remain unpersuaded that Kane's account gives us what we need. My concerns are both methodological and substantive.

First, the methodological issue. In Chapter 1, Kane writes that libertarians must show both that free will is incompatible with determinism and that it can be made intelligible in a way "reconciled with modern scientific views of the cosmos and of human beings." He calls this "The Intelligibility Question." I'm not convinced that even if Kane answers the Intelligibility Question, that that answer is enough to address the core issues at stake in debates about free will. One way to see this is to think about why I'm open to the possibility that we might be agents of the sort that Kane describes. (Perhaps John Fischer is, too.) That is, I agree with Kane that, for all that has been said, it might well be true that future science will vindicate his picture in whole or in part. And it might be that he is right that it is worth wanting, incompatible with determinism, and that it makes sense of moral culpability and credit. But where Kane seems to think that this would settle the case for libertarianism, I think this leaves crucial, even essential, work uncompleted.

Here's the issue: while it might be nice for all of us if we turned out to be the kinds of agents Kane describes, it doesn't show that libertarianism is our best account of free will if it turns out that it describes a sufficient but *unnecessary* picture of free will. Suppose that, as I am inclined to think, there are multiple ways to secure the justification of our ordinary thought and talk. Let's suppose Kane's libertarian account is one of them. This would be a modest kind of victory, but ultimately a pyrrhic one if it also turns out that some alternative (and let's suppose revisionary) compatibilist account is sufficient to ground our ordinary thought, talk, and practices.

This possibility is one of the things that is harder to see if one frames the theoretical ambitions of a theory of free will by stipulating some conceptual essence or definitional target of freedom and responsibility. The theorist proceeding in this broadly conceptualist mode runs the risk of decoupling the theoretical demands from the concrete phenomena of everyday life. In turn, this makes it harder to see that the resultant account, even if true enough, might not show that it is uniquely required to get the things we want from a theory of free will.

To pick just one place where this sort of worry emerges, consider Kane's objection to "fair opportunity" models of responsibility. Kane objects that causal indeterminism would leave an agent without a fair opportunity to avoid wrongdoing. This is because Kane thinks there is a notion of fairness according to which it can only be fair to blame if one had metaphysically robust alternative possibilities of the sort secured by libertarianism. However, one might worry that this misconstrues Hart's (1961) project, as well as the projects of contemporary theorists who draw inspiration from his account.

First, although we can read notions like "fair opportunity" and "causal possibility" in strict "garden of forking paths" ways, as the incompatibilist prefers, we don't have to. Recall the video game example I describe in Chapter 4, and the more general thought, gestured at there, that there are less-demanding ways of construing these notions, construals that have a familiar role in ordinary thought and talk (for a related discussion, see Pereboom in Chapter 3, Section 6).

Second, and relatedly, I contend that Hart-style opportunity-invoking proposals – proposals which I think of as of a piece with the broadly ecological picture of responsibility that I recommend (see Nelkin and Vargas, 2024) – are better understood as inviting us to consider whether there is a notion of fairness to which we can appeal that would be sufficient to ground normative practices of fault-finding. Even if there is some independent and theoretical sense, perhaps Kane's sense of unfairness, in which negative reactions to wrongdoing would be unfair under determinism, *that's not the issue with which proposals of this sort are concerned.* Instead, the issue is something like this: given some coarse-grained notion of opportunity, and within a framework of mutual justifiability of practices that enable goods of cooperation, coordination, and moral development, is it reasonable to impose liability on wrongdoers who had available to them opportunities of such-and-such shape or quality? That's the notion of fairness or equality of opportunity that is at stake in those proposals. Highlighting the existence of different concerns about fairness and more demanding modal notions of opportunity don't address the power of the Hartian approach for providing a minimally adequate grounding for culpability and credit practices like ours.

Of course, this is just the briefest of sketches, and there is more that Kane and other critics of the Hartian approach can say. I mention it here primarily to illustrate the claim I started with at the outset, that upstream framings of the methodological stakes of the debate have consequences for the significance of how we should interpret various substantive theoretical commitments. (I'll return to the issue of fairness in Section 4.)

There is a second, broadly normative concern that is connected to how one frames the burdens for a theory of free will. Recall the point I made in Chapter 4: it is not enough to show that a particular conception of free will is compatible with determinism or a broadly scientific picture of the world. Ectoplasm does not, so far as I know, conflict with any scientific features as we now know them. (Hey, maybe ectoplasm is a form of dark matter?) But suppose we had practices that involved blame, stigmatization, and punishment up to death when people acted wrongly in a way that putatively depended on mediation by ectoplasm. The mere absence of conflict with current scientific theories does not seem enough to license our ongoing engagement of those practices. That some scientists conjecture that there could be ways to make things work, in the absence of evidence that the contentious element is present at the right places and times, seems an alarming basis on which to treat people in the ways we take to be at stake in debates about free will. Why isn't Kane's position to advocate that we suspend those practices (as Pereboom recommends), with the caveat that when we have sufficient evidence to support our ongoing participation in them, we resume them? Or, why not say whether he thinks there is some alternative basis on which we can justify our ongoing participation in those practices?

When pressed on these kinds of concerns, and about whether some other account might do better as a stopgap, Kane's reply in the first edition of this book was: "Well, I don't like any of the options. Do I have to choose *now*? Can I spend a few weeks in Hawaii while I think about it?" (Kane 2007, p. 181). He doubles down on that reply in this volume as well (Chapter 5). While I can sympathize with the difficulty of this question, it has been more than a few weeks now. Scientific confirmation remains a speculative matter, and in the meantime, according to libertarians, the everyday blame, stigma, and punishment we dole out continue to depend on our having the properties identified by libertarians. This seems to me a very bad situation for the contemporary proponent of libertarianism, something we might characterize as "the objection from moral indefensibility."

Here, I should note that there are libertarians that are prepared to grant that compatibilist accounts can secure most or all our of everyday practices (as in Speak 2004). The distinctive claim of this kind of view is that libertarianism identifies an especially valuable form of freedom that we have reason to hope for, even if it isn't necessary for our everyday practices. Such views face the challenge of articulating what the sense is in which this agency would be deeper or more valuable. Even so, such views do not face the acute problem of moral indefensibility.

Turning to some substantive details of Kane's account, I will raise questions about four things: (i) the significance of indeterminism as an obstacle, (ii) Kane's current picture of indeterminism in the timing of choices, (iii) luck and timing, and (iv) the nature of the earliest self-forming actions.

First, consider Kane's insistence that indeterminism is an impediment and side effect of agency, as such, but not a constitutive element of intentionality, voluntariness, or action. The picture seems to impose an odd double burden on agents, not just that responsibility hinges on intentional, perhaps rational, voluntary action but that it must go through *impeded* intentional, rational, voluntary action. In other words, you are responsible for what you voluntarily intend only if something not in your control impedes what you are trying to do.

Let's suppose this could ground culpability. Recall the metaphilosophical issue I pressed in Section 1: it isn't enough to show that libertarian agency can be a ground of responsibility. Given the existence of serious, less demanding proposals for grounding culpability, libertarians must show that it is the unique (or a necessary) ground for the bulk of our everyday thought, talk, and practices concerning responsibility. So, the challenge here concerns why we should think an obstacle to agency is plausibly the *unique or necessary* ground for culpability, such that it can't be gotten by some other means.

Second, consider Kane's emphasis on the idea that appropriately situated indeterminism in the timing of decisions can ground responsibility. I am unpersuaded that indeterminism over the timing of a choice is the kind of freedom sought by many, whether compatibilists or incompatibilists. Indeed, Kane's discussion of the importance of self-forming and its rootedness in the psychology of agents suggests that the heavy lifting of explaining the norma-tive authority of responsibility practices (at least those sensitive to free will) is mostly a function of the agent's psychology, including the agent's understand-ing of the world and the reasons it provides, as well as the nature and value of intentional, voluntary choices. Given that these are all things available to the compatibilist as well, it is not entirely clear why an impediment should turn those things from normatively inert grounds for culpability practices into normatively authoritative grounds for those practices.

Third, even though Kane is concerned to address various kinds of luck argu-ments as they apply to his view, it remains unclear to me why the indetermin-istic timing of a choice is any less vulnerable to complaints about luck than which of two or more choices it is that an agent makes. If luck is a problem for synchronic differences, I don't see why one shouldn't think it is equally a problem for diachronic differences.

Fourth and last, consider Kane's account of the very earliest self-forming actions. He acknowledges that "the motivations among which we choose all come from sources outside ourselves, parents, society, upbringing" (Section 24). He says several plausible things about this phenomenon, including that it has a probing or learning character, and that it gradually builds up into an accu-mulation of more robust character and purposes. He rightly notes that given this cumulative picture of agential authority, informed freedom, and responsi-bility, parents ought not hold young children fully responsible in their early formative years.

The puzzle here is not about the gradual accumulation of responsibility, but about the idea that there is *any quantum* of freedom and responsibility at the earliest point. I'd like to hear more about why, if one has freedom and responsibility in any measure at all in that first putative instance, this doesn't just give up incompatibilism's ghost. The picture seems to entail that one can get nonzero freedom and responsibility without the structures that Kane oth-erwise requires for responsibility. If that's right, it isn't clear why we shouldn't understand this picture of agency to provide the building blocks for an entirely compatibilist account of responsibility. That there is any responsibil-ity there at all seems to be to admit that responsibility doesn't require the emergent libertarian powers postulated by Kane. And, if one thinks that our downstream character, dispositions, and choices are parasitic on the effects of those early stage probings – which are themselves contingent outputs of parents, society, and upbringing – it seems to move the operative ground for responsibility away from some distinctive story about the metaphysics of causation and into the compatibilist-friendly territory of some bit of psychology that speaks for the agent or is suitably connected to the agent's rational or evaluative commitments.

3   Fischer, Semicompatibilism, and Revisionism

I've long admired and been substantially influenced by Fischer's work, so I was particularly gladdened by his assessment of the ways in which our views have come to substantially converge. As Fischer notes, we either agree or have mostly compatible first-order or substantive theoretical commitments. My functionalist and instrumentalist approach and his intuition-based accounts provide compatible and potentially complementary accounts of responsibility. On the matter of the issues that separate revisionist theorizing from conventional theories, Fischer graciously signals something that might surprise some readers:

> On Vargas's definition, my theory of the central ideas – free will and moral responsibility – is explicitly revisionary. Nice to be in the club! I concede that the "garden of forking paths" model of moral responsibility, according to which it requires freedom to do otherwise (regulative control), is pervasive and a deep part of our way of conceptualizing both the forward-looking and the backward-looking aspects of agency: practical reasoning and moral responsibility. . ...
>
> My theory of moral responsibility holds that the required freedom is guidance, not regulative, control. I thus explicitly depart from a central view of common-sense and even more refined theorizing and thus count as an explicit revisionist. I do not, however, depart entirely from our ordinary analytical framework for freedom and responsibility. I am willing to take seriously, and am inclined to accept, the Consequence Argument, with its fixed past and fixed laws constraint. (Chapter 6, Section 3)

It seems that we are closer to three views on free will these days. (Perhaps Pereboom might yet be talked into getting us down to two in a third edition of this book? I feel we are close!)

I'd rather celebrate our convergences than to fixate on differences, but the latter is more in keeping with contemporary philosophical norms. So in what follows I say a bit about what strikes me as the points of separation between us – less as matters of disagreement than opportunities for further convergence.

Fischer writes:

> I suppose I'm a "conservative explicit revisionist," rather than a revolutionary one. My approach is to construct an overall theory that gives *both* the central libertarian

and compatibilist intuitions their place. . . . In my framework, I do not reject or explain away our libertarian views, but "find a place" for both these and our compatibilist views. They are not in fact in conflict. In contrast to Vargas, who seems to me more of a revolutionary revisionist, I contend that our libertarian and compatibilist views are true in their respective places. I thus do not have to "throw out" what Vargas refers to as "vast swaths" of folk thinking about freedom and responsibility (Chapter 6, Section 3)

On this issue, I think there is less daylight between our views than does Fischer. Given that Fischer thinks that the folk views invoke regulative control, and that guidance control is a re-engineering of folk concepts (see Chapter 3, Section 7), then it seems he must join me in holding that large swaths of folk thinking are either to be revised or dismissed in our construction of philosophical theories. So, I think we're in the same boat on that point, but I also think that's an okay result for revisionists. Membership has its privileges, and one feature of explicitly adopting a revisionary position on these matters is that one can lean into the recognition that practices can remain in good standing even if we have had erroneous beliefs about why that is so.

One place where I'll mark some uncertainty about the relationship of our views concerns what it means to "find a place" for libertarian intuitions, and what this means for revisionism as opposed to semicompatibilism. These issues may be linked. If one thinks, as I do, that we do well to think of free will as the minimal kind of agency, power, or capacity required to ground practices of culpability and credit then the way to understand libertarian intuitions are as intuitions about that. Contingent upon understanding free will that way, it is not clear that Fischer's revisionist semicompatibilism finds a place for libertarian intuitions that is any different from my revisionist compatibilism.

As I understand it, on neither Fischer's account nor on mine do those intuitions, powerful as they are, properly underpin a prescriptive theory of free will (understood in the general sense I have suggested). Nor do they ground an account of culpability/credit (i.e. moral responsibility). So far as I can tell, all parties can acknowledge that many of us, at least sometimes and in some contexts, have powerful incompatibilist convictions and that layperson convictions about the ability to do otherwise, free will, and moral responsibility sometimes appeal to these convictions.

One contrasting case here is Mele's (1995) "agnostic autonomism," which is neutral on compatibility debates but offers both a compatibilist and an incompatibilist theory of free will. Mele's approach seems to me to provide a place for incompatibilist intuitions in a way different way than does my proposal. Fischer is not prepared to adopt Mele's strategy either, I take it.

If we agree on the substance, what disagreement there is may simply be about the best way to frame these convictions. Fischer frames semicompatibilism as a position that "side steps" contentious debates about regulative control and what Pereboom dubs "free will AP" in exchange for a focus specifically on responsibility (Chapter 3, Section 7). That is, Fischer's semicompatibilism is silent about free will, and offers an account, instead, only of responsibility.

As a sociological matter, I am very sympathetic to the idea that the semicompatibilist framing helped focus attention on an important space of possibilities for the literature. It was, in effect, a bridge notion that helped focus attention more directly on the conditions for moral responsibility. It may continue to be ideal as a gateway to accepting commitments we agree upon. That said, I am inclined to think an explicitly revisionist framing is advantageous in at least one way, namely it frontloads Fischer's substantive commitments, given his revisionism.

If we construe free will in terms of the minimal kind of agency, power, or capacity required to ground practices of culpability and credit, as many do, then, prescriptive compatibilists about responsibility (including Fischer) must reject incompatibilist accounts of free will thus construed. That is, if one frames free will in a responsibility-centric way, then the semicompatibilism framing doesn't do much work for a (prescriptive) compatibilist. Given compatibilism's regular tarring as a kind of subterfuge, I think we do better to be forthright that we recognize libertarian intuitions but reject their authority for our theorizing about responsibility and – depending on how one understands its conceptual role – free will.

4   Pereboom's Hard Incompatibilism

Free will skepticism is the stone that sharpens all the other positions, and Pereboom's pathbreaking and careful development of the view have made it much clearer what the stakes and options are in debates about free will. I believe there are good reasons for regarding hard incompatibilism as a position of last resort, and good reason for thinking we are at some remove from positions of last resort.

Two issues seem especially salient to me. First, there are the methodological issues that arise from specifying the stakes of free will in some way that allows for the possibility that our theoretical constructions detach from everyday praise and blame practices, which I argue are the most important philosophical stakes. It seems to me that the basic desert approach employed by Pereboom runs afoul of this problem, in that it stipulates a notion of desert at stake in debates about free will and moral responsibility. While there are plausibly other notions of free will that have mattered in the literature, independent of the practical interests I have identified, I think there is good reason to think that for most of those notions (causal origination, the ability to do otherwise, etc.)

the interest in these things is robustly parasitic on responsibility and only superficially independent. That is, if you scratch a metaphysician, a concerned responsibility theorist bleeds.

Second, and more substantively, Pereboom needs an explanation of why moral anger and retribution require specifically basic desert, as opposed to *some* notion of desert, perhaps of a nonbasic variety (see also McCormick 2022: 143). At least in Chapter 3, Pereboom seems to assume that the absence of basic desert only leaves us with resources for forward-looking components of a responsibility practice (e.g. Section 4); in Chapter 7 he grants the possibility of nonbasic desert doing the work I suggest, but he thinks we do better with a purely forward-looking account responsibility with no backward-looking desert elements.

On this latter matter, I'll make three brief observations. First, there is some sense in which it is an open question about what system of responsibility practices does the best job at securing our interests. I've suggested some reasons for thinking backward-looking culpability practices are important for cooperation and coordination, and that they have a special role in shaping sensibilities and being practicable at scale in a wide range of contexts, which can include personal and impersonal relations. Pereboom has suggested that some relationships do best with only forward-looking justification at the fore. It seems to me the former is a better model than the latter when thinking about the practice as a whole. That said, the issue is an open matter, for there are plausibly both kinds of practices and in different contexts we might do better at securing what we want without backward-looking rules and in others with them.

Second, there is the issue of whether one thinks we have independent reason to prefer think more dramatic revisions where both have comparable justification. I'm inclined to accept a "less is more" principle for revision. I think more dramatic revisions are both more difficult to pull off and more uncertain in their effects. So, I think a principle of modesty in philosophical ambition favors retaining desert-based practices over Pereboom's more radical proposal.

Last, it is unclear that things really are on a par with respect to justification. That is, it is unclear we can readily do without some notion of desert, as Pereboom's picture suggests. Without some kind of desert base in our responsibility practices, we lose protections on blaming and punishing the innocent, and we might lose the ability to give expression to the backward-looking interests of victims (McCormick 2022: 200–205, 210). So, although Pereboom emphasizes the positive advantages for doing without desert (Chapter 7), I think there is a cost here, both in moral terms and in accommodating the retributive psychology we both think is widespread.

To be sure, there are dangers, moral and otherwise, in accommodating our ongoing dispositions to moral anger, as Pereboom rightly recognizes in

Chapter 3 (see also Pereboom 2021a: 3). However, the fact that individual cases are costly does not show that overall anger is not worth the cost. If I am right, anger plays a crucial role in stabilizing our social practices in ways that enable coordination and cooperation. So, abandoning anger would come at a very steep cost indeed.

Pereboom thinks that free will cannot be modeled on scientific cases like H_2O, in part because those cases produced the quick defeat of competing conceptions and there is no reason to think that the present proposal for thinking about free will in broadly revisionist, functionalist, and instrumentalist terms can produce similar convergence. Perhaps that is so, but I'm not convinced that ongoing debate is evidence that the general approach is misguided.

First, there is no guarantee that scientific proposals, even when plausibly an improvement over forerunners, receive immediate or ready uptake. To borrow Thomas Kuhn's rendering of an observation Max Planck made: science progresses one funeral at a time. Indeed, Pereboom's example of ongoing attempts to "naturalize" talk about God is one example. To the extent to which something has gone wrong in that case, it is that it is an open question whether the revised characterization is indeed doing the functional work of the older, pre-revised notion, and whether the revision is being appropriately marked. For any revisionist proposal – whether about God, free will, or anything else – the proposal must be tested, with costs and benefits carefully weighed. Nothing I have argued for should be taken to suggest otherwise. As I suggested in Chapter 4, the cases of race, gender, marriage, and so on, suggest it may be a mistake to think the general strategy is restricted to or uniquely dependent on the sciences.

Even if one were sympathetic to the proposal I have offered, one might still wonder what I want to say about Pereboom's Four Case Argument. In the first edition of this book, and in subsequent work (Vargas 2013), I emphasized that the answer to this question, especially with respect to where to locate the morally relevant difference across cases, is partly a matter of things external to what is contained in the vignettes. The instrumentalist answer is to be found in the wider moral context, and in the answer to questions about which system of responsibility would best enable those subjected to those norms to appropriately recognize and respond to relevant normative considerations. Here, I would add that the functional constraints on the responsibility system, and its role in facilitating cooperation and coordination, are also rightly considerations relevant to how we answer the question. (For an account in a similar spirit, highlighting the difference between one-off manipulations and systematic manipulations, see Latham and Tierney 2022.) In Vargas (2013), I argued that depending on how the details sort out, and depending on some further details about what is packed into the first case (e.g. should we think the manipulators in Case 1 disrupt reasons-responsiveness, enable it, or leave it untouched?), there is a morally significant difference from the standpoint of the responsibility system in Cases 1 and 2. I still think that answer is basically right, and I'm not aware of a response that explains what is wrong with this form of reply when given by anyone with my kinds of commitments.

That said, I think there are at least three further things worth noting that bear on how we ought to think about the Four Case Argument. These include the role of revisionism, the significance of the normative ecology, and the possibility that whether someone has free will is sometimes vague.

First, recall that, with respect to folk intuitions, the dialectical positions of revisionism about free will and responsibility is akin to that of physics: folk intuitions are mostly beside the point. That we struggle to identify a morally significant difference between Pereboom's cases might well be like laypersons or students struggling to identify where a steel ball will first land when it is dropped from a fast-moving car. Is it behind the point where it was dropped, at the point where it was dropped, or ahead of where it was dropped?

I regularly ask this question of undergraduates, and even when there are lots of STEM students in the classroom, it is not uncommon for most students to get this question wrong. This is a famously difficult case to get right from the armchair, precisely because our intuitions about physics are unreliable. So, by my lights, folk intuitions about thought experiments have only limited authority in illuminating questions about the nature of free will and determinism. They are, at best, provisional starting places. (Also, the answer is ahead of the point where the ball was dropped from the moving car, because of momentum.)

There is a second thought that can help sharpen the dialectic. Here, and in other work (Vargas 2013, 2018; Nelkin and Vargas 2024), I have emphasized an ecological conception of moral responsibility, according to which there are agent-based features (including free will, understood as a form of reasons-responsiveness) and context-based features (i.e. the presence of normatively adequate options). On this picture, the normative ecology matters in assessing responsibility. Because the justified rules governing responsibility practices are, in part, matters of how such rules operate in a community with this or that history, and with these and not those normative problems, the shape of the answer is subject to details that are abstracted away in a thought experiment like the Four Case Argument.

In general, what we are looking for are disruptors to the kinds of things that matter for the practice; plausibly, these include active interference but do not include the forces at work in situations of an everyday familiar sort. Where we are postulating a world in which disruptors are very common, there is a choice-point: either have the practice be indifferent to that fact (so, perhaps a strict liability picture in those cases, which is arguably how negligence works) or else have the practice treat disruptors as generating an excuse – at the cost of cutting against the ordinary epistemology of responsibility and of threatening one of the important goods of blame (i.e. of angry blame about culpability shaping our deliberative landscape).

To see how this works, let's stipulate that the context of disruptors is relatively close to our own situation. From the standpoint of coordination and cooperation among human beings, there is an especially notable and important distinction we should track. One idea is the idea of active intervention into someone's deliberations, and (nonculpably acquired) dispositions, where that intervention precludes consideration of deliberatively relevant opportunities that matter for relevant moral concerns (i.e. rational impairments). A different idea is intervention that leaves intact ordinary, unimpaired dispositions that are suitably sensitive to the kinds of considerations and coarse-grained opportunities at stake in responsibility practices that enable cooperation, coordination, and the attunement of moral sensibilities. Where the former raises problems that matter for coordination and cooperation, one might think the latter does not. If that's right, then this provides a principled basis for distinguishing between the cases.

There is a third and final thing to note about the presumptions built into the Four Case argument. As I suggested in Chapter 4, we ordinarily make distinctions about culpability in scalar ways, both as an epistemic matter and as a matter of the metaphysics underwriting these normative considerations. If one thinks that free will is a scalar matter and/or that moral responsibility is a scalar matter (as many of us do), then there is some reason to reject the demand that we identify some "bright line" difference between the cases. In an important sense, the matter may be vague, as Santiago Amaya (accepted for publication) has argued. Thus, the demand to identify a bright line difference may depend on smuggling in the presumption that free will is not vague in this way.

5 Fairness Under Determinism

Even after giving a thoughtful hearing to prescriptively compatibilist accounts, those gripped by incompatibilist convictions may yet be bothered by the thought that this all ignores the underlying worry that there is something fundamentally unfair or unjust about blame and punishment if the universe is deterministic. Some may think that no amount of explanation in terms of the goods or values secured by thinking about freedom and responsibility in compatibilist-friendly terms undermines that thought. For those readers, prescriptively compatibilist accounts fail to grapple with the *real* or *ultimate* ground of dissatisfaction with compatibilism. That dissatisfaction is rooted in the awareness of an ineradicable injustice in holding those culpable who were determined to act as they have. Anchoring justifications in their utility or moral

value to cooperative human life ain't nuthin', but it only obscures without eliminating the injustice from the standpoint of the universe.

I used to be convinced by something like this before finding my way to a
revisionary picture of free will. Although I think there are some things that can
be said to motivate abandonment of the idea under consideration, I do not
think the concern is one that easily goes away for those who have it. In the end,
it may be a brute thought that demands to be taken as a primitive for any theorizing by those so gripped. Perhaps the most we can hope for is something like
a slow-moving gestalt-shift in one's understanding, a transformation from seeing the arrangement of things one way to seeing them in another. Here are
some considerations that moved me, albeit slowly over time.

Although I recognize the objection from fairness, I am not convinced that
we who have felt it can entirely make good on the thought. To the extent to
which the objection requires that we take up something like the standpoint of
the universe, or some perspective entirely detached from the social conditions,
needs, values, and deliberative frameworks of valuing beings, I start to lose my
grip on how to think about the putative unfairness of the universe. The kinds
of differences that are matters of injustice are the ones that are entangled with
our shared cooperative lives and our exercises of reasoning, valuing, norm-
structured agency. It does not seem to me an injustice that lions are stronger
than humans or that some planets have more natural resources than ours, and
so on. These things can only become matters of injustice if we exercise (or had
exercised) some control over those facts or their significance for us. It is from
this practical standpoint that questions of injustice arise.

(There are, of course, religious pictures according to which the distribution
of resources across planets and the comparative physical powers of animals is a
matter of the machinations of some supernatural agent, or group of agents.
Depending on the details, this could render these issues a matter of injustice,
and if so, we would have returned to the terrain of theological fights about free
will. Here, though, I will only repeat what I said in Chapter 4, about the proper
restriction of this account to a less sectarian set of concerns.)

So, again, something like the Euthyphro dilemma emerges. Even if an imagined standpoint of the universe raises worries about injustice, we can ask why
that should matter to us. If the answer is that the concern is proper only from
that *sui generis* standpoint, it is not clear why this provides creatures like us with
sufficient reason to care. If the answer is that it connects to our practical interests, then this is the standpoint from which the question is to be adjudicated.
And it is within this latter framing that the putative unfairness of blaming and
punishing can be directly addressed.

Notice that there is a burden on the proponent of the unfairness worry: what
needs to be shown is that, within the framework of our practical interests,
blaming is indeed morally arbitrary. Yet, an easy path to that thought is what is

blocked by accounts like mine, accounts that offer a story about the normative ground of blame. That is, our interests in cooperation and coordination, in the goods these things secure, and in having moral considerations-responsive agents show that even for deterministic agents blaming need not be morally arbitrary. Blame isn't some arbitrary imposition, untethered from systematic justification or cut off from explanation of its token-level truth conditions. It isn't an unfair way of treating people who are, perhaps, causally determined to act wrongly via a chain of causes extending back prior to their birth. Instead, it is our way of managing our (perhaps) deterministic but complex functioning under the conditions we face. These practices are the way we shape ourselves and the way we enable our collective self-organization, and thereby generate goods that we value and have reason to value.

On this way of putting things, what makes blaming fair, or at least not unfair, is a two-pronged matter. First, there is a broadly constitutive consideration (i.e. that these practices just are the way we form, shape, and direct our moral agency, given the kinds of psychological architecture we have). To seek something different is to imagine a radically different picture of the human; and as Strawson suggested, it is not obvious how we could evaluate such an alternative, given what we are. Second, what burdens a justified responsibility system imposes (blame, potential eligibility for punishment, employment of specific notions of control and ability) are far exceeded by the benefits it bestows both individually and collectively (including the goods of cooperation and coordination, predictability, and control over liability, and again, the formation of moral sensibilities). If we had a workable set of alternatives to our blame- and desert-based responsibility system, something that could function at scale and across a wide range of contexts, then the unfairness complaint might have teeth. If there were no reason to care about moral agency, then perhaps brute fairness considerations would have decisive weight. As things stand, though, it is not unreasonable to organize ourselves into blame- and desert-based ways. If one is fond of philosophically underpowered but ancient and rhetorically satisfying ideas, one might even say we are determined to find such forms of self-organization appealing.

The critic might yet object that, even so, there is still some real (if difficult-to-isolate) sense in which it is unfair that we punish one wrongdoer and excuse another who is coerced when both are equally determined. If this is tacitly an appeal to some intuition rooted in convictions about the standpoint of the universe, then without further argument this is a cheat. Yet, our objector might try to press the thought that the unfairness worry is *internal* to our practical standpoint, as opposed to external, or otherwise independent of our interests in the goods of responsibility. She might insist that the goods I have pointed to – considerations of moral value, self-management, the goods of social life, and so on – do not eradicate some practical and ineliminable concern about the unfairness of blame and what follows under determinism. The goods I have identified can only trade off against that basic practical concern, piling value on one side of a scale of values.

In response, again, it would be good to have some account of why the unfairness concern has authority for us, and why it should matter to what we think and do. Simply pointing to a contested conviction as basic isn't obviously illuminating on the matter of its authority for us, and as we have seen, our overcoming received convictions has often been the first step toward a deepened understanding of the world. Still, perhaps it *is* a matter of balancing goods on a normative scale. If so, though, the scale does not favor the objector's account. Fairness is a value, but it is only one, and it is not implausible that it is outweighed by the plurality of values secured by free will and justified responsibility practices, including the shaping of our agency and the possibility of stable forms of cooperation and coordination and the goods they enable.

One could yet insist on fairness as a supreme value that trumps all other values, no matter how great and central to human lives. As a matter of practical reality and theoretical ramifications, the appeal of such a view seems minimal. Such a view entails that we should prefer a fair universe with low well-being over a universe with tremendous well-being and even the smallest instance of injustice. If that's what it takes to sustain the worry about the unfairness of blaming under determinism, then my proposal strikes me as advantaged on this matter.

6   Some Concluding Observations

If you've made it this far in the book, you've seen a range of different approaches to free will. (Also, thanks for reading this far.) No matter which view you find most satisfying – or, perhaps, least unsatisfying – it is undoubtedly true that if you continue to wrestle with these issues, you will come across new puzzles and new arguments that might alter the balance of considerations. You may eventually find yourself reconsidering some principle or argument that, once appealing and forceful, now strikes you as unobvious or implausible. In turn, this may alter your sense of which view has the most to be said for it.

The seeming unavoidability of this experience when wrestling with free will can strike some as itself a serious problem. Our individual and collective inability to readily reach decisive conclusions that command the convergence of all learned opinions can be disappointing and frustrating. There is even a view in the philosophical literature according to which the apparent irresolvability of debates about free will is characteristic of a wider and deeper problem with philosophy itself (McGinn 1993; van Inwagen 1996).

I do not think things are so dire as that. Expert disagreement is a feature of virtually every active field of research, and it seems unavoidable in any field that takes as its subject matter human social and moral life. Complex phenomena that interact with social meaning and values tend to be marked by interpretive and explanatory gaps that provide the fuel for roaring disagreements. Even so, this doesn't mean that we do not make progress, that we do not construct better theories that capture more of the phenomena, and that we do not over time succeed in achieving an enriched understanding of things.

The inevitability of disagreement can obscure the tremendous progress we have already made on a variety of philosophical fronts. We have, for example, increased our collective understanding of the nature(s) of free will, of the shape of the problem space, of the challenges of different methodological approaches, and of what might count as answers to the puzzles raised by our understanding of the world and the place of free will in it. More controversially, I am inclined to think that there *is* a growing consensus about those approaches to free will issues that are promising and those that are not. For example, few compatibilists today think the free will problem is resolved by appealing to a simple conditional analysis of "can," and considerably fewer libertarians seem comfortable appealing to properties radically discontinuous with what we think we might find in a responsible science. Sixty years ago, there was nothing like the degree of convergence we now have about these things.

Even in the lifespan of this book since it was first conceived and updated, a considerable (if incomplete) consensus has emerged among its authors about what is and is not at stake in debates about free will. Nearly all the authors agree that significant swaths of moral life seem comparatively well supported because there are robust forward-looking justifications for many of our responsibility practices. We can and do disagree about how much of ordinary practice cannot be accounted for in these terms, and we can and do disagree about how much revision in thought and practice is required to address that remainder. But again, ongoing disagreement is compatible with important points of convergence, progress toward convergence, and a deepened understanding of the nature of free will and its import.

Even so, it may be that someday these things will be overturned by some new insight or new conceptual revolution that reshapes our sense of the problem and what would count as a solution. If this volume spurs you to contribute to that possibility, then this too might be its own kind of progress.

Appendix: Some Free Will Debates

The diagram that follows presents some of the positions that have developed in the philosophical literature on free will over the past 75 years or so. It is necessarily partial, in that there are both many more positions and considerably more representatives of the various positions than are indicated here. Still, our hope is that this gives some sense of the wider theoretical landscape in which to situate the views represented in the current volume.

The main positions can be distinguished by their answers to the question of whether free will is compatible with the thesis of determinism. Incompatibilists answer no, compatibilists answer yes, and there are various minority positions that resist the question, insisting that it contains mistaken presumptions, that it is too coarse-grained, or that it is typically understood in some way that fails to capture some important set of theoretical options.

On the incompatibilist side of the diagram, there are two main options: libertarianism, and various forms of free will skepticism or eliminativism.

Libertarianism: although it does not loom large in this volume, it is customary to distinguish between various forms of libertarianism, the most significant of which have been "noncausal," "event causal," and "agent-causal" accounts. Noncausal accounts hold that freely willed decisions or actions are not or need not be caused by anything. Event-causal accounts hold that freely willed decisions or actions consist in being appropriately caused by agent-involving events.

Four Views on Free Will, Second Edition. John Martin Fischer, Robert Kane, Derk Pereboom, and Manuel Vargas.
© 2024 John Wiley & Sons Ltd. Published 2024 by John Wiley & Sons Ltd.

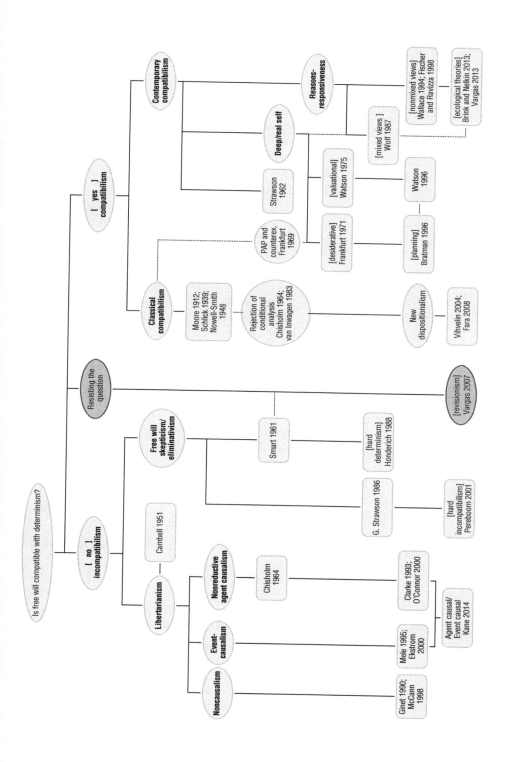

Agent-causal accounts hold that freely willed decisions or actions consist in causation by agents or effects of agents, as opposed to events. In this volume, Kane argues for a view he characterizes as "agent causal/event causal libertarianism."

Free will skepticism/eliminativism: traditionally, this position was taken by people who maintained that determinism is true (hard determinism). Contemporary instances of free will eliminativism have tended to favor views according to which free will is either impossible or we lack it whether or not determinism is true (as in Strawson 1986) or where it is unlikely to be satisfied (as in Pereboom 2001). In this volume, Pereboom argues for "hard incompatibilism."

Among approaches that resist the question, the representative version of such a view in this volume is Vargas's version of **revisionism**. Vargas maintains that debates about free will have failed to distinguish between various questions, including the question of what we think or believe about free will, and what we ought to think or believe about free will. On the first question, he favors libertarianism. On the latter, he favors a form of compatibilism.

On the compatibilist side of the diagram, we distinguish between **classical forms of compatibilism**, including more recent efforts in that spirit, that tended to focus on the analysis of "could have done otherwise" and contemporary forms of compatibilism that have sought to provide an account of what features of agents and/or social practices could ground free will and moral responsibility. Notable developments in the compatibilist side of the diagram include Frankfurt's (1969) effort to generate counterexamples to the principle of alternative possibilities (PAP) and Strawson's (1962) generative discussion of responsibility and the reactive attitudes.

Within **contemporary compatibilism**, there have been two dominant approaches. The first approach (deep self, real self, or self-expression views) emphasizes some privileged set of psychological features that constitute or are authoritative for the agent. There are different ways to regiment this idea, with different accounts appealing to desires, values, and plans to ground the privileged set of psychological features. The other main approach emphasizes reasons-responsiveness.

Initially, reasons-responsiveness was proposed as a supplement, and not as an independent alternative, to real self views (these are marked as "mixed views" on the diagram). Subsequent developments of the view did not appeal to the psychological structures characteristic of real self views. More recently, reasons-responsiveness views have been supplemented by appeals to the moral or more generally normative "ecology" or context of action. In this volume, Fischer's semicompatibilist account of responsibility emphasizes "moderate reasons-responsiveness."

Bibliography

Alicke, Mark D. (2000). Culpable control and the psychology of blame. *Psychology Bulletin* 126: 556–574.

Amaya, Santiago. (accepted for publication). "Free will" is vague. *Philosophical Issues*.

Anglin, W.S. (1991). *Free Will and the Christian Faith*. Oxford: Oxford University Press.

Aristotle (1985). *Nicomachean Ethics* (tr. Terence Irwin). Indianapolis: Hackett.

Arneson, Richard J. (2003). The smart theory of moral responsibility and desert. In S. Olsaretti, (ed.), *Desert and Justice*. Oxford: Oxford University Press, pp. 233–258.

Atmanspacher, Harald. (2020). Quantum approaches to consciousness. In Edward N. Zalta (ed.), *The Stanford Encyclopedia of Philosophy*. https://plato.stanford.edu/archives/sum2020/entries/qt-consciousness/, accessed 31 August 2023.

Ayer, Alfred J. (1954). Freedom and necessity. In *Philosophical Essays*. London: Macmillan, pp. 271–284.

Baker, Lynne R. (2006). Moral responsibility without libertarianism. *Noûs* 40: 307–330.

Balaguer, Mark. (2010). *Free Will as an Open Scientific Problem*. Cambridge, MA: MIT Press.

Balaguer, Mark. (2014). Replies to McKenna, Pereboom, and Kane. *Philosophical Studies* 169(1): 71–92.

Bennett, Jonathan. (1980). Accountability. In Zak Van Straaten (ed.), *Philosophical Subjects*. Oxford: Clarendon Press, pp. 14–47.

Bentham, Jeremy. (1823/1948). *An Introduction to the Principles of Morals and Legislation*. New York: Macmillan.

Bergson, Henri. (1889). *Essai sur les données immédiates de la conscience*. Paris: F. Alcan; translated as *Time and Free Will* (trans. F.L. Pogson, 1910). London: Allen & Unwin.

Four Views on Free Will, Second Edition. John Martin Fischer, Robert Kane, Derk Pereboom, and Manuel Vargas.

© 2024 John Wiley & Sons Ltd. Published 2024 by John Wiley & Sons Ltd.

Berman, Mitchell. (2008). Punishment and justification. *Ethics* 18: 258–290.

Bicchieri, Christina. (2017). *Norms in the Wild*. New York: Oxford University Press.

Bishop, Robert C. (2011). Chaos, indeterminism and free will. In R. Kane (ed.), *The Oxford Handbook of Free Will*, second edition. Oxford: Oxford University Press, pp. 84–100.

Björnsson, Gunnar and Derk Pereboom. (2014). Free will skepticism and bypassing. In W. Sinnott-Armstrong (ed.), *Moral Psychology: Volume 4*. Cambridge, MA: MIT Press, pp. 27–35.

Björnsson, Gunnar and Derk Pereboom (2016). Traditional and experimental approaches to free will. In Wesley Buckwalter and Justin Sytsma (eds.), *The Blackwell Companion to Experimental Philosophy*. Oxford: Blackwell Publishers, pp. 142–157.

Björnsson, Gunnar and Karl Persson. (2012). The explanatory component of moral responsibility. *Nous* 46(2): 326–354.

Björnsson, Gunnar. (2022). Experimental philosophy and moral responsibility. In Dana K. Nelkin and Derk Pereboom (eds.), *The Oxford Handbook of Moral Responsibility*. New York: Oxford University Press, pp. 494–515.

Bobzien, Suzanne. (1998). *Determinism and Freedom in Stoic Philosophy*. Oxford: Oxford University Press.

Bohm, David. (1952). A suggested interpretation of quantum theory in terms of hidden variables: Parts 1 and 2. *Physical Review* 85: 166–193.

Bratman, Michael. (1996). Identification, decision, and treating as a reason. *Philosophical Topics* 24(2): 1–18.

Bratman, Michael. (2022). *Shared and Institutional Agency: Toward a Planning Theory of Human Practical Organization*. New York: Oxford University Press.

Brembs, B. (2011). Towards a scientific concept of free will as a biological trait. *Proceeding of the Royal Society B: Biological Sciences* 278: 930–939.

Brink, David. (2021). *Fair Opportunity, Responsibility and Excuse*. Oxford: Oxford University Press.

Brink, David and Dana Nelkin. (2013). Fairness and the architecture of responsibility. In David Shoemaker (ed.), *Oxford Studies in Agency and Responsibility: Volume 2*. New York: Oxford University Press, pp. 283–313.

Buckareff, Andrei A. (2017). A critique of substance causation. *Philosophia* 45: 1019–1026.

Burgess, Alexis, Hermann Cappelen, and David Plunkett (eds.) (2020). *Conceptual Engineering and Conceptual Ethics*. Oxford: Oxford University Press.

Campbell, C.A. (1951). Is "free will" a pseudo-problem? *Mind* 60(240): 441–465.

Campbell, Joseph. (1997). A compatibilist theory of alternative possibilities. *Philosophical Studies* 88: 319–330.

Capes, Justin. (2013). Mitigating soft compatibilism. *Philosophy and Phenomenological Research* 87: 640–663.

Capes, Justin. (2023). *Moral Responsibility and the Flicker of Freedom*. New York: Oxford University Press.

Carson, Hampton L. (1917). The trial of animals and insects: A little known chapter of mediaeval jurisprudence. *Proceedings of the American Philosophical Society* 56(5): 410–415.

Caruso, Gregg D. (2012). *Free Will and Consciousness: A Determinist Account of the Illusion of Free Will*. Lanham, MD: Lexington Books.

Caruso, Gregg D. (2017). Public health and safety: The social determinants of health and criminal behavior. *ResearchLinks Books*. https://ssrn.com/abstract=3054747, accessed 26 September 2023.

Caruso, Gregg D. (2018). Skepticism about moral responsibility. In Edward N. Zalta (ed.), *The Stanford Encyclopedia of Philosophy*. https://plato.stanford.edu/entries/skepticism-moral-responsibility/, accessed 26 September 2023.

Caruso, Gregg, (2020). Justice without retribution: An epistemic argument against retributive criminal punishment. *Neuroethics* 13(1): 13–28.

Caruso, Gregg D. (2021). *Rejecting Retributivism: Free Will, Punishment, and Criminal Justice*. Cambridge: Cambridge University Press.

Caruso, Gregg D. and Derk Pereboom (2022). *Moral Responsibility Reconsidered*. Cambridge Elements Series. Cambridge: Cambridge University Press.

Cherry, Myisha. (2021). *The Case for Rage: Why Anger is Essential to Anti-Racist Struggle*. New York: Oxford University Press.

Chesney, Eugene J. (1939). The concept of *mens rea* in the criminal law. *Journal of Criminal Law and Criminology* 29(5): 627–644.

Chisholm, Roderick. (1964). Human freedom and the self. The Lindley Lecture, Department of Philosophy, University of Kansas; reprinted in Gary Watson (ed.), *Free Will*. Oxford, Oxford University Press (1982), pp. 24–35.

Chisholm, Roderick. (1976). *Person and Object*. La Salle, IL: Open Court.

Clarke, Randolph. (1993). Toward a credible agent-causal account of free will. *Noûs* 27: 191–203.

Clarke, Randolph. (1996). Agent causation and event causation in the production of free action. *Philosophical Topics* 24: 19–48.

Clarke, Randolph (1997). On the possibility of rational free action. *Philosophical Studies* 88: 37–57.

Clarke, Randolph. (2003). *Libertarian Accounts of Free Will*. New York: Oxford University Press.

Clarke, Randolph. (2005). An argument for the impossibility of moral responsibility. *Midwest Studies in Philosophy* 29: 13–24.

Clarke, Randolph. (2014). *Omissions: Agency, Metaphysics, and Responsibility*. Oxford: Oxford University Press.

Clarke, Randolph. (2019). Free will, agent causation, and "disappearing agents." *Noûs* 53(1): 76–96.

Cohen, E. (1986). Law, folklore, and animal lore. *Past & Present* 110: 6–37.

Copp, David. (1995). *Morality, Normativity, and Society*. Oxford: Oxford University Press.

Copp, David. (2008). "Ought" implies "can" and the derivation of the principle of alternative possibilities. *Analysis* 68: 67–75.

Corradini, Antonella and Uwe Meixner (eds.) (2014). *Quantum Theory Meets Philosophy of Mind*. Berlin: De Gruyter.

Cushman, Fiery. (2015). Punishment in humans: From intuitions to institutions. *Philosophy Compass* 10(2): 117–133.

Cyr, Taylor. (2020). Manipulation arguments and libertarian accounts of free will. *Journal of the American Philosophical Association* 6(1): 57–73.

Davidson, Donald. (1963). Actions, reasons, and causes. *Journal of Philosophy* 60: 685–700.

DeCaro, Mario. (2021). Machiavelli's Lucretian view of free will. In V. Prosperi and D. Zucca (eds.), *Lucretius, Poet and Philosopher: Background and Fortunes of the De Rerum Natura.* Berlin: De Gruyter.

Deery, Oisín and Eddy Nahmias. (2017). Defeating manipulation arguments: Interventionist causation and compatibilist sourcehood. *Philosophical Studies* 174(5): 255–276.

Deery, Oisín. (2021). *Naturally Free Action.* Oxford: Oxford University Press.

Della Rocca, Michael. (1998). Frankfurt, Fischer, and flickers. *Noûs* 32: 99–105.

Demetriou, Kristin. (2010). The soft-line solution to Pereboom's four-case argument. *Australasian Journal of Philosophy* 88: 595–617.

Dennett, Daniel C. (1984). *Elbow Room.* Cambridge, MA: MIT Press.

Dennett, Daniel C. (2003). *Freedom Evolves.* New York: Viking Press.

Dennett, Daniel C. and Gregg D. Caruso. (2021). *Just Deserts.* Cambridge: Polity Press.

Descartes, René. (1639–40/1996). *Meditations on First Philosophy.* Cambridge: Cambridge University Press.

d'Holbach, Paul-Henri Thiry. (1770). *Système de la Nature, ou Des Loix du Monde Physique et du Monde Moral.* Amsterdam: Marc-Michel Rey.

Doris, John (2015a). *Talking to Our Selves: Reflection, Ignorance, and Agency.* Oxford: Oxford University Press.

Doris, John. (2015b). Doing without (arguing about) desert. *Philosophical Studies* 172: 2625–2634.

Dorr, Cian. (2016). Against counterfactual miracles. *Philosophical Review* 125: 241–286.

Doyle, Robert. (2011). *Free Will: The Scandal of Philosophy.* Cambridge, MA: I-Phi Press.

Du Bois, W.E.B. (2017). *The Souls of Black Folk.* New York: Penguin Books.

Ekstrom, Laura W. (2000). *Free Will: A Philosophical Study.* Boulder, CO: Westview.

Ekstrom, Laura W. (2019). Toward a plausible event-causal indeterminist account of free will. *Synthèse* 196: 127–144.

Ellis, G.F.R. (2009). Top-down causation and the human brain. In Murphy, Nancey, G.F.R. Ellis, and Timothy O'Connor (eds), *Downwards Causation and the Neurobiology of Free Will.* Berlin: Springer Verlag, pp. 31–52.

Enoch, David, T. Fisher, and L. Spectre. (2021). Does legal epistemology rest on a mistake? On fetishism, two-tier system design, and conscientious fact-finding. *Philosophical Issues* 31(1): 85–103.

Everett, Hugh. (1957). "Relative state" formulation of quantum mechanics. *Reviews of Modern Physics* 29: 454–462.

Fara, Michael. (2008). Masked abilities and compatibilism. *Mind* 117: 843–865.

Farrell, Daniel M. (1985). The justification of general deterrence. *Philosophical Review* 104: 367–394.

Fehr, E. and S. Gächter (2002). Altruistic punishment in humans. *Nature* 415: 137–140.

Feinberg, Joel. (1970). Justice and personal desert. In *Doing and Deserving: Essays in the Theory of Responsibility.* Princeton: Princeton University Press.

Feltz, Adam. (2013). Pereboom and premises: Asking the right questions in the experimental philosophy of free will. *Consciousness and Cognition* 22(1): 53–63.

Finch, Alicia and Ted Warfield. (1998). The mind argument and libertarianism. *Mind* 107: 515–528.

Fischer, John Martin. (1982). Responsibility and control. *Journal of Philosophy* 79: 24–40.

Fischer, John Martin. (1994). *The Metaphysics of Free Will*. Oxford: Blackwell Publishers.

Fischer, John Martin. (2003). "Ought-implies-can," causal determinism, and moral responsibility. *Analysis* 63: 244–250.

Fischer, John Martin. (2004). Responsibility and manipulation. *The Journal of Ethics* 8: 145–77.

Fischer, John Martin. (2006). *My Way: Essays on Moral Responsibility*. New York: Oxford University Press.

Fischer, John Martin. (2009). *Our Stories*. New York: Oxford University Press.

Fischer, John Martin. (2012). *Deep Control: Essays on Free Will and Value*. New York: Oxford University Press.

Fischer, John Martin. (2016a). *Our Fate: Essays on God and Free Will*. New York: Oxford University Press.

Fischer, John Martin. (2016b). How do manipulation arguments work? *The Journal of Ethics* 20(1–3): 47–67.

Fischer, John Martin. (2021). Initial design, manipulation, and moral responsibility. *Criminal Law and Philosophy* 15(2): 255–270.

Fischer, John Martin. (accepted for publication, a). The resilience of moral responsibility. In Taylor Cyr, Andrew Law, and Neal A. Tognazzini (eds.), *Freedom, Responsibility, and Value: Essays in Honor of John Martin Fischer*. New York: Routledge.

Fischer, John Martin. (accepted for publication, b). Moral responsibility skepticism and semiretributivism. *Harvard Review of Philosophy*.

Fischer, John Martin and Mark Ravizza. (1998). *Responsibility and Control: A Theory of Moral Responsibility*. Cambridge: Cambridge University Press.

Fischer, John Martin and Neal A. Tognazzini. (2011). The physiognomy of moral responsibility. *Philosophy and Phenomenological Research* 82(2): 381–417.

Focquaert, Farah. (2019). Neurobiology and crime: A neuro-ethical perspective. *Journal of Criminal Justice* 65. doi: 10.1016/j.jcrimjus.2018.01.001.

Frank, Robert H. (1988). *Passions Within Reason*. New York: Norton.

Frankfurt, Harry G. (1969). Alternate possibilities and moral responsibility. *Journal of Philosophy* 66: 829–839.

Frankfurt, Harry G. (1971). Freedom of the will and the concept of a person. *Journal of Philosophy* 68: 5–20.

Franklin, Christopher. (2011). Farewell to the luck (and mind) arguments. *Philosophical Studies* 156(2): 199–230.

Franklin, Christopher. (2018). *A Minimal Libertarianism: Free Will and the Promise of Reduction*. New York: Oxford University Press.

Ghirardi, Giancarlo, Alberto Rimini, and Tullio Weber. (1986). Unified dynamics for microscopic and macroscopic systems. *Physical Review D* 34: 470–491.

Ginet, Carl. (1962). Can the will be caused? *The Philosophical Review* 71: 49–55.

Ginet, Carl. (1966). Might we have no choice? In Keith Lehrer (ed.), *Freedom and Determinism*. New York: Random House, pp. 87–104.

Ginet, Carl. (1990). *On Action*. Cambridge: Cambridge University Press.

Ginet, Carl. (1997). Freedom, responsibility, and agency. *The Journal of Ethics* 1: 85–98.

Ginet, Carl. (2007). An action can be both uncaused and up to the agent. In Christoph Lumer and Sandro Nannin (eds.), *Intentionality, Deliberation, and Autonomy*. Farnham: Ashgate, pp. 243–256.

Glimcher, Paul. (2005). Indeterminacy in brain and behavior. *Annual Review of Psychology* 56: 25–56.

Goetz, Stewart. (2008). *Freedom, Teleology, and Evil*. London: Continuum.

Goldberg, Julie H., Jennifer S. Lerner, and Philip E. Tetlock. (1999). Rage and reason: The psychology of the intuitive prosecutor. *European Journal of Social Psychology* 29: 781–795.

Graham, Peter. (2011). "Ought" and "ability." *Philosophical Review* 120: 337–382.

Greene, Joshua. (2008). The secret joke of Kant's soul. In Walter P. Sinnott-Armstrong (ed.), *Moral Psychology: Volume 3*. Cambridge, MA: MIT Press, pp. 35–79.

Greene, Joshua and Jonathan D. Cohen. (2004). For the law, neuroscience changes nothing and everything. *Philosophical Transactions of the Royal Society of London: Series B-Biological Sciences* 359: 1775–1785.

Greenspan, Patricia. (1988). *Emotions and Reason: An Inquiry into Emotional Justification*. London: Routledge.

Griffith, Meghan. (2010). Why agent-caused actions are not lucky. *American Philosophical Quarterly* 47: 43–56.

Haas, Daniel. (2013). In defense of hard-line replies to the multiple-case manipulation argument. *Philosophical Studies* 163: 797–811.

Haji, Ishtiyaque. (1998). *Moral Appraisability*. New York: Oxford University Press.

Haji, Ishtiyaque (2000). Libertarianism and the luck objection. *The Journal of Ethics* 4(4): 329–337.

Haji, Ishtiyaque. (2002). *Deontic Morality and Control*. Cambridge: Cambridge University Press.

Haji, Ishtiyaque. (2009). *Incompatibilism's Allure*. Toronto: Broadview Press.

Hameroff, Stuart. (1998). Quantum computation in brain microtubules? The Penrose-Hameroff "Orch OR" model of consciousness. *Philosophical Transactions of the Royal Society London A* 356: 1869–1896.

Hameroff, Stuart and Roger Penrose. (1996). Conscious events as orchestrated space-time selections. *Journal of Consciousness Studies* 3: 36–53.

Harris, Sam. (2012). *Free Will*. New York: Free Press.

Hart, H.L.A. (1961). *The Concept of Law*. Clarendon Press.

Hart, H.L.A. (1968). *Punishment and Responsibility*. New York: Oxford University Press.

Hartman, Robert J. (2016). Against luck-free moral responsibility. *Philosophical Studies* 173(10): 2845–2865.

Healey, Richard. (2012). Quantum theory: A pragmatist approach. *British Journal for the Philosophy of Science* 63(4): 729–771.

Healey, Richard. (2017). *The Quantum Revolution in Philosophy*. Oxford: Oxford University Press.

Heisenberg, Martin. (2013). The origin of freedom in animal behavior. In A. Suarez and P. Adams (eds.), *Is Science Compatible with Free Will?* New York: Springer, pp. 95–103.

Hieronymi, Pamela. (2001). Articulating an uncompromising forgiveness. *Philosophy and Phenomenological Research* 62: 529–555.

Hobbes, Thomas. (1654). *Of Libertie and Necessity: A treatise, wherein all controversie concerning predestination, election, free-will, grace, merits, reprobation, &c., is fully decided and cleared, in answer to a treatise written by the Bishop of London-Derry, on the same subject.* London: W.B. for F. Eaglesfield.

Honderich, Ted. (1988). *A Theory of Determinism.* Oxford: Oxford University Press.

Hooker, Brad. (2000). *Ideal Code, Real World: A Rule-Consequentialist Theory of Morality.* Oxford: Oxford University Press.

Horst, Steven. (2011). *Laws, Mind, and Free Will.* Cambridge, MA: MIT Press.

Hume, David. (1739/1978). *A Treatise of Human Nature.* Oxford: Oxford University Press.

Hume, David. (1748/2000). *An Enquiry Concerning Human Understanding.* Oxford: Oxford University Press.

Hunt, David. (2000). Moral responsibility and unavoidable action. *Philosophical Studies* 97: 195–227.

Hunt, David (2005). Moral responsibility and buffered alternatives. *Midwest Studies in Philosophy* 29: 126–145.

Hurley, S. (2013). The public ecology of responsibility. In C. Knight and Z. Stemplowska (eds.), *Responsibility and Distributive Justice.* Oxford: Oxford University Press, pp. 188–215.

Jackson, Frank. (1998). *From Metaphysics to Ethics: A Defense of Conceptual Analysis.* New York: Oxford University Press.

Jedlicka, Peter. (2014). Quantum stochasticity and (the end of) neurodeterminism. In Antonella Corradini and Uwe Meixner (eds.), *Quantum Physics Meets the Philosophy of Mind.* Berlin/Boston: Walter de Gruyter, pp. 183–197.

Jeppsson, Sofia. (2020). The agential perspective: A hard-line reply to the four-case manipulation argument. *Philosophical Studies* 177(7): 1935–1951.

Juarrero, Alicia (1999). *Dynamics in Action.* Cambridge, MA: MIT.

Kane, Robert. (1985). *Free Will and Values.* Albany, NY: SUNY Press.

Kane, Robert. (1996). *The Significance of Free Will.* New York: Oxford University Press.

Kane, Robert. (2005). *A Contemporary Introduction to Free Will.* Oxford Fundamentals of Philosophy Series. Oxford: Oxford University Press.

Kane, Robert. (2007). Response to Fischer, Pereboom, and Vargas. In J.M. Fischer, R. Kane, D. Pereboom, and M. Vargas. *Four Views on Free Will.* Malden, MA: Wiley-Blackwell, pp. 166–183.

Kane, Robert. (2009). Libertarianism. *Philosophical Studies* 144: 35–44.

Kane, Robert. (ed). (2011). Rethinking free will: New perspectives on an ancient problem. In *The Oxford Handbook on Free Will*, second edition. Oxford: Oxford University Press, pp. 381–404.

Kane, Robert. (2014). New arguments in debates on libertarian free will: Responses to contributors. In D. Palmer (ed.), *Libertarian Free Will: Contemporary Debates.* Oxford: Oxford University Press, pp. 179–214.

Kane, Robert. (2016). On the role of indeterminism in libertarian free will. *Philosophical Explorations* 19(1): 2–16.

Kant, Immanuel. (1781/1787/1987). *Critique of Pure Reason* (trans. Paul Guyer and Allen Wood). Cambridge: Cambridge University Press.

Kant, Immanuel. (1785/1981). *Grounding for the Metaphysics of Morals* (trans. J. Ellington). Indianapolis: Hackett.

Kant, Immanuel. (1797/2017). *The Metaphysics of Morals* (trans. Mary Gregor). Cambridge: Cambridge University Press.

Kearns, Stephen. (2012). Aborting the zygote argument. *Philosophical Studies* 160: 379–389.

Kelly, Daniel. (2022). Two ways to adopt a norm: The (moral?) psychology of internalization and avowal. In Manuel Vargas and John Doris (eds.), *The Oxford Handbook of Moral Psychology*. New York: Oxford University Press, pp. 285–309.

Kelly, Erin. (2009). Criminal justice without retribution. *Journal of Philosophy* 106: 440–456.

Khoury, Andrew. (2014). Manipulation and mitigation. *Philosophical Studies* 168(1): 283–294.

King, Matthew. (2013). The Problem with manipulation. *Ethics* 124(1): 65–83.

Kleiman, Mark. (2009). *When Brute Force Fails: How to Have Less Crime and Less Punishment*. Princeton: Princeton University Press.

Koch, Christoph. (2009). Free will, physics, biology and the brain. In Nancey Murphy, G.F.R. Ellis, and Timothy O'Connor (eds), *Downwards Causation and the Neurobiology of Free Will*. Berlin: Springer Verlag, pp. 120–134.

Laplace, Pierre-Simon. (1814/1951). *A Philosophical Essay on Probabilities* (trans. F.W. Truscott and F.L. Emory). New York: Dover Books.

Latham, A.J. and Tierney, H. (2022). Defusing existential and universal threats to compatibilism: A Strawsonian dilemma for manipulation arguments. *Journal of Philosophy* 119(3): 144–161.

Latham, Noa. (2004). Determinism, randomness, and value. *Philosophical Topics* 32(1/2): 153–167.

Layser, David. (2022). *Do We Have Free Will?* Cambridge, MA: I-Phi Press.

Lazarus, Richard. (1991). *Emotion and Adaptation*. Oxford: Oxford University Press.

Lehrer, Keith. (1968). "Can's without 'if's." *Analysis* 24: 159–160.

Leiter, Brian. (2007). Nietzsche's theory of the will. *Philosophers' Imprint* 7: 1–15.

Lemos, John. (2018). *A Pragmatic Approach to Libertarian Free Will*. New York: Routledge.

Lenman, James. (2006). Compatibilism and contractualism: The possibility of moral responsibility. *Ethics* 117: 7–31.

Levy, Neil. (2003). Contrastive explanations: A dilemma for libertarians. *Dialectica* 39: 51–61.

Levy, Neil. (2011). *Hard Luck: How Luck Undermines Free Will and Moral Responsibility*. Oxford: Oxford University Press.

Lewis, David. (1981). Are we free to break the laws? *Theoria* 47: 113–121.

Lewis, David. (1986). Events. In *Philosophical Papers: Volume 2*. New York: Oxford University Press, pp. 241–269.

Lewis, Peter J. (2016). *Quantum Ontology: A Guide to the Metaphysics of Quantum Mechanics*. New York: Oxford University Press.

Locke, John. (1690/1975). *An Essay Concerning Human Understanding* (ed. Peter H. Nidditch). Oxford: Oxford University Press.

Lucretius. (50 BCE/1998). *On the Nature of the Universe* (trans. Ronald Melville). Oxford: Oxford University Press.

Lycan, William G. (1987). *Consciousness*. Cambridge, MA: MIT Press.

Madigan, T. (accepted for publication). Two dimensions of responsibility: Quality and competence of will. *Journal of the American Philosophical Association*.

Maoz, Uri and Walter Sinnott-Armstrong. (2022). *Free Will: Philosophers and Neuroscientists in Conversation*. New York: Oxford University Press.

Matheson, Benjamin. (2016). In Defense of the four-case argument. *Philosophical Studies* 173(7): 1963–1982.

McCann, Hugh. (1998). *The Works of Agency*. Ithaca, NY: Cornell University Press.

McCormick, Kelly. (2016). Revisionism. In Kevin Timpe, Meghan Griffith, and Neil Levy (eds.), *The Routledge Companion to Free Will*. New York: Routledge, pp. 109–120.

McCormick, Kelly. (2022). *The Problem of Blame: Making Sense of Moral Anger*. Cambridge: Cambridge University Press.

McGeer, Victoria. (2012). Co-reactive attitudes and the making of moral community. In R. Langdon and C. Mackenzie (eds.), *Emotions, Imagination, and Moral Reasoning*. New York: Psychology Press, pp. 299–326.

McGeer, Victoria. (2015). Building a better theory of responsibility. *Philosophical Studies* 172(10): 2635–2649.

McGeer, Victoria. (2019). Scaffolding agency: A proleptic account of the reactive attitudes. *European Journal of Philosophy* 27(2): 301–323.

McGinn, Colin. (1993). *Problems in Philosophy: The Limits of Inquiry*. Cambridge, MA: Blackwell.

McKenna, Michael. (1997). Alternative possibilities and the failure of the counterexample strategy. *Journal of Social Philosophy* 28: 71–85.

McKenna, Michael. (2000). Assessing reasons-responsive compatibilism. *International Journal of Philosophical Studies* 8: 89–114.

McKenna, Michael. (2005). Where Frankfurt and Strawson meet. *Midwest Studies in Philosophy* 29: 163–180.

McKenna, Michael. (2008). A hard-line reply to Pereboom's four-case argument. *Philosophy and Phenomenological Research* 77: 142–159.

McKenna, Michael. (2009). Compatibilism and desert: Critical comments on *Four Views on Free Will*. *Philosophical Studies* 144: 3–13.

McKenna, Michael. (2012). *Conversation and Responsibility*. New York: Oxford University Press.

McKenna, Michael. (2014). Resisting the manipulation argument: A hard-liner takes it on the chin. *Philosophy and Phenomenological Research* 89: 467–484.

McKenna, Michael. (2019). Basically deserved blame and its value. *Journal of Ethics and Social Philosophy* 15: 255–282.

McKenna, Michael. 2020. Punishment and the value of deserved suffering. *Public Affairs Quarterly* 34(2): 97–123.

McKenna, Michael. (2021). Wimpy retributivism and the promise of moral influence theories. *The Monist* 104(4): 510–525.

McKenna, Michael and Derk Pereboom. (2016). *Free Will: A Contemporary Introduction.* New York: Routledge.

Mele, Alfred. (1995). *Autonomous Agents: From Self-Control to Autonomy.* Oxford University Press.

Mele, Alfred. (1996). Soft libertarianism and Frankfurt-style scenarios. *Philosophical Topics* 24: 123–141.

Mele, Alfred. (1998). Review of Robert Kane's *The Significance of Free Will. Journal of Philosophy* 95: 381–384.

Mele, Alfred. (2003). Agents' abilities. *Noûs* 37: 447–470.

Mele, Alfred. (2006). *Free Will and Luck.* New York: Oxford University Press.

Mele, Alfred. (2008). Manipulation, compatibilism, and moral responsibility. *The Journal of Ethics* 12: 263–286.

Mele, Alfred. (2009). *Effective Intentions.* New York: Oxford University Press.

Mele, Alfred. (2013). Free will and neuroscience. *Philosophic Exchange* 43: 1–17.

Mele, Alfred. (2017). *Aspects of Agency: Decisions, Abilities, Explanations, and Free Will.* New York: Oxford University Press.

Milam, Per-Erik. (2016). Reactive attitudes and personal relationships. *Canadian Journal of Philosophy* 42: 102–122.

Miller, E. and J. Cohen. (2001). An integrated theory of pre-frontal cortex function. *Annual Review of Neuroscience* 24: 167–202.

Miller, L. (2020). *Why Fish Don't Exist: A Story of Loss, Love, and the Hidden Order of Life.* New York: Simon & Schuster.

Monsó, S. and K. Andrews. (2022). Animal moral psychologies. In Manuel Vargas and John Doris (eds.), *The Oxford Handbook of Moral Psychology.* New York: Oxford University Press, pp. 109–120.

Moore, G.E. (1912). *Ethics.* Oxford: Oxford University Press.

Moore, Michael. (1987). The moral worth of retribution. In Ferdinand Schoeman (ed.), *Responsibility, Character, and the Emotions.* Cambridge: Cambridge University Press, pp. 179–219.

Moore, Michael. (1998). *Placing Blame.* Oxford: Oxford University Press.

Morris, Herbert. (1968). Persons and punishment. *The Monist* 52: 475–501.

Morris, Stephen. (2018). The implications of rejecting free will: An empirical analysis. *Philosophical Psychology* 31(2): 299–321.

Morse, Stephen J. (2004). Reasons, results, and criminal responsibility. *University of Illinois Law Review* 363: https://scholarship.law.upenn.edu/faculty_scholarship/527.

Morse, Stephen J. (2013). Common criminal law compatibilism. In Nicole A. Vincent (ed.), *Neuroscience and Legal Responsibility.* Oxford: Oxford University Press, pp. 29–52.

Morton, Jennifer M. (2011). Towards and ecological theory of the norms of practical deliberation. *European Journal of Philosophy* 19(4): 561–584.

Moya, Carlos. (2006). *Moral Responsibility: The Ways of Skepticism.* Oxford: Oxford University Press.

Murray, Dylan and Tania Lombrozo. (2017). Effects of manipulation on attributions of causation, free will, and moral responsibility. *Cognitive Science* 41(3): 447–481.

Nadelhoffer, Thomas. (2011). The threat of shrinking agency and free will disillusionism. In Lynne Nadel and Walter Sinnott-Armstrong (eds). *Conscious Will and Responsibility*. Oxford: Oxford University Press, pp. 173–188.

Nadelhoffer, Thomas. and Andrew Monroe (eds.). (2022). *Advances in Experimental Philosophy of Free Will and Responsibility*. London: Bloomsbury Academic.

Nahmias, Eddy. (2011). Intuitions about free will, determinism, and bypassing. In Robert Kane (ed.), *The Oxford Handbook of Free Will*. New York: Oxford University Press, pp. 555–576.

Nahmias, Eddy. (2014). Is free will an illusion? Confronting challenges from the modern mind sciences. In Walter Sinnott-Armstrong (ed)., *Moral Psychology: Volume 4*. Cambridge, MA: MIT Press, pp. 1–25.

Nelkin, Dana K. (2008). Responsibility and rational abilities: Defending an asymmetrical view. *Pacific Philosophical Quarterly* 89: 497–515.

Nelkin, Dana K. (2011). *Making Sense of Freedom and Responsibility*. Oxford: Oxford University Press.

Nelkin, Dana K. (2016). Accountability and desert. *Journal of Ethics* 20(1–3): 173–189.

Nelkin, Dana K. (2019). Duties, desert, and the justification of punishment. *Criminal Law and Philosophy* 13(3): 425–438.

Nelkin, Dana K. (2022). Relationships and responsibility. In Dana Nelkin and Derk Pereboom (eds.), *The Oxford Handbook of Moral Responsibility*. New York: Oxford University Press.

Nelkin, Dana K. and Vargas, Manuel. (2024). Responsibility and reasons-responsiveness. In T. Cyr, A. Law, and N.A. Tognazzini (eds.), *Freedom, Responsibility, and Value: Essays in Honor of John Martin Fischer*. Routledge, pp.37–60.

Nichols, Shaun. (2007). After compatibilism: A naturalistic defense of the reactive attitudes. *Philosophical Perspectives* 21: 405–428.

Nichols, Shaun. (2013). Brute retributivism. In Thomas Nadelhoffer (ed.), *The Future of Punishment*. New York: Oxford University Press, 2013, pp. 65–88.

Nichols, Shaun. (2015). *Bound: Essays on Free Will and Responsibility*. Oxford: Oxford University Press.

Nichols, Shaun. (2022). Moral learning and moral representations. In Manuel Vargas and John Doris (eds.), *The Oxford Handbook of Moral Psychology*. New York: Oxford University Press, pp. 421–441.

Nietzsche, Friedrich Wilhelm. (1954). *Twilight of the Idols* (trans. Walter Kaufmann). New York: Viking.

Nietzsche, Friedrich Wilhelm. (1989). *On the Genealogy of Morals* (trans. and ed. Walter Kauffman). London: Vintage Books.

Nietzsche, Friedrich Wilhelm. (1996). *On the Genealogy of Morality: A Polemic* (trans. M. Clark and A.J. Swensen). Indianapolis, IN: Hackett.

Nietzsche, Friedrich Wilhelm. (2000). *Basic Writings of Nietzsche* (trans. W. Kaufmann). New York: The Modern Library.

Nowell-Smith, Patrick. (1948). Free will and moral responsibility. *Mind* 57: 45–61.

Nussbaum, Martha C. (1997). Emotions as judgments of value and importance. In P. Bilimoria and J. Mohanty (eds.), *Relativism, Suffering and Beyond*. New Delhi: Oxford University Press, pp. 271–283.

Nussbaum, Martha C. (2016). *Anger and Forgiveness*. Oxford: Oxford University Press.

O'Connor, Cailin. (2022). Methods, models, and the evolution of moral psychology. In Manuel Vargas and John Doris (eds.), *The Oxford Handbook of Moral Psychology*. New York: Oxford University Press, pp. 442–464.

O'Connor, Timothy. (1995). Agent causation. In *Agents, Causes, and Events*. New York: Oxford University Press, pp. 170–200.

O'Connor, Timothy. (2000). *Persons and Causes*. New York: Oxford University Press.

O'Connor, Timothy (2003). Review of *Living Without Free Will*. *Philosophical Quarterly* 53: 308–310.

O'Connor, Timothy. (2008). Agent-causal power. In Toby Handfield (ed.), *Dispositions and Causes*. Oxford: Oxford University Press, pp. 189–214.

Palmer, David. (2011). Pereboom on the Frankfurt cases. *Philosophical Studies* 153: 261–272.

Palmer, David. (2021). Free will and control: A noncausal approach. *Synthèse* 198(10): 10043–10062.

Penrose, Roger. (1989). *The Emperor's New Mind: Computers, Minds and the Laws of Physics*. Oxford: Oxford University Press.

Penrose, Roger. (1994). *Shadows of the Mind*. Oxford: Oxford University Press.

Pereboom, Derk. (1995). Determinism *al dente*. *Noûs* 29: 21–45.

Pereboom, Derk (2000). Alternative possibilities and causal histories. *Philosophical Perspectives* 14: 119–137.

Pereboom, Derk. (2001). *Living Without Free Will*. Cambridge: Cambridge University Press.

Pereboom, Derk (2004). Is our conception of agent-causation coherent? *Philosophical Topics* 32: 275–286.

Pereboom, Derk. (2008). A hard-line reply to the multiple-case manipulation argument. *Philosophy and Phenomenological Research* 77: 160–170.

Pereboom, Derk. (2014). *Free Will, Agency, and Meaning in Life*. Oxford: Oxford University Press.

Pereboom, Derk. (2017a). Responsibility, agency, and the disappearing agent objection. In Jean-Baptiste Guillon (ed.), *Le Libre-Arbitre, approches contemporaines*. Paris: Collège de France, pp. 1–18.

Pereboom, Derk. (2017b). Responsibility, regret, and protest. In David Shoemaker (ed.), *Oxford Studies in Agency and Responsibility*, pp. 121–140.

Pereboom, Derk. (2018). Love and freedom. In Christopher Grau and Aaron Smuts (eds.), *The Oxford Handbook of the Philosophy of Love*. New York: Oxford University Press.

Pereboom, Derk. (2019). Free will skepticism and prevention of crime. In Gregg Caruso, Elizabeth Shaw, and Derk Pereboom (eds.), *Free Will Skepticism in Law and Society*. Cambridge: Cambridge University Press.

Pereboom, Derk. (2020). Incapacitation, reintegration, and limited general deterrence. *Neuroethics* 13: 87–97.

Pereboom, Derk. (2021a). *Wrongdoing and the Moral Emotions*. Oxford: Oxford University Press.

Pereboom, Derk. (2021b). Undivided forward-looking moral responsibility. *The Monist* 104: 484–497.

Pereboom, Derk. (2022a). *Free Will.* Cambridge Elements Series. Cambridge: Cambridge University Press.

Pereboom, Derk. (2022b). Moral responsibility, alternative possibilities, and Frankfurt examples. In Dana Nelkin and Derk Pereboom (eds.), *The Oxford Handbook of Moral Responsibility.* New York: Oxford University Press.

Pereboom, Derk. (2024). Retributivism and the relevance of metaphysics to practice. In Taylor W. Cyr, Andrew Law, and Neal A. Tognazzini, (eds.), *Freedom, Responsibility and Value: Essays in Honor of John Martin Fischer.* New York: Routledge.

Pereboom, Derk and Michael McKenna. (2022). Manipulation arguments. In Dana Nelkin and Derk Pereboom (eds.), *The Oxford Handbook of Moral Responsibility.* New York: Oxford University Press.

Perry, John. (2004). Compatibilist options. In J.K. Campbell, M. O'Rourke, and D. Shier (eds), *Freedom and Determinism.* Cambridge, MA: MIT Press.

Pettit, P. (2018). *The Birth of Ethics: Reconstructing the Role and Nature of Morality.* Oxford: Oxford University Press.

Plunkett, David (2016). Conceptual history, conceptual ethics, and the aims of inquiry: A framework for thinking about the relevance of the history/genealogy of concepts to normative inquiry. *Ergo* 3(2): 27–64.

Polkinghorne, John (ed.). (2009). Is the brain indeterministic? In *Questions of Truth.* Westminster: John Knox Press, pp. 128–135.

Priestley, Joseph. (1788/1965). *A Free Discussion of the Doctrines of Materialism and Philosophical Necessity, In a Correspondence between Dr. Price and Dr. Priestley: Part III.* Reprinted in John Passmore (ed.), *Priestley's Writings on Philosophy, Science, and Politics.* New York: Collier.

Quinn, Warren. (1985). The right to threaten and the right to punish. *Philosophy and Public Affairs* 14: 327–373.

Ragland, Clyde P. (2016). *The Will to Reason: Theodicy and Freedom in Descartes.* New York: Oxford University Press.

Rawls, John. (1955). Two concepts of rules. *Philosophical Review* 64: 3–32.

Reid, Thomas. (1788/1983). Essays on the Active Powers of Man. In Sir William Hamilton (ed.), *The Works of Thomas Reid.* Hildesheim, Germany: G. Olms Verlagsbuchhandlung.

Roberts, Robert C. (1988). What an emotion is: A sketch. *The Philosophical Review* 97: 183–209.

Roberts, Robert C. (2003). *Emotions: An Essay in Aid of Moral Psychology.* Cambridge: Cambridge University Press.

Roberts, Robert C. (2013). *Emotions in the Moral Life.* Cambridge: Cambridge University Press.

Rolls, E.T. (2012). Willed action, free will and the stochastic neurodynamics of decision making. *Frontiers in Integrative Neuroscience* 6: https://doi.org/10.3389/fnint.2012.00068.

Rosen, Gideon. (2003). Culpability and ignorance. *Proceedings of the Aristotelian Society* 103(1): 61–84.

Rosen, Gideon. (2004). Skepticism about moral responsibility. *Philosophical Perspectives* 18: 295–313.

Roskies, Adina. (2012). Don't panic: Self-authorship without obscure metaphysics. *Philosophical Perspectives* 26: 323–342.

Ryle, Gilbert. (1949). *The Concept of Mind*. London: Hutchinson Publishers.

Śāntideva. (700/1995). *The Bodhicaryāvaātra* (trans. Kate Crosby and Andrew Skilton). New York: Oxford University Press.

Sapolsky, Robert M. (2017). *Behave: The Biology of Humans at Our Best and Worst*. London: Penguin.

Sapolsky, Robert M. (2023). *Determined: A Science of Life Without Free Will*. London: Penguin Press.

Sartorio, Carolina. (2016). *Causation and Free Will*. Oxford: Oxford University Press.

Sartorio, Carolina. (2017). Frankfurt-style examples. In K. Timpe, M. Griffith, and N. Levy, (eds.), *The Routledge Companion to Free Will*. London: Routledge. https://doi.org/10.4324/9781315758206.

Satinover, J. (2001). *The Quantum Brain: The Search for Freedom and the Next Generation of Man*. New York: Wiley.

Scanlon, Thomas M. (1998). *What We Owe to Each Other*. Cambridge, MA: Harvard University Press.

Scanlon, Thomas M. (2009). *Moral Dimensions*. Cambridge, MA: Harvard University Press.

Scanlon, Thomas M. (2013). Giving desert its due. *Philosophical Explorations* 16: 101–116.

Schlick, Moritz. (1939). When is a man responsible? In *Problems of Ethics* (trans. D. Rynin). New York: Prentice-Hall, pp. 143–156.

Schoeman, Ferdinand D. (1979). On incapacitating the dangerous. *American Philosophical Quarterly* 16: 27–35.

Schopenhauer, Arthur. (1818/1961). *The World as Will and Idea* (later translated as *The World as Will and Representation*; trans. R.B. Haldane and J. Kemp). Garden City: Doubleday.

Sekatskaya, Maria. (2019). Double defence against multiple-case manipulation arguments. *Philosophia* 47(4): 1283–1295.

Shabo, Seth. (2010). Uncompromising source incompatibilism. *Philosophy and Phenomenological Research* 80: 349–383.

Shabo, Seth. (2012). Where love and resentment meet: Strawson's interpersonal defense of compatibilism. *Philosophical Review* 121: 95–124.

Shabo, Seth. (2022). Responsibility, personal relationships, and the significance of the reactive attitudes. In Dana Nelkin and Derk Pereboom (eds.), *The Oxford Handbook on Moral Responsibility*. New York: Oxford University Press.

Shadlen, Michael. (2014). Comments on Adina Roskies: Can neuroscience resolve issues about free will? In Walter Sinnott-Armstrong (ed.), *Moral Psychology: Volume 4*. Cambridge, MA: MIT Press, pp. 139–150.

Shaw, Elizabeth. (2019). Justice without moral responsibility? *Journal of Information Ethics* 28(1): 95–114.

Shoemaker, David. (2011). Attributability, answerability, and accountability: Toward a wider theory of moral responsibility. *Ethics* 121: 602–632.

Shoemaker, David. (2015). *Responsibility from the Margins*. Oxford: Oxford University Press.

Simonton, Dean K. (2004). *Creativity in Science: Chance, Logic, Genius and Zeitgeist.* Cambridge: Cambridge University Press.

Singer, Ira J. (2002). Freedom and revision. *Southwest Philosophy Review* 18(2): 25–44.

Slattery, 'Trick. (2014). *Breaking the Free Will Illusion for the Betterment of Humankind.* Decatur, IL: Working Matter Publishing.

Slote, Michael. (1982). Selective necessity and the free-will problem. *Journal of Philosophy* 79: 5–24.

Slote, Michael. (1990). Ethics without free will. *Social Theory and Practice* 16: 369–383.

Smart, J.J.C. (1961). Free will, praise, and blame. *Mind* 70: 291–306.

Smilansky, Saul. (2000). *Free Will and Illusion.* New York: Oxford University Press.

Smilansky, Saul. (2011). Hard determinism and punishment: A practical *reductio. Law and Philosophy* 30: 353–367.

Smith, Angela. (2012). Attributability, answerability, and accountability: In defense of a unified account. *Ethics* 122(3): 575–589.

Smith, Angela. (2013). Moral blame and moral protest. In D. Justin Coates and Neal A. Tognazzini (eds.), *Blame: Its Nature and Norms.* New York: Oxford University Press, pp. 27–48.

Sommers, Tamler. (2007). The objective attitude. *Philosophical Quarterly* 57: 321–341.

Sommers, Tamler. (2012). *Relative Justice: Cultural Diversity, Free Will, and Moral Responsibility.* Princeton: Princeton University Press.

Sommers, Tamler. (2022). Metaskepticism. In Dana Nelkin and Derk Pereboom (eds.), *The Oxford Handbook of Moral Responsibility.* New York: Oxford University Press, pp. 247–265.

Soon, Chun Siong, Marcel Brass, Hans-Jochen Heinze, and John-Dylan Haynes. (2008). Unconscious determinants of free decisions in the human brain. *Nature Neuroscience* 11: 543–545.

Speak, D. (2004). Towards an axiological defense of libertarianism. *Philosophical Topics* 32(1 and 2): 353–369.

Spinoza, Benedictus. (1677/1985). *Ethics,* in *The Collected Works of Spinoza: Volume 1.* Edwin Curley (ed. and trans.). Princeton: Princeton University Press.

Sripada, Chandra. (2012). What makes a manipulated agent unfree? *Philosophy and Phenomenological Research* 85: 63–93.

Sripada, Chandra. (2016). Self-expression: A deep self theory of moral responsibility. *Philosophical Studies* 173: 1203–1232.

Stapp, Henry. (2007). *The Mindful Universe.* Berlin: Springer.

Strawson, Galen. (1986). *Freedom and Belief.* Oxford: Oxford University Press.

Strawson, Galen. (1994). The impossibility of moral responsibility. *Philosophical Studies* 75: 5–24.

Strawson, P.F. (1962). Freedom and resentment. *Proceedings of the British Academy* 48: 187–211.

Stump, Eleonore. (1990). Intellect, will, and the principle of alternate possibilities. In Michael Beaty (ed.), *Christian Theism and the Problems of Philosophy.* Notre Dame, IN: University of Notre Dame Press, pp. 254–285.

Stump, Eleonore. (1996). Libertarian freedom and the principle of alternative possibilities. In Jeff Jordan and Daniel Howard Snyder (eds.), *Faith, Freedom, and Rationality.* Lanham, MD: Rowman and Littlefield, pp. 73–88.

Suarez, A. and Adams, P. (eds.) (2013). *Is Science Compatible with Free Will?* Berlin: Springer.

Tadros, Victor. (2016). *Wrongs and Crimes*. Oxford: Oxford University Press.

Tadros, Victor. (2017). Doing without desert. *Criminal Law and Philosophy* 11: 605–616.

Talbert, Matthew. (2012). Moral competence, moral blame, and protest. *Journal of Ethics* 16: 89–101.

Taylor, Richard. (1966). *Action and Purpose*. Englewood Cliffs, NJ: Prentice-Hall.

Taylor, Richard. (1974). *Metaphysics*, fourth edition. Englewood Cliffs, NJ: Prentice-Hall.

Telech, Daniel. (2020). Praise as moral address. In David Shoemaker (ed.), *Oxford Studies in Agency and Responsibility: Volume 7*. Oxford: Oxford University Press.

Tierney, Hannah. (2013). A maneuver around the modified manipulation argument. *Philosophical Studies* 165: 753–763.

Tierney, Hannah. (2014). Taking it head-on: How to best handle the modified manipulation argument. *Journal of Value Inquiry* 48: 663–675.

Tierney, Hannah and David Glick. (2020). Desperately seeking sourcehood. *Philosophical Studies* 177(4): 953–970.

Todd, Patrick. (2011). A new approach to manipulation arguments. *Philosophical Studies* 152: 127–133.

Todd, Patrick. (2012). Manipulation and moral standing: An argument for incompatibilism. *Philosophical Imprint* 12: 1–18.

Todd, Patrick. (2013). Defending (a modified version of the) zygote argument. *Philosophical Studies* 164: 189–203.

Todd, Patrick. (2017). Manipulation arguments and the freedom to do otherwise. *Philosophy and Phenomenological Research* 95(2): 395–407.

Tognazzini, Neal A. (2014). The structure of a manipulation argument. *Ethics* 124(2): 358–369.

Tse, Peter Ulric. (2013). *The Neural Basis of Free Will: Criterial Causation*. Cambridge, MA: MIT Press.

Usher, Marius. (2006). Control, choice and the convergence/divergence dynamics. *Journal of Philosophy* 304: 188–214.

Usher, Marius. (2020). Agency, teleological control and robust causation. *Philosophy and Phenomenological Research* 100(2): 302–324.

van Inwagen, Peter. (1975). The incompatibility of free will and determinism. *Philosophical Studies* 27: 185–199.

van Inwagen, Peter. (1983). *An Essay on Free Will*. Oxford: Oxford University Press.

van Inwagen, Peter. (1996). Review of problems in philosophy. *Philosophical Review* 105(2): 253–256.

Vargas, Manuel (2005). Compatibilism evolves? On some varieties of Dennett worth wanting. *Metaphilosophy* 36(4): 460–475.

Vargas, Manuel. (2007). Revisionism. In J.M. Fischer, R. Kane, D. Pereboom, and M. Vargas. *Four Views on Free Will*. Malden, MA: Wiley-Blackwell, pp. 126–165.

Vargas, Manuel. (2009). Revisionism about free will: A statement and defense. *Philosophical Studies* 144(1): 45–62.

Vargas, Manuel. (2013). *Building Better Beings: A Theory of Moral Responsibility*. New York: Oxford University Press.

Vargas, Manuel. (2015). Desert, responsibility, and justification: A reply to Doris, McGeer, and Robinson. *Philosophical Studies* 172: 2659–2678.

Vargas, Manuel. (2017). Implicit bias, moral responsibility, and moral ecology. In D. Shoemaker (ed.), *Oxford Studies in Agency and Responsibility: Volume 4*. Oxford: Oxford University Press, pp. 219–247.

Vargas, Manuel. (2018). The social constitution of agency and responsibility: Oppression, politics, and moral ecology. In M. Oshana, K. Hutchinson, and C. Mackenzie (eds.), *The Social Dimensions of Responsibility*. Oxford: Oxford University Press, pp. 110–136.

Vargas, Manuel. (2021). Constitutive instrumentalism and the fragility of responsibility. *The Monist* 104(4): 427–442.

Vargas, Manuel. (2023). Revisionism. In J. Campbell, K.M. Mickelson, and V.A. White (eds.), *A Companion to Free Will*. Oxford: Blackwell Publishing, pp. 204–220.

Vargas, Manuel (accepted for publication). Counterfactual genealogy, speculative accuracy, and predicative drift. *Inquiry*.

Vasiri, Alipasha and Martin B. Plenio. (2010). Quantum coherence in ion channels: Resonances, transport and verification. *New Journal of Physics* 12: 085001.

Vicens, Leigh and Simon Kittle. (2019). *God and Human Freedom*. Cambridge: Cambridge University Press.

Vihvelin, Kadri. (1988). The modal argument for incompatibilism. *Philosophical Studies* 53: 227–244.

Vihvelin, Kadri. (2004). Free will demystified: A dispositionalist account. *Philosophical Topics* 32: 427–450.

Vihvelin, Kadri. (2013). *Causes, Laws, and Free Will: Why Determinism Doesn't Matter*. New York: Oxford University Press.

Vihvelin, Kadri. (2016). *Causes, Laws, and Free Will: Why Determinism Doesn't Matter*, Oxford: Oxford University Press.

Vilhauer, Benjamin. (2004). Hard determinism, remorse, and virtue ethics. *Southern Journal of Philosophy* 42: 547–564.

Vilhauer, Benjamin. (2008). Hard determinism, Humeanism, and virtue ethics. *Southern Journal of Philosophy* 46: 121–144.

Vilhauer, Benjamin. (2009a). Free will skepticism and personhood as a desert base. *Canadian Journal of Philosophy* 39: 489–511.

Vilhauer, Benjamin. (2009b). Free will and reasonable doubt. *American Philosophical Quarterly* 46: 131–140.

Vilhauer, Benjamin. (2012). Taking free will skepticism seriously. *Philosophical Quarterly* 62: 833–852.

Vilhauer, Benjamin. (2013). Persons, punishment, and free will skepticism. *Philosophical Studies* 162: 143–163.

Von Stosch, Klaus, Saskia Wendel, Martin Bruel, and Alan Langerfeld (eds.) (2019). *Streit um die Freiheit*. Munich: Ferdinand Schoningh.

Wallace, R. Jay. (1994). *Responsibility and the Moral Sentiments*. Cambridge, MA: Harvard University Press.

Waller, Bruce. (1990). *Freedom Without Responsibility*. Philadelphia: Temple University Press.

Waller, Bruce. (2011). *Against Moral Responsibility*. Cambridge, MA: MIT Press.

Waller, Bruce. (2015). *The Stubborn System of Moral Responsibility*. Cambridge, MA: MIT Press.

Walter, Henrik. (2001). *Neurophilosophy of Free Will: From Libertarian Illusions to a Concept of Natural Autonomy*. Cambridge, MA: MIT Press.

Wang, Shawn Tinghao (2021). The communication argument and the pluralist challenge. *Canadian Journal of Philosophy* 51(5): 384–399.

Watson, Gary. (1975). Free agency. *Journal of Philosophy* 72: 205–220.

Watson, Gary. (1987). Responsibility and the limits of evil. In Ferdinand Schoeman (ed.), *Responsibility, Character, and the Emotions*. Cambridge: Cambridge University Press, pp. 256–286.

Watson, Gary. (1996). Two faces of responsibility. *Philosophical Topics* 24: 227–248.

Wegner, Daniel. (2002). *The Illusion of Conscious Will*. Cambridge, MA: MIT Press.

Whittle, Ann. (2010). Dispositional abilities. *Philosophers' Imprint* 10: 1–23.

Widerker, David. (1987). On an argument for incompatibilism. *Analysis* 47: 37–41.

Widerker, David. (1995). Libertarianism and Frankfurt's attack on the principle of alternative possibilities. *Philosophical Review* 104: 247–261.

Widerker, David. (2000). Frankfurt's attack on alternative possibilities: A further look. *Philosophical Perspectives* 14: 181–201.

Wittgenstein, Ludwig. (1953). *Philosophical Investigations*. Oxford: Blackwell.

Wolf, Susan. (1980). Asymmetrical freedom. *Journal of Philosophy* 77: 151–166.

Wolf, Susan. (1987). Sanity and the metaphysics of responsibility. In F.D. Schoeman (ed.), *Free Will*. Cambridge: Cambridge University Press, pp. 46–62.

Wolf, Susan. (1990). *Freedom Within Reason*. Oxford: Oxford University Press.

Zagzebski, Linda. (1991). *The Dilemma of Freedom and Foreknowledge*. New York: Oxford University Press.

Zagzebski, Linda. (2000). Does libertarian freedom require alternate possibilities? *Philosophical Perspectives* 14: 231–248.

Zawidzki, Tadeusz. (2013). *Mindshaping: A New Framework for Understanding Human Social Cognition*. Cambridge, MA: MIT Press.

Index

Note: Page numbers in *italic* refer to figures; Page numbers followed by "n" refer to endnotes.